Managing Federalism

STUDIES IN INTERGOVERNMENTAL RELATIONS

Managing Federalism

STUDIES IN

INTERGOVERNMENTAL RELATIONS

Arnold M. Howitt

Harvard University

a division of
Congressional Quarterly Inc.
1414 22nd Street, N.W., Washington, D.C. 20037

Printed in the United States of America

Library of Congress Cataloging in Publication Data

Howitt, Arnold M., 1947-

    Managing federalism.

    Bibliography: p.
    1. Federal government — United States — Case studies. I. Title.
JK325.H68   1984   353.9′29′0926   83-15046
ISBN 0-87187-277-3

For Matthew and Molly

TABLE OF CONTENTS

Managing Federalism: An Overview   1

I. The Dynamics of Federalism:
Federal, State, and Local Perspectives   37

    1. The Maternal and Child Health Block Grant
       In Washington State and Seattle   39

            The Cast   42
            Chronology   43
            The Case   44
            Exhibits   66
            Discussion Questions   70
            Suggestions for Further Reading   70

    2. The Kentucky Small Cities
       CDBG Demonstration   71

            The Cast   74
            Chronology   75
            The Case   77
            Exhibits   96
            Discussion Questions   105
            Suggestions for Further Reading   105

    3. The Environmental Protection
       Agency and Transportation Controls (A,B,C)   107

       Part A   The Cast   110
               Chronology   111
               The Case   113
               Exhibits   135
               Discussion Questions   136
               Suggestions for Further Reading   136

       Part B   The Cast   137
               Chronology   137
               The Case   139

	Exhibits	156
	Discussion Questions	158
	Suggestions for Further Reading	159
Part C	The Cast	159
	Chronology	160
	The Case	161
	Discussion Questions	179
	Suggestions for Further Reading	180

II. The System at Work   181

4. Restricting Traffic on Washington Street   183

	The Cast	185
	Chronology	186
	The Case	187
	Exhibits	202
	Discussion Questions	203
	Suggestions for Further Reading	203

5. Community Development in Gainesville (A,B,C)   205

Part A	The Cast	207
	Chronology	208
	The Case	209
	Discussion Questions	239
	Suggestions for Further Reading	239
Part B	Chronology	240
	The Case	240
	Discussion Questions	245
	Suggestions for Further Reading	245
Part C	The Cast	246
	Chronology	246
	The Case	247
	Discussion Questions	264
	Suggestions for Further Reading	264

III. Community Involvement in Federal Programs   265

    6. Extending the Red Line to Arlington   267
            The Cast   269
            Chronology   270
            The Case   271
            Exhibits   298
            Discussion Questions   300
            Suggestions for Further Reading   301

    7. Citizen Participation in Oxford   303
            The Cast   306
            Chronology   307
            The Case   307
            Exhibits   317
            Discussion Questions   320
            Suggestions for Further Reading   321

PREFACE

This book deals with *public management* in the intergovernmental system. Most academic studies of federalism adopt a theoretical perspective or analyze intergovernmental relations at a high level of abstraction. This book has a different purpose. It is intended to give its readers an understanding of the intergovernmental system's operating practices and problems *from the viewpoint of the people who must make the system work,* whatever its imperfections. This perspective is important for citizens concerned about the future of federalism and for individuals who must deal with the intergovernmental system in their work at various levels of government or in firms or organizations that interact with government.

The case studies in this book recount events that took place in Washington, D.C., in several states, and in big cities and small communities. They therefore offer an opportunity to consider the viewpoints of officials at all levels of the intergovernmental system—federal, state, and local— with particular emphasis on the latter two. The cases also deal with several substantive policy areas: community development, transportation, environmental affairs, and health and human services. Given the great diversity of American federalism, the book's coverage is inevitably selective. But these cases offer a wide array of contemporary problems to discuss and dissect.

This book was written with the firm belief that the "case method" can be an extremely useful educational tool—both for training future policy analysts and public managers and for enriching the classroom experience of liberal arts students. Case studies are not a substitute for theoretical or analytic curriculum materials, but they are a stimulating supplement. They are particularly well suited for jarring students out of passive modes of learning and preventing them from uncritically accepting generalized conclusions. Well-designed case studies can present situations that are not "predigested" analytically and that require students to engage complex problems actively. In the classroom, cases can be used as the basis for discussions, written assignments, or both.

The cases in this book have been written so that students can assume a role in the events and explain and evaluate why particular actors behaved as they did. A number of the cases, moreover, are written in a "decision-forcing" format; they conclude with a dilemma facing one or more of the actors. The intention is to compel students to confront these problems actively—to a greater degree than usually is possible in a classroom—and to force them to make choices with an understanding of some of the constraints found in "the real world."

Ultimately, this book is concerned with the issue of *managerial effectiveness* in government. It does not simplistically assume, however, that there is a single criterion against which effectiveness can be evaluated. The distinctive feature of public management—which offers both great challenge and tremendous social significance—is that it is carried on in a *political* environment where the diverse interests and values of many individuals and groups compete. What constitutes effectiveness, therefore, depends in crucial respects on one's point of view. Effective management is political as well as administrative; it must be defined in reference to a specified set of political interests and values.

While there are no absolutes in public management, there *are* sets of factors and patterns of behavior that are repeatedly important. It is a basic premise of this book that one can enhance managerial effectiveness by better understanding how the intergovernmental system functions and by better appreciating other actors' objectives and perspectives. By carefully assessing past situations, one can learn to diagnose future management problems and evaluate the options available for dealing with them.

The author and several assistants working under his direction researched these case studies. Unless otherwise indicated in the text, the sources of information were personal interviews conducted with more than 100 officials and citizens involved in the events described. These cases have been tested successfully in the classroom with students at different stages of education and of varying levels of academic ability. Student reaction has been very positive. I hope that other faculty and students find this book a helpful and stimulating educational tool.

Arnold M. Howitt
Belmont, Massachusetts
October 1983

ACKNOWLEDGMENTS

Seeing a book through to publication makes me realize how inappropriate it is to have my name alone appear on the title page. Many other people share responsibility for whatever virtues this book may have.

My most profound debt is to the more than 100 public officials and citizens who accepted an interviewer's poking, probing, guessing and hypothesizing—with almost unflagging kindness and often more interest and enthusiasm than I ever would have dreamed possible. Many are named in the text, while others—including some who have been promised anonymity—are not. But the intelligence, insight, patience, and generosity of all are genuinely appreciated.

During the years in which these cases were developed, I had the pleasure of working with eight research assistants—Richard Clarendon, Ben Dansker, Kathy Haslanger, Hester McCarthy, Ron McQuaid, Ernie Niemi, Kay Rubin, and Isaac Shapiro—each a graduate student in planning or public policy at Harvard University. Their specific roles in researching and writing this book are noted at the beginning of each case study. As substantial as their intellectual contributions were, however, I am equally thankful for their comradeship. We spent many hours together: planning, traveling, interviewing, discussing, speculating, arguing, and—above all—laughing. This book would not exist without their help, and they certainly made the work far more fun to do.

My colleagues in the City and Regional Planning program at Harvard, now partially dispersed, are an unusually stimulating and generous group. Over the years I have enjoyed their company, both professionally and personally. Several of them—Jim Brown, Fred Doolittle, Tony Gomez-Ibanez, Jeff Prottas, Avis Vidal, and Steve Yaffee—deserve particular mention for their personal support or comments on the materials in this book. To John Kain, who brought us together, I owe an even greater debt because as friend and mentor for seven years he has been a continual source of encouragement and counsel.

Several hundred students in Harvard's planning, public policy, and public administration programs and in its Extension School have used these cases in various courses. It was for them that the cases were written, and their reactions and probing comments have strengthened this book.

No work in the academic world is easily done without financial support. My heartfelt thanks are therefore due to several Harvard administrators— John Kain, Hale Champion, Stephanie Gould, and Charles Kireker—for tangible backing for curriculum development. The John F. Kennedy School of Government, through Dean Graham T. Allison, has generously granted permission for my cases to be used in this book. Some of the case research was supported by grants given to Harvard by the U.S. Department of Housing and Urban Development (HUD), and the Urban Mass Transportation Administration (UMTA) of the U.S. Department of Transportation (DOT). The views expressed in this book, however, do not necessarily reflect those of HUD, UMTA, or DOT.

My thanks are due, also, to Martha Derthick, who originally sparked my interest in intergovernmental relations when I was her graduate student and teaching assistant.

Joanne Daniels, Sue Sullivan, and Mary McNeil of CQ Press have been enthusiastic and intelligent editors—and patient beyond belief. I am grateful for their help in transforming my typings into a book. It was no mean feat. Two no-longer-anonymous reviewers—Don Kettl of the University of Virginia and Larry O'Toole of Auburn University—deserve thanks, too, for their perceptive criticisms of the original manuscript.

Last, and least only in physical stature, Matthew and Molly Howitt have contributed to this endeavor with ingenuous ease. It is to them—in thanks for the warmth and laughter they bring to my world—that I dedicate this book, with love.

Notwithstanding these individuals' many contributions, I must insist on their not-at-all-ritualistic absolution from responsibility for whatever errors or misinterpretations may remain in this book. Those are mine alone.

Arnold M. Howitt
Belmont, Massachusetts
October 1983

Managing Federalism

STUDIES IN INTERGOVERNMENTAL RELATIONS

Federalism: An Overview

By the design of its founding fathers, the United States is a *federal* system—a union of separate states that acknowledges the sovereignty of a central (or national, or federal) government but retains certain authority for each individual state. Exactly how that system of government works, however, has evolved throughout U.S. history. Sometimes change has been gradual—by the accretion of individual laws, administrative practices, and judicial decisions; sometimes it has been more dramatic—swept along by waves of legislation, as in the New Deal or Great Society years, or once, in the Civil War, by force of arms. Today the federal system is far more complex than the founders of our republic could have foreseen. It involves a complicated *division of legal authority* between the states and the national government on one hand, and the states and local governments on the other; tangled *fiscal relationships* between the national government and the states, between the national government and localities, and between the states and localities; extensive *administrative and regulatory ties* among these government entities; and dynamic *political interdependencies* among elected and appointed officials at all levels of government. Taken together, these aspects of American federalism can be thought of as *intergovernmental relations.*

This book focuses on a major facet of intergovernmental relations—the ties between the federal government and state and local governments. This by no means exhausts the topic of federalism; we might also consider interstate relations, state-local relations, and interlocal relations. But the federal role in dealing with subnational units of government is an extremely important aspect of contemporary American federalism.

Few areas of domestic policy and government exist in which the federal government plays no part. In Fiscal Year (FY) 1984 the federal government will spend more than $95 billion on aid to states and localities. This money supports myriad programs and projects that directly or indirectly benefit American citizens. It provides financial assistance, medical care, housing, social services, job training, and food to needy individuals. It supports many basic services that all citizens use such as schools, libraries, public health care, fire protection, and public transportation. It helps states and localities build major physical facilities: highways, bridges, tunnels, transit systems, dams, water treatment plants, sewer systems, and parks. It helps older U.S. cities rebuild deteriorating business and residential districts, and it helps newer cities develop the basic infrastructure that permits growth. Beyond fiscal assistance, moreover, the federal government plays a major regulatory role—for example, by promoting a clean and healthy environment or seeking to eliminate discrimination in education, housing, and employment.

Today, therefore, the federal government is a ubiquitous presence in state and local affairs. For the most part we take for granted the benefits that federal financial aid and regulation provide, but few would contend that Americans are not better off as a result of the national government's help. Nonetheless, there are doubts about how well the intergovernmental system functions.

No one working from a blank page would design the federal system as it exists today. Most government officials and a number of other observers believe that it operates far less effectively than it could. Politically, many bemoan either federal restrictions on state or local autonomy or the unequal access to public services endured by citizens because the nation's governmental authority is fragmented. Nearly every observer has proposals for tinkering with the intergovernmental system, and some advocate its radical transformation. But there are few, if any, ideas that win support from all of the constituencies concerned with making the federal system work better. This lack of political consensus probably guarantees that comprehensive reform lies beyond our grasp, but one can be sure that pressures will continue unabated for changes in intergovernmental policy and in the way the federal system is managed.

If our goal is improving the effectiveness of intergovernmental management, we need a realistic understanding of how the federal system works. The case studies in this book cover a range of problems of contemporary federalism. While the cases deal with specific events in specific places, the reader should not lose sight of the broader issues of intergovernmental management that are illuminated here: 1) *To what extent ought the federal government prescribe the objectives of intergovernmental programs?* Should it specify in detail the purposes for which grants-in-aid should be spent and the methods by which state and local governments should administer them? Or should it provide financial resources to these governments with no more than a broad statement of how they should be used? 2) *Does the federal government have the political and administrative capacity to "steer" state and local program management?* What political forces at the national level shape the way in which the federal government administers these programs? What tools—for example, statutes, administrative regulations, and grant-in-aid forms—does it have for defining its expectations for intergovernmental programs? How are federal executive branch personnel organized to oversee state and local program implementation? What role does Congress play in the administration of intergovernmental programs? How do the federal courts affect the management of grant-in-aid programs? 3) *How do federal program initiatives fit into on-going political and administrative processes in state and local governments?* How does a new federal program affect the interests and power of various political and bureaucratic actors in these governments? What is required to get the new program adopted and implemented at the state or local level? What changes in government structure and function are involved? When Congress or a federal executive agency makes major changes in an existing intergovernmental program, how does this affect state and local program administrators and constituencies? 4) *How can citizens influence the development and implementation of federal programs?* How do public officials take account of public opinion in planning intergovernmental programs? Can citizens be directly and effectively involved in developing and managing these programs? What recourse do citizens have if they are unhappy with the direction of an intergovernmental program?

The case studies in this volume give the reader a perspective on the federal system from the standpoints of federal elected officials and program managers, state and local administrators and legislators, and the citizens who are affected by intergovernmental programs. Therefore, a reader who works through this book carefully will understand more clearly both the strengths and limits of the intergovernmental system.

The remainder of this introductory chapter provides a context for the more detailed and operationally oriented case studies that follow. It first recounts briefly the history of federal programs for state and local governments, then describes the political setting in which intergovernmental programs are enacted and administered, and finally outlines the principal managerial issues that confront program administrators at each level of government.

The Evolution of the Intergovernmental System[1]

Intergovernmental relations have changed greatly since the late eighteenth and early nineteenth centuries — a fact that is linked closely to the expansion of the federal government's role in domestic policy and to the overall growth of government in American society. As public institutions have come to play a larger and larger part in our lives, the ties among different levels of the federal system have become closer and more complex.

From the Early Days to the Twentieth Century

In the first days of the new nation and during most of the nineteenth century, the level of interaction between the federal government and the states was quite low compared with what it was to become. Historians have termed this a period of "dual federalism," in which the two levels of government had largely separate sets of functions. By the latter part of the nineteenth century and the early decades of the twentieth century, however, a new pattern of "cooperative federalism" began to emerge in which the national government and the states shared responsibility for a growing number of functions, jointly financing them and managing them with some degree of federal supervision.

Intergovernmental relationships developed quite gradually at first. Government at all levels was a much less prominent force in the lives of the nation's citizens during the eighteenth and nineteenth centuries. In the early years after the Constitution was adopted, moreover, the national government in the new city of Washington, D.C., performed few domestic functions, with the principal exception of the postal service. Citizens received what services there were almost exclusively from the states and localities. Given the colonial heritage of distrusting central authority and the lack of cooperative experience among the states in domestic affairs, the development of a strong federal government cut against the grain of American political beliefs. This was reflected in the relatively limited extent to which the national government became involved in the states' internal governance.

It is true that from the earliest days of the new nation the federal government made contributions to state projects or operations, usually in the form of land grants that could be sold for cash or used for projects. Most were made as one-shot grants, however, rather than on a recurring basis, and virtually no federal supervision of state activities was undertaken. Only gradually, as the federal government asserted a stronger role in domestic affairs, did the patterns of cooperative federalism begin to develop. Not until 1862 did the Morrill Act establish a more modern grant-in-aid program—to support education in the agricultural and mechanical arts. With this program Congress made land grants to raise funds for construction of college facilities, laid down general rules about the nature of the programs to be offered, and required annual expenditure reports from the states. Not until 1887, however, did the Hatch Act provide the first *annual cash* grant to the states—for support of agricultural experiment stations. A small number of cash grant programs followed, and the rudiments of the categorical grant system—including federally defined objectives, minimum program standards, and federal oversight of state administration—began to develop.

At the outset of the new century, however, these grants were making a limited impact on a government system simpler than today's. Less than 1 percent of state and local revenues were provided by the federal government, and its grants accounted for little more than 1 percent of federal expenditures.

The grant-in-aid system grew more significantly, but still slowly, during the first three decades of the twentieth century. Changing political attitudes, activist presidents such as Theodore Roosevelt and Woodrow Wilson, and— not least—the establishment of a federal income tax to generate more revenue, made possible an expansion of the federal domestic policy agenda. Congress enacted a number of new grant programs, most importantly a highway construction grant that distributed funds according to a three-factor legislative formula, matched state expenditures on a 50-50 basis, and imposed planning and administrative requirements on the states. There were also new grants for forestry, the agricultural extension service, vocational education and rehabilitation, and maternal and infant care. When the Depression descended on the country in 1930, 15 grant programs existed—with highway construction being by far the largest—totaling $200 million and 4.9 percent of federal budget outlays.

The New Deal's Legacy

President Franklin D. Roosevelt's New Deal was a major turning point in intergovernmental relations. Under the pressure of a national economic crisis, the federal government vastly expanded the scope of its domestic programs, including aid to state and local governments. The New Deal thus represented a major reorientation of political attitudes by American citizens and policy makers alike. There was an increasing philosophical acceptance of government activism, in general, and federal activism, in particular. Between 1933 and 1938 Congress created 16 grant-in-aid programs, as well as a number of temporary emergency grants. This greatly increased the scope and dollar amount of federal aid. A one-year peak of almost $2.2 billion was reached in 1935 when several emergency programs were in full swing. By the late 1930s, the federal government was regularly spending about $1 billion annually on aid to state and local governments.

For the intergovernmental system, the Social Security Act of 1935 was by far the most important legislation of this period, laying the foundation for a national social welfare system that remains largely intact today. The Social Security Act established categorical programs for aid to the aged, blind, and dependent children; unemployment insurance; child welfare programs; and programs for maternal and child health and crippled children's services.

The New Deal programs involved departures from previous practice in several important respects. One was the growing link between the national government and local governments. Between 1932 and 1936 the amount of federal aid received by local authorities increased from $10 million to $229 million. Previously, to the extent that it reached the localities, federal aid was channeled through the states. Now money began to flow directly to local governments or to quasi-independent local agencies, for example in the public housing program enacted in 1937. The New Deal programs also enlarged the federal government's supervisory role. The authorizing statutes tended to mandate planning activities and impose other administrative requirements on the recipient governments. As a result, permanent grant programs began to develop substantial bodies of administrative regulations, and federal officials began to become more active in their oversight responsibilities.

The New Deal period also clarified the legal authority for federal grant-in-aid programs, which some believed were an unconstitutional imposition of federal power on the states. In 1936 the U.S. Supreme Court held in *United States v. Butler* that the Constitution permits federal expenditures in policy areas that go beyond the federal government's enumerated powers. In the following year in *Steward Machine Co. v. Davis* the Court also held that the grant-in-aid device did not coerce the states into accepting federal intrusion that otherwise would be unconstitutional. As a consequence of these cases, the grant-in-aid mechanism was, in effect, freed from the strictures of the Tenth Amendment, which reserves to the states powers not specifically enumerated in the Constitution as a federal prerogative.

World War II interrupted the growth of the intergovernmental grant system, despite the creation of several temporary aid programs oriented toward the war effort. Federal financial assistance to states and localities averaged just under $1 billion until 1946.

The Postwar Period

For almost 20 years after the conclusion of World War II, American government wrestled with the legacy of the New Deal's domestic policy innovations. The Democrats lacked the political strength to enhance dramatically the initiatives taken during the Depression but pressed for selective expansion. The Republicans, once in power, made no attempt to dismantle New Deal programs wholesale; they even supported increased financial aid and some new program ideas. During the Truman, Eisenhower, and Kennedy administrations, therefore, the intergovernmental grant system grew gradually but steadily—both in the number of individual programs and in the amount of financial resources provided. Table 1 on pages 8 and 9 shows this growth in dollar terms and as percentages of total federal outlays, state and local expenditures, and gross national product (GNP). Until 1958, the total merely kept up with the economy's rate of expansion, hovering around a level of 1 percent of the gross national product. Between 1959 and 1962, however, in the last years of the Eisenhower administration and the early years of the Kennedy administration, that figure increased to about 1.4 percent of GNP as a number of new grants were created.

During the postwar period, the trend toward direct aid to municipal governments or autonomous local agencies continued with the enactment of grants for airport construction in 1946, urban renewal in 1949, and urban planning in 1954. But the largest fiscal commitment of this era was made in 1956 to the interstate highway program, whose funds went to state governments.

Overall, by the end of 1962, the federal government supported a total of 160 grant-in-aid programs at an annual cost of $7.9 billion.

Grant System Growth Accelerates

During the four-year period from 1963 to 1966—the last year of President John F. Kennedy's administration and the first three of the new Johnson administration—the intergovernmental grant system underwent an explosive spurt of growth in the number of programs and the level of federal financial aid. The Democratic party's domestic legislative agenda had been stalemated in Congress during the initial years of Kennedy's term but began to move during the final year. Then, under the impetus of Lyndon B. Johnson's legislative leadership and the landslide Democratic victory in 1964, Congress enacted grant-in-aid programs at an astounding pace. These included legislative landmarks—such as Medicaid, the Elementary and Secondary Education Act, and the Model Cities program—as well as many smaller initiatives tailored to the interests of relatively narrow constituencies. In just four years, 219 new grant programs were created, with 109 being enacted in 1965 alone. As Table 1 shows, federal aid to states and localities almost doubled from $7.9 billion in FY 1962 to $13.0 billion in FY 1966. Although the rate of real growth, controlling for inflation, was not so remarkable, it still amounted to more than a 50 percent increase. By the end of 1966, there were 379 grant-in-aid programs for state and local government.

The Great Society represented a significant turning point in the development of the intergovernmental system. By moving into many new policy areas and greatly extending its involvement in others, the federal government became a far more significant—and highly active—presence in the daily lives of state and local officials and in the delivery of government services to citizens. The relationship with local government, in particular, was altered significantly. As the country politically recognized an "urban crisis," many of the new grant programs were set up to provide aid directly to municipal governments or local agencies rather than through the states as intermediaries.

This growth of the intergovernmental system was highly controversial, reflecting deep-rooted differences in political philosophy. The Great Society programs were a triumph for those who believed that the federal government should establish national goals and standards for social welfare and civil rights. They believed that neither state-by-state variations in political belief nor fiscal capacity should prevent any citizen from having a full opportunity to develop his potential and to enjoy the benefits of the nation's prosperity. Others believed with equal fervor in a decentralized federal system in which local

Table 1: Federal Grants in Historical Perspective
(Dollar Amounts in Billions)

Federal Grants-in-Aid (Current Dollars)

Fiscal Year[1]	Amount	As a Percentage of		
		State-Local Receipts from Own Source[2]	Total Federal Outlays	Gross National Product
1902	$ 7 million	0.7	1.4	n.a.
1913	12 million	0.6	1.7	n.a.
1922	108 million	2.1	3.3	n.a.
1932	232 million	3.0	5.0	0.4
1940	0.9 billion	8.3	1.0	0.9
1945	0.9	8.9	1.0	0.4
1950	2.3	10.4	5.3	0.8
1955	3.2	11.8	4.7	0.8
1956	3.7	12.3	5.3	0.9
1957	4.0	12.1	5.3	0.9
1958	4.9	14.0	6.0	1.1
1959	6.5	17.2	7.0	1.4
1960	7.0	16.8	7.6	1.4
1961	7.1	15.8	7.3	1.4
1962	7.9	16.2	7.4	1.4
1963	8.6	16.5	7.8	1.5
1964	10.1	17.9	8.6	1.6
1965	10.9	17.7	9.2	1.7
1966	13.0	19.3	9.6	1.8
1967	15.2	20.6	9.6	2.0
1968	18.6	22.4	10.4	2.2
1969	20.3	21.6	11.0	2.2
1970	24.0	22.9	12.2	2.5
1971	28.1	24.1	13.3	2.7
1972	34.4	26.1	14.8	3.1
1973	41.8	28.5	16.9	3.3
1974	43.4	27.3	16.1	3.1
1975	49.8	29.1	15.3	3.4
1976	59.1	31.1	16.1	3.6
1977	68.4	31.0	17.0	3.7
1978	77.9	31.7	17.3	3.7
1979	82.9	31.3	16.8	3.5
1980	91.5	31.7	15.8	3.6
1981	94.8	29.4	14.4	3.2
1982	88.8	25.4	12.1	2.9
1983 est.*	93.5	n.a.	11.6	2.9
1984 est.*	95.9	n.a.	11.3	2.7

* 1983 and 1984 estimates based upon OMB assumptions published in the FY 1984 *Budget.* Grant-in-aid figures from *Special Analysis H*, Table H-7; federal outlays from *Budget*, Summary Table 23; GNP and GNP deflator figures from *Budget*, Section 2, page 9. See *Special Analysis H* for explanation of differences between grant-in-aid figures published by the National Income and Product Accounts, Census, and OMB.

[1] For 1955-1976, years ending June 30; 1977-1982 years ending September 30.

Federal Grants-in-Aid (Constant Dollars)
(1972 Dollars, GNP Deflator)

Fiscal Year	Amount	Percent Increase or Decrease (−)	Estimated Number of Federal Grant Programs
1902	n.a.	n.a.	n.a.
1913	n.a.	n.a.	n.a.
1922	n.a.	n.a.	n.a.
1930	n.a.	n.a.	15
1939	n.a.	n.a.	n.a.
1945	n.a.	n.a.	n.a.
1950	n.a.	n.a.	n.a.
1955	$ 5.3	n.a.	n.a.
1956	5.9	11.3	n.a.
1957	6.2	5.1	n.a.
1958	7.4	19.4	n.a.
1959	9.6	29.7	n.a.
1960	10.2	6.3	132
1961	10.2	-0-	n.a.
1962	11.2	9.8	n.a.
1963	12.0	7.1	n.a.
1964	13.9	15.8	n.a.
1965	14.7	5.8	n.a.
1966	16.9	15.0	n.a.
1967	19.2	13.6	379
1968	22.5	17.2	n.a.
1969	23.4	4.0	n.a.
1970	26.2	12.0	n.a.
1971	29.3	11.8	n.a.
1972	34.4	17.4	n.a.
1973	39.5	14.8	n.a.
1974	37.7	−4.6	n.a.
1975	39.6	5.0	448
1976	44.7	12.9	n.a.
1977	48.8	9.2	n.a.
1978	51.8	6.1	498
1979	50.7	−2.1	n.a.
1980	51.2	1.0	n.a.
1981	48.5	−5.3	539
1982	42.6	−12.2	441[3]
1983 est.*	42.9	0.7	n.a.
1984 est.*	41.8	−2.6	n.a.

[2] As defined in the national income and product accounts.

[3] Seventy-nine programs had been folded into nine block grants, and at least another twenty six programs had not been funded as of Nov. 1, 1981.

Source: Bureau of the Census, *Historical Statistics of the United States,* part 2 (Washington, D.C.: U.S. GPO, 1975), 224, 1114, 1126; Advisory Commission on Intergovernmental Relations, *Significant Features of Fiscal Federalism, 1981-82* (Washington, D.C.: U.S. GPO, 1981).

preferences and priorities, reflected by political institutions closer to the people than members of Congress and bureaucrats in Washington, should determine the extent and character of government activity. For these individuals, the increasing number of programs and directives emanating from the nation's capital were an affront—and even a danger to the continued viability of the federal system. By no means did the successful enactment of President Johnson's legislative program prevent these philosophical differences from being played out at the state and local level, too.

More was involved, however, than a clash of political philosophies. In a more mundane sense: did the individual programs created in Washington work as intended when implemented in dozens or hundreds or thousands of state and local sites? And in a more fundamental sense: what were the limits of purposeful government intervention in the social, economic, and political lives of its citizens? Could sweeping national purposes actually be effectively achieved by planned government activity?

In the early stages of this explosive growth in the grant system, however, neither Congress nor the executive branch gave much thought to the administrative complexity of intergovernmental relations. The system grew in an uncoordinated, almost haphazard fashion. Taking its cues from President Johnson, the preeminent legislative tactician of his generation, the administration focused on getting new programs through Congress. Understanding the fragility of a president's leadership of Congress, even with an extraordinary legislative majority, the administration did not want to lose the historic opportunity to refashion the role of the federal government in domestic policy. It worried much less about the coherence of the programs it entreated Congress to enact.

As a consequence of rapid growth, though, the intergovernmental system was becoming far more difficult to manage—both from the federal perspective and the state and local side. The proliferation of grant programs meant that federal agencies were responsible for administering a larger number of separate programs, working with a larger number of governmental units, and overseeing the expenditure of increasing amounts of federal money. These programs, moreover, were more complex than many of their predecessors. Given the political climate of the day, Congress tended to prescribe in greater detail both the goals and administrative means of the programs, and it delegated to federal executive agencies a great deal of authority for further specifying program purposes and operating procedures through administrative regulations. A high percentage of the new programs, moreover, involved *project* grants to which state and local governments had no automatic entitlement; they had to apply to the federal agency responsible for administering the grant, competing with other states and localities for grant support.

This gave federal administrators a substantial amount of discretion in—and responsibility for—choosing recipients.

From the other side, state and local officials of nearly all political persuasions found the weaknesses of the intergovernmental system increasingly troublesome. As grant programs proliferated throughout the 1960s, a single jurisdiction might be eligible for literally dozens—perhaps hundreds—of programs. There was little standardization, however, in the way that the federal government administered these grants. Each program tended to have its own application procedures, budget cycle, fiscal arrangements, restrictions on expenditures, planning requirements, program regulations, and accounting procedures. Even multiple grant programs administered by the same federal agency tended to have many differences. The regulations, moreover, were often a moving target subject to frequent revision. As a consequence, local grant recipients often felt awash in red tape, burdened by program requirements that seemed ill-suited to their jurisdictions or ran counter to their sense of appropriate policy. Many disdained the grantsmanship that was increasingly necessary to secure discretionary grants from federal agencies or feared that they lacked the grantsmanship skill. Many also were deeply disturbed by the new political pressures caused by citizen participation requirements, which mandated the involvement of ordinary citizens in policy making and administration of grants and began to be included frequently in federal programs with the Economic Opportunity Act of 1964.

Chief executives—whether elected or appointed—found it particularly difficult to deal with the intergovernmental system. Grants frequently went directly to the agencies that ran federal programs, giving their bureaucratic leaders a relatively independent source of funds—and power. It therefore was difficult for the chief executive to exert central managerial control over their policies and activities. By dramatically increasing the stakes of city affairs, moreover, new federal programs tended to induce greater public participation in politics, even aside from the impact of citizen participation regulations. The task of political leadership therefore became more complex and problematic.

To some extent the Johnson administration came to recognize these difficulties and took some tentative steps to ameliorate them. Several grant programs—notably the Partnership for Health Act of 1966, the Model Cities program in that same year, and the Safe Streets Act of 1968—either consolidated preexisting categorical programs into broader purpose grants or gave the recipient government substantially more discretion in how federal funds could be used. The Model Cities program, among others, gave chief executives clearer responsibility and authority. The Intergovernmental Cooperation Act of 1968, moreover, provided for some rationalization of the grant system, including the framework for the A-95 review process (named after the federal regulations that operationalized it) by which municipal chief executives could comment on proposed federal grant programs in their metropolitan areas. Even taken as a whole, however, these measures did little to make the intergovernmental system easier to manage.

Notwithstanding these problems, the Great Society programs developed a strong constituency—in part because they gave recognition to social and political problems that governors, mayors, and other state and municipal officials felt pressure to act on; and in part because of the growing financial stake that these officials had in intergovernmental aid. The share of state and local funds that was supplied by federal grants grew steadily. In FY 1962 federal aid was equal to 16.2 percent of the revenue that state and local governments raised from their own sources; by FY 1968 that figure had reached 22.4 percent. For many financially troubled big city governments, federal funds represented an even more substantial percentage of municipal revenue. Moreover, not only did federal aid have a very great fiscal impact, but it also provided chief executives with much of the funds available for policy innovation. Money from the city's regular revenue sources usually was committed already to on-going functions, but federal aid could be applied to new activities that would demonstrate the creativity and resourcefulness of the chief executive.

The Nixon-Ford 'New Federalism'

With the election of President Richard Nixon in 1968 and the return of the Republican party to power in the federal executive branch, many thought that Great Society programs would be pruned severely and that the intergovernmental system as a whole would be subject to significant retrenchment. These expectations proved too simple. The president did seek substantial change in the structure of the grant system and hoped to rein in its fiscal growth. But determined Democratic congressional majorities strongly resisted many of Nixon's proposals and, in fact, enacted a number of new grant programs.

President Nixon made reform of the intergovernmental grant system one of the principal elements of his domestic policy. He emphasized grant consolidation, reduction of federal regulation, and, consequently, more freedom for state and local governments to set priorities for their programs. To effect this policy, Nixon proposed both *general* revenue sharing (in which states and localities would receive funds with virtually no restrictions on how they might be used) and *special* revenue sharing (in which existing categorical programs would be consolidated into a broad purpose grant in a particular policy area—for example, education—with relatively few federal restrictions on its use). To the extent that state and local officials believed that these changes would give them more flexibility in using federal money, they were warmly disposed to the president's proposals. Congress, however, was reluctant to give up federal control over the expenditure of federal funds and suspicious of how state and local officials would use more discretion; it resisted the president's initiatives for the most part. In 1972, however, Congress was persuaded to adopt general revenue sharing when a coalition of state and local leaders, spearheaded by Democratic big city mayors, organized a massive lobbying campaign to support it. The six special revenue sharing proposals languished in committee, but ultimately Congress adopted several *block* grant compromises that consolidated some grants while providing for more federal regulation than the special revenue sharing proposals had intended. Block grants were enacted in several areas—in 1973 the Comprehensive Employment and Training Act (CETA) for manpower programs and Title XX of the Social Security Act for social services, in 1974 the Community Development Block Grant (CDBG)—while leaving the existing collection of categorical programs largely intact in other areas. (The latter outcome was the same when President Gerald R. Ford subsequently proposed block grant consolidations similar to Nixon's initiatives.) Moreover, despite the administration's reluctance to see the grant system expand, Congress continued to enact new categorical programs. Among these, for example, were three counter-cyclical programs intended to ameliorate the impacts of a national economic recession. As a result, the number of separate grant-in-aid programs jumped from 379 in 1967 to 448 in 1975.

On the administrative front, the Nixon administration experimented with methods to strengthen chief executives' managerial role in the grant system and, more generally, sought to reduce the amount of federal regulation. Congress, however, did not fully share the latter goal. Largely as a result of congressional initiatives, a number of *cross-cutting* regulations were drafted in areas such as antidiscrimination, environmental protection, and employment practices. (This layer of regulations applied across the board to all or most grant programs, not just to ones that specifically included such provisions in their authorizing statutes.) While not a new practice, such regulations became a far more common device in the 1970s and consequently were seen as increasingly burdensome by state and local officials. Even the new block grants, which began life with a relatively simple regulatory framework, accumulated restrictions as early operating experience made executive branch monitors and congressional overseers dissatisfied with certain aspects of their performance.

Contrary to most observers' expectations when President Nixon was elected, the federal government's fiscal commitment to the intergovernmental system continued to grow at a rapid pace during the Nixon-Ford administrations. As Table 1 shows, the national government transferred $20.3 million to the states and localities in FY 1969—the last fiscal year of President Johnson's term. By fiscal year 1975—the last budget approved under President Nixon—

that amount had climbed steeply to $49.8 billion. Even correcting for the inflation rate in this period, that represented a cumulative increase of 69 percent in real dollars—a rate of expansion about equal to the 68 percent increase in real dollar aid during the Johnson years. By President Ford's last budget in FY 1977, the amount of intergovernmental aid had increased further to $68.4 billion—or an increase of about 23 percent in real dollar resources during the Ford administration. In only one of the eight years of Republican rule did the real resources devoted to intergovernmental aid decrease—in FY 1974, by 4.6 percent. Overall, the amount of intergovernmental aid provided by the federal government climbed from $20.3 billion in FY 1969 to $68.4 billion in FY 1977—an increase of nearly 109 percent in real dollars.

The Carter Years

The intergovernmental trends of President Jimmy Carter's administration are not clear-cut. In important respects he was an activist in intergovernmental affairs in the tradition of Lyndon Johnson. He worked at strengthening White House liaison with the nation's governors and mayors, secured enactment of major new programs (the Urban Development Action Grants, for example), modified existing ones (such as the Community Development Block Grant), promoted a strong federal regulatory role (for example, in targeting resources on needy citizens and geographic areas), and sought to generate consensus both within his administration and among other intergovernmental political actors for meaningful administrative reforms of the system. Although the exact expansion of categorical grant programs attributable to the Carter years is not available, the number of federal programs increased from 448 in 1975 to 498 in 1978 and to 539 in 1981.

Yet because he was cautious economically and faced tight fiscal conditions, President Carter's administration first slowed the rate of growth of federal aid to states and localities and then stabilized it. As Table 1 indicates, federal aid increased from $68.4 billion in FY 1977 to $94.8 billion in FY 1981, the year of Carter's last budget. That growth was largely inflation driven, however; there was almost no change in the amount of real resources provided in intergovernmental aid. More pertinently, the last three years saw a net decline in real resources of about 6 percent. The modern highwater mark of federal aid to states and localities—in real dollars— was reached in FY 1978. In light of President Ronald Reagan's subsequent policies, the Carter administration can be seen as a transition point between an era of steady expansion (that began in the postwar period and accelerated greatly during the Johnson, Nixon, and Ford years) and an era of retrenchment.

Reagan's New Federalism

President Reagan entered the White House with firm views and strong campaign commitments about intergovernmental relations. As governor of California during the late 1960s and early 1970s, Reagan had watched with dismay—politically and philosophically—as President Johnson's Great Society programs had grown in number and scale, bringing the federal government increasingly into policy matters that had been largely, if not exclusively, the province of state and local authorities. As governor, too, he had chafed at federal intrusions into his own state's affairs—quarreling, most notably, with the Office of Economic Opportunity over California's rural legal assistance program. These experiences, as well as his underlying conservative political views, led Reagan to make reform of the intergovernmental system one of the earliest and highest priorities of his presidency.

At their heart, the president's New Federalism proposals were designed to reduce the role of the national government in domestic policy. His plans had several dimensions. First, he intended to reduce the amount of money that the federal government would provide to states and localities, making them rely to an increasing degree on their own revenue sources. Second, in the areas in which the federal government continued to play a role in financing state and local programs, he intended to diminish the detail in which it prescribed program purposes, design, and management through statute and administrative regulations. Third, he planned to reduce federal monitoring of and intervention in state and local program execution.

During President Reagan's first year in office his principal method of achieving these purposes was to propose the consolidation of a number of existing federal categorical grants-in-aid into a smaller number of block grants. The broader purposes of these grants would give states and localities more freedom to manage their programs according to their own priorities, the new federal legislation and implementing regulations would contain fewer administrative strings, and the consolidation would permit the president to reduce the overall level of the federal budget for intergovernmental aid and the federal bureaucracy that administered it.

In many respects President Reagan's proposals were consistent with the direction of federal policy under his two Republican predecessors, Richard Nixon and Gerald Ford. Grant consolidation and reduction of federal constraints also had been important policy goals of their administrations. President Reagan's plans differed, however, in the importance he attached to cutting the amount of federal intergovernmental expenditures; his predecessors, after all, had presided over a substantial increase in the level of federal aid to states and localities. The Reagan proposals also differed in the key role he assigned to state government as the conduit through which federal aid would flow. Nixon and Ford had been party to the creation of direct federal-local programs—for example, the Community Development Block Grant (CDBG) and the Comprehensive Employment and Training Act (CETA). Reagan saw the states as the primary recipients of aid, who would then have the option to "pass through" assistance to local governments or selected private institutions or organizations.

The reaction to President Reagan's proposals was heated, both in Washington and around the country. In the nation's capital his plans were challenged by those who believed firmly that the federal government should be responsible for establishing national policy goals and minimum standards of service to America's people and for providing whatever funding and regulatory prodding were necessary to see that states and localities achieved them. Many members of Congress and the spokesmen for a number of major lobbying groups especially were concerned that projected budget cuts would seriously harm poor people if the states were unwilling or unable to replace federal funds for income maintenance and specialized aid programs. They worried, too, whether many states and localities would be as zealous as the federal government in protecting civil rights, preventing housing and job discrimination, and protecting the environment. In addition, many members of Congress had grave reservations about whether it would be possible to hold state and local officials appropriately accountable for their use of federal funds; they believed the level of government that raised revenue had an obligation to taxpayers to oversee its expenditure.

In state capitals and the nation's cities and towns, reaction to the president's proposals was mixed. Many public officials welcomed aspects of the president's initiatives. Most approved of his intention to reduce federal regulation and control but were extremely wary of his budget retrenchment plans. They feared that more autonomy would come only at the cost of overburdening their own budgets and forcing them to cut back services significantly or raise taxes. Some other political actors were even less enthusiastic. Many interest group leaders—particularly those who represented the poor, racial minorities, or other groups that had had a difficult time achieving influence in state and local affairs—were bitterly opposed to President Reagan's initiatives. They saw hard-won political gains, secured with the help of federal money or regulations, being swept away by "reforms" in Washington.

During 1981, President Reagan's first year in office, his plans for consolidation of categorical grant programs into a smaller number of block grants were subject to ferocious legislative wrangling. Liberal members of Congress and many interest groups fought hard to head off or modify the president's proposals. These were stalled in congressional committees during most of the year. In a dramatic push to get his tax cut and budget proposals approved through the new congressional budget process, however, the president was able to secure passage of many of his intergovernmental proposals in the Omnibus Budget Reconciliation Act of 1981, which he signed in August. That act created nine new block grants in fields such as health, education, social services, and community development by consolidating 57 previously existing categorical programs. (The president's victory was not complete, however, because Congress kept as separate grants a number of large categorical programs—for example, the major education grant—that the president had slated for consolidation.) Consistent with Reagan's views about regulation, federal agencies implementing the new block grants promulgated only a few broad regulations, leaving the recipient governments considerable latitude to interpret statutory language.

The battle over the future of the intergovernmental system was not over, however. The president regarded these initial changes as merely a starting point. In his State of the Union message in 1982, Reagan proposed sweeping changes in the grant-in-aid system. The main features of his new plan included a swap of functions between the federal government and the states and localities. The federal government would take over complete financing of the Medicaid program—the fastest-growing component of the aid system—in return for which the states would take over responsibility for 61 categorical grant programs (or what had been 125 the year before), including most of the major ones. To help the states pay for these programs, Reagan proposed a transitional trust fund that would support the programs completely for four years and then be phased out. Overall funding for these programs would drop by 25 percent over the four years.

State and local interests were overwhelmingly opposed to these ideas, as were important forces in Congress. Serious doubts existed about the adequacy of the funding sources in the trust fund and the capacity of many states ultimately to finance the programs on their own; and there was substantial local government opposition to enhanced state power over federal funds. The administration negotiated with the interest groups representing state and local governments but could find no mutually acceptable framework for enacting the president's proposals. For the most part, therefore, Congress rejected them, although Reagan won at least partial victories in the reauthorization of manpower and mass transit grants.

By 1983 the momentum behind comprehensive reform of the intergovernmental system seemed to have run out, at least temporarily. The administration proposed a new plan built around the consolidation of 34 categorical programs into four "mega-block" grants that took account of some of the reasons for opposition to the previous year's proposals. But it did not put anywhere near so much political energy into its efforts to move them through Congress, and the opposition remained steadfast. As the 1983 congressional session resumed in the fall, most knowledgeable observers expected these proposals to suffer largely the same fate as the earlier version. Nor did they think it likely that Congress would be disposed to enact major intergovernmental reforms in a national election year, even if President Reagan once more submitted proposals in 1984. If sweeping alterations in the grant system were to come, most observers believed, it would happen only if the 1984 elections brought President Reagan back to office with enhanced congressional support.

Despite disappointments in effecting structural reform in the intergovernmental system, however, Reagan had important effects on administrative and fiscal relations with state and local governments during his first three years as president. Through both legislation and regulatory action, the Reagan administration reduced the amount of federal control over state and local affairs. As Table 1 shows, moreover, a period of growth in the amount of federal aid that had continued almost uninterrupted since the end of World War II—for more than 35 years—was at least temporarily reversed. Reagan's first budget (for FY 1982) saw a decline in the aggregate amount of federal aid from $94.8 billion to $88.8 billion, a cutback of 12.2 percent in real dollar terms; and his subsequent budgets kept the fiscal pressure on state and local governments, proposing virtually no growth in real resources for intergovernmental aid. Whether that trend of increasing aid has been broken over the long haul cannot be foreseen, but the president's program represented the greatest shift in direction for the intergovernmental system in nearly a generation.

The Political Environment of Federalism

To understand the processes of contemporary intergovernmental relations, we must look more closely at the political actors who make policy in Washington and in state capitols and city halls throughout the United States.

Policy Making in Washington

The intergovernmental grant system has no centralized structure of policy making and management. No one in the White House, in the executive branch as a whole, or in Congress oversees the system in its entirety. In fact, except for a handful of groups—primarily a few less powerful congressional committees, the Advisory Commission on Intergovernmental Relations (ACIR), and the lobbying groups for generalist officials in state and local government—no institution is regularly much concerned with the intergovernmental system's overall functioning. Consequently, it operates in a highly dispersed and fragmented fashion. On a day-to-day basis, hundreds of intergovernmental programs are administered by officials in a variety of bureaus in many executive agencies. Agency staff in Washington are aided by federal employees in the field, in regional and area offices across the country. These efforts are overseen by the members and staff of numerous congressional subcommittees under the watchful eyes of lobbyists for the hundreds of interest groups whose members are affected by federal programs. To a large degree, therefore, management of the intergovernmental system is the task of specialists in the bureaucracy, congressional subcommittees, and interest groups. Each group of specialists is one of the fabled *iron triangles*—powerful, decentralized, policy-making networks that, in effect, govern federal action in their delimited spheres of influence. Even during the intermittent times when new legislation is proposed or existing programs are revised, these actors remain key players, often dominant over more visible policy makers in the nation's capital.

It is true that a president motivated to manage intergovernmental policy—as Lyndon Johnson, Richard Nixon, and Ronald Reagan have been at times—has unusually good resources to dominate the process. If he wishes, a president can pull policy planning and legislative strategy making into the White House. He can use his personal staff, personnel from the Office of Management and Budget (OMB), or executive agency staff to develop proposals for new programs or to revise existing ones. He can control the timing of debate by including his initiatives in his State of the Union address or a special presidential message to Congress. By commanding the news media's attention, he can focus the public's attention and frame its perception of the issues. Thus he can set the agenda of discussion and, within limits, have a major impact on the ultimate outcomes. Overall, the many formal and informal powers of his office make the president a formidable participant in policy negotiations about the intergovernmental system.

Yet having the nation's chief executive fully engaged is not the normal state of affairs in intergovernmental policy making. As much as a president may wish to concentrate on domestic matters, he is invariably pulled by the modern world into the realm of foreign affairs. Even on the domestic agenda, intergovernmental policy is not likely to compete with, let alone overshadow, problems of the national economy (such as inflation, unemployment, or recession) or with many other possible issues that may have more impact on the president's effectiveness and political fortunes. Therefore, having a president intensely involved in intergovernmental policy making, while not a rare event, is likely to be a fleeting phenomenon—a feature of the moment, not of the long haul.

Usually the White House staff and the Office of Management and Budget bear the primary burden of developing and proselytizing for a "presidential" policy. Compared with the times when they have the unquestioned attention and backing of the president, however, they have much less capacity to press for cooperation from the executive agencies and to bring

19

congressional and interest group participants into agreement on legislation or administrative policy.

Even during the president's activist periods, the "iron triangles" are an essential element in the policy-making process. Although some presidents, most notably Lyndon Johnson, have sometimes intentionally "frozen out" the agencies from administration strategy making, the bureaucracy is typically too important an actor to ignore. Its prominence stems from substantive and political expertise. The agencies understand the policy area in question as well as anyone in Washington, they have operated existing programs, and they have the knowledge to develop and assess policy options. On a day-to-day basis the agencies' administrative process is likely to be the main political arena for intergovernmental policy. Except in a handful of cases that involve extremely powerful interest groups, therefore, the agencies are more likely to know the constellation of concerned groups and to have better contacts with them than anyone at the White House. This expertise can be invaluable in winning approval of a policy initiative.

Congressional committees, and especially subcommittees, are also normally key actors in intergovernmental policy making, even when a president is seeking to assert his leadership. The committee structure is the repository of expertise in Congress. It is the realm of members who, particularly in the House of Representatives, often have devoted years to studying the issues in a policy area and knowing the relevant interests. Committee staff, which has gotten far more numerous in the past 20 years, is the technical counterweight to the executive agencies, giving members of Congress the benefit of professional and political expertise. While President Reagan was able to sidestep the committee structure in 1981 by using the budget reconciliation process to enact major proposals that had not been reported to the floor by the substantive legislative committees, that course of action is not likely to be open too often in the future. President Reagan was in an unusually strong political position at the time. Moreover, because subverting the committee structure is not in Congress's institutional interests, congressional leaders of both parties are not likely to countenance Reagan's tactics on a frequent basis.

As the intergovernmental grant system expanded rapidly during the 1960s and 1970s there was an explosive growth in the number of organized interests represented by lobbyists in Washington. By and large, these lobbyists are professional staff of the interest groups, but some are lawyers or public relations agents on retainer. Most of these groups are highly specialized and connected with one or a few grant programs. They include professional associations (the American Planning Association, the National Association of Housing and Renewal Officials), industrial groups with stakes in specific program areas (such as real estate interests concerned with community development policies), and organized clients (such as welfare rights groups).

There are also a number of well-known groups that have a broader concern with intergovernmental issues. Prominent among them are the organizations often labeled the "PIGs" or Public Interest Groups, which represent generalist public officials—governors, mayors, city managers, legislators. These groups include the National Governors' Association, the National Conference of State Legislatures, the National League of Cities, the U.S. Conference of Mayors, the International City Management Association, and the National Association of Counties.

In recent years, moreover, as the grant system's growth has slowed and reversed, as budgets at all levels of government have gotten tighter, and as regional rivalries have intensified, a number of new generalist groups representing particular geographic areas (the Northeastern Governors' Association and the Northeast Coalition of Municipalities) or specialized interests (rural or suburban communities, for example) have formed. Finally, there are special interest groups whose concerns cut across the range of domestic policy, including intergovernmental programs. These include some of the more visible lobbying groups in Washington—such as the NAACP, the AFL-CIO, and the U.S. Chamber of Commerce—as well as some less visible but influential groups concerned with topics such as environmental or economic development policy.

Outside of the routine intergovernmental policy-making networks lies another important set of political actors—the federal courts. As legislation establishing new programs has proliferated, as more decisions regarding the distribution of funds and the writing of program regulations have been delegated to executive agencies, and as more cross-cutting laws and regulations in areas such as civil rights and environmental protection are written, the judiciary has become an increasingly significant arena for settling disputes among the other actors in the intergovernmental system. While the basic constitutionality of the grant-in-aid system has long since been established by the Supreme Court, there is a continuous stream of litigation involving the interpretation of statutes and regulations and challenging various procedural practices of federal agencies.

The policy-making process described above helps account for two prominent characteristics of the intergovernmental system: the proliferation of separate grant programs and the difficulty of achieving comprehensive reform of the grant system. The underlying reason for this is that it is in the interest of each corner of the iron triangles to secure and maintain specialized attention to their concerns.

The structure of the federal executive branch promotes specialization and decentralization. Federal departments and agencies are divided into smaller bureaucratic units, many of which are given responsibility for (and therefore develop a stake in) individual grant programs. The people who work in these bureaus already are or soon will become specialists, too, by virtue of their professional training and experience or their job responsibilities. They therefore naturally think in terms of relatively narrow categories of government activity, a perspective reinforced by their dealings with concerned parts of Congress and lobbying groups. To counterbalance this fragmentation, the executive branch has only the president and his staff, particularly the Office of Management and Budget. But the president's own attention is often diverted, his personal staff is small and naturally oriented toward the president's priorities of the moment, and OMB primarily is inclined to concentrate more on the overall size of the budget than on the structure of programs. As a result, the forces promoting centralization tend to be much weaker than the countervailing pressures.

Congress's structure and operating procedures display a similar bias. The power of the committee system already has been noted. Along with the continued prominence of the seniority system in apportioning influence in Congress, this creates strong career incentives for individual members to devote their time and attention to relatively narrow segments of national policy. A member of Congress's relations with the voters creates similar incentives. A member campaigning for reelection wants to cite substantive accomplishments achieved during his service in Washington. That is far easier to do when he can point to his own bill dealing with an identifiable problem.

Such concern also is likely to earn the gratitude and support of the specialized interest groups that lobby in Washington. They, too, are concerned mainly with relatively narrow policy matters. The more broadly gauged groups may be more powerful, on the whole, than most of the highly specialized groups; but their concern and influence also is likely to be spread over a wider range of issues—and hence diluted. A group like the AFL-CIO can afford to commit only a limited amount of its resources to intergovernmental policy, and even a group like the National Governors' Association is concerned with a wide range of intergovernmental issues. More focused groups can concentrate their efforts. On a given public policy question, therefore, a relatively small, publicly invisible, and highly specialized interest group may well have more influence over Congress's decisions than the larger, better known, less specialized groups that have limited resources to devote to the matter.

Together, the forces promoting specialization in intergovernmental policy help account for the fragmentation of the grant system into hundreds of categorical programs. These forces provide the seemingly inexorable pressure that generates more categorical programs, and their entrenched support for *their* programs makes it difficult to win backing for more flexible grant mechanisms. In fact, massive efforts at grant consolidation—although probably the only way of winning more than limited attention from the president— also have the effect of mobilizing large numbers of specialized groups in opposition, each concerned mainly with the threat to its own particular interests. It is extremely difficult to mobilize enough political support to enact any major change in the intergovernmental system such as revenue sharing or a specific block grant proposal. Efforts, like President Reagan's, to thoroughly reorganize the system are not inevitably doomed as a result; but they must contend with opposing political forces that, in the aggregate, are quite powerful in Washington.

The State and Local Political Environment

The fundamental feature of policy making and management at the state and local level is its extraordinary diversity. As a result of the United States' tradition of federalism and the historical development of our institutions, we have a bewilderingly complex structure of subnational government. Fifty state governments are just the beginning. The United States also has an incredible quantity of separate substate governments, including 3,042 counties, 18,862 municipalities, 16,822 townships, 15,174 school districts, and 25,962 special service districts—or a total of 79,862 substate government units.[2] As a result of their separate development, moreover, these entities have varying responsibilities and powers. Consequently, one of the most basic—yet profound— insights that one can have into state and local government is that just because a particular policy or institutional practice appears in one location does not necessarily mean that it exists or operates in a similar fashion in another.

The States. Although the states are the primary recipients of federal aid, they lost relative standing to local governments during the 1960s and 1970s as more federal programs bypassed state government. That trend may be changing because the Reagan administration has emphasized the states again as the major aid recipients. Despite some backpedaling on this point in 1983 as local government opposition stalled his New Federalism program in Congress, President Reagan remained committed to strengthening the state role in managing federal intergovernmental programs.

Within state government, the executive branch generally has been the dominant force in dealing with intergovernmental programs. In many states the legislature does not appropriate federal funds; rather, grant allocation is an executive branch matter. As a result, legislatures usually have had a more distant and casual view of the intergovernmental system. An exception to this pattern, which is quite important in some circumstances, is when legislators must enact a formula for distributing federal grant funds that are to be *passed through* to localities. Then their involvement can be quite intense and the politics quite heated. Moreover, experience shows that if the states are given more discretion over the use of federal aid—as they were under several of the block grants that were enacted by the Budget Reconciliation Act of 1981— many legislators will demand a larger role in allocating federal grant funds.

Governors sometimes have played a marginal role in managing federal programs, too. With categorical grants going directly to state agencies in many cases and with federal program restrictions severely limiting state discretion in using funds, governors frequently have deferred to their agency heads in routine dealings with the intergovernmental system. They have, however, played a major role as spokesmen for the state's interests on major issues with the federal government and in lobbying for enhanced fiscal support from Washington. Like legislators, moreover, governors are likely to take a more aggressive role in managing federal grants if the president succeeds in giving the states more discretion over the use of intergovernmental aid.

Deference to specialists in state agencies frequently has made state bureaucrats' ties to their counterparts at the federal and local levels at least as important an influence on program decision making and administration as the policy guidance of state elected officials. The community of interest existing among these program managers, their shared work experience, and often their common educational backgrounds have been an influential force in shaping program implementation.

Given 50 state political systems, it is difficult to generalize about interest group activity at the state level. The constellation of interest groups that participate in policy making in state capitals is often not so diverse and competitive as in Washington, but the types of interests and their general influence tend to follow similar patterns.

The Localities. Far more diverse than even the states, local governments have become extremely important actors in the intergovernmental grant system. During the 1960s and 1970s a number of major grant programs were designed to channel funds directly to local governments rather than funneling them through the states. Far larger sums of money now flow into local coffers. Moreover, even in many program areas where money is given to the states initially, funds often are passed through to the localities that actually deliver the services.

From the local perspective, uneven coverage is an important feature of the grant system. The nation's cities have been eligible for many programs, and the larger ones have been virtually assured of access to major programs whether or not they were project grants. Medium-sized communities have been entitled by law to fewer grants, and they have been less likely than the larger cities to receive discretionary funds from federal agencies. As a consequence, each of these communities tends to have had experience with a smaller number of programs than the larger cities. Small communities, for their part, have had very spotty exposure to the grant system, with some having virtually no experience with discretionary programs. By and large, the smaller the community, the less likely it is to have significant skills in securing discretionary federal grants.

Authority in local government tends to be more centralized than it is in state government and, as a result, chief executives (whether elected mayors or appointed managers) have tended to have a larger role in administering federal programs than have governors. They, too, however, have had to wrestle with the fragmentation of power resulting from specialist control of categorical programs. Expertise and access to money—both of which have been conferred on some officials by virtue of their stewardship of federally supported programs—are important sources of political power, and municipal chief executives have had to contend with these centers of influence.

In many jurisdictions that have received federal grants, the experience has changed the face of municipal government. New functions have been added as federal grants have induced involvement, and the bureaucratic structure of local government similarly has been remodeled in response to federal programs. What is created by federal money, however, can be threatened by changes in funding. Hence urban renewal agencies that came into existence because of a federal program frequently found themselves substantially transformed, if not abolished, when the renewal program gave way to the CDBG program.

Federal grants have spawned an explosion of citizen involvement in local affairs in many cities. This is true not simply because of public participation requirements in many grant programs, although these have had an important effect, but also because federal money and the attention it helped focus on local affairs was responsible for increasing the perceived stakes of local politics. Thus more citizens felt it was worthwhile—even essential—to make their voices heard and their votes felt in municipal affairs. Many individuals who rose to prominence in city politics during the 1960s and 1970s—especially among disadvantaged racial and ethnic minorities—got their political beginnings from their involvement in intergovernmental programs. Many contemporary urban leaders began as protesters against the urban renewal or highway programs or as citizen participants in the antipoverty program.

Overall, the rapid expansion of the grant-in-aid system has changed state and local government in numerous ways. Most obviously, these governments have grown in number of employees and range of functions, aided to a substantial degree by federal funds. But federal program impacts go beyond their financial effects. Topics of federal interest have become matters of state and local concern, too. Federal initiatives have helped focus attention on issues such as fighting poverty, protecting water and air quality, and promoting neighborhood economic development. The federal government thus has been a major force in setting the state and local policy agenda. Federal initiatives also have altered patterns of political participation, especially in local government. The cumulative federal impact on the intergovernmental system, therefore, has been enormous.

Management Issues

Many aspects of intergovernmental relations arise from federal efforts to mandate state and local activities consistent with a more or less precisely defined set of federal goals. Most often this is done by offering federal financial support—that is, a grant-in-aid—as an inducement to voluntary compliance with various conditions attached to the grant. Sometimes the federal government issues a direct order—through statutes and administrative regulations—that is binding whether or not grants are involved. Ideally from the federal perspective, in either case, states and localities become the national government's administrative agents in carrying out federally defined purposes. In fact, however, intergovernmental relations are far more complicated. State and local governments have their own objectives, which do not necessarily coincide with federal purposes; they are far from being passive servants of federal directives. As a result, the relationship between federal officials on one side, and state and/or local officials on the other, is characterized by political bargaining and a persistent search for better leverage over one's partners.

Consequently, one can regard management in the intergovernmental grant system from two points of view. The "top down" perspective is held by federal officials (or state officials dealing with localities) responsible for ensuring that the recipient governments carry out the program in a way at least minimally consistent with the objectives set in Washington. The basic managerial problem from this standpoint is how to induce and assist the multitude of individual jurisdictions receiving support from the particular programs—as many as the approximately 35,000 recipients of general revenue sharing funds—to work toward federal goals. To accomplish this task, federal program managers have various administrative resources to influence policy choices and program implementation at lower levels of the federal system. These include the several types of grant-in-aid, substantive and procedural regulations, monitoring and enforcement methods, and technical assistance.

The "bottom up" perspective is that of the state or local officials responsible for administering the grants received from a higher level of government. Their basic managerial problem is to make the program work for their own government's purposes while still satisfying the requirements and expectations of the grantor. Given the character of the grant system, they must make a *multitude* of separate grant programs operate effectively for a *single* jurisdiction. This requires skills in grantsmanship, constituency building, program implementation, and administrative coordination.

Federal Policy Instruments

From the federal perspective, operating intergovernmental programs can be thought of as a process of *indirect management,* in which program administrators must induce administrators at other levels of government to pursue federal purposes. Over time, the federal government has developed a variety of policy instruments designed for indirect management tasks.

Forms of Grants-in-Aid. As described above, the intergovernmental grant system has evolved over many decades with periodic accretions of new programs and intermittent revisions of existing ones. There is no standard form of grant-in-aid; rather there are about 450 separately authorized programs, each of which has its own statutory characteristics. With full respect for this variation, however, one can usefully categorize grant programs along two dimensions.

The first dimension is the degree of discretion that federal administrative officials have in distributing funds. At one end of this continuum are *formula* grants, defined by the fact that their authorizing legislation specifies unambiguous principles by which funds should be apportioned to eligible jurisdictions. The distribution formula may be a simple one—based solely on population, perhaps—or it may be far more complex, taking account of factors such as percentage of population living in poverty, number of transit trips taken each day, or rate of unemployment. Where a fixed amount of money is appropriated for the program, the formula enables a jurisdiction to determine quite closely what share of the total pie it is entitled to. The determining character of this type of grant, from our perspective, is the fact that federal administrative officials are given virtually no discretion in allocating funds to recipients. (For present purposes, where a program involves *open-ended reimbursement*—as in some income maintenance and medical assistance programs, for example—it is regarded as a variety of formula grant.)

At the other end of this continuum are *project* grants. Congress gives the executive branch considerable latitude in determining which states or localities will receive funds—and how much they will get. Such a program's authorizing statute generally lays down standards of eligibility and broad criteria for allocating grants but gives officials in the responsible federal agency the final word in distributing the money. Typically, the agency will elaborate on the eligibility standards and program criteria in administrative regulations and then determine the grant "winners" through a competitive application process.

Between the extremes of pure "formula" and "project" grants are several variants. Some programs, such as the Small Cities Community Development Block Grant, for example—allocate funds to the states by formula and then permit discretionary distribution on a project-by-project basis to specific local governments.

Analytically, the significance of this dimension of administrative discretion lies in the potential influence it gives to federal program managers. The power to determine which jurisdictions receive federal funds and how much they get gives program managers a substantial amount of leverage over the state and local governments that want to get initial access to a grant and keep it in subsequent years. Federal program managers can use that leverage to shape grantees' policy choices and administrative behavior. (Such latitude on the federal side makes the grant system less predictable from the perspective of state or local program managers. Their efforts to gain a favorable response from federal authorities later will be termed "grantsmanship.")

The second dimension that helps to characterize intergovernmental grant programs involves the degree of restriction imposed on the use of federal funds. At one extreme of this continuum are *categorical* grants, so called because recipients can use the money only for certain clearly specified categories of expenditure. The restrictions can be quite narrow. For example, until the program was consolidated into another one by the Reagan administration, the U.S. Department of Education administered a small grant program that promoted education in the metric system of measurement. Or, moving away from the extreme end of our analytic dimension, categorical purposes may be somewhat broader—for example, grants for Aid to Families with Dependent Children (AFDC) or for highway construction.

At the other end of this dimension is the general revenue sharing program in which federal funds can be used for virtually any state or local government purpose. The various *block* grant programs—the Social Services Block Grant (formerly Title XX), the Community Development Block Grant, and the Job Training Partnership Act (successor to CETA)—give state and local recipients a good deal of latitude in determining spending priorities within a broad policy area specified by federal legislation.

In this dimension, too, considerable variation exists along the continuum. Congress is quite imaginative in the type and range of restrictions that are written into legislation establishing grant programs. The significance of the distinction, as in the case of the other dimension identified above, is the potential for federal influence. The farther along the continuum toward the categorical end that a grant program falls, the more state and local policy choices and administration will be constrained by federal preferences.

Aside from the nature of the grant itself, federal administrators have a variety of other policy instruments and administrative procedures that can be used to influence the behavior of state and local grant recipients. These tools involve the federal government's authority to issue administrative regulations, monitor program implementation, and oversee grantees' financial management practices. To help understand the process of federal influence, we can classify these tools as eligibility requirements, application review and approval processes, performance controls, and financial controls.

Eligibility Requirements. Access to federal funds can be controlled by statutory or administratively imposed eligibility requirements of several types.

These may be substantive—relating to specific features of the recipient jurisdictions' social or economic circumstances. For example, the program may require that the populations of state or local government applicants be experiencing unemployment above a certain specified rate or that water quality be below particular standards. Eligibility requirements can be institutional or procedural, too. Among the most common of these is the requirement in a number of grant programs that there be a single state agency responsible for carrying out the program; that means that the federal government wants to make sure that one administrative entity at the state level is the center of authority for the program and can be held accountable by federal program monitors. Such eligibility requirements enhance federal influence both by targeting aid on jurisdictions that meet certain criteria of need and by ensuring that applicants satisfy prerequisite standards for their administrative structures and procedures.

Application Review and Approval. Virtually all grant programs require potential recipients to submit formal applications to establish their eligibility and to meet any other requirements specified in the statute or administrative regulations. In some cases, as for general revenue sharing, this application procedure is a pro forma requirement; there is no significant weeding out of applicants. Especially for project grants, however, the application process can be a critical step in determining whether a particular jurisdiction will receive a grant.

In most situations the federal agency specifies the form and content of the grant application, indicating what kinds of information must be supplied. This may require a significant commitment by the applicant in collecting data to document eligibility and need and in developing specific plans for how the federal funds would be spent. Many programs demand detailed budgets as well as supporting narrative to describe proposed program purposes and activities. For some large-scale federal programs—notably in the environmental and transportation policy areas—elaborate interagency and interjurisdictional planning requirements also must be fulfilled to qualify for federal aid.

The completed application is then submitted to the federal agency—sometimes an area or regional office, sometimes headquarters in Washington—for review. For formula grant programs, where eligibility is usually not in doubt, this review may be quite perfunctory and is aimed merely at verifying that statutory or regulatory requirements are minimally fulfilled. It is not aimed at evaluating the quality of the application. For project grant programs, however, this review process is critical to the applicant jurisdiction's chances of actually receiving funds. Depending on how competitive the process is for a particular grant, applications may be subjected to intensive review and evaluation. Before reaching a final decision, the federal agency may choose to conduct on-site investigations to gather more information about the applicant's proposals. Final decisions by the federal agency may involve considerable negotiations with the applicant to bring the proposal into closer conformance with federal expectations.

Such an application process potentially gives federal administrators a good deal of leverage over state and local applicants. A jurisdiction eager to win a grant presumably will devote considerable effort to finding out what criteria, both formal and informal, will be applied to evaluation of its proposal. It can learn this both from its own sources of information and from the various public interest groups (PIGs), such as the National Governors' Association or the National League of Cities, that maintain Washington lobbying and intelligence-gathering offices to serve their members. To increase the chances of securing a grant, a jurisdiction is likely to tailor its application to the perceived preferences of the federal decision maker. This behavior is known as *grantmanship*. As a result, the federal agency can gain significant influence over the content of the state or locality's program.

Performance Controls. Once a grant has been given, federal administrators have different policy instruments to influence state and local program implementation. The first are rules governing management of that grant. These may be expressed in formal *administrative regulations* issued by the federal grant-giving agency according to statutory procedures and carrying the force of law, or they may be promulgated less formally as *guidelines* that carry less legal weight but that state the agency's expectations in writing. Such regulations or guidelines may be substantive (interpreting the meaning of the statute, specifying required and proscribed program activities, listing allowable and not allowable expenditures, laying down standards of education or experience for certain types of program personnel) or they may be procedural (describing required accounting practices, prescribing citizen participation mechanisms, specifying forms of administrative organization, or explaining procedures for changing budget allocations).

Over time the volume of program regulations and guidelines has a tendency to expand. For a new program, especially, there may be too little experience at the federal level to prescribe operating procedures or substance in detail. As a program develops a track record and as congressional observers and executive branch monitors detect practices that they regard as distortions or evasions of federal intent, they tend to adopt more detailed regulations to prevent such behavior by grant recipients. The aggregate volume of regulations can reach staggering proportions, as was the case for the urban renewal program that operated from 1949 until it was absorbed in the Community Development Block Grant in 1974. The regulations for urban renewal ultimately filled a shelf length of looseleaf binders.

Not all federal guidance to states and localities comes in writing. By a variety of informal communications from Washington headquarters (and often from the federal agency's regional or area offices), the program's state and local managers learn about federal preferences and intent and often get preliminary intelligence about proposed or planned program changes.

In many programs the federal agency does more than communicate its formal and informal expectations about program performance. To gauge results the agency may collect data about grant recipients' management of the program. This is done, first, by soliciting written reports from the state and local agencies implementing it. These may be followed up by field inspections so that the federal agency gets first-hand information and can verify claims made in the jurisdictions' reports. The quality and aggressiveness of such review varies widely among grant programs, depending on the availability and skills of agency staff, the political sensitivity of the program, and the incumbent administration's philosophical orientations about federal influence. In some grant programs federal monitoring is extremely sketchy — nearly nonexistent—while in others it is careful, thorough, and probing in at least a few exemplary sites.

Financial Controls. Closely allied with these performance controls are several varieties of financial control tools that can be powerful sources of influence on state and local program managers. The first, operative in some categorical grant programs, is the requirement of federal approval to "draw down" funds for upcoming expenditures. In the urban renewal program, for example, federal officials used this method extensively to keep close watch on the content and progress of individual renewal projects in successive phases of development. More commonly, federal agencies require an annual plan tied to the program's budget submission.

In extreme circumstances where federal officials believe that program regulations have been seriously violated, the federal agency can threaten or actually withhold future grant payments. Such actions are not taken lightly because of the damage that can be done to the program itself, to the program's beneficiaries, or to the working relationship between federal officials and their state or local counterparts. Significant damage also can result from the hornets' nest of political trouble that can be stirred up by a jurisdiction's congressional representatives. A more likely course of action for a federal agency dissatisfied with state or local performance would be to hold negotiations on the issue in hope of securing rectification of the matter and a pledge of future compliance with federal requirements. The possibility of a cutoff of federal financial support most likely would be an unstated premise of these negotiations. Only after exhausting the possibilities of negotiation is a federal agency likely to threaten fund withholding—and even less likely to actually attempt to do it.

31

Auditing program expenditures is another type of financial control that is more frequently—though still not extensively—applied. Federal auditors from the agency that provided the grant sample the books of grantees to determine whether program expenditures have been made in accordance with federal requirements. If discrepancies are found, either because of loose management or purposeful evasion of regulations, the federal agency can selectively seek repayment of the funds in question or deduct the amount from future grant payments. This control is a potentially useful device for steering the state or local grant recipient toward approved program practices and for deterring other jurisdictions from similar deviations. Auditing also is done by the General Accounting Office (GAO), a staff arm of Congress, as a form of oversight of federal administrative performance. The audit results are used by Congress to help determine whether statutes need to be revised and whether federal executive agencies are handling their supervisory roles effectively. In yet another use of this control technique, the federal government has expanded use of auditing by states and localities themselves by including a requirement for regular audits as a condition for receipt of general revenue sharing grants. This makes it possible for local legislatures and interested members of the public, as well as federal officials, to monitor the use of a jurisdiction's revenue sharing funds.

Technical Assistance. While not so clearly an instrument of policy control as the tools discussed so far, technical assistance can be at least a moderately influential device for shaping the behavior of grant recipients. The term "technical assistance" here does not necessarily mean aid in utilizing arcane technological innovations or technical information but can instead refer more broadly to outside support in adopting any management or program practices not currently in use in the jurisdiction or in improving the effectiveness of existing practices. Technical assistance can be a means of persuading state or local officials that new methods make sense, thus affecting the policy choices or administrative routines of their government.

State and Local Management

On the whole, for state and local program administrators, managing intergovernmental grant programs raises a different range of problems than it does for their counterparts in the federal government. When state and local governments actually operate programs they are engaged in *direct*, not indirect, management. They must worry about delivering housing services to citizens, or building public facilities, or sponsoring urban redevelopment. The management processes involved are fundamentally different from those used by federal officials trying to steer state or local actions. (The state role is a partial exception. To the extent that state government passes federal grants through to localities without actually operating programs itself, or originates aid programs for localities with its own money, its role tends to resemble the federal government's. This role requires the indirect management techniques described above.)

The state and local perspective varies, too, because these governments are likely to have at least partially different goals from their federal counterparts. Nonetheless, they must remain sensitive to the outlook of their financial benefactor. As a consequence, managing intergovernmental programs requires conforming sufficiently to federal requirements to maintain or expand the state or locality's access to federal funds while simultaneously using those resources to serve the jurisdiction's own policy and political purposes. The management outlook of grant recipients, therefore, deserves a more detailed examination.

Grantsmanship. Given the intergovernmental system's reliance on hundreds of categorical programs, state and local officials have had to develop skills in grantsmanship to take advantage of this source of fiscal assistance. Grantsmanship refers to the set of activities required to secure and retain intergovernmental grants, including intelligence gathering about federal program priorities, proposal writing, plan drafting, budget construction, negotiation with federal program managers, political support building, progress report preparation, and financial accounting. Taken as a whole the skills of a grantsman are part political and part bureaucratic—with neither side predominating. While securing some types of grants does not require these skills to a high degree, officials who by experience or natural inclination are strong in these areas are more likely to be successful in developing federal financial support.

Constituency Building. Grantsmanship is not the only aspect of managing intergovernmental programs that requires significant political skills. Starting a new program or substantially expanding an existing one demands more than monetary resources, as helpful as they may be. Federal grants are an inducement to undertake policy innovations only if there are individuals or organizations that are demanding or can be persuaded to support the ultimate product of the program. Consequently, the program manager guiding his agency into new activities must carefully build political support for his endeavor—both *within* government among elected policy makers and bureaucrats and *outside* of it among those elements of the public that will benefit in some fashion from the program's operation. These political chores need not necessarily fall to an administrative official; they may, in fact, be the province of an elected executive or a legislator. But making a new program take root in government requires that some set of senior officials makes a priority out of developing a coalition of support.

Developing Implementation Capacity. Building a government program means developing a bureaucratic unit with the staff, financial capacity, and organizational routines sufficient to implement and maintain it. That task can be exceedingly complex and time consuming, and describing it thoroughly goes well beyond the scope of this essay. It involves, however, all of the basic functions of public management: planning, personnel development and supervision, fostering an organizational structure appropriate for their work, budgeting and financial management, development of organizational control systems, operations management, performance monitoring, and program evaluation.

Implementation capacity may involve more than public agencies themselves. It has become increasingly common for states and localities to contract with private nonprofit organizations to deliver to citizens services paid for with federal funds. This strategy affords more flexibility than using government agencies and employees; no longterm commitment exists to retain the workers or the programs, and it is often possible to bypass restrictions such as civil service regulations. Use of private organizations, however, raises many issues of management control. Can government be certain that its resources are being used for the intended purposes? Using private organizations to supplement government's implementation capacity involves yet another form of indirect management.

The Case Studies

The remainder of this book presents a series of case studies on federal programs. The complexity of today's intergovernmental grant system and the diversity of state and local government in the United States pose a variety of significant problems for public managers, including the individuals who march across the pages of this book. A reader who tries to empathize with the decision makers whose administrative and political dilemmas are presented here should come away with a greater appreciation for the realities of "managing federalism."

The cases that follow are arranged in three sections. The first group of cases—"The Maternal and Child Health Block Grant in Washington State and Seattle," "The Kentucky Small Cities CDBG Demonstration," and "The Environmental Protection Agency and Transportation Controls"—is intended to convey a sense of how actors at several levels of the federal system perceive and react to a particular set of policy problems. A reader can jump back and forth from the perspectives of federal, state, and local participants to appreciate how their roles and orientations mesh or collide. The second group of case studies—"Restricting Traffic on Washington Street" and "Community Development in Gainesville"—aims at illustrating the problems of putting a federal program into effect at the local level. These cases show in some detail the processes of grantsmanship, coalition building, and development of implementation capacity. Finally, the third set of cases—"Extending the Red

Line to Arlington" and "Citizen Participation in Oxford"—is concerned with the relationship of ordinary citizens to federal programs. They show how community residents may respond to federal initiatives, both in spontaneous fashion and in more structured ways.

Together these cases provide a reader with considerable information to probe the broad issues of intergovernmental management. Understanding these issues better is an important first step toward becoming a more effective participant in intergovernmental program management. It is also a useful step for either citizens or policy makers concerned with improving the way the system functions.

NOTES

1. This section draws heavily on materials in *Categorical Grants: Their Role and Design,* Advisory Commission on Intergovernmental Relations (Washington, D.C.: Government Printing Office, 1977), 15-47; and *Toward a Functioning Federalism,* David B. Walker (Cambridge, Mass.: Winthrop Publishers, 1981), 19-131.

2. This tally dates to 1977. See *State and Local Roles in the Federal System,* Advisory Commission on Intergovernmental Relations (Washington, D.C.: Government Printing Office, 1981), 228.

I. The Dynamics of Federalism: Federal, State, and Local Perspectives

1. THE MATERNAL AND CHILD HEALTH BLOCK GRANT
IN WASHINGTON STATE AND SEATTLE

2. THE KENTUCKY SMALL CITIES CDBG
DEMONSTRATION

3. THE ENVIRONMENTAL PROTECTION AGENCY
AND TRANSPORTATION CONTROLS (A, B, C)

1. The Maternal and Child Health Block Grant in Washington State and Seattle

INTRODUCTION

When President Reagan announced his "New Federalism" proposals in early 1981, his message stirred intense interest in state capitols and city halls nationwide. The prospect of widespread change in the intergovernmental grant system was a matter of critical concern to governors, mayors, state and local legislators, and program managers. The federal government's involvement in state and local programs is so pervasive—both in financing and in setting policy for service delivery—that comprehensive reform of the grant system promised (or threatened) significant changes in nearly every corner of government.

By implementing the New Federalism, Reagan hoped to reduce the national government's role in domestic affairs. As the Nixon and Ford administrations had tried before, the Reagan administration planned to cut back on federal prescription of program purposes, design, and management. Consolidating many categorical grants into a smaller number of block grants would give states and localities greater latitude to define their own goals within broad limits; and the reduction of federal statutory injunctions, regulatory restrictions, and program reporting and monitoring would permit them to administer programs more freely. But the president's plans went beyond the diminution of federal constraints on program management to include significant reductions in the *amount* of intergovernmental aid. Although the growth of intergovernmental aid had slowed during the Carter administration (and declined modestly in real dollar terms), Reagan's intention to make sharp cutbacks was a major departure from a previous generation of presidential practice.

As Congress wrestled with Reagan's proposals throughout most of 1981, state and local officials watched closely—and warily. Events in Washington, D.C., caused many questions to be raised. What legislation ultimately would emerge from Congress? To what extent could officials influence its content through lobbying? What consequences would it have for the amount of federal aid they could expect in coming years? To what extent would it require alterations in the structure and content of the services they provided to the public? Would there be opportunities to make program changes that they had long desired? Would the New Federalism create numerous policy and political problems?

As officials pondered these questions and others, it became obvious that their answers varied according to the level of government in which they worked and the specific jobs they held.

From the state perspective, the New Federalism was a mixed blessing. In most states, officials at all levels were shocked to think of losing federal funds after many years of increased intergovernmental revenues. That prospect was worsened by the fact that the national economic recession had exposed most state governments to severe fiscal stress as their tax revenues failed to meet budget targets and as citizens-in-need demanded more public services. Whatever theoretical views on federalism they held, governors and other key administrators still had to manage their states' budgets. Reduced federal funding meant they would have to improve productivity, or cut back on services, or find new or enhanced revenue sources elsewhere.

Most top state officials, however, welcomed the idea of grant consolidation and increased reliance on block grants as a way of giving their governments greater latitude in managing federal funds. This reduction in program restrictions was seen as a positive step; the states would have the chance to respond more closely to their own priorities in the programmatic and geographic distribution of federal funds. In most states, officials valued program discretion even at the risk of increased constituency pressure from groups wanting funds used for their "pet" programs; these organizations could no longer be told that "the Feds mandated it."

At middle levels of state government, however, the prospect of looser federal controls was less clearly a benefit. There the bureaucracy's structure often corresponded closely to that of federal program support, with specific organizational units mainly administering particular federally financed programs. Program managers in these bureaus, who often chafed at how the administrative constraints created by federal regulations prevented them from running their programs as they felt would be proper, were likely to be pleased at the relaxation of federal oversight. On the other hand, to the extent that previously earmarked money might now be spent for other purposes, some of these bureaus might lose influence within their agencies—and perhaps even be threatened by the phasing out of their programs if money were reallocated for other purposes.

To a degree, many of these same considerations applied to local governments. Like state leaders, most mayors, county executives, and other local policy makers were concerned first of all with the fiscal implications of the president's proposals. Federal budget cuts simply added to the fiscal squeeze that preoccupied most of them. In many cases, already faced by a revenue gap that would force them to increase taxes or cut services, local chief executives and their top administrators were grimly aware of how reduced federal aid would exacerbate their problems.

Their feelings about block grants, however, were more mixed than the governors'. Reductions in federal oversight and regulation were welcome; but, the extent to which the federal hand would be replaced by state supervision, as it would be under the president's plans, made many local executives uneasy. As onerous as federal restrictions might be, local governments had established expectations about and working relationships with the federal agencies that ran intergovernmental programs. The president's proposals largely would wash away these expectations and make contacts with federal officials far less useful. In many cases, moreover, local leaders were apprehensive about substituting this "known quantity" for an uncertain relationship with a state government newly empowered by its control of federal funds—especially when state-local relations in the past often had been rocky. Even when local officials were used to dealing with the state agency that would manage a new block grant, they could no longer expect to be "protected" by federal regulations and monitoring that previously had constrained state officials' actions.

Under the president's New Federalism the game would be played with new rules. State spending priorities might not be the same as federal priorities. Localities might find not only that the amount available for a particular program area was being cut by the federal government but also that the state was choosing to spend what funds there were for some other purpose—or in some other location. The danger of this happening probably was greater under conditions of fiscal stress because the states' directly-financed services were likely to be hard pressed to maintain their levels of activity. Local officials feared that state administrators would be tempted to use their new control over federal funds to divert funds away from local governments in order to support traditional state programs.

Not only local government officials had such fears. Some federal grants went directly to private, nonprofit organizations such as hospitals or community health centers. If state governments secured control of this money under the New Federalism, then the affected nonprofit would have to lobby for its share and might, in fact, face drastic reductions in its budgets or even a total cutoff of federal funds.

In the case study that follows, "The Maternal and Child Health Block Grant in Washington State and Seattle," we can see how these alternative perspectives on Reagan's New Federalism were played out in one program area in one state. This case affords a good opportunity to see how both state and local policy makers reacted to the shift in structure and control of health grants, what tensions these changes created within state government, and what pulling and hauling resulted between state authorities and officials in Seattle.

THE CAST

John Spellman	governor of Washington State
Alan Gibbs	secretary of Social and Health Services
Judy Merchant	special assistant to Alan Gibbs
Dr. John Beare	director, Division of Health Services, Department of Social and Health Services (DSHS)
Dr. Robert Leahy	director, Office of Community Health Services, DSHS Division of Health Services
Dr. Peter Pulrang	staff member, DSHS Office of Community Health Services
Patricia Snyder	staff member, DSHS Office of Community Health Services
Kenneth Miller	budget director, DSHS
Charles Royer	mayor of Seattle
William Stafford	director, Seattle's Office of Intergovernmental Relations
Jill Marsden	director, Seattle Division, Seattle/King County Public Health Department
DSHS	Department of Social and Health Services
Title V	section of federal Social Security Act that provided funds for health care to mothers and children

CHRONOLOGY

<u>1981</u>

February
President Reagan sends his Program for Economic Recovery, including a plan for a New Federalism, to Congress.

Alan Gibbs becomes secretary of Social and Health Services in the new administration of Gov. John Spellman of Washington State. He is faced immediately with the task of planning for federal budget cutbacks and begins formulating procedures for systematically determining DSHS priorities.

Officials in Seattle city government map strategy for influencing and adapting to likely changes in federal grant programs.

March-April
John Beare, director of the DSHS Division of Health Services, begins setting priorities for his division's programs. He considers cutbacks in funding for Seattle.

May
Gibbs announces a plan for cutback priority setting and outlines steps to be followed until September.

June
Officials from the DSHS Division of Health Services inform Seattle that it should expect a 31 percent cutback in funds for maternal and child health care.

June-July
Officials from Seattle and the division debate the appropriateness of these cutbacks.

July
Gibbs issues DSHS "program perspective," outlining in general form the department's program priorities.

Congress enacts the Omnibus Budget Reconciliation Act, which creates nine new block grants including one for maternal and child health programs.

July-August
Gibbs solicits public comment on the DSHS program perspective while DSHS division directors work on detailed budgets for their programs.

September
Seattle makes a last appeal to preserve funding while Gibbs and his staff prepare the final budget.

In 1981 during his first seven months as secretary of the Department of Social and Health Services (DSHS) in Washington State, Alan Gibbs had faced a looming budget crisis. President Ronald Reagan's proposals to cut federal domestic expenditures and consolidate many grant-in-aid programs for state and local governments into a few, broad-based "block" grants seemed likely to affect Gibbs' department in major ways—most significantly by cutting its federal revenues by about $110 million over a two-year period. Because these cuts came in the wake of a severe recession in the state, which had already forced state budget cutbacks and threatened still more, the potential disruption of DSHS programs was immense.

As a consequence of the federal grant consolidation, however, Washington State's officials had unprecedented discretion in deciding how to reduce their program expenditures. Although the officials by no means had a totally free hand, the new block grants allowed them to spend money across the boundaries of the predecessor categorical programs; they no longer were obligated to use funds for closely circumscribed federal purposes. Gibbs, therefore, could recommend to the governor cuts that largely reflected *state* spending priorities, not federal requirements.

Along with greater freedom in spending federal grant money, though, came vulnerability to pressure from the many program constituencies that depended on federal funds. These interests—including service recipients, service providers, professional groups, local and county governments, and other concerned citizens—had their own sense of what social needs were most pressing and therefore how federal money ought to be spent. Their clamoring made the job of setting priorities for DSHS a difficult task—and a politically risky one for a new administrator from out of state.

Gibbs had faced these problems with skill, establishing a comprehensive budget review and priority-setting process that gave the department's varied constituencies a full opportunity to join in the policy debate. Now, in September 1981, assisted by his department's top administrators, he had to make hard decisions about which programs to cut.

No decision was tougher than how to allocate funds from the new Maternal and Child Health Block Grant to the city of Seattle and surrounding

This case was written by Arnold M. Howitt.

King County for their joint mothers' and young children's programs. Seattle had been a statewide leader in providing prenatal care to low-income pregnant women and following up with well-baby clinics and other medical programs for their offspring. Because of the city's aggressive attack on these health problems and the concentration of low-income people in the city, Seattle had received the lion's share of federal funds allocated to Washington State under the categorical grant programs that had preceded the Maternal and Child Health Block Grant. Now, with the freedom to reallocate federal money, Gibbs' Division of Health Services wanted to shift resources away from Seattle/King County to other communities that had not offered so wide an array of services to their needy citizens. Such a decision would not come without a fight. Seattle's Mayor Charles Royer and his staff, as well as officials from the Seattle/King County Public Health Department, had lobbied hard to preserve their share of federal funds, arguing strenuously that the Seattle area should not be punished for its concern and success in providing health care.

Faced with pressure both from within his own department and from the state's major metropolitan area, Gibbs methodically pondered his options.

The Federal Policy Context

Secretary Gibbs' policy choices and budgetary dilemmas were shaped in important ways by events in Washington, D.C., where the president and Congress had spent much of 1981 sparring over proposals to redesign the nation's intergovernmental grant system.

The Reagan Administration's 'New Federalism'

On February 18, 1981, just one month after becoming president, Ronald Reagan presented his "Program for Economic Recovery" to a joint session of Congress and a national television audience. As the centerpiece of his first year's legislative program, the president proposed a substantial reduction in personal and business income taxes, significant cuts in federal domestic expenditures, and a "New Federalism" to be achieved by restructuring grant-in-aid programs for state and local governments.

The heart of the New Federalism was the consolidation of many existing categorical grant programs into a smaller number of block grants. Categorical programs allocate money for specific and relatively narrow purposes—for example, to combat a particular disease or to educate a specified target group such as handicapped children. Block grants, in contrast, give discretion to recipient governments to spend funds in a broader functional area—for example, community development or social services.

President Reagan made the case for block grants on the basis of reducing costs, improving efficiency, giving states and localities greater flexibility, and decentralizing policy-making authority. Over the next two months the White House made detailed proposals to put the president's ideas into operation. As a first step toward the New Federalism, the administration wanted to "fold" 84 existing grant programs into seven block grants: two for education, one for community development, one for social services, two for health services, and one for energy and emergency assistance.

The two health grants—one for health services and the other for preventive health—were designed to consolidate 25 categorical programs, each of which delivered care to specific target populations defined variously by age, income, occupation, place of residence, health status, or disease category. These grants had no uniform administrative structure. Some gave money to the states according to a congressionally enacted formula, while others required detailed applications for specific projects. Some grants went to state governments for their own purposes or to be "passed through" to local recipients, while others went directly from the federal government to local governments or nonprofit institutions. Most of the grants had unique planning requirements and idiosyncratic regulations and administrative features.

Existing Maternal and Child Health Programs

President Reagan's proposals came after nearly 70 years of federal involvement in maternal and child health services. Beginning with the establishment of the Children's Bureau in 1912, the federal government has played a major role in creating an array of state and locally provided health programs. The Sheppard-Towner Act of 1921 was the first vehicle to distribute federal funds—to states that established programs to reduce infant mortality rates among the urban poor—but the Social Security Act of 1935 set the modern pattern of aid. Title V, drafted by the Children's Bureau, provided grants to states for prenatal care for pregnant women and for well-baby and well-child clinics for their children. Title V also created a Crippled Children's program to aid both the handicapped and victims of chronic diseases. As a whole, Title V substantially strengthened the federal role by making receipt of funds contingent on state acceptance of federal regulations about planning and delivery of the health services. Each state's share of the total federal appropriation was set by a statutory formula.

Throughout the 1960s the federal government expanded its efforts. Title V was amended in 1963 to create the Maternity and Infant Care and the Children and Youth programs, which permitted the federal government to contract directly with private institutions or government entities other than the states to provide specific maternal and child health services. These funds were distributed as project grants, thereby giving federal administrative officials wide discretion in selecting recipients rather than making them distribute funds according to the Title V formula. In the 1960s and early 1970s, other categorical grants were established, including programs for supplemental security income for disabled children, lead paint poisoning prevention, genetic disease screening, dental health, sudden infant death syndrome (SIDS) counseling, hemophilia treatment, family planning, and adolescent pregnancy prevention and counseling.

In 1975, with President Gerald R. Ford pressing for grant consolidation, Congress folded five project grant programs into the basic Title V formula. As a result, states were required to use their Title V allotments to support at least one project—somewhere within their jurisdictions—in each of five program areas: maternity and infant care, infant intensive care, family planning, children and youth, and dental health. The states were expected to target these projects on localities with concentrations of low-income persons. The remaining categorical programs continued to exist separately.

Congressional Debate

President Reagan's block grant proposals were designed to rationalize administration of these and other health programs by combining them into two larger grants that would give state governments more control over funds and greater program discretion. These plans swiftly came under fire from various beneficiaries of the categorical programs, professional groups, state and local officials, and other concerned interests. They charged that the block grants would jeopardize important programs that some states would not support if left on their own, that needy groups and the politically impotent would lose services, that the states would waste money through poor management or steer it to political uses, or that some states would discriminate against minorities in disbursing funds. They also charged that the president was greatly exaggerating the administrative cost-savings possible by consolidating existing grants.

The congressional battle over President Reagan's tax cuts, budget reductions, and block grant proposals was long and fierce. The Republican-controlled Senate was more inclined to accept the block grant concept than the Democratic-controlled House of Representatives, but both houses of Congress favored more "strings" (regulatory restrictions) than the administration desired. The outcome hung in doubt until the summer of 1981.

Cutback and Block Grant Planning

As the president lobbied for his program in Congress, top officials in Washington State government and in the city and county governments in Seattle spent many hours pondering how the president's proposals might affect their current operations and finances, and how they might influence the national government's final decisions.

Alan Gibbs and the DSHS

In Olympia, Washington State's capital city, the national Republican tide in 1980 had carried in a new Republican governor and GOP majorities in both houses of the state legislature. Commentators regarded Gov. John Spellman, former chief executive of King County (the largest county in the state, containing the city of Seattle and its surrounding suburbs), as a political moderate slightly to the left of his Republican compatriots in the legislature.

Among the new governor's initial responsibilities was the selection of a secretary for the state's mammoth Department of Social and Health Services, which had approximately 12,000 employees and an annual budget of $1.3 billion. DSHS was created in 1970 to consolidate management of the state's human service programs. It contained operating divisions responsible for income-maintenance programs such as Aid to Families with Dependent Children and Medicaid, social services, public health, juvenile rehabilitation, developmental disabilities, vocational rehabilitation, and mental health. (Education, employment, and community action programs never had been included in DSHS, and in 1980 a separate Corrections Division was established to run the state prisons.) The DSHS central office in Olympia housed the secretary, deputy secretary, two assistant secretaries, and the division directors, as well as a variety of staff who worked in budget and personnel. Six regional offices also existed to supervise 63 district offices around the state. These district offices delivered services directly to citizens. In addition DSHS worked closely with a wide range of private, nonprofit agencies and county and city governments that provided services on a contract basis with state-provided funds.

To head this giant agency, Governor Spellman turned to Alan Gibbs. Secretary Gibbs—an out-of-stater and registered Democrat—was a seasoned public administrator with executive experience in federal, state, and local government. After earning a bachelor's degree in labor and industrial relations in the mid-1960s, he worked for the National Labor Relations Board and the Equal Employment Opportunities Commission in both Washington, D.C., and Alabama. From 1970 to 1973 he held several senior health administration posts under Mayor John V. Lindsay in New York City, and from 1974 to 1977 he was the number-two administrator in the New Jersey human services agency. During the Carter administration he returned to national government as assistant secretary of the Army. He had visited Washington State only once before arriving to become secretary of DSHS in February 1981.

The Fiscal Outlook at DSHS. From the outset Gibbs was compelled to concentrate on budget problems; even without the proposed federal cuts, he confronted a tight fiscal situation. Shortly before he arrived in Washington, state tax shortfalls and DSHS budget overruns had forced reductions in department services for the final six months of the 1979-1981 biennial state budget, which would end on June 30, 1981. The state's severe economic recession had caused the tax shortfalls. As a result, some of the expenditure overruns had been uncontrollable. Both the AFDC program for unemployed parents and Medicaid had seen their caseloads soar as a result of the poor economic conditions. But there had been other DSHS cost overruns due to weak management controls in the Corrections Division and in homemaker services for the aged and disabled. In response, the legislature had appropriated a small supplementary budget but also had forced DSHS to make deep program cuts. These included terminating the AFDC programs for unemployed parents (which eliminated aid for 26,000 people), and terminating general financial assistance for adults (which eliminated benefits for 8,000 more people), reducing Medicaid benefits for 14,000 people, terminating homemaker services for 4,000 people and reducing the services available to 2,000 to 4,000 others. These cuts had been hard on DSHS clients and had damaged the morale of the agency's employees.

The immediate future did not look better. Contemplating President Reagan's budget proposals in February 1981, Gibbs knew that federal cutbacks could have an important effect on the 1981-1983 state budget soon to be enacted by the legislature. If the president's plans were adopted, Washington State stood to lose about $110 million in federal aid over the two-year budget period.

Planning for Budget Reductions. Secretary Gibbs saw President Reagan's block grant proposals as primarily

> a budget problem, since 45 percent of DSHS funds came from the federal government.... We knew there was no chance of state funds to make up for the lost federal dollars. We faced a conservative legislature and poor economic conditions, so it wasn't politically possible to get significant tax increases.

Gibbs saw this as a long-run problem, not just a temporary dislocation. "I saw the problem as positioning DSHS for the next several years," he recalled. "Reagan was in many respects continuing what Carter had started: putting a lid on the growth of federal aid. This problem was going to last for a long time."

Given the likely effects of more budget cutbacks, Secretary Gibbs wanted to take a careful, analytic approach to the planning. He did not want policy choices made in the same way that earlier budget reductions had been decided upon. "Those were done with a meat ax. They were big decisions, but there was little analysis of what the impacts would be," he said.

As an alternative, Gibbs had a firm sense of how he wanted to handle further budget reductions:

> In making the cuts, we could have gone three ways. First, we could have reduced our budget in the mirror image of the federal cutbacks. Whatever programs they cut, we could have cut proportionately. Or, we could have reduced all programs across-the-board by an equal percentage, say 5½ percent. But we rejected both of those alternatives. Instead we wanted to establish priorities, identify low priority services, and then switch state money around to make up for federal reductions in high priority areas.

Gibbs had no illusions that this process would be simple, "Government is not good at setting priorities and concentrating resources." He knew that decision making on cutbacks would mobilize numerous interest groups—and their allies in the state bureaucracy and legislature—to resist budget reductions in their favored programs. Knowing that budget making is inherently political—it determines the allocation of public benefits to competing claimants—Gibbs feared that generalized cutbacks might engulf DSHS in bitter wrangling among the most powerful interests, making it impossible to establish priorities rationally and difficult to keep the agency functioning effectively after the cuts were made.

Gibbs had substantial experience in budgeting. He had used the planning-programming-budgeting system (PPBS) in New York City, zerobase budgeting (ZBB) in New Jersey, and both systems in the Pentagon. Although convinced that systematic budgeting was a valuable activity, he also was aware that these techniques had serious problems and limitations. Had he not faced the need for sharp cutbacks at DSHS, he probably would have moved more slowly in establishing a priority-setting budget system for the agency.

Moving fast, though, did not mean moving unilaterally. From the beginning Gibbs believed that he had to keep the people involved—both inside and outside the agency—informed of what he was doing and convinced that he was making sensible and fair decisions.

Gibbs turned for help to Judith Merchant, a senior DSHS program manager whom his predecessor had assigned to plan for the new block grants. Consulting with senior DSHS officials over the next several months, Gibbs and Merchant developed plans for a formal cutback decision-making process. In many respects this process resembled the zero-base budgeting system that President Jimmy Carter had installed in the federal government, but Gibbs made no use of that term.

By early May, Gibbs was ready to go public with his plans. He widely distributed a memo to state and local officials and interested citizens explaining the need for careful planning of cutbacks. Citing the difficult fiscal pressures that DSHS faced, the memo nonetheless noted that the block grant mechanism proposed by President Reagan might permit handling the new round of cutbacks without severe service reductions:

> Block grants imply substantially reduced or eliminated federal regulations and oversight. This should permit the department to integrate its state and federal appropriations, to alter traditional categorical program approaches, and to develop a strategy for agency-wide reallocation of resources.

Gibbs' memo explained who would be involved in the decision making. The DSHS executive committee (consisting of Gibbs, the deputy secretary, and two assistant secretaries) would be at the center, giving DSHS program managers guidance on planning and making final decisions. These top DSHS officials would be aided by the agency's experts on the budget and on relevant federal and state law. At the next level of the DSHS hierarchy, divisions and bureaus—for example, the Health Services Division and its Office of Community Health Services—would be responsible for developing detailed programs and budgets. Both the agency's top policy makers and its operating managers would consult DSHS regional administrators and a variety of existing DSHS advisory committees.

To coordinate DSHS's planning with other government entities, Gibbs also established an Interagency Task Force composed of representatives from the governor's office, the Department of Employment Security, the Department of Planning and Community Affairs, the State Office of Financial Management, the legislature, the Association of Washington Cities and the Washington State Association of Counties (both organizations representing local governments), the state Superintendent of Public Instruction, and the U.S. Department of Health and Human Services (HHS) regional office. Gibbs wanted to keep these organizations well informed of DSHS plans so that he could head off in advance any political and bureaucratic opposition.

Gibbs' May memo outlined a series of steps to implement the budget reductions:

> The process for reallocating funds will begin by requiring program directors to prioritize state service responsibilities without regard to cost. This step will facilitate a dialogue regarding general social, health, and administrative problems which DSHS should address, the principal measures or actions it should take to alleviate these problems, and identification of realistic options available to the department. Programs serving the same clients or responding to similar kinds of needs will be expected to confer and propose coordination or consolidation. This initial step will help formulate a department policy statement which must be met and client groups that must be served.
>
> Concurrently, each program will begin building a budget that ultimately will display its services at different funding levels. Each level will reflect program and department priorities for clients and/or services and will contain descriptions and data describing the impact of the reduced funding.

Gibbs established a firm time schedule for the budget review process:

1. By June 15 each DSHS program director would submit to Gibbs an analysis of several related topics: client needs, the department's current service responsibilities, their impact on the community, their connection to DSHS's statutory or other legal obligations, and the administrative support requirements of these services.
2. These documents would be submitted to relevant DSHS advisory committees for comment.
3. By July 1 the department's executive committee would develop an integrated, department-wide "program perspective" identifying basic client needs and service responsibilities to give overall guidance to the program directors who would be responsible for detailed planning.
4. By mid-August each program would submit a detailed budget showing alternative levels of expenditure. Gibbs required each program to show its service priorities at a level of appropriation equal to 60 percent of that available in the 1981-1983 biennial budget and then at several intermediate levels up to the full amount.
5. By mid-September the DSHS executive committee would review each program budget and develop a department-wide budget.
6. The revised programs and budgets would be submitted to the governor for review and approval by September 15 so that DSHS could be ready when the anticipated federal cutbacks went into effect on October 1, at the start of the federal fiscal year.

Planning in the DSHS Division of Health Services. During the early months of 1981, as Secretary Gibbs strove to develop a central budget cutback strategy, DSHS program directors in Olympia—the people immediately responsible for managing specific state programs—were independently assessing how federal cuts would affect their operations.

Dr. John Beare, a 16-year DSHS veteran and director of the Division of Health Services, was among these. The division had four offices in addition to a small director's staff: epidemiology and laboratory facilities, environmental health, planning and development, and community health services. The division had a total budget of $81 million for 1981-1983, of which 77 percent was allocated to the Office of Community Health Services, which awarded contracts to county health departments and other health-care providers. About $20 million of the division's biennial budget was allotted to a variety of maternal and child health programs.

In March and April, while preliminary guidance was forthcoming from Secretary Gibbs, Dr. Beare began planning in his division. First, he ordered each office to prepare data about the programs they operated. Then he convened an in-house committee, consisting of representatives from each office plus three members of his own staff, to develop criteria by which priorities could be assigned to each of the division's programs. Working with materials submitted by each office, this group made a preliminary ranking of the division's 69 programs and developed rough budget allocations for each program based on the assumption of a 25 percent reduction in federal funds.

At this point Dr. Beare and his staff were uncertain how priorities set at the division level would figure in Secretary Gibbs' decision making. They also were uncertain whether the secretary's avowed intention of reallocating state funds to make up for federal reductions in high-priority areas would have any practical impact on their own programs. Traditionally, the divisions in DSHS had operated quite independently; previous secretaries had done relatively little to disturb program decisions and relative shares of budgets set at the division level. Past experience, therefore, led Beare to expect that relatively few changes would be made in his division's priority rankings and that there would be little, if any, central reallocation of funds. Consequently, the division's budget review went one step further by considering not only the programmatic distribution of funds, but also the allocation of money among geographic areas of the state.

For several years the Office of Community Health Services had been concerned that the city of Seattle was receiving too large a share of federal maternal and child health funds, mainly because of the special project requirements of Title V funding. The fact that three of the five special projects were located in Seattle—either because federal officials had dictated that choice when the projects were established (as in the case of the maternity and infant care and children and youth projects) or because the only facilities in the state appropriate for the project were located in the city (as in the case of the infant intensive care project)—meant that 46 percent of the state's Title V funds went to Seattle.

Dr. Robert Leahy, director of the Office of Community Health Services, and his staff had wanted to shift some of these funds from Seattle to other areas of the state that, for lack of funds or public commitment, had a need for better maternal and child health care. As Dr. Leahy argued, "There were areas other than Seattle which had large deviations from the normal infant mortality or morbidity figures." Consequently, with the promised flexibility of President Reagan's block grants and the expected elimination of the special projects requirement, Leahy and his staff planned to reduce Seattle's share of the state's allotment for maternal and child health programs.

A Wary City Watches
Developments in Washington, D.C., and Olympia

Alan Gibbs and other top state officials were not the only ones carefully tracking federal government developments in the wake of President Reagan's budget reduction and block grant proposals. In Seattle—Washington State's largest city with a population of 494,000—Mayor Charles Royer and his staff were monitoring closely the progress of the president's plans in Congress and trying to assess the likely consequences for the city's own budget and programs. Not only might changes in federal policy reduce the funds that Seattle received directly from the federal government, but they also might affect the flow of money and the nature of programs run by the state government in Olympia.

A journalist turned politician, Mayor Royer was intensely interested in national urban policy. Beginning his fourth year as Seattle's mayor, he was an officer of both the National League of Cities and the U.S. Conference of Mayors—the two principal lobbying groups for the nation's municipalities. At Royer's direction, during the early months of 1981 mayoral staff watched the growing national debate over the president's budget and New Federalism proposals.

The main responsibility fell to the city's Office of Intergovernmental Relations, headed by William Stafford, which oversaw Seattle's contacts with the federal and state governments and with various metropolitan organizations and officials. Stafford, a young businessman who had become involved in Seattle politics in the early 1970s, was now a veteran of city government, having served in the same position for several years under Mayor Royer's predecessor.

Stafford's task had two dimensions: forecasting the programmatic and financial effects that the proposed changes in federal law would have on city government operations and devising a strategy to influence decision making in Washington, D.C. On the basis of formal legislative proposals and informal intelligence gathered from several sources in the nation's capital, Stafford and his staff fed information to key city department administrators, letting them know how federal law and funding levels might change, and helping them assess what this would mean for their agencies. These assessments, in turn, helped Mayor Royer, Stafford, and others develop positions to influence the debate in Washington, D.C. Their strategy depended on keeping influential members of Congress informed of the mayor's views on the federal budget and block grants, working through the national mayors' organizations to influence congressional decisions, and trying to get the urban viewpoint across to the general public through speeches and guest newspaper columns.

Although he was worried about the impact of federal budget reductions on Seattle, Mayor Royer was not a reflexive opponent of the block grant concept. His administration's experience with the Community Development Block Grant, a program enacted in 1974, had convinced him that there were great advantages in the flexibility of the block grant mechanism. But the mayor had grave reservations about the form of block grant that President Reagan was proposing.

Royer first was concerned about whether the block grants would target enough money to big cities. As he wrote to U.S. Rep. James R. Jones, D-Okla., chairman of the House Budget Committee:

I believe that the block grant mechanism can be extremely effective if adequate resources are made available, and if there are assurances that large cities will receive their fair share. Urban centers that have unique problems, such as refugees, large numbers of low-income residents, and higher unemployment rates, must be considered according to their individual circumstances.

He also was worried about the role of state government. As he wrote to Henry M. Jackson, Washington State's influential senior U.S. senator:

The block grant concept will be most successful if allocations come directly to the cities based on a formula related to need. Without such a formula, many cities which have severe problems will lose most of the resources they presently have under categorical funding. For several years, the cities have been able to deal directly with the federal government on block grants. If the state is going to become the administrative intermediary, it will be a step away from local flexibility and control and will add needless administrative costs.

Block Grants and the Public Health Department. Because health programs figured prominently in President Reagan's proposals, Mayor Royer's aide, Bill Stafford, enlisted the help of administrators in the Seattle/King County Public Health Department.

The Public Health Department operated as a joint enterprise of the city and county. (In 1980 King County had a total population of about 1.3 million, including Seattle, or about 31 percent of the state's entire population.) The Public Health Department was an organizational hybrid. It operated several centrally administered, countywide programs—including the medical examiner's office, emergency medical services, an alcoholism and substance abuse program, sewage and solid waste disposal, and various inspectional programs. Personal health services—such as family planning, prenatal and pediatric care, immunizations, nutrition, dental care, geriatric programs, and venereal disease prevention and treatment—were delivered through two geographically organized operating divisions. The Seattle division managed three local health service centers in the city, and the county division ran three more in the parts of King County outside of Seattle.

Seattle received federal funds from Title V and other categorical programs for maternal and child health care in several ways. The bulk of the money came to the Public Health Department through a contract with the state DSHS. Under this contract the Public Health Department ran two of the required Title V special projects—a maternity and infant care project through which prenatal and obstetrical services were provided to high-risk pregnant women in several target neighborhoods, and a children and youth project that provided comprehensive health care to children living in the Rainier Valley in southeast Seattle. In addition to these projects, the Public Health Department received federal funds through the state for clinic and home visits to pregnant women, services to crippled children, and counseling for families stricken by sudden infant death syndrome. Some of this money was channeled through independent health organizations, including several large private hospitals. Indirectly, these funds helped support a network of 20 neighborhood health and dental centers that served the city.

DSHS provided federal Title V money to two health care providers in Seattle other than the Department of Public Health. University Hospital—an affiliate of the University of Washington Medical School—ran an infant intensive care program, which was another of the Title V special projects; and the Odessa Brown Center, originally established under the federal Model Cities program, received a direct contract from DSHS to provide prenatal care in its area of the city.

In February 1981, to support Stafford's lobbying efforts in Washington, D.C., and the city's own fiscal contingency planning, Jill Marsden, director of the Public Health Department's Seattle division, began to project how various federal legislative proposals would affect the department's budget and its service delivery capacity. Born and educated in England, Marsden had worked in health planning and administrative jobs in the Seattle area for about a dozen years; she and Stafford had collaborated several times before on federal grant projects.

The impact of the Reagan proposals proved difficult to forecast, involving a good deal of guesswork both because the ultimate form of congressional action was unknown and because the state might have substantial discretion in making its own policy choices before passing any funds on to the Public Health Department. Marsden and her staff performed several analyses as Congress deliberated over the next several months. As spring turned to summer, though, her attention and Stafford's shifted from Washington to DSHS in Olympia.

Breaking the News to Seattle. When Secretary Gibbs' formal planning memo was issued in May, the DSHS Health Services Division had a substantial head start in preparing the required "program perspective." As instructed by Gibbs, Dr. Beare sent this document, which identified the division's programs and reported its preliminary priority rankings, to the six DSHS regional offices for comment by their management coordinating committees and citizen advisory committees; he also sought feedback from other sources in the state's public health community.

Dr. Beare's division, however, had gone further than Gibbs had directed by developing preliminary budget allocations to its programs under the assumption of a 25 percent reduction in federal funds. On the basis of his past experience, Beare believed that little central reallocation of funds would occur and that therefore his division's recommendations would be accepted largely in the final decisions. Consequently, in late May 1981 the Division of Health

Services decided to brief county health departments about what effects the new federal policies were likely to have on their allotments from the state.

On June 1 Dr. Peter Pulrang and Patricia Snyder from the DSHS Office of Community Health Services met with top administrators from the Seattle/King County Public Health Department and from Mayor Royer's office. From the local perspective the message was grim. Pulrang and Snyder described the decision making occurring in DSHS. They explained that program decisions were not final but suggested that the department should prepare for cuts. In DSHS's judgment, Seattle/King County was getting too large a share of the state's federal allotment. As a result, while the cutbacks for other jurisdictions generally would be about 25 percent, Seattle/King County would sustain a total cut of about 31 percent in its maternal and child health programs. Pressing for an explanation, the local officials were told that DSHS health programs were being evaluated carefully for "need, performance, availability of alternative sources, and prior funding commitments." Bill Stafford recalled that

> It was hard to get them to be explicit about their reasoning. It was not clear why we were getting a disproportionate cut. It seemed that they were trying to get the basic level of services up statewide, and there were some counties that had no maternal and child health programs. We were putting in local funds in this area and others were not. I said to them, "You're in effect penalizing us, rather than rewarding us, for doing that."

The meeting left the Seattle/King County officials quite concerned about the prospects of their programs.

Jousting Over Budget Allocations. Throughout the summer the Seattle/King County Health Department and the DSHS Division of Health Services corresponded about the division's program priorities and its planned cuts in the department's allocation of federal funds.

On July 2 the division sent the department its program perspective, prepared for Gibbs, for comments. This document identified 69 programs whose overall goal was to "preserve, protect and promote the life and health of the people of the state." To set priorities for the required cutbacks, the division identified five criteria: community protection, long-term consequences, benefits to clients, appropriateness of Division of Health intervention, and effectiveness. It then divided these 69 programs into four categories of need: essential, high, medium, and a group that could be eliminated. (See Exhibit 1, pp. 66-67.)

This document caused consternation in the Public Health Department. In general, officials there were mystified about how the division's specific priorities emerged from the state criteria because there was no elaboration of what the criteria meant or how the rankings were done. Inspecting the priority statement, they concluded that general preventive services, including client-oriented and environmental services, were accorded relatively lower priority than laboratory services and certain specialized programs such as genetic screening. This ranking made little sense to them. They also were concerned that no cost data was included to allow them to compare the costs and benefits of various programs. Furthermore, the program perspective gave them no clue why Seattle's funding for maternal and child health care was being cut back more drastically than other localities'.

Consequently, two weeks later the department wrote to Secretary Gibbs, outlining its concerns about the division's program perspective and, separately, to the division, challenging the rationale for the 31 percent cut in funds. The second letter argued that

> A high proportion of the [King County] population consists of socially and economically disadvantaged people whose health promotion, preventive care and basic medical service needs are not met by the private sector. These people depend on the public sector for health care. Their number is growing and public sector resources are diminishing.

Citing a variety of statistics about infant mortality (especially in the black and Asian populations of the inner city), the Asian refugee problem, and the shortage of resources exacerbated by cutbacks, the letter asserted that Seattle and King County had a greater concentration of need than any other area in the state. Consequently, the letter asked for a detailed breakdown of funds available for maternal and child health programs for each county in the state, for more detailed information about the criteria or allocation formula used in determining these funding levels, and for more specific definitions of both "performance and prior funding commitment" (two of the criteria cited in Pulrang and Snyder's visit). This information would help the city understand why the Health Services Division felt it was receiving more than its share of funds.

In late July the division replied in two separate letters. One responded to questions about priorities by describing a point system used by the division's staff, but it gave no information whatever about Seattle's programs' individual scores on each criterion or about how these scores were determined. The second letter, after taking issue with some of the department's data, argued that the ultimate allocation of funds depended on judgment, not just statistics:

> The allocation of funds is a difficult task. We do not approach it with a simple mechanistic formula based on such things as population or resources alone. We do study various indices of health and mortality; review these with local communities; and assess local interest in and ability to address health service issues. . . . Finally we exercise our best collective judgment and allocate the funds for which we were given responsibility.

In conclusion, the division finessed the distribution issue:

Our proposed allocation for King County is not based upon a judgment that you are receiving more than a fair share of the funds available, but rather on the fact that other counties of the state have serious problems with the health of mothers and children and need to do something about them, just as you do.

Officials in the Seattle/King County Public Health Department regarded these responses as totally unsatisfactory. By this time, however, Secretary Gibbs was issuing a department-wide priority statement that formed the basis for public hearings around the state. Although the status of the Division of Health Services' document was not entirely clear, the secretary's priority statement seemed to supersede it.

A Department-Wide Program Perspective

Although the planning process in the division ran parallel to that in other parts of DSHS, Dr. Beare and his staff had stepped ahead of the timetable that Secretary Gibbs had laid out for formulating and publicizing their budget. As far as DSHS's top administrators were concerned, no budget allocations were established firmly yet; these awaited further progress in setting department priorities. Gibbs first wanted agreement on more general principles.

As Gibbs recalled, "The reactions of program managers to the budget process were mixed. The program perspectives developed by each unit varied tremendously in quality." These documents were sent out to the regional offices in mid-June for comments by the management coordinating committees and by the citizen advisory committees. At headquarters Gibbs met personally with each program manager in the department and with each region's top officials.

Then the secretary and his top staff worked on a department-wide priority statement. In effect this document would present the DSHS rationale for its mission and lay out in general form the department's spending priorities. As Gibbs' special assistant Judy Merchant recalled:

The result of the public consultation was surprising. There was not much controversy over what the department ought to do. There was a strong consensus on priorities, despite the fact that there is an urban liberal/rural conservative split in the state.

By late July, Gibbs had distributed publicly a formal statement about the department's mission and priorities. This document explained why budget cutbacks were necessary and described the internal planning that DSHS had been conducting. It identified three general categories of DSHS services: protection of the general public, protection of people unable to care for themselves, and protection of needy persons. Then it specified an ordered set of priorities.

The first priority, "basic life support services," was defined as "those services designed to ensure provision of essential food, shelter, medical care, and physical safety for persons unable to do so for themselves." These included protective services for children and frail, aged, and mentally disabled persons; financial assistance for needy single-parent families, the aged, the blind or disabled, unemployable adults, refugees, and those needing emergency assistance; food stamps for low-income families; residential care for children, the aged, and the disabled; preventive and immediate medical care for needy persons; and infectious disease control.

In the second-priority area were "services to avoid or reduce the need for basic life support services." These included employment counseling and training for low-income or disabled persons; maintenance of independent living for disabled persons; family crisis intervention; community outpatient services for the mentally ill or alcohol or drug abusers; preventive or restorative medical care for the needy; family planning; nutritional programs for the aging; adoption of children with special needs; and support services for the elderly and handicapped persons at risk of institutional placement.

In the third-priority category were "services designed to improve access to the service delivery system." These included information and referral services, advocacy or ombudsman services for the elderly and disabled, volunteer programs for persons in institutions, demonstration projects, and outreach programs.

The document then described the next steps that Gibbs intended to take. It announced that "decision packages" were being prepared in every program area and that these would be examined according to general guidelines for making cuts in selected programs, eliminating nonessential regulatory programs, establishing fees for certain services, increasing services provided by local governments or charitable organizations, increasing volunteer activity to offset reduced state services, and improving DSHS efficiency.

Next the document identified more than 100 specific possibilities for cutting the DSHS budget. In health services, for example, it raised the possibility of reducing the scope and level of personal health services such as family planning, crippled children's services, and maternal and child health care.

Finally, the program perspective discussed an issue closely related to the block grant mechanism. As Judy Merchant recalled, "There was a high degree of anxiety, especially in the social services area, about whether the block grants would take money away from local agencies [that had previously gotten funds directly from the federal government, rather than through the state as intermediary]." Given uncertainty about the state's intentions, there was great concern that some of these agencies might not survive. To reassure these agency officials, the program perspective declared that DSHS intended to fund these agencies for at least a year but at a level reduced in proportion to the overall loss of federal funds.

Public Participation. From the beginning of the planning process, Gibbs had intended to build in substantial opportunities for public participation. In retrospect, he cited several motivations:

> First, there was a long history of citizen participation in Washington throughout state government. There are numerous boards and commissions attached to state agencies. There is also the tradition of the citizen initiative, where both positive and negative legislation can be placed on the election ballot. That history dictated an approach that involved participation. Second, DSHS already had 36 formal advisory committees on various issues and a variety of ad hoc committees, plus its regional advisory committees. Third, I believe firmly that while bureaucrats have detailed expertise, they don't have a corner on the market of ideas. Involving citizens can sometimes generate some ideas that no one else has thought of and also identify some poor ones that may have been proposed by the department. Their comments can be a help, too, in gauging the political realities surrounding program changes. Finally, DSHS was held in very low regard around the state. It was seen as a large, rambling, inefficient bureaucracy. The legislature, for example, had in the past accused the department of lying to it. Generally, there was an enormous credibility problem, and participation could help us deal with that.

Consequently, DSHS distributed its priority statement widely. About 8,000 copies were mailed around the state to people likely to be interested in the department's decisions. These included various professional groups (such as health care officials and social workers), client groups, vendor or provider groups, municipal officials, county commissioners and administrators, and various nonprofit agencies and citizen groups.

The public had several opportunities to comment on the priorities and cutback issues contained in the program perspective. The department held six formal public meetings, one in each region of the state, chaired by a top executive of the department. Somewhat nervous about possible adverse reactions, Gibbs scheduled all of these meetings for the evening of August 6 as a way of minimizing the negative publicity that might appear in the press if the DSHS plans got a hostile reaction. Gibbs feared a sequence of newspaper stories recounting protests and accusations. However, there was little hostility expressed at the meetings. Gibbs also made an effort to consult personally with several important constituencies that had particular concerns. Those constituencies included Mayor Royer and top officials from the city of Seattle, the leaders of all United Way organizations in the state, the statewide Health Coordinating Committee, and the state's four health planning agencies.

DSHS received more than one thousand letters about the program perspective. Gibbs had the letters summarized and categorized so that he and his colleagues would understand the scope and intensity of public opinion.

Congress Enacts the Block Grants

In late July 1981 a congressional conference committee finally reached agreement on President Reagan's tax, expenditure reduction, and New Federalism package. The president signed the massive Omnibus Budget Reconciliation Act with triumph on August 13.

Congress gave the president less than he had requested in his original block grant proposal. The act created nine new block grants by consolidating 57 existing categorical programs. In modifying the administration's plan, Congress cut less money, excluded a number of categorical grants (including some of the larger ones), and attached more regulatory "strings" to the new block grants than the president had wanted. Nonetheless, the block grants represented significant change, affecting $7.5 billion of the $88 billion in federal aid to states and localities that Congress had authorized in fiscal year 1982.

In the health field Congress enacted four block grants instead of the two that the administration wanted. The Preventive Health Block Grant consolidated eight programs, including emergency medical services, hypertension control, rodent control, fluoridation, and rape prevention. Five programs were merged into an Alcohol, Drug Abuse, and Mental Health Block Grant. Two programs—community health centers and primary care research and demonstrations—were merged into a Primary Care block grant. Finally, seven categorical programs were combined into a Maternal and Child Health block grant.

This new Maternal and Child Health Block Grant consolidated Title V, including the five special projects, and six related grant programs: Supplemental Security Income for crippled children, lead paint poisoning prevention, genetic disease screening, sudden infant death syndrome counseling, hemophilia treatment, and adolescent pregnancy prevention and counseling. The new grant allocated funds to the states according to a statutory formula. In accord with the block grant philosophy, the states were free to use these funds for any purposes consistent with the broad goals stated in the act. (Funds could not be used, however, for most inpatient services, cash payments to recipients of health services, capital expenditures, or research and training at profit-making private health facilities.) The total congressional authorization for the block grant was $373 million.

Congress, however, imposed more administrative restrictions on the states than the Reagan administration had wanted. Each state would have to spend $3 of its own for every $4 of federal funds it received. To receive funds each state would have to submit an annual plan identifying the "intended use" of federal funds. It also would have to file assurances that the state would distribute funds fairly among individuals, areas, and localities needing services; spend a "substantial" proportion on the old Title V programs including "special consideration" for the five special projects; spend a "reasonable" proportion on the specific purposes enumerated in the act; use a sliding,, income-related, fee scale for any user charges imposed on service recipients; and participate in certain coordination activities. Finally, the state would have to file an annual report to the federal Health and Human Services Department on how it spent its money and have a biannual audit done on its expenditures. Despite these requirements, however, the overall planning, application, and reporting regulations were less extensive than those under the predecessor programs. In sum, the new Maternal and Child Health Block Grant gave the states more discretion and less federal supervision than they previously had been accustomed to, but it did not offer either the program scope or degree of freedom that the president had proposed.

Making Budget Decisions

With the legislation thus defined, the task of establishing DSHS priorities became paramount. Throughout July and August each DSHS program division worked hard on the next step of Secretary Gibbs' planning process: making detailed budget proposals. Each program director was expected to identify 40 percent of his budget to be cut, indicate his priorities for incremental funding additions, and build the budget back up to its original level. Gibbs wanted each manager to identify concrete expenditures that might be reduced and to establish clearly priorities for his or her division's activities.

Therefore, each program director was instructed to develop a set of "decision packages." Each decision package indicated a program activity, its cost, the actual services provided, and any consequences of eliminating the service. Each program director then ranked the decision packages according to the priorities established in the department-wide program perspective. He then was to submit the ranked set of decision packages to the DSHS central budget office.

Gibbs and other top-level DSHS staff found the resulting decision packages a useful tool. As Ken Miller, the DSHS budget director, recalled:

> In general, the decision packages constructed by the divisions were astonishing in quality. There has been a tendency in other organizations that have tried similar budgeting methods to do what Gibbs calls "gold-watching"; that is to identify high priority programs as areas for cuts, hoping the decision makers won't do it, and sending up garbage as supporting analysis. Relatively little of that happened in DSHS, and much of what was done of that sort was weeded out by the line managers, as well as the central staff.

For DSHS as a whole, 250 decision packages were prepared. The Division of Health Services submitted 14 decision packages, including 10 that potentially affected maternal and child health programs in Seattle. These decisions included cuts in Seattle's basic program for high-risk pregnant women and children, the targeted maternity and infant care project, Supplemental Security Income for crippled children, the genetics screening program, and the prenatal program. (See Exhibit 2, pp. 67-69.)

In late August, Gibbs published a booklet that showed each of the 250 decision packages, without disclosing the operating divisions' priority rankings. Although not so widely distributed as the program perspective, the decision packages were sent to a wide range of individuals and organizations, including all DSHS advisory committees and major governmental units. Gibbs made no effort to keep them secret. As he remembered: "Anyone who wanted to see the detailed decision packages could have gotten access to them. Xerox machines around the state were going feverishly."

Seattle's Last Appeal. Secretary Gibbs continued to make himself accessible to people who wanted to express their views about the budget. He consulted personally with all program managers in DSHS and with a number of outside constituency groups.

On September 4 Gibbs and several senior DSHS staff conferred with Mayor Royer and his staff in Seattle. Gibbs explained the status of his decision making, and the mayor once more sketched out the city's concerns. Royer was worried, first, that budget cutting in DSHS would result in some responsibilities being transferred from state to local government with no state financial resources to support them—at a time when local governments also were squeezed for money. As Royer noted in a follow-up letter to Gibbs, "To assume that local governments can pick up an activity if they want to, is tantamount to terminating the program." Second, Royer was concerned with the balance in funding between state institutions, such as mental health facilities, and community services, which had tended to be local responsibilities. He urged Gibbs to be evenhanded in apportioning cuts in these two sectors. Third, Royer raised the issue of how block grant funds would be allocated within the state. His follow-up letter argued:

> We see a tendency to support cuts of a larger percentage in grants for the major recipients, particularly in the area of block grant legislation. The purported objective of the State is to provide for minimum levels of service through a uniform statewide approach to a particular problem. Although this appears to be a rational way to deal with a problem, it has the negative effect of siphoning off money from the major cities and counties to offset the impacts of federal budget reductions on smaller cities and counties. To guarantee minimum program levels especially for jurisdictions that make no real effort to support an activity, is patently inequitable. This pattern of allocation, combined with the possible elimination of programs targeted to special populations in the metropolitan areas, could be devastating to a select number of communities.

At the meeting Royer's staff called attention to a number of decision packages that would cut funds for programs in Seattle. They presented analyses of the likely impacts of these budget reductions on Seattle's programs and citizens and argued strongly that these were undesirable. The meeting offered a chance to reiterate their arguments about the planned reductions in maternal and child health care for the city.

Final Decisions. The final task of establishing priorities for DSHS services and making reductions in the department's budget fell to a group of eight senior staff—including Secretary Gibbs; his deputy and assistant secretaries; Judy Merchant, special assistant for block grant planning; Ken Miller, the budget director; the DSHS legislative liaison officer; and the DSHS controller. This group met for long hours during late August and early September, mulling over the decision packages, the priority rankings of the DSHS program directors, and a multitude of public comments. The question of maternal and child health services was one of the more important matters in dispute, with clear lines of demarcation between the Division of Health Services and the city of Seattle. The issues were focused—and the time had come to decide.

EXHIBITS

Exhibit One:
Preliminary Priority Ranking
of DSHS Division of Health Services Programs

Essential

Immunization
Genetics Program
Health Education

Radioactive Materials Control
Reference Bacteriology Laboratory
Immunofluorescence Laboratory

T.B. Control
Maintain State/Local Delivery System
Virus Isolation & Identification Lab.
Lab Quality Assurance

Vital Records
Infectious Disease Epidemiology
Mycobacteriology & Mycology Lab

Dental Rinse
X-ray Control/X-ray Compliance
Local Health Dept. Management Support

Family Planning
Water Facilities Improvement
Center for Health Statistics

MCH
Occupational/Environmental Disease Epidemiology
Enteric Lab
Virology, Serology Lab

VD
Occupational Health
Chronic Disease & Special Investigations Epidemiology
General Serology Lab
Metabolic Disorders Lab

High

Crippled Children's Services
Water Facilities Funding

WIC
Shellfish (Environmental Health)
Shellfish & Paralytic Shellfish Lab
Food Service

Environmental Rad. & Emergency Response
Employee Health Promotion Project
Bioassay Water Bacteriology

On-site Sewage
Chemical Hazards
Inorganic Chemistry/Environmental Radiation Testing
Organic Chemistry/Pesticide Lab

Refugee Health
Health Facilities Survey
Lab Quality Assurance/Water Lab Certification
Emergency Medical Services

Pesticide and Vector Control
Personal Care Facilities Survey

Certificate of Need
Construction Review
Consultation and Development

Water Systems Compliance
Water Systems Coordination

Medium

Water Supply Operations

Parasitology Lab

EFSEC
Health Policy Planning

Hypertension
Perinatal Programs
Uranium Mill Control Program

SSI—Disabled Children
Kidney Disease

Diabetes Demo Project
State Institutions Env. Inspections

Eliminate

Health Facilities Inv. & Plant Evaluation

Waterborne Disease Study

Low-Level Rad. Waste

School and Physical Hazards

Swimming Pools

Transient Accommodations

Exhibit Two:
Excerpt from DSHS Division of Health Decision Packages

Decision Package

Reduce the scope and level of personal health services, such as family planning, crippled children, and maternal and child health.

	TOTAL	STATE	FEDERAL Block	Categorical
Personal Health Services:				
Mentally Retarded, Adolescent, Impaired Child Health Projects*	$ 841,308	$ 0	$ 841,308	$ 0
Genetics	120,000	0	51,432	68,568
Tuberculosis Control	60,000	60,000	0	0
SSI/Disabled Children's Program #1	278,000	0	278,000	0
Maternal and Infant Project*	292,500	0	292,500	0
Health Education #1	58,000	58,000	0	0
Crippled Children's Services	987,000	0	987,000	0
Perinatal Program #1	50,000	0	50,000	0
Venereal Disease Control	175,350	31,500	0	143,850
Maternal and Child Health	1,140,520	0	1,140,520	0
Health Education Services #2	140,000	0	135,000	5,000
SSI/Disabled Children's Program #2	330,000	0	330,000	0
Perinatal Programs #2	309,606	0	309,606	0
Family Planning Option 1	2,757,394**	50,100	450,900	2,256,394
Option 2	3,258,394**	100,200	901,800	2,256,394
Option 3	3,759,394	150,300	1,352,700	2,256,394
TOTAL	$14,557,466	$450,100	$7,120,766	$6,986,600

The individual units in this decision package are ranked in priority order.

Final reductions to both block grant and categorical programs will be adjusted to reflect actual federal allocations.

This decision package contains $5.2 million of the $7.2 million in the division affected by block grant language in the new federal budget.

* See pp. 68-69 for detailed program description.

** More than one mutually exclusive option; subtract to avoid double count when calculating division total.

[Exhibit 2 Cont.]

Mentally Retarded, Adolescent, Impaired Child Health Projects

Division/Bureau: Division of Health.

Issue: Eliminate Mental Retardation, Adolescent, and Improved Child Health Projects.

Present Services: Mentally Retarded and Adolescent Projects — provides for health care for children and adolescents, particularly the mentally retarded and those with multiple handicaps, and the provision of consultation services in these areas by professionals throughout the state. Follow-up services for high-risk newborns.

Improved Child Health Project — to develop a coordinated, integrated system of comprehensive health care for high-risk mothers and infants in four northwest Indian tribes including well child clinics; prenatal care supplemental to obstetric care provided by local private physicians, and health, nutrition and education services.

Proposed Service: Elimination of programs.

Impact:
   a. Clients: 7,958
   b. Fiscal: Total: $841,308 grants and subsidies
              Federal: $841,308 (Title V)
   c. FTE: None
   d. Other services (state or local): Elimination will increase demand for services on Title XIX, Developmental Disabilities, COH, Neuromuscular Centers, SSI, Seattle-King County Health, Skagit and Whatcom Health Departments, and the University of Washington.

Required Statute/WAC Changes: None, assuming federal government will address necessary changes in Title V law

Potential Implementation Problems: Resistance by affected Indian Tribal Councils and University of Washington

Estimated Effective Date: October 1, 1981

Maternity and Infant Project

Division/Bureau: Division of Health

Issue: Reduction in the Maternity and Infant Care Project would eliminate services for the entire second year of the biennium.

Present Services: The Maternity and Infant Care Project, as part of the Seattle-King County Department of Public Health, provides comprehensive obstetric services to medically high risk, low income pregnant women in southeast, southwest, and central Seattle. Clinics are located at Harbor-view Hospital and Columbia Health Center. Complete prenatal care, delivery, and follow-up services for both mother and infant are currently provided by an interdisciplinary team to approximately 300 medically and/or socially high risk women. The Project also provides diagnosis and screening services for pregnant women residing in the catchment area who request Project services.

Proposed Service:
Option #1: Reduction eliminates the project entirely by the second year of the biennium.

Option #2: Continue the services in some form with costs absorbed by MCH block grant funds awarded to King County and/or health department funds.

Impact:
a. Clients: approximately 300 low income high risk women for prenatal care, 300 infants and 300 women for screening and referral services

b. Fiscal: $292,500 total grants and subsidies
$292,500 (MCH block grant)

c. FTE: 0

d. Other services (state or local): Increasing burden for maternity services will be placed on community health clinics and MCH programs operated by health clinics in Seattle

Required Statute/WAC Changes: None

Potential Implementation Problems: None

Estimated Effective Date: September 1, 1981.

Discussion Questions

1. What are the main arguments in favor of and against the grant consolidation proposed in President Reagan's New Federalism?

2. What were the major risks and opportunities for Alan Gibbs, a new manager from out of state, in initiating the block grant and cutback planning process?

3. What was the likely "executive strategy" underlying the planning process that Gibbs devised?

4. In what way did the cutback planning process appear important to Drs. Beare and Leahy and their staffs? Why did they get "out in front" of the schedule that Gibbs was laying out for DSHS as a whole?

5. Describe the strategy followed by Mayor Royer and his staff to deal with the situation following President Reagan's New Federalism proposals.

6. How reasonable was it for Seattle's officials to demand a detailed explanation of the grounds on which the Division of Health Services was planning to reduce its funding? Should the division have had a precise formula for distributing federal funds? Why or why not?

7. What functions did the public participation process serve for Gibbs?

8. How should Gibbs make his final decisions?

Suggestions for Further Reading

Ellwood, John William, ed. *Reductions in U.S. Domestic Spending.* Transaction Books, 1982. A description of the 1981 federal budget cuts and a preliminary assessment of their impacts on state and local governments.

Nathan, Richard P., and Doolittle, Fred C. *The Consequences of Cuts.* Princeton Urban and Regional Research Center, 1983. An analysis of the effects of President Reagan's New Federalism programs, based on field studies of state and local governments in 14 states.

Pyhrr, Peter A. "The Zero-Base Approach to Government Budgeting." *Public Administration Review,* January/February 1977, 1-8. The developer of ZBB describes and advocates the budgeting method that President Carter used in Georgia state government and later introduced to the federal government.

2. The Kentucky
Small Cities CDBG Demonstration

INTRODUCTION

The Reagan administration's "New Federalism" policies aim at enhancing the authority of state and local governments over intergovernmental programs by reducing federal influence. The previous case, "The Maternal and Child Health Block Grant in Washington State and Seattle," examines some of the consequences of this transfer of responsibility—most notably, the resource allocation choices that must be made when federal restrictions on program expenditures are relaxed. As new program arrangements take effect, however, resource allocation decisions become only one aspect of the altered management situation. Changes in program structure also affect other administrative practices and relationships.

The following case study, "The Kentucky Small Cities CDBG Demonstration," describes a precursor of President Reagan's New Federalism: an experimental program initiated in two states by the federal Department of Housing and Urban Development (HUD) during the Carter administration to give state administrators more opportunity to influence community development in their small cities and towns. By looking closely at how HUD's demonstration changed the Small Cities Community Development Block Grant (CDBG) program, we can explore several general issues that arise in the transfer of policy making and administrative authority from federal to state officials.

The idea of reducing federal control over intergovernmental grants leaves open the question of whether the states or local governments will gain the most influence. This depends, first, on the preexisting structure of the grant program. In some programs the federal government gives money to the states, which implement the programs directly through their own agencies and personnel. In other programs federal funds go initially to the states, which then allocate it to local governments, which in turn implement the program. (In this situation, the states play a "pass-through" role, although they also may regulate and monitor local program management.) In yet other programs, federal money goes directly to local governments with the states left out of the administrative chain. In principle, federal control could be reduced while leaving any of these program structures intact. In fact, however, the Reagan administration's approach has tended to favor strengthening *state* governments rather than localities. (That approach was moderated, though, in the administration's legislative proposals of 1983, which, for other reasons, did not survive congressional scrutiny.)

In the "Maternal and Child Health Block Grant" case study, Washington State's Department of Social and Health Services (DSHS) secured greater influence over programs that, in the main, it previously had run itself or passed through to local governments. DSHS administrators therefore were quite familiar with the programs' characters and existing operating procedures. In the "Kentucky Small Cities CDBG Demonstration" case study, however, Kentucky officials took on managerial responsibilities with which they had had little experience. Hence the change from federal to state administration of the Small Cities CDBG program involved a more demanding managerial transition. Moreover, as in any transfer of decision-making authority, this switch had important political implications.

In originally enacting the Small Cities Community Development Block Grant program in 1977, Congress opted for a direct federal-local program structure. In a competitive project grant-giving process, HUD gave funds directly to communities that submitted successful proposals. The demonstration program's genesis indicated that the choice of such a program structure was not a politically neutral decision. The principal group that lobbied for creation of the demonstration program—the Council of State Community Affairs Agencies (COSCAA)—aimed to create a state role in managing the community development program both as a way to establish that the states had the administrative capacity to do so and to make a claim for more state policy-making influence in the program. That claim challenged other interests, though. The National League of Cities (NLC), one of the major advocates of local government interests, feared that a larger state role, at least in some states, would mean either the neglect of municipal interests or the injection of narrow political considerations into the administration of the Small Cities CDBG program. The jousting between COSCAA and NLC, while relatively tame, shows the potential for state-local conflict in the design of the New Federalism and indicates how interest groups lobby in Washington, D.C.

The Kentucky demonstration's genesis makes clear, too, the tensions that can arise within a federal agency over the transfer of authority for a grant program. On one hand, some administrators resist such a transfer because they fear that the states or localities lack the administrative competence to run the program, that state or local politics will significantly distort program choices, federal purposes (in this case, benefits for low- and moderate-income families) that initially led Congress to enact the program. On the other hand, others in the federal agency are more sympathetic to the idea of giving increased discretion to the states and localities. They may feel that their colleagues' fears are either unfounded or are outweighed by other reasons to transfer program authority.

This case study also highlights an important issue in managing intergovernmental programs: the selection of recipients of discretionary grants. At the federal level, this issue arises in selecting the sites of the demonstration project. The choice of Kentucky and Wisconsin illustrates the layering of programmatic and political factors that frequently structure such decisions. At the state level the issue arises in a somewhat different context: Kentucky's selection of the recipients of the Small Cities CDBG grants themselves. The case describes the development of an elaborate set of procedures and criteria designed to minimize purely political considerations.

Among the more important issues considered in this case study are the administrative problems faced by Kentucky in taking over a grant program for which it previously had had no responsibility. Because the Small Cities CDBG program had involved a direct federal-local relationship, the demonstration required Kentucky to undertake a number of new management activities. Throughout the demonstration year, the state had to cope with staffing problems and with the development of new policies and administrative procedures. Kentucky's difficulties in simply taking over the CDBG *selection* process suggest how much more would be involved in assuming full responsibility for the program—including financial management and project monitoring—under the Reagan administration's 1981 legislation. The issue of administrative capacity is therefore critical in considering New Federalism policies, not because the states inherently lack the ability to take a larger role in managing intergovernmental programs, but because that capacity must be developed rather than presumed.

This case study also considers political relationships that may affect the success of a transfer of authority for a grant program. Some Kentucky municipalities distrusted Governor John Y. Brown's administration, fearing that the CDBG program would be politically manipulated. The demonstration's managers went to considerable lengths to dispel these concerns. It becomes clear that building effective working relationships—not only with the municipalities themselves, but also with interest groups representing local government and officials such as community development directors—constitutes a demanding but essential task for state program managers.

Finally, the demonstration program's progress shows the extent to which intergovernmental relations are often a matter of inter*bureaucratic* relations. Aside from the personal acquaintance of HUD's James Forsberg and

Kentucky's Sally Hamilton, the case shows the close working relationships that developed between HUD's area office and Kentucky's Division of Community and Regional Development (DCRD). Their cooperation—forged through similarities in their staffs' professional backgrounds and policy goals—helps account for the satisfaction that those involved felt with the demonstration; it perhaps accounts as well for the comparatively small changes in selection criteria made by Kentucky. As in other situations, these relationships may overshadow the influence of generalist officials like the governor, who in this case made little effort to shape the substance of the demonstration.

THE CAST

Robert Embry	HUD assistant secretary for Community Planning and Development
James Forsberg	director of the HUD Small Cities CDBG program
Trudy McFall	director of HUD's Office of Planning and Program Coordination
Dennis Carr	director of HUD's Kentucky Area Office's Division of Community Planning and Development
Michael Brintnall	staff member in HUD Office of Evaluation
John Y. Brown	governor of Kentucky
Ralph Coldiron	director, Kentucky Division for Community and Regional Development
Sally Hamilton	assistant director of DCRD and principal architect of the Small Cities CDBG in Kentucky
Sheila Etchen	staff member in DCRD
Joseph Marinich	executive director of COSCAA
Marvin Tick	staff member of COSCAA
B. J. Reed	staff member of NLC
HUD	U.S. Department of Housing and Urban Development
CDBG	Community Development Block Grant program

COSCAA	Council of State Community Affairs Agencies, a lobbying group
NLC	National League of Cities, a lobbying group
DCRD	Kentucky Division for Community and Regional Development
Area Development Districts (ADD)	regional planning agencies in Kentucky

CHRONOLOGY

1977	Congress enacts the Small Cities CDBG Program, which creates a state entitlement/city competitive grant program.
1978	Council of State Community Affairs Agencies (COSCAA) lobbies HUD for a state role in community development programs; it secures a promise from HUD Assistant Secretary Robert Embry that some involvement will be arranged.
	Embry assigns Trudy McFall, director of Planning and Program Coordination, and James Forsberg, director of Small Cities CDBG, to develop regulations for a demonstration in which two states would be responsible for selecting Small Cities CDBG recipients.
1979-1980	Internal debate occurs within HUD—with outside involvement by COSCAA and the National League of Cities—over the desirability and nature of the demonstration.
1980	
April	HUD issues formal regulations for the demonstration and writes a letter to each state's governor inviting an application to participate.
May	Kentucky submits an application for the demonstration, one of nine states to do so.
July	HUD selects Kentucky as one of four semifinalists in the competition.

August	Kentucky Gov. John Y. Brown asks President Jimmy Carter to help the state get selected as one of the demonstration sites, which Carter does.
September	Kentucky is formally notified that it has been selected as a demonstration site along with Wisconsin.
	Sally Hamilton, assistant director of Kentucky's Division for Community and Economic Development, begins planning for implementation of the demonstration.
October-November	DCRD staff, with help from local officials and HUD area office staff, develop revised selection criteria.
November-December	DCRD staff conduct an outreach effort to inform local governments about the new program regulations and encourage their applications for a Small Cities CDBG grant.

1981

January	DCRD receives 112 preapplications and begins to evaluate them.
March	DCRD selects the winners, submits them to HUD for approval, and then has them announced to the public.
April	With President Ronald Reagan's proposal for a state takeover of the Small Cities CDBG pending in Congress, HUD accelerates its evaluation of the demonstration in Kentucky.
July	Congress approves the president's proposal, giving the states the option of taking over complete administrative responsibility for the Small Cities CDBG Program.
	Sally Hamilton at DCRD in Kentucky ponders how administratively to handle the complete takeover of the program.

THE CASE

In the fall of 1981, spotting another article in the *Lexington Herald* about the Reagan administration's plans for a "New Federalism," Sally Hamilton thought again of the excitement and unexpected twists of her recent past. Less than one and a half years earlier, in April 1980, she had been working in the Small Cities Division at the U.S. Department of Housing and Urban Development (HUD) in Washington, D.C., on leave from her job in Kentucky government. After just five months in Washington, she was offered the chance to return to Kentucky as assistant director of the state Division for Community and Economic Development. There Hamilton was put in charge of applying for a program—the Small Cities Community Development Block Grant (CDBG) Demonstration—administered by her former office in HUD. Under the demonstration, two state governments would assume responsibility for selecting the communities in their states that would receive Small Cities grants, a task usually performed by HUD's area offices. Although all other administrative responsibilities—for example, monitoring the grants after they were allocated—would remain with HUD, the demonstration offered states their first opportunity to participate in a program that previously had been run on a direct federal-local basis.

With the help of Kentucky Gov. John Y. Brown's lobbying, Kentucky was chosen as a site for the demonstration. Hamilton directed the project—a job that placed exhausting demands on her and her small staff. Although begun in the last year of the Carter administration, the demonstration was one of the few operating examples of how the newly elected Reagan administration might administer its New Federalism program. The demonstration became a topic of national discussion, and the staff's long hours proved rewarding when local governments showed they preferred state to federal administration.

The promise of the demonstration became a reality when Congress enacted some of the Reagan administration's New Federalism proposals as part of the Budget Reconciliation Act, signed by the president in August

This case was written by Isaac Shapiro under the supervision of Arnold M. Howitt, with editorial assistance by Charles F. Kireker. The work was financed under a grant from the U.S. Department of Housing and Urban Development for use in the Program for Senior Executives in State and Local Government, John F. Kennedy School of Government.

1981. The bill contained provisions giving states the option to take over completely the Small Cities CDBG program, including selection of grant recipients, monitoring of project implementation, and management of finances. Instead of simply reworking the selection process begun under the demonstration, Hamilton would have to focus on the larger task of managing the state's entire Small Cities grant program.

Background on the Small Cities CDBG Program

Prior to 1974 the federal government's community development grants were subjected to tight federal control. Federal funds were allocated to both large and small cities through categorical grant programs. Under these, cities applied on a project-by-project basis for federal support. Federal officials decided whether a particular proposal met the criteria and policy purposes of the corresponding federal program.

Pressed by the Nixon administration to reduce the federal role in managing intergovernmental aid programs and to increase the responsibility of state and local governments, Congress enacted the Housing and Community Development Act of 1974. Although the act provided no role for the states, it gave large cities (defined by Congress as those with more than 50,000 in population) substantially more discretion over their community development programs. The 1974 act combined a group of HUD's categorical grant programs—including urban renewal, Model Cities, water and sewer grants, public facilities loans, open space grants, and rehabilitation loans—into one formula block grant whereby all large cities received an "entitlement" automatically, based on a statutory formula. Because these cities could spend their block grant subject only to broad federal restrictions, local discretion was enhanced. The federal government no longer controlled which cities and projects received grants.

The 1974 act did not substantially increase the discretion of *small cities,* however. Congress established a pool of funds to serve small cities' development needs but prescribed different methods of distributing them. Small cities that had received HUD housing and community development grants in the preceding five years were given temporary entitlement status. For two years these 740 small cities were guaranteed funding equal to the average annual level of grants they had received over the last five years; then their entitlements were totally phased out over the following few years. The 1974 act did not provide short-term entitlements to the approximately 18,000 small cities that had not received HUD categorical grants during the preceding five-year period. Instead, cities completed with each other on a project-by-project basis for a limited amount of federal money.

In subsequent years considerable political pressure was exerted to put aid to small cities on firmer footing. In 1977 amendments to the Housing and

Community Development Act created a new Small Cities CDBG program allocating $1 billion to a combination State Entitlement-City Competitive system. Each state received an entitlement according to a formula based on several factors—population, the extent of overcrowded housing, and the state's poverty level. Small cities interested in receiving funds then could compete for grants from the state pool.

In each state four separate Small Cities CDBG competitions were held: for metropolitan, single-purpose grants (roughly 10 percent of the funds); nonmetropolitan, single-purpose grants (roughly 20 percent of the funds); metropolitan, comprehensive grants (roughly 20 percent); and nonmetropolitan, comprehensive grants (roughly 50 percent). Metropolitan grants were for small cities located in metropolitan areas. Single-purpose grants were for individual projects such as a new public building. Comprehensive grants were applied to projects intended to "address a substantial portion of the identifiable community development needs of defined, concentrated area(s)" and that involved two or more related but independent activities.

In each category Small Cities grants targeted aid to low- and moderate-income individuals. Specifically, the regulations for the Small Cities CDBG program stated five objectives:

1. To support realistic and attainable strategies for expanding low- and moderate-income housing opportunities,

2. To promote expansion of housing choice for low- and moderate-income persons outside areas of minority and low- and moderate-income concentrations or in revitalizing neighborhoods,

3. To promote more rational land use,

4. To provide increased economic opportunities for low- and moderate-income persons,

5. To correct deficiencies in public facilities that affect the public health or safety, especially of low- and moderate-income persons.

The regulations also stated that program design "as a whole must principally benefit low- and moderate-income persons and directly impact on the applicant's needs." Thus programs must "either benefit low- and moderate-income persons, or aid in the prevention or elimination of slums and blight, or meet other community development needs having a particular urgency." Examples of Small Cities CDBG projects in Kentucky included a new sewer system for Murray (population 13,537) and a housing project for low- and moderate-income persons in Bowling Green (population 38,800).

The Small Cities program was administered by the U.S. Department of Housing and Urban Development as a direct federal-local program. The 40 HUD area offices, whose jurisdictions roughly correspond to state boundaries, rated the applicants for each state, selected the winners, and oversaw the implementation of community development projects. State governments had no role in managing the program.

The first and most important step in applying for a grant was the submission of a preapplication by a small city to its HUD area office. The preapplication contained a description of the intended project, including a cost analysis and explanation of how it would serve community development needs. The area offices used a nationwide point system developed by HUD headquarters in Washington, D.C., to rate the preapplications, which were compared only within each state. Points were awarded on the basis of local need (as measured by both the percent and absolute number of people in poverty), the expected impact of the project, and previous local housing and equal opportunity performance. More preapplication points were awarded if the degree of poverty in a city, the ability of the program to address this and other community development needs, and the success of previous housing and equal opportunity programs were greater. (See Exhibit 1, pp. 96-101.)

The HUD area offices then asked the highest scoring preapplicants to submit full applications. However, most of the screening occurred at the preapplication stage. HUD area offices merely reviewed the full applications—which explained grant proposals in much greater detail than preapplications—to confirm that the proposed project was both workable and satisfied all federal regulations. Unlike preapplications, the full applications did not compete with others for selection. On only a few occasions did an area office reject a full application because it did not meet federal guidelines. The preapplicants selected to submit full applications were thus almost always the ultimate grant recipients.

Within each HUD area office, the Division of Community Planning and Development was responsible for managing the Small Cities program, as well as several other HUD programs—the CDBG entitlement program for large cities, the Urban Development Action Grant program, the Section 312 Housing Rehabilitation program, and the Section 407 Disaster Fund program. In Kentucky the Division of Community Planning and Development spent 70 percent of its time on the Small Cities CDBG program and 30 percent of its time on other programs.

Dennis Carr, director of HUD's Kentucky area office's Division of Community Planning, organized the 21 members of his staff into three groups: the program unit, the special programs unit, and the program support or technical unit. The program unit consisted of one supervisor and five community planning and development representatives who acted as HUD's principal contacts for individual projects. They monitored progress both through site visits and written or verbal communication; if localities had questions about their projects, they contacted their community planning and development representative. The representatives responded if they could or referred the questions to the appropriate program specialist. The special programs unit was comprised of four specialists and a supervisor; individuals in this unit specialized in projects such as economic development or rehabilitation. Members of the technical unit performed several functions; for example, its two fiscal experts handled project financing. The technical unit also included a supervisor, general program aide, engineer, and acquisition and rehabilitation expert. The Planning and Community Development Division maintained three general clerical positions and relied on an environmental expert from a different division.

Because the division's Small Cities responsibilities included tasks other than the selection of grant recipients, Dennis Carr estimated that only about 10 percent of his staff's time was spent on the selection process. The 21 staff members in his office thus spent slightly more than two man-years annually on the selection process.

Genesis of the Demonstration

Although the 1977 Housing and Community Development Act excluded the states by establishing a direct, federal-local Small Cities program, Congress had left open the possibility of a modest state role. Section 104(e) of the act gave the secretary of HUD the option of involving states in the selection of grant recipients:

> The Secretary may provide an opportunity for the states . . . to participate in the selection process for funding such small city grants. Such participation may include, as determined practical by the Secretary, the incorporation of state growth and resource coordination policies in funding decisions on such grants, or such other arrangements, excluding administration of the grants referred to in the preceding sentence, as the Secretary deems appropriate.

Among the state and local interest groups that lobbied in Washington, the Council of State Community Affairs Agencies (COSCAA) was most in favor of the secretary's exercising the Section 104(e) option, thereby encouraging the development of a federal-state-local Small Cities program. COSCAA's membership consisted of state Community Affairs agencies whose responsibilities included housing programs and community and economic development efforts. Joseph Marinich, COSCAA's executive director from 1974 to 1980, recalled, "Prior to the 1976 presidential election, we were negotiating with the Ford administration to have the states take over the administration of the Small Cities program. If Ford had been reelected, I believe these negotiations would have proved successful."

But Jimmy Carter—a Democrat who was less committed to increasing state power—won the 1976 presidential election. After the 1977 Housing and

Community Development Act passed, Marinich and members of COSCAA lobbied HUD for state involvement in the Small Cities program. He later explained COSCAA's interest:

> From a strategic perspective, we felt having a foot in the door was crucial, that it would give states the opportunity to demonstrate their administrative ability. This would help us educate HUD as to the ability and importance of states, a vital objective since HUD tended to ignore the state perspective in favor of the local perspective.

> We were confident that state administration would be preferable for a number of reasons. We felt states had more specific experience working with the unique needs of localities than did the federal government. We also felt that states can establish flexible and streamlined regulations targeted towards the diverse needs of localities, whereas the HUD Area Offices relied on often inapplicable nationwide criteria. Finally, all politics are local, and a political relationship has been established between states and localities in the administration of other programs that leads to state responsiveness to local needs.

In response to these lobbying efforts, Robert Embry, HUD's assistant secretary for Community Planning and Development, promised COSCAA that he would work on finding a role for the states. What this role would be, though, was left undefined in 1978 while both COSCAA and HUD worked on expanding the state role in community development programs through the State Incentive Grants Bill. This bill would have provided incentive funds to states that reoriented their development programs toward poor people and distressed areas. When Congress failed to enact the bill, Embry kept his commitment to Marinich, agreeing to a demonstration program in which states would be involved in selecting Small Cities CDBG recipients.

Embry assigned Trudy McFall, director of HUD's Office of Planning and Program Coordination, to develop regulations guiding the demonstration. McFall had recently joined HUD, having previously worked as a housing official with the Metropolitan Planning Council in St. Paul, Minnesota. McFall strongly supported expanding the states' role in community development programs. She believed that nationwide rules did not work, that HUD civil servants were not always in touch with local needs, and that separate state standards incorporating state priorities were preferable.

Within HUD, however, McFall had few allies who supported a state role: "Besides me, there was very little support in HUD for involving the states in the Small Cities CDBG program. Bob Embry was for a role for the states more than anyone else, and he was only about 33 percent for such a role." She thus relied on COSCAA's Marinich to help convince other HUD officials that state participation was desirable and that the demonstration should be quickly undertaken.

James Forsberg, director of the Small Cities program since its inception in 1977, and his Small Cities staff were assigned to work closely with McFall and her staff on developing regulations for the demonstration. Forsberg, who had worked in HUD area offices for five years and at HUD headquarters for three years, was opposed to the demonstration. He felt that Small Cities CDBG should remain a federal-local program:

I was opposed to the demonstration initially because I felt the Small Cities CDBG program was already running well. I also saw the Small Cities program as a federal program with the federal objective of community development geared towards low- and moderate-income individuals. I felt federal administration could best meet these goals, while the states might have objectives which conflicted with these goals.

Forsberg also was concerned about fears expressed by HUD area officials and some local governments that states might politicize the selection process, that grant recipients would not be fairly judged, and that the process would become a political power game. They also feared that involving the states in the selection process only would add another layer of undesired bureaucracy and red tape.

The interest group representing the small cities—the National League of Cities (NLC)—had mixed feelings about involving the states in the Small Cities program. B. J. Reed, a senior staff associate at the NLC, summarized the localities' reservations:

Localities are very concerned about any proposed increases in the role of the states in federal programs. Up until the 1930s the states turned their backs on the cities. This was part of the impetus for the New Deal and the expanded role of the federal government. Since the 1930s there hasn't been any groundswell—on a broad basis—of state responsibility and administrative capacity.

Nonetheless, the NLC supported the demonstration as long as it was assured in the demonstration's regulations that local interests would not be ignored by the states participating in the project.

Although Embry committed HUD to the demonstration in 1978, internal opposition turned developing the demonstration's regulations into a drawn-out process. Numerous drafts were written and circulated within HUD, and often to interest groups such as COSCAA and the NLC. McFall argued for a demonstration that placed few restrictions on participating states, and Forsberg argued for a demonstration that would tighten federal controls. The lengthy bureaucratic struggle culminated in a final discussion of the objectives of the demonstration. McFall recalled:

I felt that the purpose of the demonstration was an attempt to share power. Jim Forsberg argued that it should help increase funding to low- and moderate-income individuals. Bob Embry was sort of for both objectives, but in the end when it became clear that the low- and moderate-income objective would not be met he said, "O.K. We'll try sharing power and see how it works."

On April 22, 1980, almost two years after the demonstration's conception, CDBG regulations were published in the *Federal Register*. They included a provision requiring that a consensus of a state's localities favor state participation before joining in the demonstration; this provision satisfied the NLC's concerns.

Simultaneously, HUD sent each state a letter describing the demonstration and offering an opportunity to apply. In Kentucky, Governor Brown's office received the letter and referred it to the Division for Community and Economic Development. (See Exhibit 2, pp. 101-103.)

The Demonstration in Kentucky

Brown's election in 1979 brought an energetic and ambitious individual to Kentucky's governor's office. Before entering politics, Brown had built Kentucky Fried Chicken into one of the largest fast-food franchises in the country, owned the Boston Celtics, and married Phyllis George—a former Miss America turned sportscaster. In seeking the governor's job, he relied on a media campaign featuring himself and his wife. A Democrat, Brown was known to have presidential ambitions.

The predominantly rural state of Kentucky (population 3.5 million) can be divided into three distinct regions. Kentucky received its nickname, "The Bluegrass State," from the first region. Located in central Kentucky, the Bluegrass area boasts relatively good agricultural conditions and a prominent horse breeding industry. The region contains Kentucky's two largest cities and the state capital: Louisville (population 310,000, located on the western edge of the Bluegrass area), the rapidly growing city of Lexington (population 193,000), and Frankfort (population 22,000, the state capital.) The second region, western Kentucky, is less prosperous than the Bluegrass region but contains some wealthy agricultural counties. It also encompasses substantial coal production areas. Coal is most important in the hilly, poverty-stricken region of eastern Kentucky. Better known as part of Appalachia, this region is marked by small, rural towns. Overall, in 1980, almost two-thirds of Kentucky's population could be found in its 450 small cities.

These communities have substantial housing and community development needs. According to a 1970 national study, Kentucky's nonmetropolitan areas had the highest percentage of houses without plumbing, the tenth highest percentage of overcrowded housing, the fifth highest percentage of population in poverty, and the fourth lowest per capita income. The communities in the Appalachian region of eastern Kentucky were especially destitute.

Kentucky's state-level housing and community development programs were the responsibility of the Division for Community and Regional Development (DCRD). DCRD's 62 employees administered funds received from the Appalachian Regional Commission, a federally financed program that targeted money to the Appalachian region of eastern Kentucky, and from the HUD 701 program, which supplied localities with general planning funds. DCRD also acted as a liaison between Kentucky's communities and HUD.

Kentucky as a Demonstration Site

Ralph Coldiron, director of DCRD's Division for Community and Economic Development, initiated Kentucky's interest in the Small Cities CDBG Demonstration. He placed his new assistant, Sally Hamilton, in charge of Kentucky's application. Hamilton was well prepared for the task. After receiving her Ph.D. in German and teaching the language, she entered Kentucky's Department of Local Government, the organizational predecessor to DCRD, in 1975. In late 1976 Hamilton was appointed head of the Housing and Community Development Unit. The unit's responsibilities included providing technical assistance to communities, administering a housing rehabilitation program, assisting in housing relocation, and monitoring the 701 program. Its four or five staff members also acted as a liaison among communities, Area Development Districts (ADDs),* and the HUD area office.

In November 1979 Hamilton left Kentucky for HUD headquarters in Washington, D.C., having been selected to the competitive one-year Intergovernmental Management Program. In the Small Cities division she worked on research projects and helped write regulations for the Small Cities CDBG Demonstration. But she became bored in Washington and jumped at the opportunity to return home to Kentucky as assistant director of the Division for Community and Economic Development. When she arrived back in Kentucky in May 1980 she found on her desk a letter—which she had helped compose during her stint at HUD—written by the agency and sent to all governors. The letter invited the states to participate in the demonstration. The application procedure required states to explain why they wanted to participate in the demonstration, to describe their housing and community development efforts, to outline how they would achieve local consensus on state participation, and to provide assurances that they had the staff capacity and financial resources to participate in the project. (See Exhibit 2, pp. 101-103.)

Kentucky was one of nine states to apply. Forsberg of HUD's Small Cities division suggested that "Two criteria in particular scared off other

---

* The 15 Area Development Districts, established by the Kentucky legislature, coordinated areawide planning. Part of this responsibility included applying for federal grants.

states from applying. First, the states had to provide their own administrative funds to run the program. Second, the criteria said states also would be evaluated on whether they would increase funding to distressed places." Marvin Tick, COSCAA's legislative affairs coordinator, believed that only nine states applied because of the administrative funding provision: "States felt, why should they do HUD's job for them for free?" In turn, Reed of the NLC felt the dearth of applications indicated a lack of state commitment to the localities: "If the states won't pay the administrative costs for staffing the selection process, then what is their commitment to small cities?"

Having received all the applications by early June, the HUD central office moved on to the next step: whittling down the list of applications to four semifinalists. A small group at HUD read all the applications, focusing on each state's administrative capacity and political conditions. States that lacked previous administrative experience with housing and community development programs were eliminated. The central office also relied on HUD area office field personnel to assess administrative capacity and to determine in which states politics might interfere with a fair selection process. After all the applications were read, the small group at HUD sat down with Assistant Secretary Embry and made its recommendations. On July 16, with little dispute, they decided upon the four semifinalists: Kentucky, New Mexico, South Dakota, and Wisconsin.

In Kentucky the demonstration application had become a priority of Governor Brown's. Prior to the Democratic National Convention in August, Brown spoke with President Carter requesting that Kentucky be selected as a demonstration site. President Carter's subsequent directive filtered down to Embry, McFall, and Forsberg; and Kentucky became one of the sites for the demonstration. The ultimate selection of Wisconsin—which had the best-written application—and Kentucky did not occur without one last stand by Forsberg. McFall described the meeting:

> Jim made one last plea to Bob Embry that none of the states were good enough to be selected, that none of the applicants addressed the selection criteria of helping low- and moderate-income persons significantly more. This notion was a false one. The states could not promise other big changes in what they would do, that they would commit substantial amounts of new funds to community development just to participate in the demonstration. Well, Bob said that as long as we are this far down the pike, we are going to go with the demonstration.

Kentucky informally learned of its selection in early August and received public notification on September 5. Forsberg was responsible for overseeing the demonstration for HUD. In Kentucky, Hamilton was responsible for administering the program.

Designing the Demonstration

Despite the interest in the demonstration indicated by Governor Brown and by Coldiron, Hamilton received little guidance either on what the specific objectives of the demonstration should be or on how it should be run. Thus, when she informally learned of Kentucky's selection in early August, Hamilton focused on defining the state's objectives. Sheila Etchen, Hamilton's principal aide in administering the demonstration, recalled:

> No objectives for running the program were coming down from the Executive Office. So, we determined the objective of the demonstration would be to make the Small Cities CDBG system more responsive to local needs. We didn't feel HUD had failed in the past; the HUD area office had good rapport with the localities. But we also felt the national selection criteria weren't always applicable to Kentucky. For example, the system didn't adjust for the conditions of eastern Kentucky where land is expensive and hard to build on and where spot rehabilitation is required, with a broken down shanty right next to a $200,000 home.

The objectives did not go much beyond making the system more responsive to local needs. Hamilton felt a cautious approach to modifying the selection system was appropriate. Essentially satisfied with the HUD system, she felt that given the lack of lead time and administrative resources, it would be foolish to redesign the selection system with more lofty goals in mind.

Hamilton indeed was shorthanded at DCRD. In addition to Sheila Etchen, Hamilton's staff included Guy McElfrish, who was on loan from the HUD area office in Louisville, and Al Andrews, the staff engineer. For additional assistance Hamilton borrowed Ed Holmes, a planner from the Bluegrass Area Development District (ADD), for five months. Because of the short-term nature of the demonstration, Hamilton's only alternative was this patchwork staffing approach; she could not add permanent personnel to run a temporary demonstration. Hamilton and her staff would work almost double the number of hours that the HUD area office spent on the selection process, but Kentucky nevertheless needed additional help to run the demonstration. First, the state had the extra burden of both devising and explaining a new selection system. Second, Kentucky lacked the expertise and experience of the HUD area office in running the program. Finally, Hamilton would not have access to additional staff during "crunch" times, whereas the HUD area office's Division of Community Planning and Development could throw all 21 staff members into the selection process if necessary, as it often did to rate the preapplicants.

In designing the demonstration, Hamilton thus had to consider how to adjust for her staff shortage. She also had to consider her relationships with HUD officials. Because of their work together at HUD, she could count on close communication with Forsberg. The relationship between Kentucky and

Dennis Carr, director of the Community Planning Division in the HUD area office, also had been congenial. In addition, two requirements in the demonstration's regulations encouraged Hamilton to design an administrative structure that included close cooperation with HUD officials. HUD had to verify that a local consensus existed for the new selection criteria and to approve the selected grant recipients.

Finally, Hamilton had to consider the viewpoints of the various local governments and regional agencies concerned with community development. Most notably, she communicated with both the individual members of the ADDs and the lobbying organization of the area development districts; with the Kentucky Municipal League, which represented the views of cities; and with the state Community Development Association, whose membership consisted of all the community development directors in Kentucky. Although these officials knew little about the demonstration at the time of Kentucky's selection, Hamilton soon began to solicit their views. She remembered:

> There was lots of tension about how the demonstration would be run. Local officials, CD directors, and mayors were all concerned that the program would be very political. They thought the demonstration would be shaped to meet the objectives of Governor Brown—who greatly emphasized economic development—and not the needs the localities felt were most important.

Hamilton thus decided upon the central strategy she would use in the demonstration: she would develop a consensus among local, state, and HUD area office officials. She recalled, "to calm the fears of the local officials and because we thought it was the best approach in any case, that if we worked together we could run the program better, we decided to establish a joint process. We hoped to work with both local and HUD officials." A consensus process also dealt well with many of Hamilton's other concerns. For example, local officials' suggestions would help adjust the selection system to local needs, and relying on nonstate officials' time and needs might help compensate for the small DCRD staff.

Administering the Demonstration

Having defined the demonstration's objectives and decided upon a general administrative approach, Hamilton went to work on a broad outline of the selection process, including a detailed time schedule for the three basic steps of the demonstration: 1) designing new selection criteria, 2) establishing an outreach process to explain the new selection criteria to potential applicants, and 3) selecting the winning applicants.

Designing New Selection Criteria

Hamilton knew that devising selection criteria for the Small Cities program would not be an easy task. Although it might be easy to reach agreement on general principles—for example, that the criteria should make the Small Cities program more responsive to local needs—it would not be easy to develop a consensus behind specific changes and to ensure that the new criteria would be fair and objective.

With these difficulties in mind, Hamilton established two committees: a technical committee with expertise in community development to discuss and design specific selection criteria, and a policy advisory committee to assess the general implications of any proposed changes. To be consistent with the consensus approach, she chose local officials as committee members. The technical committee was composed of six area development district directors who had backgrounds in long-range, general community development planning, and six community development association members who were familiar with Small Cities CDBG projects and were experienced in applying for grants.

In a meeting chaired by Hamilton, the technical committee met for two days in September to establish new selection criteria. The committee went through HUD's selection system step by step, voting on each provision separately. Hotly disputed issues included the number of bonus points a proposal should receive if it had an Areawide Housing Opportunity Plan (AHOP),* the number of objectives a proposal had to achieve to be considered a comprehensive project, and the need indicators (for example, percentage of people in poverty versus the absolute number of people in poverty) that should be used. The central argument throughout these two days was whether to tamper with a familiar system that most involved felt was fair. Ultimately, the committee chose to maintain the basic structure of the nationwide system.

The proposed selection criteria then were submitted to the policy advisory committee, which was to assess the general character of the proposed selection criteria. Members of this committee came from all major community development interest groups in Kentucky: the Kentucky Municipal League, ADD directors, the Kentucky Association of County Officials, the state Community Development Association, the Kentucky Council of ADDS, and the state government. At their meeting in late September, state officials explained the criteria at length to the committee, and its members were asked to consider the proposed system until a subsequent meeting was held in late October.

In the meantime approximately 500 copies of the selection criteria were distributed statewide for comments to mayors, community development

---

* HUD encouraged, but did not require, metropolitan areas to formulate Areawide Housing Opportunity Plans (AHOPs), which were difficult to develop because of insufficient housing. An AHOP consisted of an areawide housing strategy including, in particular, a strategy to expand housing opportunities for minorities. In the Small Cities' metropolitan competition, a small city participating in an AHOP could receive bonus points. Because only one Kentucky metropolitan area had an AHOP, many local officials disliked this bonus point provision.

directors, and other interested officials. Of the 50 officials who replied, 49 generally favored the proposed criteria, and only one was negative.

The policy advisory committee met on October 28 to review the local officials' comments and to decide upon the final selection criteria. Policy advisory committee members felt comfortable with the nationwide system, so they were quick to agree to the slightly modified version proposed by the technical committee.

The Outreach Program

With the final criteria established, the state began in early November to explain the demonstration and the new selection system to local governments. Because some small cities did not understand or were unaware of the old selection system, DCRD instituted an outreach program. Hamilton, Etchen, McElfrish, Carr, and two other HUD area office staff members conducted four regional training sessions, each attended by 30 to 40 potential applicants.

As part of this outreach effort, Hamilton's staff responded to applicants' questions and, as necessary and when time permitted, visited applicants. (Altogether, the state visited 35 applicants.) Etchen described the outreach process:

> During the demonstration, the state was involved in a different kind of technical assistance. In the past, technical assistance was specialized. For instance, we might help a locality calculate the cost of a relocation proposal. This year we provided technical assistance on program design, on how to put the projects together. For example, if a small city was trying to decide which of two programs to apply for, they would call us and we would help them make this decision.

Selecting the Winners

In late January DCRD received 112 preapplications. With $10.25 million in grant money to allocate (the other $17.5 million of Kentucky's Small Cities CDBG grant money was allocated to continuations of projects selected in previous years), Kentucky ultimately would select 18 new grant recipients from these preapplications. (See Exhibit 3, p. 104.)

Determining the number of points a preapplication received was a two-part process. First, the needs and the bonus point sections—60 percent of the potential points a preapplication could receive—were determined. The points were calculated by the HUD area office computer because they followed a strict formula. For example, a preapplication received a certain number of points depending upon the percentage of people living in poverty in the small city, say 10 points if 8 percent, 12 points if 10 percent, and so on.

Calculating program impact points (40 percent of a preapplicant's potential point total) required subjective judgments—for example, assessing how well the proposed project addressed small city problems as defined by

HUD regulations. Hamilton and Etchen set up four ratings teams to determine program impact points—one each for comprehensive, housing, public facility, and economic development proposals. Each panel was made up of three members—representing DCRD, HUD, and local government—who rated the preapplications in their areas of expertise. This joint review was consistent with Hamilton's consensus approach; and, as she recalled, "DCRD did not have the resources to fill the 12 positions internally."

By early March the preapplication scores had been compiled, and DCRD and HUD officials embarked on site visits to the 30 applicants with the highest preapplication point totals. A preapplication could not gain points as a result of a site visit, but it could lose points if it was found to be inaccurate or if the proposed project was problematic. For example, one site lost points because there were no provisions for water supply in a proposed housing project.

After the site visits DCRD selected the grant recipients. For each category of competition, the preapplication with the most points would be a winner, as would the preapplications next on the list, until funds for that category were exhausted. The last preapplication selected might have its project scaled down so that the amount of funds allocated did not exceed that category's budget.

DCRD then submitted its recommendations to the HUD area office for final approval. This approval was given and, in late March, the Kentucky congressional delegation notified the 18 winning preapplicants.

The Process Appraised

Throughout the selection process Hamilton communicated closely with all interested parties. She and Forsberg spoke frequently about the demonstration, and Forsberg came to Kentucky to attend the second policy advisory committee meeting and to observe the rating teams. The state also worked closely with the HUD area office, whose staff attended meetings of the technical and policy advisory committees and worked jointly with DCRD during the training sessions, rating procedure, and on-site visits. Etchen believed this joint process strengthened federal-state relations: "When you work day-in, day-out, from sunup to sundown, with other individuals, soon you either cannot stand them, or you grow to like them. Fortunately, in the case of HUD area office staffers, the latter occurred."

The consensus process also benefited state-local relations. Local officials were glad to have their say as members of the various committees and appreciated the training sessions. As Anna Jean Tackett, head of the State Community Development Association and a member of the technical committee, recalled:

I felt the state's cooperation with local representatives such as the state CD Association made the demonstration successful. The training sessions were good, and Sally Hamilton and Sheila Etchen were accessible. Given this cooperation, I think it is better to have the state administer the Small City CDBG program; it better understands the different and unique needs of local communities.

Events in Washington, D.C.

After President Ronald Reagan's inauguration in January 1981, a different attitude toward federal programs dominated Washington. The new president, a former two-term governor of California, strongly believed that the federal government should turn power back to states and localities. Accordingly, the Reagan administration submitted a proposal to Congress that would combine many federal categorical grants programs into several general block grants, the administration of which would be delegated to the states. Reagan's proposal offered states the option to assume complete administrative control of the Small Cities CDBG program. In April the proposal still awaited action by Congress. It was expected to pass the Republican-dominated Senate with ease but to face stiff opposition in the Democratic-controlled House.

At the same time, the administration's attitude on federalism affected HUD's operations. Forsberg, who remained in his job after the change in administrations, explained, "HUD's objectives changed with the new administration. Whereas under Carter the stress was on low- and moderate-income individuals, under Reagan, the crucial issue is local choice. That is, let the states decide themselves what problems are most critical." Hamilton put the change succinctly, "HUD's now a new ballgame. There's no Bob Embry saying, 'Low-Mod, Low-Mod, Low-Mod.' "

HUD's Office of Evaluation began to review the demonstration results in this context. An unexpected turn of events hastened the completion of the review. HUD Secretary Samuel Pierce was asked about the demonstration by a congressional committee. Consequently, the executive office at HUD requested that the Office of Evaluation produce its report on the demonstration immediately. Judith Hamburger of the Office of Evaluation recalled, "The Office of Evaluation originally hoped to keep the demonstration report quiet and technical and intended to write the report in September. But the executive office wanted the report for a speech and for Congress, so we put out an interim evaluation in a three-and-a-half-day crash."

The hastily composed interim evaluation was based on a survey of localities in Kentucky and Wisconsin. The authors summarized its central conclusion in the overview: "The principal findings at this time are that local officials in Kentucky had very positive opinions about state administration of the selection system, understood state objectives, and believed the system would achieve its objectives." Fifty-eight percent of the localities surveyed said they preferred Kentucky to administer the selection process, 25 percent favored HUD, and the remainder had no opinion. The demonstration's popularity was attributed to Kentucky's outreach program.

The evaluation did not attempt to judge the quality of the projects selected, a much more difficult task that could not be undertaken until the projects were completed. In addition, because the grant recipients in Wisconsin had not been selected at the time, the evaluation highlighted only the Kentucky demonstration. Preliminary findings indicated that Wisconsin had changed the selection process more substantially than had Kentucky. State officials also had worked less closely with their local counterparts and the HUD staff.

Despite the preliminary and partial nature of the findings, the interim evaluation soon "popped up everywhere," as Michael Brintnall of the Office of Evaluation recalled. Articles in housing and community development journals and newspapers, as well as individuals at HUD and in Congress, generally acclaimed the demonstration as a success. They primarily based their opinion on its popularity among Kentucky localities. The political impact of the demonstration's success was limited but positive. Tick, the legislative director of COSCAA, explained, "The demonstration did not have a huge political impact; though, as an example of a state successfully operating part of a federal program, it did give the Reagan administration some armament."

Supporters of increasing state responsibility also felt the demonstration indicated that states had the administrative capacity to assume greater responsibility. Forsberg of HUD's Small Cities division was transformed into an advocate of state control. "The demonstration has shown two states have the administrative capacity to take over more responsibility," he said. "Indeed, the argument by the cities that states lack administrative capacity is not the real issue; their real concern is the fear of the unknown."

On the other hand, some observers cited reasons why the demonstration's results did not support a substantial increase in the authority of state governments. They argued that Kentucky and Wisconsin were atypical; that their administrative capacity and commitment to community development exceeded that of other states. Reed of the NLC agreed with this argument. He also noted the limited applicability of the demonstration:

> The demonstration should not be used to justify complete state administration of federal programs. In the demonstration, there were many controls by HUD, including the local consensus requirement. If strict federal controls are maintained, the NLC can accept increased state responsibility; the possibility that controls will not be maintained is the NLC's greatest concern.

93

Moreover, the demonstration had allowed Kentucky and Wisconsin to assume control only of the selection process; most of the responsibility for the Small Cities CDBG program—such as fiscal management and project monitoring—remained with the HUD area office. In contrast, the 1981 Reagan administration proposal allowed states fully to take over management of the Small Cities program. Finally, HUD's Dennis Carr in the Kentucky area office commented, "I would like to make two qualifications regarding why folks preferred state administration of the program. First, the survey was taken before the grant winners were selected. Second, Kentucky did not make any big changes in the point selection system." Under the Reagan administration proposal, states would be able to make any changes in the selection system they desired.

The fate of the Reagan administration's Small Cities proposal was decided when the Budget Reconciliation Act passed Congress in late July 1981. Cuts in the federal budget were the main focus of the bill. But the 300-page bill also contained many of the Reagan administration's pet proposals, including a modified Small Cities CDBG program. In future years, therefore, states would have the option of assuming complete responsibility for the program.

Hamilton Ponders the Future

In the spring of 1981 Sally Hamilton was busy answering inquiries about the demonstration. Her office was bombarded with phone calls from community development officials from across the nation, and she was called to testify before the House Subcommittee on Housing and Community Development. She also organized a conference on the demonstration for officials from southeastern states.

From April to late June, Hamilton operated under the assumption that the demonstration would continue in Kentucky, but that in the upcoming fiscal year the state would not assume any responsibilities for the Small Cities CDBG program beyond administering the selection process. Yet the demands upon Hamilton and her staff were unexpectedly intensified. Upon learning of the passage of the budget bill and the consequent changes in the Small Cities CDBG, the state of Kentucky decided to assume full control of the program.

In planning for Kentucky's administration of the program, Hamilton first thought back on the results of the demonstration. She was aware of the interim evaluation report and also knew that both the Kentucky Municipal League and many members of the State Community Development Association were in favor of the demonstration. She knew the consensus process had had much to do with their positive attitude. However, she also had received some negative feedback on the program from western Kentucky. For example,

Richard Rector, the community development director from Bowling Green since 1970, remarked:

> Though the demonstration worked out pretty well in Kentucky last year, and Sally Hamilton and Sheila Etchen did an excellent job, I have some problems with the demonstration specifically and state administration of the Small Cities program in general. First, there's a big potential problem of the governor eventually getting involved and the process becoming political; this can happen whenever a governor is given discretion over a lump sum of money. Second, with ADD members sitting on rating teams and also submitting preapplications, sweetheart deals are a possibility. Third, the governor went ahead with the demonstration without considering administrative capacity, and the state had zero to zip experience.

Hamilton also reflected on the costs of running the demonstration. She calculated that 3.5 man years of administrative time, plus travel expenses, cost the state $75,000. This figure did not include HUD's costs or the state's opportunity costs resulting from Hamilton's and Etchen's having to drop other activities. The federal government, however, would pick up half the administrative costs in the next year.

In planning for new program responsibilities, Hamilton reviewed the methods that the HUD area office had used to administer the Small Cities CDBG program. She knew that Dennis Carr believed that it would take the state 17 people to effectively administer the Small Cities CDBG program; compared with HUD's staffing, he estimated the state could get by with one fewer supervisor, one fewer community planning and development representative, one fewer special programs staffer, and no general program aide in the technical assistance unit.

Hamilton, however, did not have 17 individuals with experience in the Small Cities program available to her. Two staff members who had worked on the demonstration, Guy McElfrish and Al Andrews, had left DCRD. Only three remaining individuals—Etchen and two of her assistants—were familiar with the Small Cities selection process. In addition, although other DCRD staffers had technical assistance experience, Hamilton realized with trepidation that DCRD lacked any experience with program monitoring or with direct fiscal management of grants.

Finally, Hamilton formulated her own objectives. She was ready to make major changes in the selection process:

> Last year the main change in the selection process was a change in the people running the program. This time we want to radically change the process. We know it will take three or four years of changes before we fine-tune the selection process.... One of our main objectives this year is to develop a system so we will fund on the basis of quality of a project instead of funding how well preapplications are prepared; potentially good projects should not be rejected because a small city does not know how to fill out a preapplication.

95

Etchen further defined DCRD's objectives:

> We didn't change the selection process too much the first year because we didn't want to go like gangbusters, we wanted to walk before we ran. . . . This year one problem we would like to correct is that last time around there was generally a lack of a balance in the type of projects funded; for example, there were not enough economic development projects and too many housing rehabilitation projects.

At the same time, because DCRD lacked experience in monitoring and fiscal management, and because in early September HUD's regulations for the new program were not yet completed, Hamilton expected to move with care on these aspects of administering the Small Cities program.

EXHIBITS

Exhibit One:
National Selection Criteria For Small City Block Grants

Selection System for Comprehensive
Grants Metro and Non-Metro

[HUD guidelines under the Housing and
Community Development Act of 1977]

Preapplications are rated and scored against each of the following factors. All points for each factor are rounded to the nearest whole number. The maximum score possible is 940 points for metropolitan applicants and 920 points for non-metropolitan applicants.

	Points
a) Need — absolute number of poverty persons	75
b) Need — percent of poverty persons	75
c) Program Factor — Impact of proposed program	400
d) Benefit to low- and moderate-income persons	200
e) Outstanding performance:	
Housing	100
Local equal opportunity efforts	50
f) Areawide Housing Opportunity Plan (AHOP)	20
(metropolitan applicants only)	

g) Energy conservation or production   20

       Total points:
       (Non-Metro)   920

    (Metro)   940

Preapplications from counties in behalf of themselves, or joint preapplications in which a county is participating, are scored separately with respect to the needs factors.

(a) Need — absolute number of poverty persons (75 points). All applicants are compared in terms of the number of persons whose incomes are below the poverty level. Individual scores are obtained by dividing each applicant's number of persons in poverty by the greatest number of persons in poverty of any applicant and multiplying by 75.

(b) Need — percent of poverty persons (75 points). All applicants are compared in terms of the percentage of their population below the poverty level. Individual scores are obtained by dividing each applicant's percentage of persons in poverty by the highest percentage of persons in poverty of any applicant and multiplying by 75.

(c) Program factor — impact of the proposed program (400 points). Each applicant shall select four program design criteria from among the following eleven. *The State* shall measure the impact of the program on low- and moderate-income persons for each of the program design criteria selected, based on the results to be achieved in relation to the amount of funds requested, the number of persons to benefit given the type of program, the nature of the benefit, additional actions that may be necessary to fully resolve the need, previous actions taken by the applicant to address the need, whether displacement will be involved and what steps will be taken to minimize involuntary displacement and to mitigate its adverse effects or related hardships, environmental considerations, and where appropriate, site selection standards. Each applicant must use specific measurable terms to explain how its program benefits low- and moderate-income persons.

(1) Program design criteria.

    (i)   Supports comprehensive neighborhood conservation, stabilization, and/or revitalization.

    (ii)   Provides housing choice on a regional basis; or implements a HUD-approved Areawide Housing Opportunity Plan.

    (iii)   Provides housing choice within the community either outside areas with concentrations of minorities and low- and moderate-income persons or in a neighborhood which is experiencing revitalization and substantial displacement as a result of private reinvestment, by enabling low- and moderate-income persons to remain in their neighborhood.

(iv) Supports the expansion of housing by providing additional housing units not previously available.

(v) Addresses a serious deficiency in a community's public facilities.

(vi) Expands or retains employment opportunities.

(vii) Attracts or retains businesses which provide essential services.

(viii) Removes slums or blighted conditions.

(ix) Resolves a serious threat to health or safety.

(x) Supports another Federal *and/or State* program or programs being undertaken in the community or deals with the adverse impact of another recent Federal action. The other Federal *and/or State* program or action must be of substantial size or impact in the community in relation to the proposed program.

(xi) Supports energy production or conservation.

(2) Rating and ranking methods. This factor requires a two-step rating process. First, the potential of the proposed program of activities to achieve the results intended by each selected criterion when considered in relation to other communities addressing the same criterion is assessed. A numerical value is assigned, based on the following:

	Points
The results would have insignificant impact	0
The results would have minimal impact	2
The results would have a moderate impact	4
The results would have a substantial impact	8

After each of the four criteria selected by an applicant is rated and a value assigned, the total is added (Program Impact Score maximum is 32). Then, the actual points are determined by dividing each applicant's Program Impact Score by the highest Program Impact Score achieved by an applicant and multiplying the result by four hundred.

(d) Benefit to low- and moderate-income persons (200 points). All applicants are scored in terms of the percent of funds benefiting low- and moderate-income persons. Determining the percentage of funds benefiting low- and moderate-income persons requires three steps. First, the amount of funds to benefit low- and moderate-income persons for each activity is determined by dividing the number of low- and moderate-income persons by the total number of persons to benefit from the activity and multiplying by the amount of Small Cities Program funds requested for that activity. Then, these amounts for each activity are added and divided by the total amount of requested Small Cities Program funds. This number multiplied by 100 is the percentage of funds benefiting low- and moderate-income persons. Costs of planning, management, and administration may not be included in this computation.

Points for benefit to low- and moderate-income persons are awarded to each applicant as follows:

	Points
100% — 75% Benefit to low- and moderate-income	200
74% — 50% Benefit to low- and moderate-income	100
49% — 25% Benefit to low- and moderate-income	10
24% — 0% Benefit to low- and moderate-income	0

The appropriate median income amounts for low- and moderate-income are supplied by HUD. Where appropriate, HUD may modify the geographic area used in the definition of low- and moderate-income persons.

(e) Performance in housing and equal opportunity (150 points) — (1) Housing efforts (100 points).

(i) Fifteen points for each of the following criteria are awarded to each applicant that demonstrates outstanding performance in:

(A) providing housing for low- and moderate-income families located in a manner which provides housing choice either in areas outside of minority and low- and moderate-income concentrations or in a neighborhood which is experiencing revitalization and substantial displacement as a result of private reinvestment, by enabling low- and moderate-income persons to remain in their neighborhood; or if the community is predominantly inhabited by persons who are members of minority and/or low income groups. HUD shall assess the extent to which assisted housing is distributed throughout the community.

(B) integrated occupancy by race and ethnicity in assisted housing projects and, if the applicant has a Section 8 Existing Housing Program, evidence of locational choice in the Section 8 Existing Housing Program demonstrated in the occupancy of units.

(C) active enforcement of a fair housing ordinance at least equivalent in scope and coverage to Title VIII of the Civil Rights Act of 1968.

(D) implementation of a HUD-approved New Horizons Fair Housing Assistance Project (or demonstrated participation in a HUD-approved county/State/Regional New Horizons Project) or a fair housing strategy that is equivalent in scope to a New Horizons Project.

(ii) Twenty points for each of the following criteria are awarded to each applicant that demonstrates outstanding performance in:

(A) meeting its large family housing assistance needs in relation to that proportion of need.

(B) carrying out housing assistance goals from previous HAP(s) or, if the applicant has no prior HAP, meeting a significant proportion of its housing assistance needs.

(2) Local Equal Employment and Entrepreneurial Efforts (50 points).

  (i)   Twenty-five points are awarded to each applicant that demonstrates that its percentage of minority permanent employees (20 hours per week or more) is greater than the percentage of minorities within the SMSA for metropolitan applicants, unless the percentage of minority population in the community itself exceeds that of the county or SMSA, in which case minority employment must generally reflect the minority population of the community.

  (ii) Twenty points are awarded to each applicant that demonstrates that at least five percent of all its contracts based on dollar value have been awarded within the past two years to minority owned and controlled businesses, providing the applicable percentage of minority population is five percent or less. If the applicable percentage of minority population exceeds five percent, then the applicant must have a corresponding percentage of its contracts awarded to minority businesses; however, twenty percent of the total dollar value of its contracts awarded to minority business enterprise will be sufficient for award of points for any applicant. The applicable percentage of minority population is the percentage of minorities in the applicant's jurisdiction, or in the county for nonmetropolitan applicants, or in the SMSA for metropolitan applicants, whichever is higher.

  (iii) Five points are awarded to each applicant that demonstrates that at least five percent of its deposits from all sources, measured as an average in a minority owned and controlled financial institution. The year measured is the year ending the date the preapplication is due.

(f) Areawide Housing Opportunity Plan (metropolitan applicants only, 20 points). *Twenty* points are awarded to each metropolitan applicant that is in its first year of participation in a HUD-approved Areawide Housing Opportunity Plan (AHOP). Each applicant which has been a participating jurisdiction in a HUD-approved AHOP for more than one year is awarded the *twenty* points if the areawide planning organization with the approved AHOP certifies that the applicant is adequately carrying out its responsibility to implement the AHOP. An applicant which is a participating jurisdiction in an AHOP but which is not adequately fulfilling its commitments to implement the AHOP is awarded zero points. The time period considered is measured from the date of written HUD approval of the AHOP to the date the preapplication is due.

The Area Office may reject the certification by the areawide planning organization if there are data or facts available to the Area Office which indicate that a community is not carrying out its responsibility to implement the AHOP.

(g) Energy conservation or production (20 points). Twenty points are awarded to each applicant that demonstrates that its proposed program will promote energy conservation or support energy production in the applicant's jurisdiction.

Exhibit Two:
Letter Explaining Demonstration to Governors

Department of Housing and Urban Development
Washington, D.C. 20410

[April 1980]

Office of the Assistant Secretary
For Community Planning and Development

Dear Governor Brown:

In response to the President's urban and rural policy initiatives and [as] part of its effort to forge a closer partnership with States, HUD is planning to respond to a request from the Governors to conduct a demonstration program designed to involve one or two States more directly in the selection of the small cities to receive Community Development Block Grants. (The Community Development Block Grant program will award nearly $1 billion to small cities this year.) HUD's primary purpose in undertaking this demonstration is to determine whether increased State participation can further such objectives as more effective targeting and coordination of Federal and State resources to communities with the greatest need, more responsiveness to State and local priorities and plans, and greater commitment of State resources to housing and community development.

I am writing you and all other Governors to determine your interest in having your State participate in this demonstration effort. States will be selected to participate through a competitive process that emphasizes existing State efforts to assist communities with the most pressing problems of distress. HUD is inviting State participation in this demonstration project on a strictly voluntary basis and we will not be able to provide States with additional funds to cover the administrative costs associated with State involvement in the ranking and selection process for Small Cities CDBG applications.

The demonstration program is intended to give the States selected the greatest involvement permitted under the Housing and Community Development Act in recommending both metropolitan and non-metropolitan small city applicants to receive grants. I want to emphasize that an absolute prerequisite for any State to be selected will be a clear indication that there is a clear consensus on the part of affected local governments for the State assuming this role in the small cities selection process.

The States chosen may modify the selection criteria, may design a system and procedures for selecting applications, and will manage, to a significant degree, the preapplication and selection process. These activities will be done in close consultation with the local HUD Area Office. Once the State-proposed procedures and selection criteria are approved by HUD and gain the acceptance of local government, the State will conduct the preapplication and selection process and rank all the applications. HUD will review the State's recommendations and fund those applications in rank order. Thus, the State could develop selection criteria which would support its own priorities, consistent with the block-grant program legislative mandates and national objectives. In evaluating State applications, we will be concerned with the degree to which a State demonstrates outstanding performance in:

(1) Providing State funds for low- and moderate-income housing and community development which aid distressed places and expand choice;

(2) Using plans, policies and programs that constitute a State strategy that serves as the basis for State decision-making; and

(3) Demonstrating a system for targeting State resources to distressed communities, including cities over 50,000 population, and to low- and moderate-income persons and minorities.

We will also be looking for:

(4) A clear indication of how the State expects to be able to demonstrate a consensus among eligible small cities grant applicants and recipients for the extent and type of State participation being proposed, and

(5) Strong assurances that the State has the staff capacity and financial resources to undertake the demonstration since additional State administrative costs will not be provided by HUD or chargeable to Small Cities CDBG funds.

Enclosed is a copy of the regulations for this demonstration project that were published in the *Federal Register* in April and a submission format for the competitive application process. The submission format includes a description of the way we would expect to measure a State's performance on the five criteria listed above. I hope, in assessing whether to seek to participate in this effort, you will look closely at the criteria and make a realistic appraisal of your State's record in relationship to other States. I do not think it is to either the State's benefit or HUD's to encourage large numbers of States to compete when we only expect to be able to involve one or two States.

In addition to responding to each of the criteria, please include a discussion of how you would expect to see the selection criteria for Small Cities Block Grants changed, what changes in emphasis and impact you feel you might wish to achieve if your State had more direct involvement in the program, and how this relates to the State's strategy. We are particularly interested in learning what added resources and other benefits your more distressed communities could expect to receive as a result of your participation in this demonstration. We appreciate that at this time you could not be expected to have detailed answers for these questions, but would like to obtain your preliminary thoughts on what you would expect as a result of increased State involvement.

If you think you may wish to participate in this effort, I would like an expression of interest by May 30. Since gathering some of the information requested in the submission format may require some time, we are prepared to accept the best estimates available for this initial expression of interest.

We will evaluate the responses that are received and make a preliminary determination of those States that appear to be most competitive. To save other States time and expense, we will request final proposals only from a limited number of the States, probably no more than five. It is HUD's intention to ask them to submit final proposals in August and to select the one or two States to participate in September.

The selected States will then have to develop and gain acceptance for their selection criteria and procedures from affected communities as well as HUD and demonstrate consensus to HUD. We would expect the State to participate in the FY 1981 selection cycle which occurs in the fall of 1980.

We look forward to your response and involvement in this demonstration effort to permit States an opportunity for more direct involvement in HUD programs toward our common goal of aiding distressed places and people.

If you personally have any questions I hope you will call me. Trudy McFall, my Director of Planning and Program Coordination, also is available to answer questions.

Sincerely,

Robert C. Embry, Jr.
Assistant Secretary

Exhibit Three:
Kentucky Small Cities Program Preapplication Breakout

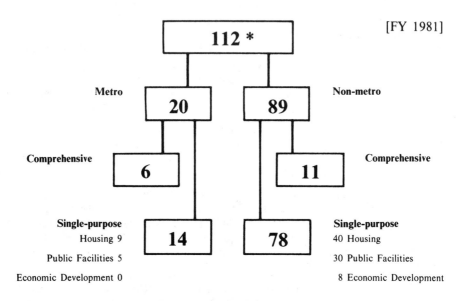

[FY 1981]

112 *

Metro — 20   89 — Non-metro

Comprehensive — 6   11 — Comprehensive

Single-purpose
Housing 9   14   78   40 Housing
Public Facilities 5   30 Public Facilities
Economic Development 0   8 Economic Development

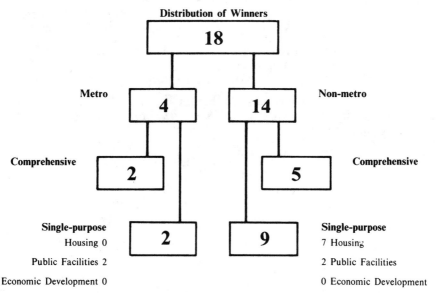

Distribution of Winners

18

Metro — 4   14 — Non-metro

Comprehensive — 2   5 — Comprehensive

Single-purpose
Housing 0   2   9   7 Housing
Public Facilities 2   2 Public Facilities
Economic Development 0   0 Economic Development

* 3 Pre-apps were disqualified due to past performance problems

Discussion Questions

1. Why did HUD Assistant Secretary Robert Embry agree to establish the Small Cities CDBG Demonstration?

2. How can one explain Trudy McFall's and James Forsberg's contrasting views about the wisdom of the demonstration?

3. Why would Kentucky (or the other states that applied) want to participate in the demonstration?

4. What factors accounted for Kentucky's selection as a demonstration site?

5. Once Kentucky was selected as a site, what key decisions did Sally Hamilton and other Kentucky administrators have to make about the way they would conduct the program?

6. What administrative resources were most important in enabling Kentucky to run the Small Cities CDBG demonstration?

7. Evaluate Hamilton's strategy of making very few changes in HUD's project selection criteria.

8. Why did the demonstration become more important and "visible" when the Reagan administration took office?

9. What additional administrative capacity—in terms of personnel and functions—must Hamilton develop in her agency to permit Kentucky to take over the Small Cities CDBG program fully and effectively?

Suggestions for Further Reading

Kettl, Donald F. *Managing Community Development in the New Federalism.* New York: Praeger Publishers, 1980. An account of what the federal government intended to accomplish in establishing the Community Development Block Grant program and how CDBG was implemented in four Connecticut cities.

Pressman, Jeffrey L. *Federal Programs and City Politics.* Berkeley: University of California Press, 1975. Chapter 4, "Images: Federal and Local Officials View Each Other," offers keen insight into the differing perceptions of federal and local program managers.

Williams, Walter. *Government By Agency: Lessons from the Social Program Grants-in-Aid Experience.* New York: Academic Press, 1980. Chapter 4, "The Implementation of CDBG," focuses on how HUD organized itself to manage the community development program.

Haider, Donald H. *When Governments Come to Washington.* New York: The Free Press, 1974. Describes the lobbying activities of groups such as the National League of Cities in the legislative and administrative arenas in Washington, D.C.

3. The Environmental Protection Agency and Transportation Controls

INTRODUCTION

Regulation is perhaps the most controversial aspect of contemporary intergovernmental relations—a topic that both provokes heated comments from federal officials and their state and local colleagues and engenders serious clashes over specific policies. The following three-part case study, "The Environmental Protection Agency and Transportation Controls," permits us to explore the dynamics of the regulatory process under the Clean Air Act as it unfolded at several levels of the federal system.

In general, regulation in intergovernmental programs arises from two broad imperatives. The first is the desire to set national standards for a particular program. Most federal domestic programs initially are created because a winning legislative or administrative coalition believes that some policy question—for example, housing for low-income families, highway construction, fire safety practices, or environmental protection—should not be left totally to the discretion of state and local authorities. In effect the program defines national goals that, to a greater or lesser degree, are meant to outweigh local policy preferences.

The second imperative underlying intergovernmental regulation is the method of "indirect management" that arises from our federal system. Programs are managed indirectly in that the level of government that defines the program, establishes some or all of its basic operating principles, and provides financial resources (the federal government) actually does not implement the program; that is left to state or local authorities. This decentralized management structure, so different from what exists in many other countries where the national government has a strong local presence, has deep roots in our governmental heritage and in our contemporary political values. It means, however, that national policy goals are carried out by dozens, hundreds, or even thousands of subnational units of government.

As a result of these imperatives, federal program architects use regulations as a tool for making national intent clear and ensuring that local program implementors follow it. To adopt a manufacturing metaphor, regulations permit federal program managers to define product specifications, prescribe production processes, and exercise quality control. Many federal regulations are program-specific—that is, they are written explicitly for a particular program. Another class of regulations applies across the board to all programs or to broad classes of programs. These so-called "cross-cutting" regulations became increasingly important in the late 1960s and the 1970s when their number proliferated.

Most intergovernmental regulations grow out of the grant-in-aid relationships between the federal government and states and localities. The recipient government accepts the obligation to follow the regulations as a condition of securing federal funds. In principle, this obligation is accepted voluntarily; if the grant money were not accepted, the regulations would not be binding. An important but less extensive body of regulations is not voluntary. In policy areas such as civil rights and environmental protection, for example, the federal government mandates state or local policy whether or not federal aid is involved. The transportation controls described in the following case study, "The Environmental Protection Agency and Transportation Controls," fall into the latter category.

Inevitably, the regulatory process results in a pulling and tugging within the federal system that sometimes erupts into bitter political conflict. This case study explores one such program—EPA's efforts to reduce urban air pollution, in part, by restricting auto use. By studying these events we can better understand the motivations and stakes of the principal actors at several levels of government, the constraints they faced, their influence on policy, and the requisites of effective regulatory administration.

Case A concentrates on the political and managerial problems of regulation from the federal perspective. EPA's experience shows that regulation writing often proceeds in a complex, highly pressurized, policy-making environment. Because congressional agreement often is reached at the price of statutory ambiguity, the administrative agency responsible for writing and implementing regulations may have relatively little guidance on what it should consider. The agency's own interests—in the policy at hand and in relation to other goals and programs—inevitably color its deliberations. In a controversial policy area such as air quality, the agency may find its actions scrutinized by the White House and its staff arms, such as the Office of Management and Budget (OMB). Congress, acting through influential individual members, its committees, or as a legislative body as a whole, may try to oversee agency execution of policy, and its influence will loom large because of its budgetary authority and its capacity to amend the statutes on which administrative regulations rest. Outside of the government but closely attuned to its deliberations, a constellation of interest groups may be clamoring for varying interpretations of the law or for different degrees of toughness in enforcement. Finally, the courts, removed at one level from the political fray, may offer an alternative channel of access to policy making for claimants who cannot win their point in legislative or administrative politics.

Against this political backdrop, the program manager's task of writing regulations often proves difficult. First, the goals of the program may be subject to varying interpretations. To the extent that Congress papered over its own conflicts with ambiguous statutory language or with rhetoric enshrining multiple and inconsistent objectives in the bill, the program manager must either operationalize these goals or finesse the issue with ambiguity of his own. Second, the program manager must deal with the "empirical complexity" of the world; that is, he must make sense of the myriad social and economic circumstances that frame the policy problem he faces. Often he will find it extremely difficult to secure basic information about the nature and extent of the problem, let alone to disentangle the causal relationships among elements of the problem and its environment. Third, the program manager must design appropriate policy instruments to accomplish his regulatory goals; he must define exactly what state and local agencies are required to do. This is difficult enough when effective means are known and available, but it becomes even more difficult to select the "technology" of regulation when problem causes and solutions are uncertain—as is so often the case in domestic policy arenas. Finally, designing policy instruments is made more problematic by the vast variation in structure and authority in state and local governments that must implement the regulatory program; what might be appropriate regulations in 14 states may be ill-conceived for others.

Like any regulatory program, EPA's new transportation controls confronted an existing system of transportation policy and politics in each state to which the regulations applied. Case B examines the regulatory process in the Boston area from the perspective of Massachusetts' governor and secretary of transportation. It is by no means certain that such officials will enthusiastically implement a regulatory program, thus committing their energy, political resources, and prestige to support a federal agency's agenda. Their cooperation is likely to depend on how they gauge the impact of the federal rules on their own programs and objectives, and whether they sense political gain or loss in association with the regulations. In any event, such officials are not likely to serve as passive agents of federal will. They either will strive to use the federal initiative for their own purposes or maintain a discreet distance from the regulatory process in order to disclaim responsibility for its results. The choice may be difficult, however, as Case B reveals in examining

Governor Sargent's and Secretary Altshuler's approach to transportation controls.

The federal regulatory role does not end with the promulgation of formal rules. State and local performance must be monitored, and, where noncompliance goes beyond acceptable limits, enforcement actions may be required. Case C follows the implementation of transportation controls in Massachusetts from the perspective of EPA's Boston regional office, which took the lead in pressing to meet the federal clean air standards. This part of the case study permits us to assess the factors that affect the success of a regulatory program. These include, in this example, the scale of the regulatory effort, the adequacy of the federal agency's administrative apparatus, its seriousness about enforcement, the probability of state and local compliance or evasion, and the incentives that the federal agency can offer to induce state and local cooperation. Case C also returns to the theme of "indirect management" by examining the implementation of various control measures such as downtown parking restrictions, an auto-restricted zone, and express bus lanes. Inevitably, EPA was dependent on other levels of government to carry out the projects associated with the regulatory effort.

Taken as a whole the three parts of "The Environmental Protection Agency and Transportation Controls" provide a multi-faceted view of intergovernmental regulation—a view that allows us to see both its political and administrative dimensions and to assess the roles of actors at all levels of the federal system.

The Environmental Protection Agency and Transportation Controls (A)

THE CAST

Edmund S. Muskie	U.S. Senator from Maine; chairman of the Public Works Subcommittee on Air and Water Pollution; leading environmental advocate in Congress and potential presidential candidate in 1972
William D. Ruckelshaus	EPA administrator
Robert Fri	acting administrator of EPA
EPA	U.S. Environmental Protection Agency

OMB	U.S. Office of Management and Budget, a White House executive office agency
SIP	State Implementation Plan required under the Clean Air Amendments
TCP	Transportation Control Plan required under Clean Air Amendments
Riverside v. Ruckelshaus	federal court decision requiring EPA to propose a TCP for Los Angeles
NRDC v. EPA	federal court decision requiring EPA to force states to submit TCPs.

CHRONOLOGY

<u>December 1969 — December 1970</u>	Congress considers and enacts revisions of the Clean Air Act.
<u>1970</u>	
July	President Nixon proposes creation of the Environmental Protection Agency (EPA) in a reorganization message to Congress.
December	EPA officially comes into existence.
	President Nixon signs the Clean Air Amendments.
<u>1971</u>	
January	EPA Administrator Ruckelshaus proposes ambient air quality standards as required by the Clean Air Amendments.
April	EPA issues draft regulations governing preparation of State Implementation Plans (SIPs), requiring transportation controls.
August	EPA's final SIP regulations relax but do not eliminate the transportation control requirements.
Fall	Ruckelshaus decides that the states may submit

separate Transportation Control Plans (TCPs) to EPA by February 15, 1973, rather than include them in the SIPs due January 30, 1972.

1972

January   Due date for state submission of SIPs to EPA.

February   Congressional oversight hearings on implementation of the Clean Air Amendments.

May   Ruckelshaus refuses to grant automakers a one-year extension of the deadline for emission control devices.

Ruckelshaus grants 17 states a two-year extension (from 1975 to 1977) for achieving the clean air standards.

September   A federal appeals court decides in *Riverside v. Ruckelshaus* that EPA must promulgate transportation controls for Los Angeles.

1973

January   Ruckelshaus announces the Los Angeles TCP.

A federal appeals court decides in *NRDC v. EPA* that EPA had no authority to extend the deadline for submitting TCPs or to give blanket extensions until 1977 for achieving clean air standards. The ruling requires the states to submit TCPs by April 15, 1973.

April   Under court pressure Ruckelshaus grants automakers a one-year extension for complying with the Clean Air Amendments.

Deadline for states to submit TCPs.

Robert Fri becomes acting administrator of EPA after Ruckelshaus is appointed director of the FBI.

June   Deadline for EPA to approve or disapprove state TCP submissions.

THE CASE

Squinting into the glare of the television lights, William D. Ruckelshaus, administrator of the U.S. Environmental Protection Agency (EPA), shuffled his papers and prepared to begin the press conference at Los Angeles' Biltmore Hotel on January 15, 1973. He had come to California to announce a sweeping set of proposed federal regulations aimed at drastically reducing the use of motor vehicles in the Los Angeles basin. Flanked by aides from EPA's Washington and regional headquarters, Ruckelshaus explained that Congress, by enacting the Clean Air Amendments of 1970, had committed the nation to strenuous efforts to reduce metropolitan air pollution, a major portion of which was caused by the automobile.

Among the measures needed to achieve the required air quality standards in Los Angeles, he stated, were the mandatory installation of emission control devices on all existing autos and the imposition of stringent gasoline rationing. These and other possible transportation controls were intended to curb auto use by more than 80 percent during the months of May to October when pollution problems were most serious. Ruckelshaus acknowledged that such restrictions might have "severe" and "costly" effects on the Los Angeles area.[1] As noted in the proposed rules:

> ... vehicle owners may have to assume the direct costs of emission abatement equipment to bring their vehicles into compliance. Second, reduction in the mobility of workers and consumers could have a major impact on the economic fabric of the community. Third, interference with the ability of citizens to move freely will alter the lifestyle of the region.[2]

Admitting that he personally had "grave reservations" about the plan, Ruckelshaus counseled that "this is not a time for panic." Public hearings would be held on the proposed regulations, comments were welcome, and revisions in the rules could be expected. Nonetheless, he cautioned, sweeping changes in auto use in Los Angeles were necessary; the Clean Air Amendments left him no choice but to impose stringent restrictions.[3]

This case was written by Arnold M. Howitt and Richard P. Clarendon, with the research assistance of Ernest G. Niemi. Portions of this research were completed under grant MA-11-0007 from the Urban Mass Transportation Administration, U.S. Department of Transportation.

113

Reaction to Plan

Reaction to the Los Angeles plan was swift and hostile. Public hearings on the proposed regulations, reported one journalist, "brought an immediate negative reaction from wide sectors of the community"; and California's political leaders harshly attacked EPA's plan. Los Angeles Mayor Sam Yorty called it "shocking" and "economy destroying," while U.S. Senator John Tunney found the plan "drastic and nonsensical." Jesse Unruh, a candidate for mayor, thought that a 20 percent reduction might be possible but predicted "quite possibly a revolution" and "armed raids on gasoline stations" if the 80 percent restriction were put into effect.

The Greater Los Angeles Chamber of Commerce forecast the destruction of 400,000 jobs in the region. Even California environmental groups were reluctant to endorse completely what one spokesman termed an "unrealistic" plan. As a *Los Angeles Times* editorial observed, "The consensus has it that the Environmental Protection Agency's proposal to ration gasoline sales in Los Angeles during the six smoggiest months of the year is economically unrealistic." [4]

Notwithstanding these reactions and the reservations of Ruckelshaus and other EPA policy makers, the agency felt compelled by the clear language of the Clean Air Amendments and the order of a federal court to forge ahead with drastic motor vehicle restrictions for Los Angeles. As one official concluded:

> This is the crunch. This is the first dramatic confrontation between the federal government and the states on the 1970 act. People have to come to grips with the question of what price they want to pay for what benefits. [5]

Creation of EPA and
Enactment of the Clean Air Amendments

Public concern about environmental quality burst to the forefront of national domestic policy in 1970. Maine's Sen. Edmund S. Muskie, then considered the most likely Democratic presidential nominee in 1972, already had made himself a national spokesman on this issue during the 1960s by sponsoring and shepherding through Congress several major pieces of environmental legislation. In 1969 Congress initiated and enacted the National Environmental Policy Act (NEPA), which created the Council on Environmental Quality in the Executive Office of the President and mandated the preparation of environmental impact statements for federally funded development projects. Signing that bill on January 1, 1970, President Richard Nixon recognized the potency of environmental sentiment. He sought to recover the political initiative in February by sending Congress a message proposing 37 executive and legislative actions to protect the environment. Environmental policy seemed to command the public's attention as few other issues could—a fact confirmed by the observance of "Earth Day" on April 22. Across the country tens of thousands of citizens gathered in a series of demonstrations both to celebrate the nation's bountiful natural resources and to insist that this heritage be protected. Their concern both symbolized and further stimulated the intensity of feeling about the environmental issue.

The Birth of EPA[6]

One consequence of the president's eagerness to act decisively was close scrutiny of the federal government's existing institutional structure for making policy and running environmental programs. Finding these responsibilities divided among many federal agencies, the president's Advisory Panel on Executive Organization recommended in April that these organizational fragments be pulled together into a single, independent federal agency. President Nixon concurred, directing the Office of Management and Budget (OMB) to draft a formal plan. On July 9 the president submitted Executive Reorganization Plan No. 3 of 1970 to Congress, proposing the creation of the Environmental Protection Agency. A presidential message accompanying the plan explained its rationale:

> Our national government today is not structured to make a coordinated attack on the pollutants which debase the air we breathe, the water we drink, and the land that grows our food. Indeed, the present governmental structure for dealing with environmental pollution often defies effective and concerted action.

> Despite its complexity, for pollution control purposes, the environment must be perceived as a single, interrelated system. Present assignments of departmental responsibilities do not reflect this interrelatedness. . . .

> In organizational terms, this requires pulling together into one agency a variety of research, monitoring, standard-setting and enforcement activities now scattered through several departments and agencies. It also requires that the new agency include sufficient support elements—in research and in aids to State and local anti-pollution programs, for example—to give it the needed strength and potential for carrying out its mission. The new agency would also, of course, draw upon the result of research conducted by other agencies. . . .

> As no disjointed array of separate programs can, the EPA would be able—in concert with the States—to set and enforce standards for air and water quality and for individual pollutants. This consolidation of pollution control

authorities would help assure that we do not create new environmental problems in the process of controlling existing ones. . . .

As prescribed by the statute governing executive reorganizations, the president's plan went into effect October 2 in the absence of congressional action to disapprove it. EPA officially would come into being on December 2.

The new agency was an uneasy amalgam of staff and programs previously located in 15 separate federal agencies. EPA had a total budget of $1.4 billion. Its 5,743 employees worked in 157 different places, ranging geographically from a floating barge off the Florida coast to a water quality laboratory in Alaska. In Washington, D.C., alone there were 2,000 employees scattered across the city in 12 separate office buildings. EPA's tasks were equally diverse. The fledgling agency confronted an agenda of problems, including water and air pollution, solid waste, pesticides, radiation, and noise hazards. It operated 21 grant programs and consulted 90 advisory panels composed of government, science, and industry representatives.

Chosen by the president to head EPA as its first administrator was William Doyle Ruckelshaus, a 38-year-old, Harvard-trained lawyer from Indiana. After briefly practicing law in his family firm, Ruckelshaus had been named a deputy attorney general of Indiana. In 1966 he was elected as a Republican to the state legislature and was chosen majority leader only one year later. Politically ambitious, he challenged Indiana's Democratic incumbent U.S. Sen. Birch Bayh in 1968 but was defeated. The newly elected Nixon administration brought him to Washington anyway—to the Justice Department as assistant attorney general in charge of the Civil Division. Ruckelshaus' environmental credentials were slim. In the early 1960s as deputy attorney general of Indiana, he had drafted the state's air pollution control law and represented the board of health in water pollution abatement cases. Therefore, ardent environmentalists were wary when President Nixon named him EPA administrator.

Ruckelshaus, however, was determined to be an aggressive agency manager and a forceful advocate for environmental interests, even if the White House pressed him to be moderate in his enforcement actions:

> I could see some enormous difficulties if they were going to give lip service, as everybody was doing at that stage, to the problems of the environment, and then try to get the administrator of that agency to act as a front man for that lip service when in fact he wasn't implementing these acts or doing what he was supposed to do. I thought that would be just disastrous.[7]

Making EPA into a functioning agency was an enormous task. All the while keeping its current operations going, Ruckelshaus had to worry about recruiting able people to staff the agency's key administrative posts and a number of important middle-management jobs. He needed to develop an administrative structure that would fashion the disparate fragments of old organizations into a cohesive EPA structure. He had to see that a variety of management systems—personnel, fiscal, procurement—were developed effectively. To improve agency communications and morale, he needed to get EPA's Washington staff relocated into a single headquarters complex. And, perhaps most important, he had to launch the agency's program and regulatory initiatives in a way that would win public confidence and help EPA build a supportive political constituency.

Structurally, Ruckelshaus reshaped EPA into both substantive and functional units. There would be separate divisions, each headed by an assistant administrator, for major program areas such as air and water pollution. There also would be separate units for key agencywide functions such as enforcement and management.

Since EPA was the first major new federal line agency created by the Nixon administration, its institutional structure was greatly influenced by the emerging doctrine of the "New Federalism." The agency had 10 regional offices located in major cities across the country. These offices housed a substantial portion of EPA employees, consistent with the administration's wish that it have decentralized operations to foster close working relationships with state and local governments. Unlike many other federal departments, which had highly centralized management structures, EPA had administratively strong regional administrators who played key roles in policy formulation and implementation. While various branches in EPA's Washington headquarters offered guidance to their counterparts in the regions and monitored their operations, they did not exercise direct authority over them. Decision-making power in EPA was exercised by the administrator through his regional administrators.

The Clean Air Amendments of 1970

Public concern with air pollution was fueled by a growing body of scientific evidence suggesting that smog—technically the result of nitrogen oxides (NO_x) and hydrocarbons (HC) reacting with sunlight—had serious long-term impacts on health, particularly in exacerbating respiratory and cardiovascular problems. Along with factories and power plants, the major culprit in creating smog and other air pollutants was the automobile, specifically the internal combustion engine. As public awareness of the problem increased, pressure mounted for the government to control this health hazard.

"The history of federal intervention in pollution control," two careful analysts have observed,

> ... has been one of gradual steps, first toward study, then toward modest intervention, then toward more far-reaching controls. Each step has been

accompanied by the announcement that primary responsibility lies with state and local government, but each has eroded state and local authority more than previous measures—and precisely because experience revealed, in the congressional judgment, an inability on the part of lower levels of government to carry out the responsibilities Congress had left to them.[8]

Congress Acts

Prior to passage of the Clean Air Amendments of 1970, Congress had enacted several pieces of air quality legislation.[9] The Air Pollution Control Act of 1955 had established a federal program of research, training, and demonstrations. It was followed in 1963 by the Clean Air Act, which gave the federal government limited enforcement authority to regulate emissions from "stationary" sources of air pollution such as industrial plants. That bill was strengthened two years later with "mobile" source controls in the Motor Vehicle Air Pollution Control Act, which authorized the Department of Health, Education, and Welfare (HEW) to establish automobile emission standards. In 1967 the Air Quality Act expanded HEW's role to include oversight of state standards for ambient air quality.

As chairman of the Subcommittee on Air and Water Pollution of the Senate Public Works Committee, Senator Muskie had emerged during the 1960s as the principal congressional advocate of environmental legislation, including the air quality bills. Muskie's rise to prominence as the leading contender for the 1972 Democratic presidential nomination, following his campaign as Hubert H. Humphrey's vice presidential running mate in 1968, roughly paralleled the flowering of environmental policy as the nation's premiere domestic issue.

By 1970, however, his leadership of the environmental forces was under challenge from several sides. In December 1969, about the time that Muskie was introducing legislation to modify the Air Quality Act, the House of Representatives stole the legislative initiative from him when the Subcommittee on Public Health and Welfare of the Interstate and Foreign Commerce Committee held hearings in preparation for revisions of the act. President Nixon followed suit in January by devoting most of the domestic part of his State of the Union message to environmental issues and then submitting a 37-item package of specific proposals in February. Among these proposals was one calling for a 90 percent reduction in federal emission standards by 1980, a more stringent plan than Muskie's own. The House subcommittee, which resumed hearings in March, reported an air quality bill to the floor in June. This bill would have required the federal government to set air pollution standards, mandated state plans to achieve these standards, required federal emission tests of new motor vehicles, and authorized $575 million over three years to pay portions of the air quality planning costs of state governments. Within one week the bill was adopted overwhelmingly by the House.

In the Senate, Henry M. Jackson, D-Wash., chairman of the Interior Committee, made several environmental proposals that seemed to threaten the jurisdiction of Muskie's subcommittee; and Gaylord Nelson, D-Wis., in August introduced a bill to ban the internal combustion engine by 1975. The most painful blow, though, came in May when a Ralph Nader study group published *Vanishing Air,* a report that accused Muskie first of knuckling under to industry while shepherding the Air Quality Act of 1967 through Congress and then of watching passively as experience proved the bill inadequate.

Senator Muskie's Subcommittee on Air and Water Pollution also held hearings in March 1970 but moved more slowly than the House. It did not send its draft bill to the full Public Works Committee until late August. That bill, however, with far tougher provisions than either the Nixon administration's proposals or the House version, represented a major departure from past congressional efforts to improve air quality. It called for strict new emission standards based on public health requirements rather than either technological or economic feasibility; it also set tight deadlines for achieving the standards, removed most executive branch discretion in administering them, and authorized stiff fines for violations. The Muskie bill was altered only slightly by the full Public Works Committee and was then adopted by the Senate in September by a 73-0 vote.

While a House-Senate conference committee met to resolve differences between the versions enacted by each chamber, the Nixon administration appealed for relaxation of the deadlines for automotive emissions and for granting more discretion to those who would administer the act. Virtually all of the administration's proposals were rejected by the conference committee, however, which instead adopted a bill almost entirely conforming to the Senate's bill. Both the House and the Senate then approved the conference draft. President Nixon signed the act on December 30, 1970.

Aside from the general climate of public opinión favoring environmental protection, the Clean Air Amendments were helped through Congress by several circumstances. Meteorological conditions produced severe air pollution along the entire East Coast while the act was being considered, and the 1970 Collegiate Clear Air Car Race seemed to prove that a cleaner automobile could be developed. Environmental groups lobbied intensively for retention of the tough provisions of the Senate bill; but the auto industry was relatively restrained, apparently recognizing the public mood and fearing an outright ban on the internal combustion engine.[10]

The Statute's Provisions

The Clean Air Amendments[11] mandated sweeping action by federal officials, state governments, and the automobile industry, under tight deadlines and with little opportunity for administrative discretion. (See Exhibit 1, pp. 135-136.) The act instructed the EPA administrator to establish national ambient air quality standards (NAAQS) for each pollutant deemed hazardous to public health and to ensure their achievement no later than 1977.

The act further required the states to develop state implementation plans (SIPs) detailing air pollution control measures necessary to achieve the NAAQS. And the statute required the auto industry to manufacture vehicles that would cut carbon monoxide (CO) and hydrocarbon (HC) emissions to 10 percent of their 1970 level by the 1975 model year and reduce nitrogen oxides (NO_x) equally by 1976.

This requirement placed the auto makers under strong pressure because no generally accepted technology existed for achieving the 90 percent reduction in hazardous emissions. By adopting a "technology-forcing" strategy, Congress assumed that the industry would prove innovative under strict statutory obligations. The act therefore gave the EPA administrator little flexibility in enforcing the standards—only the right to grant a one-year extension of the deadlines.

While the administrator's discretion was greater in setting permitted levels of pollution, he was given a limited set of *criteria* for developing the standards. The statute held that "National primary ambient air quality standards ... shall be ambient air quality standards the attainment and maintenance of which in the judgment of the Administrator, ... and allowing an adequate margin of safety, are requisite to protect the public health." That meant that any criteria other than health effects (for example, cost, impact on economic activity or social life) were irrelevant to the standard-setting process. The EPA administrator was not permitted to make tradeoffs among other possible values.

To pursue these air quality goals, Congress required each state not in compliance to prepare a state implementation plan (SIP), spelling out precisely what steps would be taken to reduce pollution, including establishment of emission standards at least as stringent as the federal ones for both stationary and mobile pollution sources. To achieve these standards, the Clean Air Amendments required:

> ... emissions limitations, schedules, and timetables for compliance with such limitations, and such other measures as may be necessary to insure attainment and maintenance of such ... standard, including, but not limited to, land-use and transportation controls. ...

The SIPs also were required to provide "necessary assurances that the State will have adequate personnel, funding, and authority to carry out such implementation plan."

Once SIPs were prepared, the EPA administrator was required to evaluate them according to the statutory criteria. If a state failed to submit a SIP, or submitted a plan not meeting the criteria and then failed to revise it within 60 days, the administrator was obligated to propose and promulgate *under federal authority* regulations that would fulfill the mandates of the act. Thus, in the absence of satisfactory state action, EPA was mandated to *supersede* state authority.

The Clean Air Amendments laid out an ambitious timetable for compliance:

1. 120 days after enactment of the act, the EPA administrator was to establish national ambient air quality standards (NAAQS).

2. Nine months after the NAAQS were set, states were to submit SIPs.

3. Four months after submission of the SIPs, EPA was to approve or disapprove them.

4. Three years after the SIPs were approved (roughly by mid-1975), the NAAQS were to be achieved.

The act, however, permitted the EPA administrator to grant a state a two-year extension if necessary technology was not ready and "the State has considered and applied as a part of its plan reasonably available alternative means of attaining such . . . standard."

To enforce its provisions, the Clean Air Amendments provided EPA with authority to issue compliance orders and bring civil suits against violators. These procedures, however, were cumbersome. Upon discovering a violation of a SIP, the administrator was empowered to issue a notice of violation to both the violator and the state. If after 30 days the violation was not cleared up, the administrator could issue a compliance order or bring suit. If violations were so widespread that the administrator believed them to result from state failure to enforce the SIP, he could declare a "period of federally assumed enforcement" during which he might issue compliance orders or bring suit against violators without first issuing a notice of violation. EPA compliance orders, though, could not take effect until the person affected "has had an opportunity to confer with the Administrator concerning the alleged violation." A civil suit, seeking a temporary or permanent injunction against prohibited acts, could be brought in federal district court (with EPA being represented by the U.S. Department of Justice). If successful, such suit would punish any violator who had persisted in prohibited behavior after being issued a compliance order, or 30 days after notification during a period of federally assumed enforcement; a violator was subject to fines up to $25,000 per day of violation, or imprisonment for up to one year, or both. These civil suit provisions, however, were subject to the usual delays of crowded court dockets and the appeals process.

The Clean Air Amendments did not depend entirely on EPA to initiate enforcement. Congress granted standing to any citizen to bring a civil suit in federal court against any violator or "against the administrator [of EPA] where there is alleged a failure of the administrator to perform any act or duty under this Act which is not discretionary. . . ." In deciding such suits, "the district courts shall have jurisdiction . . . to enforce such an emission standard or limitation . . . or to order the administrator to perform such act or duty. . . ."

Implementing the Clean Air Amendments of 1970

In signing the Clean Air Amendments on December 30, 1970, President Nixon was forced to approve a far more stringent bill than he would have preferred. Responsibility for implementing the act now fell to the fledgling EPA, which had begun operations *less than one month earlier.*

While the act was extremely specific in some respects, it was very vague about at least one type of pollution control measure: transportation controls. Aside from brief language in the section on SIPs that required "such measures [in addition to emission limitations] as may be necessary to insure attainment. . . , including, but not limited to, land use and transportation controls," the statute was silent about restrictions on auto use. Congressional debate on the Clean Air Amendments did little to illuminate this provision, except for brief references to traffic controls that might prove necessary in some urban areas. Few members of Congress had any inkling what controls EPA ultimately would propose.

EPA Acts Promptly

The Clean Air Amendments imposed early and rigid deadlines on EPA's administrator—deadlines that would have been difficult enough for an established agency to meet, let alone a brand new one. Within 30 days of the president's signing—that is, by January 30, 1971—Ruckelshaus was obliged to propose national ambient air quality standards (NAAQS) reflecting the public health criterion in the amendments; within 90 days more, he was to promulgate formal federal regulations containing any revisions in the proposed standards he deemed appropriate as a result of public comment.

Ruckelshaus decided that it was critical to meet this schedule to build public respect for EPA as a strict guardian of environmental interests—a decision that accorded well with the general thrust of his early months at the agency.* As Ruckelshaus recalled later:

---

* Within his first weeks on the job, for example, Ruckelshaus initiated suits against the cities of Atlanta, Detroit, and Cleveland as well as against the Jones and Laughlin Steel Co. and U.S. Plywood-Champion Papers Co.—all for alleged violations of water pollution statutes. In its first two months of existence, EPA began five times as many enforcement actions as its predecessor agencies together had initiated in any previous two-month period.

For purposes of agency credibility it was important to meet those deadlines at the beginning of the agency. I think that in achieving some of them we may have made some mistakes by doing things faster than we were ready to move wisely, but that *had* to be weighed against the fall-out of not meeting the deadline, which could have been deadlier to the agency.

This attitude was formed in large part by the vigilance of environmental interest groups and their tendency to categorize public officials as either "tough" or "soft" on polluters. Because these groups had ready access to the national press, they could largely define for the general public what was "tough" (and therefore "good") environmental regulation. As Ruckelshaus viewed it, "We couldn't afford even the *appearance* of being soft." [12] Consequently, Ruckelshaus promulgated NAAQS for hydrocarbons, photochemical oxidants, and carbon monoxide according to the statutory schedules. EPA also proceeded to propose guidelines to the states on how to prepare their SIPs, due on January 30, 1972. On April 7, 1971, the agency issued draft regulations regarding the SIPs. These regulations would have required states whose pollution problems were too severe to be corrected solely by emissions standards for new motor vehicles, to place in their SIPs various measures "including, but not limited to" conversion of commercial and governmental vehicle fleets to low-emission fuels or engines, and methods of reducing auto use, such as commuter taxes, gasoline rationing, parking limitations, staggered work hours, and restrictions on vehicle idling time. It also would have required the states to demonstrate that the agencies charged with enforcing the SIPs had sufficient legal authority to mandate the elements of the plan.[13] For the first time, therefore, EPA was explaining how it intended to interpret the words "transportation controls" in the Clean Air Amendments. At least in the short run, though, that interpretation did not stick.

The 'Quality of Life' Review. After formally being proposed by EPA, the SIP guidelines were submitted for review to a special interagency task force, directed by staff from the Office of Management and Budget (OMB) that the Nixon administration had established to scrutinize all EPA regulatory activities. This "quality of life" review, as it became known, was created to give other federal agencies whose programs were affected by EPA regulations a chance to comment before they were formally promulgated; it was intended to ensure that legal, economic, budgetary, and other policy implications of EPA regulations were assessed. Ruckelshaus initially welcomed the "quality of life" review because he lacked complete confidence in the bureaucracies he had inherited from HEW and other federal agencies; they had on the payroll experts on air and water quality engineering and on the health impacts of pollution, but they lacked persons with skills in systems analysis, economics, and other scientific areas. Even though critics inside EPA as well as outside the executive branch charged that the Nixon administration was trying to restrain or "water down" environmental regulation, Ruckelshaus, who retained ultimate statutory authority to promulgate EPA's regulations, believed that the "quality of life" review gave him useful information to weigh along with public comments on proposed rules. [14]

In the case of the planning regulations for the SIPs, the OMB-managed review and numerous comments from the states resulted in changes in the provisions for transportation controls when final regulations were issued on August 14, 1971. Mention of specific control measures was replaced by more general language requiring "such other measures as may be necessary," and the requirement that the state have legal authority for transportation controls "in hand" was replaced by the injunction that "such plan shall set forth the State's timetable for obtaining such legal authority as may be necessary...." [15] EPA also promised to develop information to help the states forecast how various transportation controls would affect pollution levels.

In the fall of 1971, EPA's requirements for transportation controls were relaxed still further to give the states more time to develop plans. After continued state complaints and the agency's own failure to develop adequate technical guidelines to help the states forecast what impact specific control measures would have on air pollution, Ruckelshaus decided that too little experience with transportation controls existed to permit the states to devise appropriate measures and predict their effects. He therefore modified EPA requirements for the SIPs due in January 1972. Specification of controls would no longer be mandatory: the SIP only would have to state what amount of emissions reduction would be required from transportation controls to attain the NAAQS and list the measures being considered. The states were then given more than a full year more, until February 15, 1973, to submit:

> ... definitive transportation control plans, including identification of the specific measures to be implemented, demonstration of the adequacy of these measures for attainment and maintenance of the national standards, and a detailed timetable for obtaining any necessary legal authority and taking all steps necessary to implement the various measures. [16]

Consequently, when the states submitted their SIPs in January 1972, the issue of transportation controls was left hanging.

Steering a Middle Course

Political pressure, always an element in policy making in Washington, is magnified during a national election year. In 1972 Ruckelshaus found his agency trapped between opposing forces. On one hand were those in the Nixon administration who sought to restrain EPA's regulatory activities; on the other were environmental groups and their advocates in Congress who wanted vigorous enforcement of the Clean Air Act and other environmental statutes.

Pressure from the Administration. While Ruckelshaus himself felt that delay in requiring transportation control plans was warranted, he and others in EPA were becoming troubled by White House intervention in the agency's rule-making processes, mainly through the "quality of life" review. For Ruckelshaus the review had lost much of its earlier usefulness. In October 1971 he had established an EPA Office of Planning and Evaluation that was capable of conducting independent economic impact analyses. He also had instituted an internal EPA review process to ensure that EPA engineers, scientists, economists, and lawyers were consulted before he issued regulations. In contrast, the OMB-directed review had become less and less objective: the group of individuals invited to task force meetings grew narrower, with those sympathetic or neutral to strong environmental regulation deleted from the list of invitees. By late 1971 and 1972, the "quality of life" review largely had become an administration device for obstructing stringent environmental regulations, as the environmental interest groups had originally feared. Although the White House wanted to avoid direct confrontation with the politically potent environmental movement, especially with President Nixon running for reelection in 1972, it sought to use the review process to delay and restrain EPA's regulatory activities. Some bureaucratic opponents of strict environmental controls—notably the Department of Commerce—used the review to "filibuster" proposed EPA rules.[17]

Ruckelshaus pushed, with little success, to have the "quality of life" review streamlined; but he was in a difficult position administratively. The Clean Air Amendments clearly gave the EPA administrator—not the president, OMB or an interagency committee—the authority to issue regulations. But Ruckelshaus served "at the pleasure of the president." Even though the political influence of the environmental movement could protect him up to a point, Ruckelshaus might well have been dismissed had he refused altogether to cooperate with the OMB-directed review. Instead, he accepted the necessity of interagency coordination and the consequent delays, bending to pressure for change in EPA proposals when that seemed wise or unavoidable but drawing the line on matters of principle or critical policy.

Congressional Oversight. By no means did all of the pressure on EPA come from the administration. In February 1972 the Senate Subcommittee on Air and Water Pollution began oversight hearings on the first year of implementation of the Clean Air Amendments. Environmental groups harshly criticized the federal government's performance. As the spokesman for the Natural Resources Defense Council (NRDC) charged:

> ... it is becoming painfully clear that the promise of the clean air amendments will not be fulfilled. State implementation plans ... have mostly become little more than weak-kneed apologies for each state's present program....

The major blame for this situation must be placed squarely on the Nixon administration. The White House Office of Management and Budget [and other agencies are] ... reviewing in secrecy every major action of the Environmental Protection Agency. The public is completely excluded from this review.... These agencies, acting as spokesmen for industrial interests, have effective power to veto EPA's actions. Now becoming routine, OMB review is gelding the clean air amendments.[18]

In response, Ruckelshaus emphatically denied that OMB had final say on approving the state implementation plans:

... it is not the way the process works, and the OMB will have nothing to do with the approval of each of these individual implementation plans. They will sit on a committee which we chair to review the aggregate impact of all of these implementation plans.... There is nothing about that committee which has any final authority over the approval of an individual plan. The authority is mine and mine alone.[19]

In general, Ruckelshaus insisted, the "quality of life" review was not undermining his authority. "It is not being delegated to anybody else, and if anybody tried to force me to delegate it, I could no longer function as Administrator of this Agency." [20] But Sen. Thomas F. Eagleton, D-Mo., chairing the hearings, was skeptical: "I wish I could be convinced that you are calling the shots as you see them." [21]

Two Decisions. In May 1972 Ruckelshaus faced two key issues stemming from the Clean Air Amendments—the deadline for new automobile emission standards and the approval or disapproval of the SIPs submitted in January.

The amendments required auto manufacturers to meet stringent emission standards for the 1975-1976 model years, despite the fact that appropriate pollution control equipment had not yet been developed. This "technology-forcing" provision was intended to spur innovation by the auto industry, but it contained a partial escape clause. The EPA administrator, upon petition from the industry, could grant a one-year extension of the deadlines.

Between January and April, five auto manufacturers applied for the extension. Their request was backed up by the reports both of a special committee of the National Academy of Sciences (commissioned by Congress in the Clean Air Amendments) and of the president's Office of Science and Technology—each of which questioned the feasibility of the statutory deadlines. But hearings before the Senate Subcommittee on Air and Water Pollution clearly showed that influential members of Congress were opposed to an extension.[22]

The law permitted Ruckelshaus to grant the extension only if the industry had made "good faith efforts" to achieve the emission standards. Convinced that this was not the case, the EPA administrator decided to deny the manufacturers' request and stuck with that intention despite White House pressure.[23] In announcing his decision in mid-May, Ruckelshaus noted that "while the technical feasibility of compliance is a close issue..., I am compelled to conclude that information indicating that the standards are achievable is as persuasive as is information which indicates that they are not achievable." [24]

If Ruckelshaus' refusal to grant the auto industry an extension demonstrated determination to force compliance with Clean Air Act deadlines, his second decision in May showed willingness to be more flexible in dealing with the states. On May 31 the *Federal Register* published the administrator's decisions on the state implementation plans submitted in January. Even in disapproving a number of SIPs, Ruckelshaus indicated a desire to secure voluntary compliance with statutory requirements:

> In the interest of giving States every opportunity to bring their implementation plans into full compliance with the Act..., the Environmental Protection Agency has notified States that modifications submitted after the statutory deadline for submittal of State plans would be accepted and considered.... Where such modifications affect the Administrator's approval or disapproval of a State plan or portion thereof, but are not reflected herein, appropriate changes to this part will be published as soon as the Administrator's evaluation of such modifications is completed.[25]

Thus, if a state were prepared to work on modification of its SIP, Ruckelshaus was willing to delay unilateral action imposing an EPA-developed plan, as the Clean Air Amendments prescribed. Even more important, Ruckelshaus granted 17 states two-year extensions for achieving air quality standards because of the need to implement transportation controls:

> The Administrator has determined that the lead time necessary for development, adoption, and implementation of transportation control measures generally precludes their application on any significant scale within the next 3 years, i.e., they will not be available soon enough to permit attainment of the primary standards within the time prescribed by the Act.... Accordingly, it is the Administrator's judgment that 2-year extensions are justified in cases where transportation control measures will be necessary.[26]

Thus these states would have until 1977 (not 1975) to achieve the standards.

The Courts Upset the Balance

While welcome to many state governments, Ruckelshaus' decision to allow more time for the development of transportation controls did not please the environmental movement, which felt that he had exceeded his authority under the Clean Air Amendments.

Riverside v. Ruckelshaus.[27] In September 1972 two communities in California—Riverside and San Bernardino—along with several citizens' groups filed suit in federal district court to force EPA to promulgate a transportation control plan (TCP) for Los Angeles. The suit charged that because EPA had not approved the state's plan for Los Angeles, the agency was required by the statute to draft one itself; hence its extension of the deadline for transportation controls until February 1973 was unlawful. Ruling in November 1972, the court found against EPA. The judge, under authority specifically granted the courts by the Clean Air Amendments, ordered the agency to prepare a plan for Los Angeles by January 15, 1973, that would attain the national air quality standards.

The *Riverside* decision pressed EPA staff into frantic efforts to find a way to achieve the stringent pollution reductions necessary to comply with the amendments. But, even by taking the best available estimates of the pollution problem and applying every control measure available other than strict gasoline rationing, EPA found itself far short of the air quality goals. To comply with the court order EPA would have to mandate restrictions it had sought to avoid.

New Pressure from the Administration.[28] Almost simultaneously, the agency came under a different sort of pressure. In November 1972 President Nixon won reelection in a landslide, defeating George McGovern, the Democratic nominee. Seemingly assured of four more years in office, key administration officials became bolder in trying to restrain EPA.

That fall EPA had proposed that the lead content in gasoline be reduced—a policy that the "quality of life" review had opposed. In mid-December Ruckelshaus was called to the White House to meet with Domestic Council Chief John Ehrlichman, Treasury Secretary George P. Shultz, and OMB Director Caspar W. Weinberger. Insisting on his independence, Ruckelshaus successfully argued that the public health rationale for the lead reduction was so clear that he had no alternative. The others backed off, but Ruckelshaus was concerned about his isolation in the administration. Like all other presidential appointees, he had submitted a pro forma resignation after the election. Whether he fit into the second Nixon administration was uncertain.

The answer came almost immediately. Nixon's press secretary Ron Ziegler summoned Ruckelshaus to inform him that he would be permitted to stay on, but that four of his five principal subordinates would be replaced, with their successors to be chosen by the White House, not Ruckelshaus. Ruckelshaus threatened to resign under those circumstances. He demanded the right to select his own deputy and assistant administrators as well as to institute reforms in the "quality of life" review. The administration bowed, in part, to Ruckelshaus' determination. John Ehrlichman let him know that he could retain his aides, but the OMB-staffed "quality of life" review would remain.

The Los Angeles TCP. By late December 1972 EPA was hard upon the court-imposed deadline of January 15 for devising a TCP for Los Angeles. Hoping to persuade environmentalists to reduce their pressure, EPA legal staff negotiated with the plaintiffs in the *Riverside* suit. Although they pointed out the consequences of compliance, compromise was not possible. No serious thought was given to appealing the court's decision. The law was not in doubt, and, as one staff lawyer recalled, "it wasn't a situation where if we waited a few months we'd get our act together."

Pressed by the court's deadline, EPA staff in the regional office came up with a plan requiring up to 82 percent reductions in auto use, secured by gasoline rationing, during the high smog months of May through October. This proposal set off vigorous debate in EPA's Washington headquarters. In the agency's early days, Ruckelshaus had been cautious in issuing proposed regulations. To build up EPA's credibility, he had wanted to avoid having to retreat in promulgating the final regulations after public hearings; therefore he had sought to make proposed regulations as close as possible to what he thought would ultimately stick. The proposed Los Angeles TCP violated that practice. But Ruckelshaus saw no alternative given the court's decision, the unrelenting pressure from the environmental movement, and the unyielding insistence by congressional advocates that the Clean Air Amendments be enforced firmly. As one of the administrator's close aides recalled:

> Despite staff objections that such a proposal would be a folly, that it could not be implemented, that it would be laughed at, and that it might arm the enemies of clean air with a powerful club, Ruckelshaus proposed the plan.[29]

Ruckelshaus' decision led directly to his press conference in Los Angeles on January 15, 1973, and to the resulting political brouhaha—both described at the beginning of this case study. (See pp. 113-114.)

Natural Resources Defense Council v. EPA. As dramatic as the consequences of the *Riverside* case were, the decision applied only to the Los Angeles area. But just two weeks after Ruckelshaus' press conference there, another court decision wholly upset the careful balance that Ruckelshaus had sought in implementing the Clean Air Amendments.

Some months before, the Natural Resources Defense Council (NRDC), a small but energetic environmental interest group, had brought suit in federal court in Washington, D.C., challenging Ruckelshaus on grounds similar to the *Riverside* case. But this case framed the issues so that they applied nationwide. On January 31, 1973, the court decided *NRDC v. EPA* in favor of the plaintiffs. Specifically, it found that Ruckelshaus had exceeded his authority by giving the states until February 15, 1973, to file TCPs (rather than incorporating them in the SIPs due in January 1972). The court also found invalid the administrator's blanket extension from 1975 to 1977 of the deadline for achieving national air quality standards for those states needing to impose transportation controls. Consequently, the court ordered Ruckelshaus to rescind the two-year extension for compliance with the air quality standards and to demand submission of TCPs no later than April 15, 1973.

The practical import of *NRDC v. EPA* was far greater than that of the *Riverside* case. The states already had been obligated to produce TCPs by February 15, but they had assumed they were planning to achieve the pollution reductions by 1977, not 1975. Most states had found meeting the 1977 attainment deadline difficult enough. Thanks to the court's ruling, though, they did not even have the benefit of relying on cleaner-running 1975, 1976, and 1977 model vehicles to achieve some of the required reduction in air pollution. They would have to propose additional vehicle restrictions to make up the difference. In effect, the court ordered 17 states to propose measures so tough as to ensure that massive social and economic disruptions would follow. To many governors, obeying such an order was political suicide. On top of this, the court-imposed April 15 deadline required states to draft TCPs on a crash basis.

The Auto Industry Appeals.[30] Yet another court decision resulted in even more problems for EPA in regard to the TCPs. In May 1972 when Ruckelshaus had denied the auto manufacturers' request for an extension for achieving emission standards for new cars, the industry had appealed according to procedures in the Clean Air Amendments. In December the courts had ordered Ruckelshaus to reconsider his decision. When he reaffirmed his original decision, the manufacturers again sought court relief; and Ruckelshaus once more was ordered to reconsider, apparently as an invitation to change his mind. The court commented that while Congress had "deliberately designed [the emission standards] as 'shock treatment' to the industry," the provision for an extension in the Clean Air Act was a "purposeful cushion."[31]

On April 11, 1973, therefore, Ruckelshaus announced a compromise. He gave the industry a one-year extension of the deadline for meeting the emission control requirements but insisted on both stiff interim standards and the designation of California as a test site for even tougher standards. The net effect of Ruckelshaus' action, though, was to *reduce* the expected contribution of new car emissions standards on metropolitan air pollution and thereby *increase* the burden on the states to meet the statutory deadlines imposing transportation controls.

Changes in the Clean Air Act? As the court's April 15 deadline for submitting the revised TCPs approached, it became clear to Ruckelshaus and his top aides that few if any states would submit plans that satisfied the requirements of the statute. Many states simply refused to write any plan at all, while others proposed TCPs based on the assumption that the 1975 air quality goals were unattainable. EPA's leaders realized that the agency itself would have to formulate TCPs for metropolitan areas in these states just as it had for Los Angeles.

Pressed on one hand by the courts to impose severe restrictions on auto use in the nation's major cities, and confronted on the other hand by either active or passive resistance from virtually every state government, Ruckelshaus saw no reasonable alternative to amending the Clean Air Act again. In testimony to both houses of Congress, therefore, Ruckelshaus proposed changes in the statute, including relaxation of the requirement for transportation controls.

Even though many House members representing districts that feared the imposition of strict auto restrictions echoed Ruckelshaus' plea for amendments, the Senate Subcommittee on Air and Water Pollution, headed by Senator Muskie, was reluctant to take action. Recognizing that the climate of opinion had changed greatly since 1970 when the statute was enacted, Muskie and his colleagues worried that, once open to amendment, the Clean Air Act might be gutted.[32]

Ruckelshaus' appeal for amendments proved to be his final major act as EPA administrator. With the Watergate scandal beginning to emerge, President Nixon was having difficulty getting Patrick Gray confirmed by the Senate as J. Edgar Hoover's successor as director of the Federal Bureau of Investigation (FBI). Needing to find a new FBI chief with a reputation for independence, the president turned to Ruckelshaus.

When Ruckelshaus left EPA in April, Robert Fri, deputy administrator since 1971, became acting administrator. Fri had spent his entire pre-EPA career at McKinsey and Co., a leading management consulting firm. His main responsibility at EPA had been to oversee the fledgling agency's management systems, but he also had participated in policy discussions about regulatory issues. Even before Ruckelshaus resigned, Fri had made known his intention to leave government service shortly. Removing his name from consideration for permanent assignment as administrator, Fri would guide EPA for about four months until Russell Train took office as Ruckelshaus's successor.

Like Ruckelshaus, Fri believed that the Clean Air Act had to be amended; but in renewing the agency's proposals to Congress he had no more luck than Ruckelshaus had had earlier. Senator Muskie's subcommittee remained the major obstacle. As Fri recalled:

> They hated the idea. They feared other amendments, and Muskie had an environmental constituency which constrained him from taking action.... The thrust of congressional opinion—among the environmentalists in Con-

gress—was that you guys at EPA have to figure out how to make things go without any amendments to the Clean Air Act.

Revising the TCPs

While Ruckelshaus and Fri sought changes in the Clean Air Act, EPA staff coped with the court-imposed deadline of June 15 to approve or disapprove the TCPs submitted by the states. Where the plans were deficient (or where state governments had refused to cooperate), EPA had until August 15 to propose regulations that conformed to the statutory requirements. The agency's first efforts came in its 10 regional offices. However, the regional EPA staffs, by and large attuned to their regions' political realities, sent many weak plans through to headquarters in Washington. There the follow-up work was handled mainly by lawyers in the EPA general counsel's office and by staff in the air branch who consulted with the agency's central technical staff in Durham, North Carolina.

The prominence of lawyers in this work was not surprising. Lawyers normally dominate sensitive tasks in regulatory agencies, and in this situation the agency was operating under an unambiguous order from the federal courts. One EPA attorney, a self-styled environmental "zealot" who was closely involved, recalled the circumstances well:

> During May and June 1973 there was frantic staff work by a few people trying to figure out why the state plans were inadequate, which was relatively easy, and then moving pieces around to get complete plans which would satisfy the legal requirements. It was relatively easy to put together a package of restraint measures that would secure sufficient reduction in air pollutants, especially if one weren't worrying too much about whether they were feasible.

Another lawyer, also deeply involved, noted that the most careful attention went to making the plans judgment-proof. "My concern was with the technical defensibility of various regulations that would be included in the plans," the lawyer said. "This defensibility was from a legal standpoint. If there were a court challenge, would the regulations hold up?"

In many cases the draft plans that emerged from this staff work imposed strict controls on auto use. New York City, for example, would be forced to limit taxicab cruising, establish special reserved street lanes for buses, improve mass transit, reduce the number of parking spaces in Manhattan, encourage staggered work hours, charge tolls on the bridges across the Harlem and East rivers, and initiate a program to inspect auto emission control devices and to force motorists to maintain them properly. Minneapolis-St. Paul, Minnesota, as another example, would have to ban downtown parking, provide a shuttle-bus service from outlying parking areas, and begin an inspection and maintenance program. If none of the plans were as severe as the earlier Los Angeles TCP, they nonetheless were unlikely to be popular with citizens and public officials.

But that was not a concern that figured prominently among the considerations of the EPA staff drafting the TCPs. As the attorney first quoted above noted:

> There was very little high-level guidance from EPA. We were caught in the transition between Fri and Train. Lots of people in the agency thought the TCPs were a very good idea, and no one knew what it meant politically. No one worried about how the plans would be enforced, about how we could deal with so large a gap between the law and the reality of what could be done.

By early June EPA's acting administrator, Robert Fri, turned his close attention to the problem of the TCPs. It was a thorny problem, although for once EPA was getting virtually no pressure from the White House, then preoccupied with the Senate Watergate Committee's investigation.

Fri faced a court-imposed deadline of June 15 to approve or disapprove the TCPs submitted by the states in April. He had until August 15 to promulgate regulations for states that had prepared deficient transportation control plans. Strategically, Fri saw several options—each unattractive:

- He could announce that EPA would not enforce the Clean Air Act because of the unrealistically close deadlines for achieving the air quality standards. But this course of action had several drawbacks: it would not focus attention on the root of the problem—Congress's failure to amend the statute; it risked alienating the agency's main constituency, the environmental movement; and it risked lawsuits that might result in judicial rule making on issues which Fri felt merited full congressional debate.

- Fri could disapprove the deficient TCPs and then dribble out revisions for two months until the August 15 deadline. Releasing the easy TCPs first would give the agency more time to consider alternatives for the more difficult ones. However, this strategy bought only a little time without getting to the crux of the matter—the Clean Air Act's unreasonable deadlines.

- Fri could go once more to Senator Muskie's subcommittee and to the other environmentalists in Congress to let them know what consequences would result from the court's orders under the statute. Perhaps they would act to forestall the political storm that would arise when stringent TCPs were announced. But because the congressional environmentalists only had recently refused to initiate changes in the Clean Air Act, Fri was not optimistic that a fresh appeal would work.

- Finally, Fri could forcibly call congressional attention to the Clean Air Act through visible and controversial rule making, for example, by promulgating stringent TCPs all at once "to light a bonfire." This strategy, too, might prove costly: it risked making EPA look foolish and, by issuing a series of unrealistic plans, could damage the agency's credibility.

NOTES

1. *Los Angeles Times,* January 15, 1973.
2. 38 *Federal Register* 2196, 2197 (1973).
3. *New York Times,* January 16, 1973; *Los Angeles Times,* January 15, 1973.
4. These reactions are quoted in *Pollution and Policy* by James E. Krier and Edmund Ursin (Berkeley: University of California Press, 1977), 222-223; and *Los Angeles Times,* January 15, 1973.
5. Cited by Charles O. Jones, *Clean Air* (Pittsburgh: University of Pittsburgh Press, 1975), 270, as quoted in *New York Times,* January 14, 1973.
6. This section is based on material in "Design for Environmental Protection" by Gregory B. Mills and Charles J. Christenson (Boston: Intercollegiate Case Clearing House, 1975), #9-175-047, and in Peggy Wiehl and Joseph L. Bower, "William D. Ruckelshaus and the Environmental Protection Agency" (Boston: Intercollegiate Case Clearing House, 1975), #9-375-083.
7. Wiehl and Bower, "William D. Ruckelshaus and the Environmental Protection Agency," 9.
8. Krier and Ursin, *Pollution and Policy,* 200.
9. The next paragraphs are based on Jones, *Clean Air,* 175-210; and Elias Zuckerman, Philip B. Heymann et al., "Senator Muskie and the 1970 Amendments to the Clean Air Act" (Boston: Intercollegiate Case Clearing House, 1978), #9-378-572.
10. Frank Grad et al., *The Automobile and the Regulation of Its Impact on the Environment* (Norman: University of Oklahoma Press, 1975), 334; Jones, *Clean Air,* 207; and Alan Altshuler et al., *The Urban Transportation System: Politics and Policy Innovation* (Cambridge: MIT Press, 1979), 182-183.
11. PL 91-604; 84 STAT. 1676.
12. Wiehl and Bower, "William D. Ruckelshaus and the Environmental Protection Agency," 10-12. Quotations appear on p. 12.
13. 36 *Federal Register* 6682-6683 (1971).
14. Robert L. Sansom, *The New American Dream Machine* (Garden City: Anchor Press/Doubleday, 1976), 29-32. Sansom was EPA assistant administrator for air programs during the period covered by this case.
15. 36 *Federal Register* 15489-15490 (1971).
16. 37 *Federal Register* 10844 (1972).
17. Sansom, *The New American Dream Machine,* 28-34.
18. Quoted in Jones, *Clean Air,* 240-241.
19. Ibid., 243.
20. Quoted in Sansom, *The New American Dream Machine,* 36.
21. Jones, *Clean Air,* 244.
22. Ibid., *Clean Air,* 253-263.
23. Sansom, *The New American Dream Machine,* 36-38.
24. Quoted in Jones, *Clean Air,* 264.
25. 37 *Federal Register* 10842 (1972).
26. 37 *Federal Register* 10845 (1972).
27. This section is based on Krier and Ursin, *Pollution and Policy,* 217-220.
28. This section is based on Sansom, *The New American Dream Machine,* 40-43.
29. Ibid., 162.
30. This section is based on Jones, *Clean Air,* 265-269.
31. Ibid., 266.
32. Sansom, *The New American Dream Machine,* 53.

EXHIBITS

Exhibit One:
Excerpts from the Clean Air Amendments of 1970

Sec. 107. (a) Each state shall have the primary responsibility for assuring air quality within the entire geographic area comprising such State by submitting an implementation plan for such State which will specify the manner in which national primary and secondary ambient air quality standards will be achieved and maintained within each air quality control region in such State....

Sec. 110. (a) (1) Each State shall, after reasonable notice and public hearings, adopt and submit to the Administrator [of EPA], within nine months after the promulgation of a national primary ambient air quality standard ... a plan which provides for implementation, maintenance, and enforcement of such primary standard in each air quality control region (or portion thereof) within each State....

(2) The Administrator shall, within four months after the date required for submission of a plan under paragraph (1), approve or disapprove such plan or each portion thereof. The Administrator shall approve such plan, or any portion thereof, if he determines that it was adopted after reasonable notice and hearing and that —

(A) (i) in the case of a plan implementing a national primary ambient air quality standard, it provides for the attainment of such primary standard as expeditiously as possible but ... in no case later than three years from the date of approval of such plan...;

(B) it includes emission limitations, schedules, and timetables for compliance with such limitations, and such other measures as may be necessary to insure attainment and maintenance of such primary or secondary standard, including, but not limited to, land-use and transportation controls;

(C) it includes provisions for establishment and operation of appropriate devices, methods, systems, and procedures necessary to (i) monitor, compile, and analyze data on ambient air quality...;

(F) it provides (i) necessary assurances that the State will have adequate personnel, funding, and authority to carry out such implementation plan....

(4) (e) Upon application of a Governor of a State at the time of submission of any plan implementing a national ambient air quality primary standard, the Administrator may ... extend the three-year period ... for not more than two years for an air quality control region....

Sec. 304. (a) . . . any person may commence a civil action on his own behalf —

(1) against any person (including (i) the United States, and (ii) any other governmental instrumentality or agency . . . who is alleged to be in violation of (A) an emission standard or limitation under this Act or (B) an order issued by the Administrator or a State with respect to such a standard or limitation, or

(2) against the Administrator where there is alleged a failure of the Administrator to perform any act or duty under this Act which is not discretionary with the Administrator.

Discussion Questions

1. Why did EPA Administrator Ruckelshaus decide to postpone the required date for transportation control plans? How sound was this decision?

2. What role did Congress play in shaping EPA's regulatory strategy in the years following enactment of the Clean Air Amendments of 1970?

3. Was the White House's involvement in EPA's regulatory policy making appropriate?

4. How did the federal court decision in *Riverside v. Ruckelshaus* and the *NRDC* case change the circumstances surrounding development and enforcement of transportation controls?

5. What were the advantages and disadvantages of each of the options available to Acting Administrator Robert Fri in June 1973?

Suggestions for Further Reading

Advisory Commission on Intergovernmental Relations. "Protecting the Environment: Politics, Pollution, and Federal Policy." Washington, D.C.: U.S. Government Printing Office, 1981. A descriptive and analytic overview of federal environmental regulation.

Jones, Charles O. *Clean Air: The Politics of Pollution Control.* Pittsburgh: University of Pittsburgh Press, 1975. A political history of air pollution control efforts.

Orfield, Gary. *The Reconstruction of Southern Education.* New York: John Wiley & Sons, 1969. A penetrating political and administrative history of federal regulatory efforts in another highly controversial policy arena—school desegregation in the South.

Rabinovitz, Francine; Pressman, Jeffrey; and Rein, Martin. "Guidelines: A Plethora of Forms, Authors, and Functions." *Policy Sciences,* 1976, 399-416. An exploration of various forms of federal program regulations and guidelines.

The Environmental Protection Agency and Transportation Controls (B)

THE CAST

Francis Sargent	governor of Massachusetts
Alan Altshuler	Massachusetts secretary of transportation
Ray Rodriguez	EOTC staff member
Robert Fri	acting administrator of EPA
Russell Train	EPA administrator
John McGlennon	EPA regional administrator for New England
TCP	Transportation Control Plan
EOTC	Executive Office of Transportation and Construction

CHRONOLOGY

<u>1970</u>	Massachusetts Governor Francis Sargent declares a moratorium on highway construction in the Boston metropolitan area.
<u>1971-1972</u>	Boston Transportation Planning Review (BTPR) studies facilities needed in metropolitan area.
<u>1972</u> July	Sargent assigns responsibility for developing the Boston TCP to Secretary Alan Altshuler and the Execu-

	tive Office of Transportation and Construction (EOTC). Altshuler hires consultants to help in planning.
November	Sargent announces that he is cancelling construction of most planned highways in the Boston area.
December	Altshuler receives consultants' draft TCP but is greatly concerned with its feasibility and cost.

1973

January	Altshuler completes his own draft TCP but *NRDC v. EPA* upsets his planning assumptions.
February-May	Although the state formally refuses to submit the draft TCP to EPA, Altshuler works with EPA Regional Administrator John McGlennon to revise the plan.
May	EPA's Boston regional office sends draft TCP to Washington headquarters.
May-June	EPA Washington headquarters works to revise TCPs for 19 metropolitan areas.
June	EPA Administrator Fri announces 19 TCPs, including Boston's.
July	Stormy public hearing on Boston TCP.
July-August	EPA regional office and Altshuler's staff make changes in TCP in light of public comments.
September	Governor Sargent and EPA Regional Administrator McGlennon jointly announce revised TCP at press conference.
	Russell Train becomes EPA Administrator, succeding Fri.
October	Arab-Israeli war breaks out, resulting in an oil embargo on western nations.
October-November	EPA headquarters revises new TCP draft, tightening it in some places; Massachusetts officials annoyed.
November-December	Congress and the White House consider relaxation of some environmental laws.
December	Governor Sargent and Secretary Altshuler ponder whether to continue supporting the TCP.

THE CASE

*The time has come to end our love affair with the automobile ...
our addiction with the automobile and the degrading effect it has on
Boston.*

John A. S. McGlennon, EPA regional administrator

*We wanted to cooperate [with EPA] in any way that wasn't going to
destroy [Governor] Frank Sargent.*

Alan Altshuler, Massachusetts secretary of transportation

When Congress enacted the Clean Air Amendments of 1970, it mandated
strong state action to combat air pollution. Under the amendments, the states
were required to develop state implementation plans (SIPs) by January 31,
1972, declaring how they would achieve the National Ambient Air Quality
Standards (NAAQS) established for several pollutants by the federal Environmental Protection Agency (EPA). EPA expected the states to propose
"stationary source" controls on factories, power plants, and other major
polluters. Air quality conditions also would be helped by the cleaner-running
cars that the auto industry was required to produce within a few years. But
EPA knew that in the most heavily polluted metropolitan areas "mobile
source" controls—restrictions on the use of automobiles and other vehicles—
would be necessary to achieve the air quality standards by the statutory
deadlines. How would Americans respond to EPA's efforts to make substantial
changes in their lifestyles?

Massachusetts Considers Transportation Controls

Perhaps more than in any other state, Massachusetts' policy makers and
citizens were receptive to the idea of transportation controls. Well before
EPA's interpretation of the Clean Air Amendments made the issue "hot,"
Massachusetts was debating the merits of unrestricted auto use.

*This case was written by Arnold M. Howitt and Richard P. Clarendon, with the
research assistance of Ernest G. Niemi.*

Transportation Policy in Massachusetts

Throughout the 1960s Massachusetts highway planners energetically pressed ahead with plans for a series of highway construction projects to expand the network of roads in the Boston metropolitan area.[1] These projects had the enthusiastic support of many businessmen and labor unions, as well as the press, which saw them as the key to continued economic growth in the region. But, as the decade wore on, increasing numbers of people became alarmed at the destruction of neighborhoods, the displacement of residents from their homes, and the changing character of urban life as more land was taken for highway construction. Moreover, contrary to the predictions of highway proponents, traffice congestion and its attendant pollution grew worse as new highways were opened. By the end of the decade, a coalition of inner-city residents, suburbanites, advocate planners, and activist academics had formed to fight further highway construction in the Boston region. Late in January 1970—only two days after Francis Sargent, a Republican, had become governor of the Commonwealth[2]—this coalition held a mass rally on the steps of the statehouse in Boston, demanding that Sargent halt all pending highway projects in the metropolitan area.

Notwithstanding the powerful political interests—business, labor, and parts of the state bureaucracy—arrayed on the opposite side of the highway issue, Sargent decided to take a careful look at the case for further highway construction. He selected Alan Altshuler, an MIT political scientist specializing in urban affairs, to head a task force on transportation policy. Altshuler recruited task force members from business, labor, civic associations, and the academic world—none of whom previously had taken public positions on the highway issue. Sifting through the arguments presented by both sides, the task force was persuaded that highway construction decisions were made from a very narrow perspective. As a result, it recommended to Sargent that he declare a moratorium on most highway projects on the drawing boards and undertake a full-scale review based on economic and social considerations as well as transportation impacts.

Early in 1970, in the rising political temperature of an election year, Sargent accepted this advice, temporarily halting highway projects in the Boston area pending reevaluation of their purposes and justifications. Retaining Altshuler as a consultant, Sargent had him begin plans for the review. In the meantime the governor waged and decisively won his reelection campaign.

As his new term began in 1971, Sargent could approach the highway question with the relative political freedom assured by a four-year lease on the governor's office. He appointed Altshuler to the new post of secretary of transportation, heading the Executive Office of Transportation and Construction (EOTC), which oversaw the Commonwealth's several transportation agencies. By this time Altshuler had organized an unprecedented study of the

Boston highway and transit network. Underwritten by $3.5 million in funds from the U.S. Department of Transportation, the Boston Transportation Planning Review (BTPR) was to examine further highway construction in the light of the area's total transportation needs (both auto and transit) and the social and economic impacts of further development. When the results of the BTPR's careful analysis became available in 1972, Sargent found himself more and more persuaded by the arguments of those who questioned the value of more highway construction.

On November 30, 1972, in a dramatic speech to a statewide television audience, Sargent announced his intention to make the highway moratorium permanent. Going beyond his advisers' counsel, the governor said he was scrapping virtually all planned highway construction within the boundaries of Route 128 (a circumferential highway around Boston and its suburbs). Instead, he was committing those resources to extensive improvements in the region's mass transit system.

Altshuler "Discovers" the Clean Air Amendments

Throughout 1971, Massachusetts' development of the state implementation plan required by the Clean Air Amendments centered in the Bureau of Air Quality Control (BAQC) of the state's Department of Public Health. EPA simplified BAQC's task in the fall by citing the lack of appropriate technical guidelines and announcing that the SIP due in January 1972 did not have to include transportation control measures. (EPA advised the state, though, that a separate transportation control plan, TCP, had to be submitted by February 15, 1973.) The SIP was completed on schedule and substantially approved by EPA in May 1972. EPA also granted the state a two-year extension for meeting the air quality standards—from 1975 to 1977. (See "The Environmental Protection Agency and Transportation Controls (A)," pp. 125, 128.)

At the same time, EPA reminded the state that it must proceed with a TCP. John A. S. McGlennon, EPA's regional administrator in Boston, wrote to Governor Sargent:

> You are now probably all wondering what this means for Massachusetts....
> Basically, what I am saying is that it appears to me we may have to change our whole transportation philosophy. We are going to have to end in the Boston area the reliance on the automobile as the principal mode of transportation. This will have to be done in order to meet air quality standards.

Noting that "we do know that the implementation plans will have an effect on the economy," McGlennon sought to reassure state officials:

> We do not expect any mass plant closings. We do not expect any mass exodus of business and industry from Massachusetts because of the plan. We do not expect that implementation of these plans will affect the unemployment rate to any great degree.

141

In response, Governor Sargent mildly observed that

> ... the Commonwealth will accelerate our efforts to develop such a plan. However, I hope it would be possible for us to obtain a clearer indication of the degree to which the Environmental Protection Agency expects the states to reduce vehicle traffic.[3]

By mid-1972, Secretary Altshuler and the Executive Office of Transportation and Construction largely were preoccupied with assessing the findings of the BTPR and preparing for Sargent's highway construction decision. Nonetheless, the governor's office decided to assign responsibility for developing the TCP to Altshuler and the EOTC. The alternative was the Bureau of Air Quality Control, which was understaffed and had no transportation expertise. Altshuler himself had no time to spare, but he assigned Under Secretary John Doolittle and Ray Rodriguez, a young EOTC staffer, to meet with EPA regional staff and begin work on the state's TCP.[4]

Hard pressed by other tasks, Doolittle and Rodriguez looked for help in developing the TCP. Rodriguez was able to find $50,000 in federal highway planning money that—despite resistance from the state Department of Public Works—was used to hire consultants. EPA already had contracted with two consulting firms, GCA and Allen M. Voorhees and Associates, to do back-up work on a Boston TCP in case the state failed to produce an acceptable plan. EOTC piggybacked its contract with EPA's. Rodriguez recalled:

> For about two months, from about October to December of 1972, we had about 24 meetings at the state level with all sorts of people potentially involved with the TCP. EPA was always invited but only sometimes showed up. There were working sessions with the city officials of Boston and Cambridge, the Sierra Club, Associated Industries of Massachusetts, and the Registry of Motor Vehicles. In other words, we saw all of the local interest groups on both sides of the issue, as well as municipal officials and representatives from other state agencies. Even without very good data about the effects of our strategies on air quality, we were coming up with some of the strategies that were eventually adopted. These were largely brainstorming sessions.

The Consultants' Plan. In mid-December 1972, just two months before the TCP was due to be submitted to EPA, the consultants presented Altshuler with a draft plan. Seeking to control pollution through both emission control systems ("tailpipe controls") and restrictions on vehicle use, the consultants proposed several measures:[5]

1. A program, known as the "retrofit" strategy, to install emission control devices on pre-1975 vehicles. The consultants anticipated that this measure would cost owners approximately $300 per vehicle.

2. A traffic management strategy to "monitor and exclude low priority traffic" from Boston's downtown core area. This measure was linked to the following policy.

3. A licensing scheme through which drivers on a priority basis would be issued special licenses to drive in Boston's downtown core. The consultants proposed that "persons making trips deemed essential or deserving certain priorities" be allowed to enter the core area, but left unspecified which drivers fell into this category.

4. Imposition of tolls on all major radial routes into Boston to discourage unnecessary traffic. These included Routes 1 and I-93 to the north, Route 2 and the Massachusetts Turnpike to the west, and the southeast expressway (Route 3) to the south.

5. A state gasoline tax designed to curb unnecessary driving, enforced by "police border patrols" to prevent drivers from purchasing fuel out of state.

Altshuler's Draft TCP. Aghast at the potential dollar cost of these proposals and the political uproar they doubtless would engender, Altshuler began working with Rodriguez to develop a more acceptable plan for Massachusetts. He had mixed feelings about the task. On one hand, it was a complex undertaking that he had neither the technical nor monetary means to complete properly. From the BTPR, Altshuler knew that the quantitative models available for simulating the effects of auto use on air pollution were primitive and far too imprecise to permit accurate predictions of the impact of various control measures. In conducting the BTPR, moreover, Altshuler had secured $3.5 million in funds from the U.S. Department of Transportation (DOT); but for the current job he had only $50,000—not one cent of which came from EPA. There was no alternative to a "quick and dirty" study, he thought. On the other hand, EPA's insistence on a TCP was helpful reinforcement for Governor Sargent's decision only one month earlier to stop construction of more highways in the Boston region. The approach EPA advocated was largely compatible with, if more extreme than, the views Sargent had espoused in formulating his highway decision.

After more than a month of hard labor, Altshuler completed his plan in mid-January 1973. It began with the assumption that EPA's "Detroit strategy," which required the auto industry to produce cleaner vehicles starting with the 1975 model year, would greatly help Massachusetts achieve the air quality standard by 1977. The plan then proposed a set of basic measures to be enforced at all times, plus further restraints to be imposed on an intermittent basis when meteorological conditions otherwise made it impossible to maintain air quality. As summarized in Exhibit 1, p. 156, the elements of Altshuler's plan included:[6]

1. A state-run inspection and maintenance (I & M) program. Under this program, all vehicles registered in Massachusetts would be required to undergo biannual checks to ensure the proper installation and operation of their emission control devices.

2. Implementation of the state's recently unveiled $1 billion transit improvement program for the eastern Massachusetts area. Altshuler felt that this was

essential to attract additional transit riders and thus necessary to reduce further vehicular traffic.

3. A traffic management strategy to ban driving during meteorologically induced episodes of poor air quality. This measure would be applied in conjunction with the following policy.

4. A state-run "sticker plan" that separated "non-essential" vehicles into five groups, each marked by a different colored window sticker. Under this plan, on an alternating basis, one or more groups would be prohibited from traveling during poor air quality episodes.

5. A system of air quality monitoring and surveillance for episodic application of controls.

6. A freeze on the supply of parking in Boston's core areas. In his November 1972 speech Governor Sargent had broached the idea of prohibiting development of further off-street parking lots in Boston as a long-term strategy to discourage driving downtown.

7. A $1 parking surcharge on all parking in the core area to be imposed at the localities' discretion. The city of Boston supported this plan for the revenues it would earn, but Altshuler proposed it to discourage unnecessary traffic.

8. Special carpool and bus lanes on major radial highways into Boston, including the southeast expressway, Route 2, I-93, and Route 9.

Because the plan had been completed well before the February 15 deadline, leaving time for consultants to refine and document its technical assumptions, Altshuler believed the matter was well in hand:

> Our feeling was that if we had to do things other than change the pollution characteristics of automobiles themselves, then we wanted to do what was maximally compatible with Sargent's transportation policy statement of November 1972. In other words, we wanted to emphasize transit and to restrict parking in the core area of Boston. We believed that episodic controls in the context of a public health emergency were easier to enforce and cheaper than retrofit.

A public hearing on the proposed Boston TCP was scheduled for February 27.

EPA Takes the Lead

Less than two weeks after Altshuler completed his draft TCP, however, a federal court abruptly altered the Sargent administration's calculations concerning transportation controls.

The NRDC Decision

On January 31, 1973, a federal court in Washington, D.C., issued its decision in *NRDC v. EPA*. The Natural Resources Defense Council, an environmental advocacy group, had brought suit some months before charging that EPA Administrator William D. Ruckelshaus had exceeded his authority in 1) giving the states until February 1973 to submit TCPs rather than requiring transportation control measures in the SIPs, and 2) granting 17 heavily populated states a blanket extension from 1975 to 1977 of the deadline for achieving the air quality standards. Upholding the plaintiffs, the court ordered EPA to rescind the two-year extension and to demand TCPs no later than April 15. (See "The Environmental Protection Agency and Transportation Controls (A)," pp. 130-131.)

The NRDC decision dramatically changed the assumptions that had shaped Altshuler's proposed TCP in Massachusetts. In developing the plan, Altshuler had thought that implementation would prove difficult; but, counting on the 1977 deadline for achieving air quality standards, he explicitly had assumed that the cleaner-running 1975 and 1976 autos would produce significant reductions in the region's air pollution. By mandating a 1975 deadline, the court had shifted the entire burden of reducing pollution to the state. To satisfy this requirement, Altshuler saw no alternative to drafting a plan that included harsh restrictions on auto use. However, that plan would impose wholly unacceptable political risks on the Sargent administration.

With the governor's concurrence, Altshuler informed John McGlennon, EPA's regional administrator, that the state would not submit a revised TCP. Under the provisions of the Clean Air Amendments, therefore, responsibility for developing a plan would be placed squarely on EPA's shoulders. McGlennon, however, was anxious to have the state issue the Boston TCP under its own authority. Seeking to preserve the rapport he had carefully cultivated with the state, McGlennon urged Altshuler to submit his original TCP "as is," merely substituting 1975 for the 1977 attainment date. That way, McGlennon reasoned, EPA could grant the state a two-year extension on the grounds that attaining the NAAQS by 1975 was technically infeasible. Altshuler, however, rejected this ploy, fearing that further court intervention might force Massachusetts to comply with the stated 1975 goal.[7]

EPA's regional staff therefore proceeded largely on its own to develop a new TCP for Boston. Having foreseen that Massachusetts might refuse to promulgate the Boston TCP, McGlennon earlier had contracted with two consulting firms (the same ones Altshuler had used) to prepare a contingency plan. A few EPA regional staffers worked doggedly through February, March, and April, conferring widely with groups that had an interest in the TCP. Mayor Kevin White and other officials from the city of Boston, for example, let EPA know that they supported an on-street parking ban, a freeze on construction of new parking facilities downtown, and a tax surcharge on parking fees.

By May EPA's regional office had finished a draft of the TCP for Boston and had forwarded it to headquarters in Washington, D.C., for approval.

Headquarters Acts Decisively

As Massachusetts struggled to formulate acceptable transportation control measures for Boston, other states faced similar problems. In virtually all cases the result was the same: confronted with the hard deadlines created by the NRDC case, the states chose to let EPA take responsibility—and blame—for the TCPs.

Not all EPA regional offices were so firm as the Region I staff in Boston. Most of the draft plans sent to EPA headquarters in Washington were far too weak to achieve the clean air standards. During May and June 1973, therefore, staff in Washington, consulting with the agency's technical staff in Durham, N.C., reworked the plans until they conformed to the statutory requirements. This task was made even more difficult than it would have been several months earlier because in April EPA's administrator had given automobile manufacturers a one-year extension of the deadline for producing cleaner-running vehicles. But his action did not change the overall statutory deadline for achieving national air quality standards. As a result, in drafting the TCPs, EPA staff had to place a relatively heavier burden on "mobile source" restrictions. The TCPs that emerged from this process generally required very stringent control measures. (See "The Environmental Protection Agency and Transportation Controls (A)," pp. 131, 133-135.)

By early June EPA's Acting Administrator Robert Fri was pondering what he should do. The NRDC decision had given EPA until June 15 to approve or disapprove TCPs proposed by the states and until August 15 to propose alternatives if state efforts were inadequate. Assessing his options, Fri began by assuming that the Clean Air Act was gravely flawed. Its deadlines were too rigid, thereby forcing the states to restrain auto use even though a delay of a few years would allow cleaner- running new cars to reduce pollution. Fri and his predecessor, William Ruckelshaus, had tried to persuade Senator Muskie and other congressional environmentalists to initiate changes in the statute; but they had refused, fearing that opponents of the Clean Air Act would use the occasion to "gut" it.

Because of unambiguous federal court instructions on the NRDC case, Fri saw no possibility of ignoring or evading the statute's requirements. That course, moreover, would focus public and congressional attention on EPA's failures rather than on the shortcomings of the law. It also would expose EPA to judicial intervention that was insensitive to issues of implementation.

Sentiment existed within EPA to follow the court's NRDC order by issuing TCPs at intervals for different metropolitan areas until the August deadline. By announcing the easier cases first, EPA could buy time to work on the thornier problems in other areas. Fri dismissed that idea, however, because it bought only a little time and did nothing to make easier the task of imposing stringent TCPs on some urban areas.

Fri therefore decided that decisive, dramatic action was necessary:

The administrative process had to go forward until the rule making pushed Congress to the end of its rope because of the infeasibility of some of the regulations. I realized there was a need to light political bonfires even at the risk of making the agency look foolish rather than Congress.

Consequently, Fri made plans to issue a package of 19 TCPs prepared by EPA staff. To focus public attention on the issue, he sought the maximum "publicity splash" possible—no mean feat in Washington at a time when almost everyone's eyes were riveted to the televised hearings of the Senate Watergate Committee, investigating wrongdoing by President Nixon's campaign committee. By choosing June 15, a day when the committee was not in session, Fri got the splash he wanted. Newspapers and TV gave the TCPs ample "play." As a result, public reaction was swift and mainly negative—a pattern similar to what had occurred when the Los Angeles plan had been announced in January. A storm of controversy swirled around EPA.

EPA's TCP for Boston

The Boston TCP was among those Fri announced in June, and it was published in the *Federal Register* in early July. (See Exhibit 2, pp. 157-158.) Ironically, although the NRDC decision had prevented EPA from allowing the state to assume a 1977 deadline for meeting the air quality standards, the agency effectively could grant itself this two-year extension by declaring that meeting the earlier deadline was infeasible. EPA's proposed TCP had a number of similarities with the version that Altshuler had drafted six months earlier but was tougher in several key respects. The plan (summarized in Exhibit 1, p. 156) called for:

1. A modified "sticker plan" that grouped nonessential vehicles into five groups (as the state's plan would have done) to be alternately banned from the roads. Instead of being imposed only during episodes of poor air quality, however, this measure would be applied over entire seasons (for example, summer and fall, the worst seasons for air quality).

2. Parking restrictions in the core area. Specifically,
   a. A surcharge of $5.00 levied on all off-street parking.
   b. An on-street parking ban imposed from 6 to 10 a.m. and 4 to 10 p.m. Both of these measures were designed to discourage unnecessary driving into Boston's downtown core.

3. A freeze on parking supply in the core area. To discourage driving into the downtown area, this measure would prohibit development of additional off-street parking.

4. A state-administered inspection and maintenance program for all Massachusetts vehicles. This measure would require biannual inspection of pollution control devices, followed by mandatory repair if necessary.

5. Installation of emission control devices would be required for pre-1975 vehicles. This "retrofit strategy" would complement the factory installed controls on post-1975 vehicles.

6. A series of stationary source controls on dry-cleaning establishments, degreasing operations, and other large sources of hydrocarbon emissions. Although not technically transportation controls, these measures actually would account for the bulk of the reduction in this type of pollutant.

Public Hearings on the TCP

Because the Clean Air Act required EPA to solicit and consider public comments on its plans before their promulgation in final form, EPA's regional office scheduled public hearings on the Boston TCP for July 19 and 20 in Boston's historic Faneuil Hall. In preparation for the hearings, John McGlennon, EPA regional administrator, and his staff sought to drum up support and neutralize potential opposition to the plan. Hoping to elicit favorable testimony, they had briefed the staffs of U.S. Senators Edward Kennedy and Edward Brooke, Governor Sargent, and Boston Mayor Kevin White, as well as officials of other municipalities in the Boston area. To defuse anticipated objections from the business community, McGlennon met with representatives of the Associated Industries of Massachusetts and the Greater Boston Chamber of Commerce to explain the TCP's purposes. By the time the hearings began on July 19, more than 50 groups and individuals, representing a broad spectrum of interests, had signed up to comment on the TCP.

Governor Sargent led off the testimony by reiterating his position on highway construction in the Boston area, enthusiastically supporting the principles of the Clean Air Act, and then turning the floor over to his secretary of transportation. Altshuler began by supporting the objectives of the act, but soon turned his opportunity to speak into a platform for airing the state's positions on several related issues. He reviewed in detail the governor's antihighway position, his protransit proposals, and the reasoning behind them. Altshuler's testimony also provided an opportunity to vent some of the Sargent administration's dissatisfactions with federal policy. He established some political distance between the governor and EPA by offering a broad critique of the federal government's transportation and air pollution control policies. Linking transportation controls to federal funding policies, he pointed out that excluding mass transit projects from those supported by the federal Highway Trust Fund hindered attainment of air quality goals. Also, the fact that EPA in April had granted automakers a one-year extension for meeting federal emission standards, he said, hindered achievement of air quality goals by 1975 and shifted the burden of air pollution control to the Massachusetts citizens who would have to reduce use of their automobiles.

Altshuler then launched a scathing attack on EPA's plan for Boston. He criticized the "sticker plan" as "administratively infeasible to enforce."

Blasting the $5.00 parking surcharge, he labeled it "a very substantial tax on a limited segment of the population." Altshuler even portrayed the TCP as unnecessary because cleaner vehicles coming into the market in 1975 would by themselves attain the NAAQS by 1978.

Tempering his criticism, Altshuler endorsed EPA's proposed mandatory inspection and maintenance program, the off-street parking freeze, and the on-street parking ban in the core area. Lastly, he offered alternative measures developed by EOTC's staff for EPA's consideration. The $5.00 parking surcharge should be eliminated, he proposed, in favor of requiring off-street parking lots to maintain a 40 percent vacancy rate until 10 a.m. Also, requiring employers within the Route 128 perimeter to reduce their employee parking by as much as 20 percent, Altshuler claimed, would offset relaxations in other measures.

Altshuler was followed by representatives from core area cities such as Cambridge and Boston who supported EPA's plan. Boston officials particularly plugged the parking surcharge because of the increased revenues it would produce for the city. Local and statewide environmental groups also spoke in favor of the plan.

Negative testimony came largely from other elected officials and business representatives. Robert Quinn, the state attorney general and a Democratic gubernatorial hopeful, labeled the plan "unenforceable." Likewise, state Representative James Smith of Lynn termed EPA's measures "shallow . . . lacking depth, crucial backup data, and a basic understanding of transportation." Other state legislators either gave the plan lukewarm support or criticized it outright.

Business leaders vehemently opposed transportation controls in the Boston area. The state's only statewide business advocacy organization, the Associated Industries of Massachusetts, sent its lawyer, William McCarthy, to testify. Representing mainly industrial and manufacturing concerns, McCarthy scored the plan, charging:

> It is grossly unfair and discriminatory. . . . It ignores the reality facing some 289,000 industrial workers in the Route 128 area. . . . [It] could result in the loss of millions of dollars in wages and could result in serious disruption for their companies. . . .

The Culmination of EPA-State Cooperation

The EPA regional office felt that the plan had weathered the public hearings well. Aside from Altshuler's testimony, McGlennon attributed the negative remarks and criticisms of the plan to "professional lobbyists" and biased news reports about the plan's substance. In accordance with the Clean Air Act, the regional office began revising the Boston TCP in light of comments made at the public hearings. As one EPA regional staffer recalled:

149

The law requires that the TCP be adopted after the public hearing. You are not required to change anything, but, practically, you are. The plan can be challenged in court within 30 days of the final regulations. Therefore you listen to testimony to avoid being challenged in court.

The process of revision was not one of total accommodation to objections, though. As the staff member noted:

Almost everyone at the public hearing had useful suggestions to make, but so many changes were suggested that it would have gutted the plan to accept them all. Those things that had little impact on air quality were dropped out. For example, if the city of Boston said that 10 out of 200 streets that were supposed to be closed to parking should be exempted, then we were willing to do that. We paid attention to those actors with political clout: the state, Boston, Cambridge. These were all given close attention. On the other hand, we put little stock in what people from the AAA said.

For the rest of the summer, EPA regional staff consulted extensively with Secretary Altshuler as they sought to "fine tune" the TCP. Despite his doubts, Altshuler was willing to cooperate with EPA in redrafting the TCP. He still felt strongly that many elements of the plan were both desirable in themselves and bolstered Governor Sargent's controversial positions on highway construction. As long as EPA was pushing the state vigorously to restrict auto use in the Boston area, it made the job of defending Sargent's policy far easier. Altshuler had another reason, though, for working closely with EPA. Because he was far more sensitive to questions of political and administrative feasibility than the EPA regional office, he wanted to play as active a part as possible behind the scenes in revising the TCP. He felt that he thereby might help draft a plan that the Sargent administration could live with.

Throughout late July and August, the cooperative spirit on both sides paid dividends as the state and EPA agreed on virtually all provisions of a revised TCP. At a joint press conference at the statehouse on September 4, 1973, EPA Regional Administrator McGlennon unveiled the plan. Among the revisions (summarized in Exhibit 1, p. 156), were.[8]

1. A $2.50 parking surcharge to replace the earlier $5.00 fee. To make up for the increased traffic that would result from this reduction, EPA would require off-street parking lots to maintain a 40 percent vacancy rate until 10 a.m. on weekdays.

2. A "regional parking management system" proposed in lieu of the abandoned "sticker plan." This system would require employers with 50 or more workers to reduce their employee parking spaces by 25 percent or by that number necessary to reach a parking space-to-employee ratio of .75, whichever was greater.

3. The parking freeze imposed on the core area would be expanded to include Logan International Airport, the origin of a considerable amount of carbon monoxide emissions. This meant that no additional parking facilities could be constructed at Logan to discourage unnecessary future traffic.

4. A retrofit program to install catalytic converters only on 1974 vehicles, rather than on all vehicles as EPA had proposed. In addition EPA would require equipping some older vehicles with less costly emission control devices.

5. As new measures, EPA would require the state to plan and administer a carpool matching system and to provide a carpooling incentive to drivers in the form of exclusive carpool/bus lanes on the southeast expressway.

Speaking after McGlennon, Governor Sargent endorsed each of the measures in the plan, except for the retrofit requirement; the latter he thought ill-advised, but he acknowledged that the provision was necessary to satisfy the requirements of the Clean Air Amendments.

As a result of the press conference, EPA was jubilant. At last an effective Boston TCP seemed assured.

The Scheme Begins to Unravel

Only a few months after this demonstration of good will and cooperation between Massachusetts officials and EPA, a series of events threatened to undermine the arrangement.

In Washington a new EPA administrator had inherited the problems associated with the TCPs. Russell Train, former chairman of the president's Council on Environmental Quality, took over in September and remembers feeling as if he had "walked into a buzz saw." A steady barrage of complaints and pleas had been generated from mayors, governors, and members of Congress who sought some relief from the stringent plans moving toward final promulgation. On the other hand, Train's legal staff insisted that the courts had given EPA no choice but to press forward vigorously to enforce the Clean Air Act.

So far the strategy adopted by Fri in June to win changes in the Clean Air Act had not worked. Train appealed again to the environmentalists in Congress to sponsor legislation to relax transportation controls, but he enjoyed no more success than had Ruckelshaus and Fri. Despite widespread political pressure (or perhaps because of it) congressional environmentalists resisted, fearing that their colleagues would fatally weaken the regulatory process rather than simply relax the deadlines for achieving the air quality standards.

The political climate virtually changed overnight, however. On October 6, 1973, the Middle East exploded into war as Arab states took the initiative against Israel. When the United States resupplied the Israeli military, Arab producers imposed an oil embargo on the United States and other Western nations. Fuel shortages, dramatized by long lines at gas stations, soon over-shadowed all other policy issues in the United States, including air quality.

In Massachusetts the prospects for smooth implementation of transportation controls began to sour. Even before the oil embargo, leading businessmen

151

and a number of elected officials had continued unabated their attacks on the TCP. Now in the face of the embargo, the Sargent administration became more cautious. A new public hearing on the TCP scheduled for late October was canceled.

EPA regional officials pushed ahead as well as they could. Recognizing Governor Sargent's problems, McGlennon agreed to appeal to EPA headquarters in Washington to remove from the TCP the one measure Sargent had not endorsed in September—the retrofit requirement.[9]

But headquarters, although not wholly unconcerned with securing state cooperation, had a different perspective on the regulatory process. Around the country, following hearings on the proposed TCPs, EPA regional offices had redrafted the plans in light of public comments. The Boston office, like the others, had sent its draft to headquarters. An EPA attorney recalled how the TCPs then were revised:

> The general counsel's office played roughly the same role in redrafting the TCPs [as it had for the first round in the spring of 1973]. Many of the regulations drafted by the regional offices were poor efforts. It was important that they be put into legal language that would stand up in court, which meant that they had to be technically adequate. I drafted a model regulation using bus lanes as an example and that ended up being the bus lane proposal in a number of TCPs without further ado.
>
> In October 1973 I wrote several memos arguing that the TCPs had to have consistent regulations. This was an effort to bring the various plans drafted by the regions into conformity with each other so that the policies proposed for one area, or discarded as infeasible in one area, were treated the same elsewhere—for example, bus lanes or catalytic converters. Another memo argued that the technical standards used for evaluating the impact of policies should also be consistent. In other words, the same computer models or forecasting techniques would be used.

When the Boston TCP was officially published in the *Federal Register* on November 8, 1973, Massachusetts officials were shocked by its transformation. As one EOTC staff member commented:

> EPA regional had to get Washington's approval for their draft of the TCP.... The studies that had been conducted by the regional office had to be transformed by lawyers into regulations. But it is very hard to write regulations without writing substance as well.... The lawyers didn't show understanding of the transportation issues and the practical issues of the implementation of the TCP through such agencies as the Department of Public Works and the Massachusetts Bay Transportation Authority. They included absurd time schedules.

For example, some planning documents were required by December 1, barely three weeks away; a special carpool and bus lane on I-93 had to be in operation by April 15; and a system for inspecting and maintaining emission control devices on all gasoline-powered vehicles had to be developed and adopted by the state legislature by April 1. Taken as a whole, moreover, the TCP was likely to impose enormous burdens on the state budget, but EPA could provide no financial assistance to help pay the costs. Nonetheless, the TCP was now a legally binding document, backed by the authority of the federal government under the Clean Air Act.

The Sargent administration was not the only party upset by the TCP. Within 30 days of publication of the Boston TCP, nine separate lawsuits seeking to enjoin its enforcement had been filed in federal district court. One suit in particular embarrassed EOTC. The Massachusetts Port Authority, an independent state agency subject to limited supervision by EOTC, joined a coalition of airlines in suing EPA over a parking freeze that would bar construction of a planned garage at Logan Airport. (See "The Environmental Protection Agency and Transportation Controls (C)," pp. 166-167.)

In Washington the oil embargo put congressional environmentalists on the defensive. On November 7, President Nixon in a televised address to the nation called on Congress to enact emergency energy legislation "which would provide the necessary authority to relax environmental regulations on a temporary, case-by-case basis, thus permitting an appropriate balancing of our environmental interests ... with our energy requirements, which, of course, are indispensable." [10] As energy legislation moved through Congress, a number of members of Congress saw the chance to restrain EPA's transportation control policies. An amendment was added to the bill denying EPA authority to impose parking surcharges, and other amendments prohibited EPA from requiring special carpool and bus lanes on highways or requiring review of plans to construct new parking facilities.

Also in November, experts testifying before the Senate Public Works Committee were sharply critical of the catalytic converter as an emission control device. The converter itself, some scientists argued, produced hazardous sulfate emissions. Consequently, several bills were filed to prevent EPA from requiring use of the catalytic converter.

By December the fate of these measures in Congress was still in doubt, but EPA and state officials in Massachusetts and elsewhere could see that the climate of congressional opinion was changing rapidly. Even though transportation controls, such as parking restrictions, were designed to discourage vehicle use—and consequently might be regarded as energy conservation measures—Congress was unwilling to impose new hardships on American motorists already enraged by the effects of the oil embargo. It was clear, too, that the White House was ready to see the Clean Air Act weakened.

The Sargent Administration's Dilemma

By December Governor Sargent and Secretary Altshuler knew they had to rethink their position on the Boston TCP. On one hand, the governor's

153

unequivocal policy on new highway construction and transit development was a part of his record from which there was no retreat—or desire to retreat. Many of EPA's transportation control measures reinforced and made credible the rationale for his policy. Moreover, only three months before, Sargent publicly had endorsed the Boston TCP in a joint press conference with McGlennon. To back off now would expose him to charges of bad faith from environmentalists and others.

The situation had changed drastically in a relatively short time, however. As Altshuler recalled:

> We must remember that in early 1973 we didn't perceive things as we do now. The Clean Air Act looked real. Congress had passed it, the courts were forcing EPA to enforce it, Congress was indicating that it was not about to repeal the act. We felt that we should try in a serious way to come up with a compliance plan. John McGlennon was willing to have a reasonable policy pursued. He was willing to cooperate with us. . . . McGlennon's principal constraint was that he had to be able to say that Boston was in compliance with the air quality standards required by the Clean Air Act.

> That became more tenuous as time went on . . . as a result of a number of factors. One, public reaction to the TCP. Two, reports that President Nixon was going to submit revisions of the Clean Air Act to Congress. Three, reports that other metropolitan areas had been slipping on the commitments required by the TCPs there. Four, we were in the midst of an energy crisis, evidenced most clearly by the oil embargo which began in October. . . .

> It is important to understand the changing policy environment. In 1972, when the Boston Transportation Planning Review came out, the environmental movement was at its peak in the state. It was a prime good government issue, the economy was strong, there was no energy crisis. By late 1973 conditions had changed substantially. . . . Sargent couldn't be seen as hassling the public, especially if he was going to be left out on a limb by President Nixon's actions on the Clean Air Act. . . .

> By winter of 1973-1974, we also believed that many of the VMT ["vehicle miles traveled," a measure of transportation use] reductions might be achieved by energy shortages rather than by mandated changes in the TCP. . . .

> We also gradually learned political lessons about talking about VMT reductions. It was one thing to try to stop highways, another to reduce VMT. This was less obvious at the beginning of 1973 than at the end.

The administration's position on the TCP was complicated greatly by the fact that 1974 was an election year. Sargent's reelection campaign would face tough challenges from both sides of the political spectrum. Within the Republican party, conservative elements plotting to ambush Sargent in the primary election surely would castigate him for supporting stringent transportation controls that might exact a heavy toll on the state's economy. And the leading Democratic gubernatorial candidate, former State Rep. Michael Dukakis, had strongly endorsed the TCP at the public hearings in July.

With this background, Sargent and Altshuler pondered their next move on the TCP.

NOTES

1. The following four paragraphs are based on material in "Transportation Policy in Massachusetts (Note, A, B)," Kennedy School of Government (C16-75-033, 034, 035).

2. Sargent, elected as lieutenant governor two years earlier on a ticket with John Volpe, became governor when Volpe was selected as secretary of transportation in President Nixon's cabinet. Sargent would serve the remaining two years of Volpe's term and then face the voters in his own right in 1970.

3. McGlennon and Sargent are quoted by Michael Padnos and Edward I. Selig, "Transportation Controls in Boston: The Plan That Failed," an unpublished paper commissioned by the American Bar Foundation and the National Academy of Science (June 30, 1976), 11-12.

4. EOTC was at this time a very small agency. Created in 1971 (as a consequence of legislation in 1969 that reorganized state government), EOTC was responsible for coordinating the activities of the Department of Public Works (the state highway agency), the Massachusetts Port Authority (which operated Logan Airport and the Port of Boston), and the Massachusetts Bay Transportation Authority (which ran Boston's subways and buses). Because the second stage of the reorganization had not been approved by the legislature, EOTC had only about 8 to 10 staff members.

5. Padnos and Selig, "Transportation Controls in Boston: The Plan That Failed," 16-17.

6. Ibid., 17-21.

7. Ibid., 25-27.

8. Ibid., 51-59.

9. Ibid., 60-61.

10. Quoted by Charles O. Jones, *Clean Air,* (Pittsburgh: University of Pittsburgh Press, 1975), 311.

Exhibit One:
Summary of Provisions in Transportation Control Plans

Transportation Control Plan	Altshuler Draft	EPA's Proposed Plan	EPA's Final Plan	EPA's Second Proposed Plan	EPA's Second Final Plan
Date Released	Jan. '73	July '73	Nov. '73	Feb. '75	June '75
Measures Proposed:					
(1) Inspection & Maintenance Program	X	X	X		X
(2) Traffic Management Strategy	X				
(3) Air Quality Monitoring	X			X	X
(4) Parking Freeze					
(a) Core Area	X		X	X	X
(b) Logan Airport			X	X	X
(5) Parking Surcharge					
(a) $1.00	X				
(b) $2.50			X		
(c) $5.00		X			
(6) Carpool/Bus Lanes	X		X	X	X
(7) "Sticker Plan"	X	X			
(8) On-Street Parking Ban		X	X	X	X
(9) Retrofit Strategies					
(a) Vacuum Spark Advance Disconnect					
(i) Pre-1970 Models		X			
(ii) Pre-1968 Models			X		
(b) Air Bleed Emission-Control Device, 1968-71 LDV,* PRE-72 MDV**			X		
(c) Catalyzing Oxidizers					
(i) 1972-75 Models, Fleets of 10+		X			
(ii) 1969-74 Models			X		
(10) Regional Parking Management System: Employer-Enforced 25% Reduction in Employee Parking			X		
(11) 40% Vacancy in Off-Street Lots			X		
(12) Egress Toll At Logan			X		
(13) Computer Carpool Matching				X	X
(14) Employer-Enforced 25% Reduction in Single-Passenger Commuting					
(a) Mandatory Requirement				X	
(b) Goal					X
(15) Bikeways Study				X	X
(16) East Boston Controls Study				X	X
(17) Stationary Source Controls		X	X	X	X

* LDV - Light Duty Vehicle.   ** MDV - Medium Duty Vehicle.

Exhibit Two:
Excerpts from the Proposed Boston
Transportation Control Plan

(Federal Register, July 2, 1973, pp. 17691-17699)

(g) Regulation limiting on-street parking. . . . Beginning on or before May 1, 1974, the Commonwealth of Massachusetts together with the City of Boston and other political or administrative subdivisions of the Commonwealth, shall prohibit on-street parking on all streets, highways, and other roadways within the Boston core area . . . such prohibition to be in effect, as a minimum, during the hours of 6 a.m. to 10 a.m. and 4 to 6 p.m., except on Saturdays, Sundays, and legal holidays. The prohibition shall state that vehicles parked in violation of the prohibition shall be towed away, and that the owner shall be subject to a fine of not less than $50.00. . . .

(h) Regulation for parking surcharge. . . . A surcharge of $5.00 per day per vehicle . . . shall be applied . . . to any contract or other agreement among private parties whereby parking a motor vehicle in an off-street parking space is permitted by any person in exchange for consideration. Such surcharge shall be collected by the person providing the permission to park and paid to EPA or any agency approved by EPA. . . .

The surcharge provided for . . . shall be applicable, beginning December 1, 1974, to all parking at Logan International Airport between the hours of 6 a.m. and 10 p.m.; [and] to all parking arrangements within the Boston core area . . . during the hours of 6 a.m. to 10 p.m. . . .

Regulation for seasonal vehicle use prohibition program. . . . The Commonwealth of Massachusetts shall establish a seasonal vehicle use prohibition program applicable to all private light-duty vehicles which operate on streets or highways over which it, or any of its subdivisions or agencies, have ownership or control. No Later than November 1, 1974, the Commonwealth shall adopt regulations to establish such a program. The regulations shall:

(i) Provide for the division of the population of private light-duty vehicles registered within the Boston Intrastate Region into five equal groups, on a basis that is equitable and is not related to place of registration.

(ii) Provide for the issuance of windshield stickers or other appropriate identifying devices to assign the five groups to the five days of the week Monday through Friday.

(iii) Provide that, during a control period designated by the Administrator [of EPA] . . . the operation of a private light-duty vehicle within the [Boston metropolitan] area . . . on the day of the week to which such vehicle has been assigned, shall be prohibited.

On or before April 30, 1974, the Governor of the Commonwealth of

Massachusetts shall submit to the Administrator for his approval a detailed description of the legal and administrative mechanisms adopted for operating the vehicle use prohibition program....

(1) Regulation for yearly inspection and maintenance.... The Commonwealth of Massachusetts shall establish an inspection and maintenance program applicable to all light-duty vehicles which operate on streets or highways over which it has ownership or control. No later than March 1, 1974, the Commonwealth shall submit legally adopted regulations to EPA establishing such a program. The regulations shall include:

(i) Provisions for inspection of all motor vehicles at least once each year by means of an idle emission test.

(ii) Provisions for inspection failure criteria consistent with the failure of 40 percent of the vehicles tested during the first inspection cycle.

(iii) Provisions to require that failed vehicles receive, within 2 weeks, the maintenance necessary to achieve compliance with the inspection standards.

This shall include sanctions against individual owners and repair facilities, retest of failed vehicles following maintenance, a certification program to ensure that repair facilities performing the required maintenance have the necessary equipment, parts and technical skills to perform the tasks satisfactorily, and such other measures as may be necessary or appropriate.

(n) Regulation for oxidizing catalyst.... On or before May 31, 1977, all gasoline-powered fleet vehicles, and private light-duty vehicles of model year 1972 to 1975 subject to registration in the Boston Intrastate Region shall be equipped with an appropriate oxidizing catalyst control device....

After May 31, 1977 ... the State shall not register a vehicle subject to this paragraph which is not equipped in accordance with ... this section.... The failure of any person to comply with any provision of this paragraph shall render such person in violation of a requirement of an applicable implementation plan, and subject to enforcement action....

Discussion Questions

1. How did Governor Sargent and Secretary Altshuler react to EPA's transportation controls during the early development of the regulations?

2. How important a role did the EPA regional office play in the development of the Boston TCP?

3. Why were Sargent and Altshuler willing to be cooperative with and accommodating to the EPA after the *NRDC* decision had limited EPA's flexibility and after substantial public concern had emerged in Massachusetts?

4. What importance did the first public hearing on the Boston TCP have for its participants, including EPA regional officials, Sargent and Altshuler, various state and municipal officeholders, and interest group leaders?

5. By the late fall of 1973, had the balance of program and political interests for Sargent and Altshuler changed enough to pull them away from their earlier stance of cooperation with EPA?

Suggestions for Further Reading

Derthick, Martha. *The Influence of Federal Grants*. Cambridge: Harvard University Press, 1970, Chap. 8, 193-218. A now-classic exposition of the political and administrative interdependencies between federal agencies and state officials in the management of intergovernmental programs.

Krier, James E., and Ursin, Edmund. *Pollution and Policy*. Berkeley and Los Angeles: University of California Press, 1977. A detailed history of automobile pollution control efforts in California.

Nathan, Richard P., and Dommel, Paul R. "Federal-Local Relations Under Block Grants." *Political Science Quarterly,* Fall 1978, 421-442. An analysis of the regulatory disputes between federal and municipal administrators that developed in the management of the CDBG program.

The Environmental Protection Agency and Transportation Controls (C)

THE CAST

John McGlennon	EPA regional administrator for New England
Russell Train	EPA administrator
Robert Thompson	EPA assistant regional counsel, coordinator of TCP Strategy Committee in regional office
John Quarles	EPA deputy administrator
Francis Sargent	governor of Massachusetts, 1969-1974
Alan Altshuler	secretary of transportation in the Sargent administration
Michael Dukakis	governor of Massachusetts, 1975-1978

Fred Salvucci	secretary of transportation in the Dukakis administration
Kevin White	mayor of Boston
EOTC	Executive Office of Transportation and Construction
EOEA	Executive Office of Environmental Affairs
South Terminal case	federal court decision that obligated EPA to revise Boston TCP

CHRONOLOGY

1974

January-April	Disagreement arises in EPA Washington headquarters about enforcement of the TCPs; no consistent pressure exerted on regional offices to proceed vigorously.
	Boston misses early deadlines for action in the Boston TCP. EPA Regional Administrator John McGlennon decides to press hard for enforcement.
February	EPA Administrator Russell Train gives auto makers a one-year extension for achieving nitrogen oxide emission standard.
March	Train proposes that Congress extend attainment deadlines for localities with severe pollution problems, but Congress refuses.
May	McGlennon creates TCP Strategy Committee, consisting of top regional office staff; names Robert Thompson, assistant regional counsel, as coordinator.
August	EPA regional office, backed by a top Washington official, announces plan to crack down on violators of business parking restrictions; administrative snafus sabotage enforcement effort.
September	Federal court, deciding the *South Terminal* case, orders EPA to revise Boston TCP.
October	EPA regional office becomes more conciliatory; Thompson looks for "reasonable" control measures.

1975	
January	Resolving a dispute between EPA Washington head-quarters and Boston regional office, EPA Administrator Train approves a plan for Boston that falls short of attaining the air quality standards.
March	Public hearing on new Boston TCP
May	Train reaffirms support for "non-attainment" plan for Boston despite opposition in EPA headquarters.
June	Final version of the new Boston TCP published in the *Federal Register.*

THE CASE

I had immense confidence in [the TCP's] necessity because of public health. I also had great confidence in my political ability to pull it off... And I knew that I had the full authority of law, backed by the power of the federal government, to impose the plan.

John A. S. McGlennon, EPA regional administrator

By the early months of 1974 the main burden of enforcing the Boston Transportation Control Plan (TCP), promulgated officially in November 1973 by the federal Environmental Protection Agency (EPA), had fallen on that agency's New England regional office in Boston. Despite some wavering by EPA's top administrators in Washington and the increasing unwillingness of Massachusetts Gov. Francis Sargent and his transportation secretary Alan Altshuler to lend political and administrative support to the Boston TCP, EPA regional administrator John McGlennon was convinced that the plan was important and remained committed to its enforcement.

This case was written by Arnold M. Howitt and Richard P. Clarendon, with the research assistance of Ernest G. Niemi. The research was supported, in part, by grant MA-11-0007 from the Urban Mass Transportation Administration, U.S. Department of Transportation.

161

The View From Washington

By early 1974 the political climate in Washington increasingly had become hostile to EPA's efforts. Already heatedly opposed, the transportation portions of the Clean Air Act had come under even harsher attack in the wake of the Arab oil embargo begun in October 1973 as a consequence of the Mideast war. As millions of Americans angrily waited in line for hours to purchase limited quantities of gasoline, Congress debated and enacted emergency energy legislation in January 1974. Although Sen. Edmund S. Muskie and other congressional environmentalists had forestalled major weakening of the Clean Air Act, the energy act required EPA to suspend regulations imposing parking surcharges and restrictions on parking supply. Even when President Nixon vetoed this bill (for reasons unrelated to its environmental provisions), it was clear that large parts of the public wanted no further interference with its free use of automobiles, that both houses of Congress were prepared to restrain EPA's methods of enforcing the Clean Air Act, and that the White House was ready to rein in EPA's regulatory actions.

This rapidly changing political environment had important effects on decision making in EPA's Washington headquarters. Russell Train, who had become EPA administrator in September 1973, took a strong stand against serious weakening of the Clean Air Act—to the point that rumors floated around Washington that he would resign or be dismissed—but did not feel that the act was absolutely sacrosanct. Even before President Nixon vetoed the energy bill, Train had decided that EPA would refrain voluntarily from regulating parking supply or requiring surcharges; congressional sentiment was strong on that issue. He also was prepared to extend certain deadlines in the Clean Air Act. In February 1974 he gave automakers an extension for complying with the new car standards on nitrogen oxide emissions; in March he proposed to Congress that states facing extremely difficult pollution problems be given up to ten additional years to meet air quality standards.

However, in the absence of a change in the Clean Air Act, no consensus existed among top EPA staff about how to proceed with the TCPs, which already had been legally promulgated in most affected metropolitan areas. Some key staff, particularly within the air program office and the general counsel's office, believed that the agency should proceed aggressively to enforce the TCPs; less enthusiasm was apparent in other parts of EPA. A lack of consensus also existed in EPA's regional offices. Train noted that

> ... within EPA there were differences of opinion about the TCPs. As the plans were reviewed nationwide, the agency was pursuing plans in some places and not in others.... There were real differences among the regions. Where there was no enthusiasm at the regional level, we in Washington did not push too hard. In Region III, which covered Philadelphia, Pittsburgh, and Baltimore, the regional administrator was critical of our approach. He felt

that if he had to enforce the plan, it would take every political chip that the agency had. It would require enormous resources of money and personnel. The regional people were more sensitive to these issues than the headquarters staff.

As a result, recalled an EPA staff attorney in Washington deeply involved in the issue:

... the leadership of EPA did not strongly pressure the regions to enforce the TCPs in late '73 and early '74, but occasionally they issued a supportive statement if regions wanted to take the lead themselves.

Train's attention often was on other issues as 1974 wore on, so the decisions about day-to-day enforcement policy usually were made by staff and administrators within EPA's program and functional divisions. No grand design existed and there was a good deal of disagreement about tactics. Overall during 1974, remembered the lawyer quoted above:

... the top of the agency—Train and others—was not consistent in its attitudes toward enforcing the TCPs. They would take one step forward and then one back. Sometimes they would force the regions to take actions and at other times they would not.

Region I's Resolve

There was far less uncertainty in EPA's Region I office in Boston, which had responsibility for the six New England states. Indeed, regional administrator McGlennon was determined to press strongly for implementation of the Boston TCP.

McGlennon had firm roots in the Boston area and in Massachusetts politics. As a Republican, he had been elected in 1964 as a state representative from Concord, an upper-middle-class suburb of Boston. Later he had served on Gov. John Volpe's staff, and he had made an unsuccessful bid for Congress in 1968. An outspoken advocate of environmental causes—he was a member of the Sierra Club and the Massachusetts Audubon Society— McGlennon had been recommended to the Nixon administration by Massachusetts Republican leaders to head the regional office of the new Environmental Protection Agency. Energetic, politically experienced, and committed to environmentalism, McGlennon was 35 years old when appointed to the job in 1970. By early 1974 he was a seasoned federal administrator whose zeal for his work had not diminished.

McGlennon was aware that EPA headquarters had become more cautious: "EPA Washington changed its attitudes on the TCPs when Russell Train took over as administrator. Train saw the political liabilities in Congress. . . ." But McGlennon also knew that he had considerable autonomy in setting policy within the region and that a number of key officials in Washington were deeply committed to enforcing the TCPs:

> In 1974 the regional administrators were still on their own in deciding what enforcement policy to pursue—except, if they decided to issue orders against mayors or governors, they were required to clear this with Russell Train. There was not too much pushing from Washington, where EPA was willing to go with whatever policy the regional administrator thought was most sensible. Officials in Washington ... were available to back up the regional administrators if they requested it.

For his own part McGlennon was determined to press hard for enforcement of the Boston TCP. As one of his close associates in the regional office remembered: "What distinguished the EPA Region I from other regions, with the possible exception of New York, was the commitment of the regional administrator.... We were clearly the lead region in the country."

Massachusetts Balks

As 1974 progressed, it became more and more obvious that those subject to TCP regulations would not readily comply with them. On January 1, the Commonwealth of Massachusetts missed the first deadline in the plan—for submission of a compliance schedule outlining the steps that the state would take to implement the inspection and maintenance program and the emission control retrofit program for older cars required by the TCP. The Sargent administration, while still sympathetic with the goals of the TCP, was beginning to establish political distance between itself and EPA's regulatory efforts. Events in Washington had convinced the governor and transportation secretary Altshuler that the national coalition supporting the Clean Air Act—and particularly transportation controls—was breaking apart. They did not see how they could withstand political pressures in Massachusetts if the will to push ahead was evaporating in Washington. That was especially true given the upcoming gubernatorial election in the fall, when Sargent would come up against a primary challenge from a conservative Republican before facing a strong Democratic challenger. Furthermore, with the oil embargo now a factor, they believed that gasoline shortages and higher prices were more likely to restrain auto use in the Boston area than were federal regulations. This expectation was the key to their policy of curtailing Boston area highway construction. Although McGlennon and his colleagues in the EPA regional office did not conclude that the state could not be counted on for active support until spring, the direction of state policy clearing was visible before then.

On January 31 another TCP deadline passed with few signs of compliance. By that date metropolitan area business firms were to have reported to EPA how many employees and employee parking spaces they maintained. The information would enable EPA to determine which firms were subject to the TCP's requirement that employers with more than 50 employees cut parking space by 25 percent. Not wanting to establish a precedent for permitting defiance of the TCP, McGlennon and his staff sought help from two business organizations, the Associated Industries of Massachusetts (AIM), and the Greater Boston Chamber of Commerce, to make their members aware of the enforcement actions they might face for failure to comply with the reporting requirement. Although AIM and the Chamber publicized this message in their monthly newsletters, few firms filed reports. There was little agreement within the regional office about whether EPA should send warning letters to noncomplying firms demanding the reports, or whether enforcement action should be initiated immediately.[1]

The TCP Strategy Committee

Thus faced with an uncooperative state government, a resistant business community, and a staff divided over tactics to secure compliance with the TCP, McGlennon decided in May 1974 to establish a TCP Strategy Committee consisting of senior regional office personnel who could develop a cohesive agency position. The committee included the heads of several of the agency's program divisions (Air, Enforcement, Management, and Surveillance and Analysis), as well as the regional counsel, director of public affairs, director of state relations, and McGlennon himself. The committee met whenever major decisions about TCP enforcement had to be made.[2]

To coordinate the Strategy Committee and perform staff work on the TCP, McGlennon assigned Robert Thompson, assistant regional counsel, who would spend most of the next year immersed in efforts to make the Boston TCP work. During his first month on the job, Thompson attended a protest meeting called by AIM and the Chamber. The meeting attracted about 700 angry business people; and, Thompson recalled, a "feeling of panic" at what the TCP entailed permeated the room. Thompson soon began to meet with business people and municipal officials who also were supposed to reduce their employee parking. Persistent exposure to these individuals persuaded him that EPA should be more accommodating in its dealings with them, taking more time to *persuade* them to cooperate rather than trying to compel them.[3]

The Hard Line Prevails—and Fails[4]

But the dominant view in the Strategy Committee was that forceful action had to be taken to preserve EPA's credibility. It was decided that notices of violation would be sent to about 1,500 businesses thought to be flouting the TCP requirements.

Informed that Region I planned to crack down on these apparent violators, EPA's Washington headquarters saw the chance to take a strong public stand on TCP enforcement. Therefore, Deputy Administrator John Quarles, the agency's second-ranking official, came to Boston to hold a press conference with McGlennon, threatening to initiate prosecution of businesses that continued to refuse to file reports. His remarks came just one month before the Republican gubernatorial primary during a campaign in which Governor Sargent's opponent was accusing him of being antibusiness. Quarles promised a 20-day grace period before violation notices were dispatched but asserted that EPA planned to "hang tough" in enforcing the Clean Air Act.

In preparation for the mailing of violation notices, EPA regional staff routinely began to check their list of 1,500 noncomplying companies against various business directories. When a preliminary check showed that some of the companies had no local offices, others had gone out of business, and yet others had only a handful of employees, senior staff in the regional office were distressed. Quickly assembling a group of 50 secretaries and technical staff from all parts of the office, the public affairs director set them to work finding out which companies actually did business in Massachusetts and employed at least 50 people. Under this scrutiny the list of 1,500 supposed violators shrank to fewer than 300, to whom formal notices were sent. Many of these, it turned out, were exempt for various reasons from the provisions of the TCP. Ultimately, only about 25 companies continued to ignore EPA's demands for cooperation. Yet when the Enforcement Division began preparing to turn these cases over to the U.S. Attorney's office for prosecution, it was discovered that the EPA staff involved in verification—inexperienced in these tasks—had not satisfied the necessary evidentiary requirements. Every file was deficient somehow. Not even one case was referred to the U.S. Attorney.

Efforts to press state government to implement other sections of the TCP (including carpools, express bus lanes, and inspection and maintenance) likewise were stalled. Although the Enforcement Division insisted that the TCP was law and would be enforced, EPA took no steps to force compliance. McGlennon feared that filing a suit against the state during a gubernatorial election would impede rather than facilitate state cooperation.

Making matters worse was the fact that the regional office could not keep up with the administrative demands of enforcing the Boston TCP. It literally was overwhelmed by paperwork. Thousands of inquiries from employers, municipal and university officials, and concerned citizens piled up awaiting response from harried regional staff. The agency simply lacked the resources to manage the enforcement effort.

There was confusion on policy, too. In a speech to a business group, Thompson implied that a "good faith effort" at compliance would qualify a company for a hardship exemption that Quarles had mentioned in his Boston press conference. When the *New York Times* printed the story, outraged officials in Washington accused Thompson of selling out the TCP.

The South Terminal Decision[5]

In late September 1974, while these administrative and policy fiascoes were still fresh, EPA's efforts to impose transportation controls on the Boston area were profoundly changed by a U.S. Court of Appeals decision in the *South Terminal* case. The previous fall, among nine lawsuits filed against the Boston TCP within 30 days of its promulgation, was one brought by a consortium of airlines and the Massachusetts Port Authority, challenging a ban on their plans to build a parking garage for their new terminal at Logan Airport.

The court's opinion was in many respects a victory for EPA. It held that the agency had conformed to appropriate procedural safeguards in proposing the TCP by holding a public hearing and revising the plan before final promulgation. It also held that EPA had ample legislative authority in the Clean Air Act to issue such regulations. But the court's decision cited possible problems with the technical data used by EPA to justify its regulations:

> EPA is said to have overestimated the photochemical oxidant problem in the Boston region. Most pertinent are petitioners' arguments that the key ambient air quality reading taken on one day at a monitoring device located at Wellington Circle [in Medford, a town some distance from the airport] must have come from a defective instrument. This single reading . . . was the basis for a region-wide estimate of the amount of hydrocarbon reduction required. . . . Petitioners point to a computer printout taken at that monitoring station; it contains a high number of "9999" readings which may indicate instrument malfunction. . . . On the present record we cannot say with confidence that the use of a single reading from a machine as to which objective readings suggest a substantial possibility of malfunction is sufficient to support EPA's photochemical oxidant determination.

On EPA's conclusion that the restrictions at Logan Airport were essential to control carbon monoxide emissions, the court noted that this finding was based on a single air quality reading taken in Kenmore Square in downtown Boston on one day in 1970. There was no data for Logan Airport itself or for the surrounding East Boston area:

> The special qualities of carbon monoxide, as compared to photochemical oxidants, make the absence of such data critical to any argument that Logan traffic should be controlled to protect East Boston. The EPA engineer states that "carbon monoxide is a highly localized pollutant which tends to stay fairly close to where it was emitted," and a report in the record indicates that "due to the localized nature of the problem, carbon monoxide concentrations need to be controlled within areas of blocks, not entire regions."

In conclusion, the court held that

> . . . as laymen we are in no position to know how much ultimate weight to give to these arguments, based as they are on technical assumptions. We can only say that the objections as to data and methodology seem too serious to us simply to pass by; they demand investigation and answer.

The court therefore ordered EPA to hold a new public hearing on the Boston plan and to revise the TCP light of evidence gathered and presented there.

167

Region I's Attitudes Soften

South Terminal's effect on Region I was profound. Nominally, it required the agency to remonitor air quality in and around Logan Airport and to redraft the Boston TCP. Practically, however, the court's decision gave freer rein to a sense of political realism that had begun to affect Region I's thinking about transportation controls.

Revising the TCP

Robert Thompson, whom McGlennon had assigned to coordinate the TCP Strategy Committee, was a major influence on the regional office's emerging redefinition of policy. Over the summer of 1974 he had come to understand the perspectives and fears of the business community, municipal officials, and others affected by the TCP. He also had come to appreciate the limitations of EPA's own capacity to plan and enforce transportation controls. As he noted:

> Implementation of the TCP is an incredibly sophisticated problem that requires a subtle knowledge of how government agencies work and what the perspective of different kinds of agencies is likely to be. You simply can't expect EPA engineers at GS-11 or GS-12 level to comprehend or act on these things. They just can't do it. Therefore, we came to the conclusion that if this policy was going to be successful, that state people were the only people who were going to make these political and policy judgments. They had grown up with the system and had the capabilities.

Therefore, as EPA began to rethink the TCP, Thompson recalled:

> I went directly to the people who had operational responsibility: the Department of Public Works, the Registry of Motor Vehicles, engineers on the tunnels and bridges that Massport controls, the Massachusetts Turnpike Authority, the Cambridge Commissioner of Traffic and Parking, and the Boston Commissioner of Traffic and Parking. I believed that if implementation was going to be successful, we needed personal relationships, and we needed to understand the detailed implementation problems that would arise.

As revision of the TCP began, Thompson found himself

> . . . the only one in EPA who could speak to many of the people in state government. McGlennon was distrusted, regarded as imperious. The enforcement director kept threatening to sue, which shows how well he got along with state people. The air quality people had their own hands full in reassessing the technical data.

Substantively, Thompson saw his job as

> . . . finding those policies that would in fact turn out to be viable. I wanted to discover what things EPA should insist on and what policies should be abandoned. There were essentially three categories: 1) what could and should be implemented with present resources and legal authority, 2) what could and

should be implemented when resources and authority became available, and 3) those policies that neither EPA nor the state thought should be implemented because they were politically infeasible.

These efforts were made more difficult by a transition in Massachusetts government. Governor Sargent, after turning back a challenge in the Republican primary, was defeated for reelection in November by Michael Dukakis, his Democratic opponent. Dukakis had been an early proponent of transportation controls, speaking out forcefully for their adoption at EPA's public hearing in 1973. But his current views were not precisely formulated, and it took some months for his major administrators to be appointed and to begin formulating policy on the TCP.

EPA regional officials devoted many hours to negotiating with business representatives about a replacement for the policy of reducing employee parking space by 25 percent, which business hated and which EPA came to regard as inequitable in its effects. State officials eventually decided to seek a 25 percent reduction in the number of single-passenger vehicles used for commuting. To satisfy business sentiment, they decided to state this as a goal rather than as a mandatory requirement. [6]

The apparent necessity for extreme measures in the new TCP crystallized a new regional office perspective. When the Region I air branch completed its remonitoring late in 1974, the results seemed to indicate that the pollution problem in Boston was so severe that both retrofit of older cars with emission control devices and gasoline rationing would be necessary to achieve the air quality standards by the deadlines in the Clean Air Act. Senior staff in Region I, recognizing that neither control measure was politically feasible in Massachusetts, began to recommend that EPA issue a "nonattainment" plan, which would require "reasonable" control measures but would not, even on paper, achieve the statutory goals. Officials in EPA headquarters in Washington vigorously resisted that idea, arguing that the statutory requirements must be met regardless of political opposition, if only to avoid litigation by environmental groups similar to that brought in 1973 by the Natural Resources Defense Council.[7] As Thompson recalled, "In Washington they were committed to holding the line, almost to the extent of leading a religious crusade."

It took a meeting with EPA Administrator Russell Train in late January 1975 to settle the matter. Train approved a compromise under which EPA would "announce" gas rationing as a measure to be implemented only if air quality standards were not achieved. Retrofit would be promulgated in the plan but "deferred," thus signaling that EPA did not intend to force it on the state. By these means the framework, if not the reality, of an attainment plan would be preserved. Shortly thereafter, however, recalculation of the technical data showed that gas rationing was not, in fact, required—although retrofit still was.[8]

When the proposed new TCP was published in the *Federal Register* on February 28, 1975, it was a less restrictive plan than the one promulgated in November 1973. (See "The Environmental Protection Agency and Transportation Controls (B)" pp. 152-153.) It did, however, impose some stringent controls. Among the new plan's provisions (See Exhibit 1, p. 156.) were:

1. A parking ban in the downtown core area from 7:30 to 9:30 a.m. and from 4 to 6 p.m.

2. A state-administered inspection and maintenance program for emission control devices.

3. A retrofit program imposed on pre-1975 vehicles. Implementation of this measure would be deferred indefinitely.

4. A parking freeze imposed on the core area and on Logan Airport.

5. A requirement that employers take steps to reduce one-passenger commuting by 25 percent.

6. Reserved lanes on major highways for carpools and express buses.

7. A state-sponsored carpool matching program.

The Public Hearing

EPA sponsored a public hearing on the proposed new regulations in late March. Michael Dukakis, the new governor, gave a guarded endorsement to the more modest elements of the plan, but he opposed retrofit and expressed reservations about an inspection and maintenance program. Business representatives attacked the provision involving the 25 percent reduction in single-passenger commuting vehicles. Because Washington had insisted that this be a mandatory measure, not just a goal as the regional office had agreed, the business community angrily questioned EPA's good faith. The South Terminal Corporation, unwilling to surrender its planned garage, presented data disputing the need for parking controls at Logan Airport. While the cities of Boston and Cambridge and a few environmental groups lent support to the proposed TCP, little backing was shown for strong transportation controls.[9]

Showdown in Washington

Recognizing the lack of support at the public hearing, Region I officials proposed that several provisions of the TCP be revised to make them more acceptable. Because these revisions were vehemently opposed by some key officials in EPA headquarters in Washington, the issues wound up being argued before Russell Train in May 1975. McGlennon insisted that EPA should, in effect, approve a nonattainment plan containing only control measures that were "reasonable under the circumstances." He argued that gas rationing and retrofit should remain out of the TCP to avoid jeopardizing other more feasible control measures. To include rationing and retrofit merely to ward off a citizen suit, McGlennon believed, would damage the agency's credibility because EPA had no current intention of implementing them. McGlennon also argued that the 25 percent reduction in single-passenger vehicles should be dropped because of local opposition. Despite strenuous disagreement by the EPA headquarters staff, Train accepted McGlennon's positions on the Boston TCP. Shortly afterwards one of the leading EPA hard-liners on the TCPs resigned from the agency.[10] The final version of the second Boston TCP was published in the *Federal Register* on June 12, 1975.

Implementing the Second Boston TCP

With policy making for the TCP largely complete, responsibility for managing its implementation began to pass to a small "mobile source emissions" staff in the Region I air branch. Because it was impossible for these half-dozen, mid-level EPA staffers—whose responsibilities also included the other New England states—to maintain detailed, day-to-day oversight of TCP implementation, they were highly dependent on public officials in state and local government to carry out the work. The regional office's role therefore changed to one of loosely monitoring the actions of others and periodically exhorting them to press ahead.

The State's Early Implementation Efforts

Throughout much of 1974 and 1975 the responsibility for implementing the TCP was in bureaucratic limbo in Massachusetts government.

During 1974 the Executive Office of Transportation and Construction, which had played the leading role in 1973 under Secretary Altshuler, was essentially inactive on the matter of EPA's transportation controls. The one exception was carpooling—a policy that Altshuler was quite interested in. Building on a program initiated by a Boston-area television station and an auto club, EOTC developed a $600,000 carpool program that was formally adopted by Altshuler shortly before the Sargent administration left office. The main approach of the program, run by the Massachusetts Department of Public Works, was an effort to make large employers the focal point for carpool formation.[11]

As the new administration organized in 1975, Governor Dukakis chose Fred Salvucci as transportation secretary. Salvucci formerly had been a transportation adviser to Boston's Mayor Kevin White. He had watched the TCP drama closely and was both sympathetic to its goals and keenly aware of its political pitfalls. He and his staff promoted the carpool program energeti-cally and worked closely with the city of Boston in developing procedures for the downtown parking freeze and the on-street parking ban (to be described below). But Salvucci and his staff limited their involvement in TCP implemen-tation to the projects that suited their own priorities; they did not seek or accept a broader role or public identification with TCP enforcement.

As the role of EOTC diminished, the Executive Office of Environmental Affairs (EOEA) gradually took on greater responsibility. When Secretary Altshuler dropped his active role in TCP policy making and implementation in 1974, Ray Rodriguez, the aide who had done much of his TCP staff work, took a new job with Secretary of Environmental Affairs Paul Foster. But, like Altshuler, Foster was preoccupied with other matters in the election year. Rodriguez's main TCP-related work was to shepherd EPA's Robert Thompson around state government, introducing him to key people as Thompson worked to find feasible control strategies for the second TCP. EOEA was a fledgling agency at this time; the state legislature had not yet finished establishing its operating departments. In fact, legal authority to regulate air pollution then resided with a division of the state Department of Public Health, which was not part of EOEA. It was not until July 1975 that the legislature created the new Department of Environmental Quality Engineering (DEQE) by transferring the air pollution unit in the Health Department to EOEA. Governor Dukakis named David Standley, former executive director of the Boston Air Pollution Control Board, to head this new department. Standley provided a focal point for the state's involvement in the control plan's implementation, but few of his staff were equally enthusiastic about the TCP. It took Standley a while to find subordinates who shared his concern. Ultimately these included Rodriguez and Anthony Cortese, who had played a key staff role for John McGlennon in 1973 when the EPA Region I office had been writing the first TCP. By 1976, DEQE was becoming an agency that could maintain effective liaison with EPA's regional office, on the one hand, and with EOTC, the city of Boston, and others responsible for carrying out the TCP's provisions, on the other hand.

The City of Boston's Implementation Efforts

The state was not the only unit of government that took responsibility for implementing provisions of the TCP. The city of Boston under Mayor Kevin White had been a firm supporter of EPA's regulatory policies and now assumed a leading role in two areas: the off-street commercial parking freeze and the on-street parking ban during rush hours.

The Freeze on Off-Street Commercial Parking. Even before the TCP was proposed, Mayor White had committed his administration to stabilizing or reducing peak-hour auto traffic entering the central area. In 1970 he publicly had pressed Governor Sargent to declare a moratorium on highway construction in the metropolitan area and had subsequently backed the governor's decision to discontinue several specific highway projects. When EPA was formulating the first TCP in 1973, White and his transportation and air pollution advisers met with EPA regional officials to advocate a freeze on the number of general-purpose, off-street commercial parking places in the central area. The White administration believed that placing responsibility for the freeze on EPA would allow the city to avoid the political onus of imposing it.

Once the freeze was part of the TCP, administrative procedures were necessary to enforce it. Although the TCP directly regulated only state government, the city of Boston had the administrative capacity, the detailed knowledge of local conditions, and the motivation to administer the freeze. During the last year of the Sargent administration, while the first TCP was in effect, the state took no action on the freeze, and EPA gave priority to enforcing other elements of the plan. After the Logan Airport legal challenge had been decided and EPA began revising the TCP in 1975, the city of Boston continued to support the parking freeze concept. As a result, even though Congress had curtailed EPA's authority to regulate parking, the freeze requirement remained in Boston's new plan.

Despite persistent support from key figures in the White administration, however, two years passed before the freeze was fully implemented. This delay resulted from disagreement over administrative procedures rather than opposition to the policy itself. Before it would delegate legal authority to the city, the state insisted that Boston work out detailed enforcement plans. More than a half-dozen city agencies eventually became involved in these discussions, including the Traffic and Parking, Building, and Real Property departments, the Boston Redevelopment Authority (BRA), the Air Pollution Control Commission (APCC), the zoning board, and the mayor's office.

The city first decided to control the number of parking spaces through zoning regulations, a method that involved persuading the independent zoning board to make parking a conditional land use so that permits could be required. The next step was to determine which city agency would be responsible for implementation. David Standley, the state commissioner of environmental quality engineering and formerly Mayor White's top air pollution aide, believed that the Traffic and Parking Department was unsympathetic to the purposes of the freeze and that the BRA, which itself leased parking lots to private operators in several development projects, would have a bureaucratic conflict of interest.

The proposed alternative was to delegate implementation authority to the city Air Pollution Control Commission (APCC), whose small staff would be assisted by the BRA transportation planning staff, which had no direct connection with that agency's parking facilities. Traffic and Parking, however, resisted designation of the APCC as the responsible agency, and the decision was complicated by the instability of the APCC at that time. Under severe budget pressure, the mayor had sharply cut APCC staff and was seriously considering abolishing the agency; in less than two years it had had three executive directors. It was unclear whether the APCC would have the capacity to administer the parking freeze, if it survived at all.

Developing detailed administrative procedures was another problem. Before the freeze, a parking lot operator needed to obtain permits from different city agencies depending upon whether it was to be an open-air or indoor facility. These departments therefore had to agree not to issue the other permits until a "freeze" permit had been granted.

In 1976, after more than a year of disagreement, the APCC, the Traffic and Parking Department, the Building Department, and the BRA signed a memo of understanding that set out implementation procedures. Although the APCC would administer the freeze, the commissioner of Traffic and Parking would become an *ex officio* member of the APCC so that his concerns would be represented. The other departments agreed that they would not issue any permit connected with a parking facility unless the applicant had already obtained a freeze permit from the APCC. Because this procedure satisfied state environmental officials, Governor Dukakis formally delegated authority for enforcing the parking freeze to city government.

Actually implementing the freeze required further work. First, it was necessary to determine the number of parking spaces in the city as of October 1973, the date specified in the EPA regulations. Although a comprehensive inventory had been prepared in spring 1973, the BRA transportation staff had to update this work laboriously. In addition, a dozen or so parking facilities had been granted temporary permits during a "build at your own risk" period after adoption of the TCP. These operators had to apply for freeze permits from the APCC, which then conducted public hearings to consider the applications. Virtually all were approved.

In the short run, the freeze procedures seemed to work well. The city owned a "bank" of obsolete or underutilized parking lots and garages; these could be shut down to accommodate desirable new parking facilities. The long-term outlook, however, was unclear. Because plans for several major development projects called for large amounts of parking, the bank of parking lots would be exhausted eventually. It remained to be seen how the freeze process would work when difficult choices between new and existing parking facilities were made.

The On-Street Parking Ban. As a deterrent to commuters, Boston's TCP restricted parking on all central area streets from 7:00 to 9:30 a.m. and from 4:00 to 6:00 p.m. Although supporting this provision, the White administration resisted implementation until it settled a dispute with the state over financing. The Traffic and Parking Department, constrained by the city's fiscal ills, insisted that its budget could not cover the $150,000 for street signs and posts needed to mark the affected area. The state, in turn, claimed that it had no funds for this purpose. For its part, EPA could provide no grants-in-aid to expedite enforcement of the ban. Although the city ultimately found the money, months of further delays resulted because the Traffic and Parking Department could not assign enough personnel to erect the signs quickly.

Once the signs were in place, the effectiveness of the parking ban depended on vigorous enforcement. A residential sticker system was devised so that only commuters would be affected. Four agencies then shared responsibility for ticketing violators: the Police Department and the Traffic and Parking Department's meter maids had overlapping jurisdiction on most city streets; the Metropolitan District Commission (MDC), a state agency, patrolled certain major access roads to the city as well as streets within parks; and the Capitol Police covered streets adjacent to the statehouse and other state buildings. These agencies varied significantly in how energetically they enforced the regulation. Although the Boston police accepted only a small role in enforcement, Traffic and Parking reassigned a number of meter maids to cover the affected areas during the restricted hours. Because the meter maid force was being reduced for budgetary reasons, however, there were simply not enough personnel to do the job thoroughly unless other enforcement priorities were changed. Under pressure from state environmental officials, the MDC police eventually assigned five officers to enforcement duty, while the Capitol Police did little enforcement work.

Enforcement efforts generated a number of citizen complaints that helped reduce the vigor of enforcement. Within the MDC's jurisdiction, for example, a Montessori school in the Fenway district of Boston wanted to have a 15-minute parking limit so that parents could drop off children; a dental clinic wanted a two-hour parking limit to accommodate its patients; female students at Wheelock College, concerned about the safety of the subway system, resisted regulations that would prevent them from driving to school; and the Museum of Fine Arts and other local employers worried about how their workers would be affected.

In the long run, the ban's effectiveness depended on both the continued allocation of personnel by enforcement agencies and the deterrent of ticketing. Because no agency had sufficient manpower to enforce all parking restrictions in its jurisdiction, however, enforcement of *any* restriction was inevitably selective. In addition the power of ticketing as a deterrent to illegal parking was considerably reduced by the city's ineffectiveness in collecting fines for parking violations.

The Reserved Lane for Buses and Carpools[12]

The TCP required the state to initiate special reserved lanes on expressways for use only by buses and carpools. By speeding up the commuting trip for these vehicles, the intent was to encourage other motorists to leave their own autos home. EOTC completed studies of this option on a number of major arteries in the metropolitan area. In early 1976 Transportation Secretary Salvucci and Department of Public Works Commissioner John Carroll decided to undertake an experiment on the southeast expressway by instituting a reserved lane for buses and cars with three or more occupants. Although they had sufficient legal authority to implement the plan, they presented the idea for comment to leaders of the state legislature's Joint Committee on Transportation. Recognizing the potential for public controversy when expressway access was regulated, Salvucci and Carroll hoped to forestall negative legislative action: a bill that would explicitly prevent them from creating a reserved lane.

As a result of these consultations, Salvucci and Carroll decided to postpone implementation of the reserved lane until 1977. Transportation Committee leaders argued that it would be difficult to prevent restrictive legislation during an election year if the public complained vehemently. To minimize controversy in any event, they strongly recommended that the lane be voluntary—in other words, that violators not be ticketed.

Accepting a year's delay, therefore, transportation policy makers set implementation of the reserved lane for the spring of 1977. The lane would extend eight miles along the southeast expressway, beginning at a point just north of the intersection with Route 128 in Quincy and ending at the Massachusetts Avenue interchange in Boston. During the morning peak period, from 6:30 to 9:30 a.m., the far left lane on the northbound side would be open only to buses and carpools with at least three occupants. For safety reasons, motorists would have access to the reserved lane only at its entrance; officials did not want vehicles moving in and out of the expressway's high-speed lane. To separate the reserved lane from the concurrent flow of traffic each day, DPW personnel each morning would insert plastic posts into metal sleeves in the highway.

The lane was announced to the public as a temporary measure designed to reduce congestion resulting from reconstruction of the bridge decks at the Massachusetts Avenue interchange. Officials in the Executive Office of Transportation and Construction planned that, if successful, the reserved lane would be a permanent traffic control measure. To avoid federal requirements for an Environmental Impact Statement and public hearing, the project was wholly funded from the state budget.

Phase 1 of the project began May 4, 1977, one month before bridge reconstruction started. It was preceded by an extensive publicity campaign urging commuters to form carpools or consider alternate routes to Boston. Phase 2 began June 1 when bridge reconstruction commenced. During both Phases 1 and 2, compliance with the restriction was voluntary. Legislative leaders strongly preferred this arrangement, and, in any event, enforcement posed certain difficulties for EOTC. Nonetheless, state officials sought to discourage violators by stationing a police cruiser in Quincy at the reserved lane entrance.

Public reaction to the reserved lane was favorable during Phases 1 and 2. Because the lane was voluntary and seemingly necessary to prevent tie-ups during bridge reconstruction, critical comments were few. News reports and editorials supported the experiment. In the legislature, several South Shore representatives called for better transit options while the lane was in force. A bill also was filed that would have removed Department of Public Works (DPW) authority to operate a reserved lane, but legislative leaders, consistent with their agreement with Salvucci, bottled it up in committee.

Voluntary compliance with the reserved lane restrictions was far from universal. During Phase 1 only 21 percent of the vehicles in the lane were entitled to be there, and that figure declined to 19 percent during Phase 2. Overall, though, despite wholesale violations of the reserved lane restrictions, travel times were shorter for traffic in *all* lanes during Phases 1 and 2.

By midsummer, however, state officials had decided to make the restrictions mandatory and to enforce them stringently. The ready visibility of violators had evoked considerable pressure from citizens and the news media to force them to comply. With voluntary compliance declining, moreover, there was danger that the violations would degrade the service benefits made possible for buses and carpools. Informing the legislative leaders of his plans, Salvucci was counseled not to proceed, but he felt there was no choice.

Because it was too dangerous to pull violators over to the side of the road from the high-speed lane, state officials decided that the restrictions would be enforced by having police record the license numbers of noncomplying vehicles and issue a citation by mail. It took more than two months, however, to implement this decision. Although a similar system had been used for years to apprehend toll violators on the Massachusetts Turnpike, several legal issues needed resolution. Ultimately, the state attorney general held that the DPW could issue an administrative regulation making the restrictions mandatory and categorizing them as moving vehicle violations so that drivers could not ignore them like parking tickets. With this decision the DPW then had to negotiate with both the state police (whose jurisdiction covered the reserved lane section between Route 128 and Neponset Circle) and the Metropolitan District Commission police (responsible for the rest of the lane) over the feasibility of the enforcement scheme and their willingness to assign enough personnel to do the job effectively. It also was necessary to brief personnel in the several district courts that would have jurisdiction over the tickets so that they would understand the new regulation and accord priority to enforcement. Once all of these preparations were completed, the DPW made extensive efforts to publicize the new mandatory regulations through press releases, public meetings, and notification of South Shore elected officials.

Enforcement of the mandatory restrictions, marking the beginning of Phase 3 of the reserved lane experiment, began on October 18. Its impact was immediate and dramatic. Travel time in the reserved lane did not change appreciably; but, as violators shifted out of the reserved lane, travel time increased substantially in the *un*reserved lanes. For example, from 7:30 to 8:00 a.m. it rose from 24 to 40 minutes.

177

Negative publicity and citizen complaints were extensive. TV and radio coverage at the onset of enforcement highlighted the delays. The *Herald-American,* one of Boston's two daily newspapers, published front-page columns highly critical of the mandatory restrictions and within a week denounced the experiment in its lead editorial as a "flop." Angry commuters protested by telephone and letter to the DPW, Secretary Salvucci, the police, their legislators, and Governor Dukakis.

No spontaneous public support arose for the reserved lane. DPW Commissioner Carroll personally sought support from the private bus companies but with little result. Other state officials unsuccessfully sought to organize backing from bus riders and environmental groups.

As a result of the uproar, the state legislature mobilized against the experiment. A bill to ban the reserved lane altogether was reactivated, and a new proposal to permit two-occupant vehicles to use the lane was introduced.

State officials felt that neither bill was acceptable. Allowing two-occupant cars in the reserved lane would have caused enough congestion to all but eliminate the travel time improvements and make it more difficult to enforce compliance. In that event, the concept would have been discredited. Commissioner Carroll, moreover, was considering the possibility of a capital construction alternative—two new, reversible, reserved lanes to be built in the expressway median—that he feared would be jeopardized by a continuing public outcry against the current experiment. Neither did Secretary Salvucci want to waste his political resources in a doomed cause. At the same time, expressions of concern were coming from the governor's office. Facing a Democratic primary challenge in his reelection bid in 1978, Governor Dukakis was not eager to face the prospect of either vetoing or acquiescing in legislative restrictions on the reserved lane. His announced challenger, Edward King, already had made clear that highways would be an important election issue. Despite his support for the reserved-lane concept, the governor wanted to avoid becoming too closely identified with a very unpopular policy.

Given the strength of public opposition and the political circumstances, state policy makers explicitly decided to "cut their losses." Commissioner Carroll therefore announced at a November 2 legislative hearing that the reserved lane was being terminated. After only two and a half weeks of mandatory restrictions, the project had died.

The TCP in Late 1977

By the late fall of 1977—more than two years after promulgation of the second Boston TCP—the elements of the plan were in various stages of implementation. A carpool matching program was under way at EOTC; the on-street parking ban was in effect but only spottily enforced; the parking freeze was working effectively; a reserved expressway lane for carpools and buses had proven to be a political disaster. One other measure—an inspection and maintenance program for auto emission control devices—seemed hopelessly stalled in the legislature.

EPA's regional office watched these efforts, but staff limitations affected its ability to monitor, let alone actively intervene, except on infrequent occasions. EPA had long since given up its attempt to put teeth in the TCPs.

NOTES

1. See Michael Padnos and Edward I. Selig, "Transportation Controls in Boston: The Plan that Failed," an unpublished paper commissioned by the American Bar Foundation and the National Academy of Sciences (June 30, 1976), 71-73.
2. Ibid., 73-75.
3. Ibid., 74-77.
4. Ibid., 77-82.
5. Ibid., 82-88.
6. Ibid., 92-93.
7. Ibid., 93-94.
8. Ibid., 94-55.
9. Ibid., 98-101.
10. Ibid., 101-107.
11. Ibid., 89-90.
12. This section draws on information contained in Daniel Brand et al., "Southeast Expressway Reserved Lane for Buses and Carpools," presented at the Annual Meeting of the Transportation Research Board, Washington, D.C., January 1978.

Discussion Questions

1. Why did the Boston Transportation Control Plan become a matter of such high priority for John McGlennon and the EPA regional office?

2. What administrative problems arose as the regional office tried to enforce the TCP provisions? To what extent might these have been avoided?

3. What rationale did Robert Thompson have for "softening" the regional office's stance on revising and enforcing the Boston TCP?

4. Why was there so wide a policy gap between the regional office and the "hardliners" in EPA's Washington headquarters?

5. Compare and contrast the implementation problems that emerged in devising and enforcing the parking freeze, the on-street parking ban, and the reserved lane for buses and carpools.

6. Would a tougher stance by the EPA regional office have improved or accelerated enforcement of the second Boston TCP?

Suggestions for Further Reading

Berman, Paul. "The Study of Macro- and Micro-Implementation." *Public Policy,* Spring 1978. A theoretical perspective on the problems of implementing intergovernmental policy.

Berman, Paul. "Thinking About Programmed and Adaptive Implementation: Matching Strategies to Situations" in *Why Policies Succeed or Fail,* Helen Ingram and Dean Mann, eds. Beverly Hills, Calif.: Sage Publications, 1980, 205-227. An analysis of how the problems of program implementation vary under differing administrative and political circumstances.

Ingram, Helen. "Policy Implementation Through Bargaining: The Case of Federal Grants-in-Aid." *Public Policy,* Fall 1977, 499-526. An assessment of the limits of federal influence in intergovernmental program management.

McKean, Ronald N. "Enforcement Costs in Environmental and Safety Regulation." *Policy Analysis,* Summer 1980, 269-289. Analysis of an often-ignored dimension of regulatory policy making and implementation.

Sabatier, Paul, and Mazmanian, Daniel. "The Conditions of Effective Implementation: A Guide to Accomplishing Policy Objectives." *Policy Analysis,* Fall 1979, 481-504. A perspective on the factors that promote and impede successful policy implementation.

II. The System at Work: Local Implementation of Federal Programs

4. RESTRICTING TRAFFIC ON WASHINGTON STREET

5. COMMUNITY DEVELOPMENT IN GAINESVILLE (A, B, C)

4. *Restricting Traffic on Washington Street*

The federal government frequently intends that its grant programs will spur innovation in state and local government. The genesis of these programs lies in the perception by Congress or a federal agency that some issue of public policy is not being adequately handled. A new grant program may be created to encourage state and local governments to work on the problem by providing the financial means to make action feasible.

When the federal program's architects want to steer grant recipients in a particular policy direction, they are likely to choose a *project* grant as the funding mechanism. Where that policy direction is experimental, they are likely to use a special kind of project grant—a *demonstration* grant. By financing a specific program idea in a limited number of sites, a demonstration is, in one sense, a test of the idea's feasibility and effectiveness. At least as important, however, a demonstration may be part of a marketing strategy to convince state or local officials (and frequently others in the federal government) that a program merits more financial support and widespread adoption.

That marketing effort is intended to work in several phases. First, funds are given to one or more jurisdictions to induce them to adopt the program or policy innovation. Then the results of that adoption are monitored and evaluated. If the outcome is favorable, the federal agency will then try to persuade the president and Congress to provide more funds and other jurisdictions to adopt the idea.

The first step, in many ways, is most critical. Federal officials hope that enactment of a new grant program will spur local innovation by making an issue more visible and significant to public officials, interest groups, and citizens—in effect, enhancing the issue's place on the jurisdiction's policy agenda. A new grant program also can provide funds that public officials can steer to a new purpose with fewer political risks than if they were compelled to reallocate funds from an existing program or to raise new revenue through taxes. For the state or local government, therefore, the grant program is a tangible incentive to alter its existing policies.

Yet creation of a new federal program cannot guarantee that state and local governments will participate or take action consistent with federal intent. Almost never does a new federal program enter a total political or policy vacuum at the state or local level; such initiatives must fit into an on-going pattern of politics and decision making related to the grant program. Federal policy goals may be only partly, or not at all, shared by officials at other levels of government. Even if these individuals go ahead with the program, they may try to use the grant money to advance their own purposes—in addition to or instead of the federal goals. Moreover, change may seem threatening to elected officials wary of negative constituent reaction, to public agencies that hold contrary policy views or that do not wish to commit resources and energy to a new program, to interest groups that fear damage to vital concerns, and to a public-at-large often suspicious of ideas seemingly imposed from outside. It is possible, too, that even if favorable attitudes exist about the substance of the program, the grant may be an inadequate financial subsidy. As a result of these factors, the incentive effects of a federal grant are only one of a variety of forces that determine which policies are adopted and implemented.

In "Restricting Traffic on Washington Street," officials in the U.S. Urban Mass Transportation Administration (UMTA), an agency within the U.S. Department of Transportation, use a demonstration grant to solicit Boston's interest in a project to limit automobile access to the downtown shopping district. The principal focus of the case is how that grant affects the policy process in Boston's city government. It is about grantsmanship, constituency building, and the early phases of grant implementation.

By first exploring earlier attempts to make Boston's main retail area more accessible to pedestrians, the case offers insight into the attitudes of important figures in city government and the business community, their sources of policy influence, and the nature of city decision-making processes. That information helps a reader assess how the federal demonstration program might affect the city's willingness to participate in the demonstration.

Much of this case concerns constituency building. Even though favorably disposed toward UMTA's policy, the mayor and his staff were not in a position politically to impose auto restrictions against the objections of major city agencies and important sectors of the city's business community. To move forward with the auto-restriction plan, the city administration had to develop wider support for the idea.

The problem of constituency building thus highlights the critical role of *policy entrepreneurs* in promoting innovative policies. As this term's adaptation from economics suggests, policy entrepreneurs are individuals whose resources, skills, and efforts are essential to launching a new public policy "enterprise" and making it work. As the term implies, the entrepreneur's role involves the "investment" of his or her political "capital" (including time, staff, budget, and political influence) in a project that carries an inherent risk of failure but that also promises possible gain (such as advancing one's policy objectives or career). While a policy entrepreneur sometimes independently has sufficient resources to make innovation possible, the role more frequently requires skillful coalition building to bring together enough resources to proceed.

"Restricting Traffic on Washington Street" looks closely at the efforts of two policy entrepreneurs. John Sloan, the redevelopment authority staff member responsible for the Washington Street Mall project, must win support from both inside and outside city government, particularly in the business community. When UMTA later proposes a substantial expansion of the Washington Street Mall, Emily Lloyd, head of the mayor's transportation policy staff, faces an even more complex entrepreneurial challenge; she must make the plan acceptable to city government, win support in the business community, and maintain UMTA's willingness to award the demonstration grant. The possible solutions to Lloyd's dilemma suggest a good deal about the potential—and the limits—of federal aid in promoting policy innovation in state and local government.

THE CAST

Kevin H. White	mayor of Boston
Robert Vey	deputy mayor of Boston
Robert Kenney	BRA director
John Sloan	BRA project director, Washington Street Mall
William Noonan	commissioner of Traffic and Parking
Emily Lloyd	chief, mayor's transportation policy staff
Sue Clippinger	member, mayor's transportation policy staff
Alex Taft	member, mayor's transportation policy staff
Alvin Schmertzler	chairman, Winter Street Association
BRA	Boston Redevelopment Authority
CCBD	Committee for Central Business District
ARZ	auto-restricted zone

UMTA	Urban Mass Transportation Administration
Victor Gruen Associates	planning/architectural firm
Jordan Marsh	Boston department store
Gilchrist's	Boston department store
Filene's	Boston department store
Retail Trade Board	Boston merchants association
Winter Street Association	organization of small retailers

CHRONOLOGY

Late 1973	BRA Director Robert Kenney revives the Washington Street Mall concept and selects John Sloan as project manager.
January-December 1974	John Sloan begins planning for Washington Street Mall, discussing project with merchants and city departments and developing a tentative proposal.
1975	
January-July	Sloan seeks allies for his plan, including Emily Lloyd, the Winter Street merchants, and the Retail Trade Board.
July	Mayor White tentatively approves the Mall idea.
September	UMTA solicits Boston's participation in the ARZ demonstration program.
July 1975-April 1976	The BRA conducts further policy discussions with city departments and prepares detailed designs for the Washington Street Mall.
1976	
January	UMTA consultants begin site visits to select cities for detailed planning studies for the ARZ demonstration.

April	UMTA selects Boston as one of five finalists for ARZ demonstration and commences detailed planning.
April	Commissioner Noonan runs his own test of the Washington Street Mall plan; Deputy Mayor Vey gives project final approval.
July	Construction of Washington Street Mall facilities begins.
October	UMTA consultants propose extensive ARZ for downtown retail districts.

THE CASE

Washington Street is the lifeline of one of Boston's major retail shopping areas. A multitude of stores, restaurants, and entertainment spots are closely packed along its sidewalks and a number of small, adjacent side streets. The area is the home of Boston's two department store giants, Jordan Marsh and Filene's, and of dozens of smaller stores that sell everything from clothing and shoes to candy and books. It includes a number of dining and entertainment spots, including the Parker House (one of the city's finest hotels), the Orpheum Theater, and the "Combat Zone" (an "adult entertainment district" in which pornographic book stores, movie theaters, and "topless and bottomless" bars are concentrated).

In October 1976 a team of consultants working for the federal Urban Mass Transportation Administration (UMTA), a unit of the U.S. Department of Transportation, presented city officials with a dramatic plan to create an extensive auto-restricted zone (ARZ) on Washington Street and several side streets. The consultants proposed entirely closing some streets to traffic and restricting others only to transit and delivery vehicles. Throughout the entire area pedestrians would be able to move freely, aided by a shuttle bus system.

This case was written by Arnold M. Howitt and Kathryn D. Haslanger, with the research assistance of Ben Dansker, Ernest G. Niemi, and Mary McShane. Portions of the research were completed under grant MA-11-0007, from the Urban Mass Transportation Administration, U.S. Department of Transportation.

For Emily Lloyd, head of Boston Mayor Kevin H. White's transportation policy staff, and her two aides, Sue Clippinger and Alex Taft, the UMTA consultants' plan created a difficult dilemma. The proposal was consistent with the mayor's long-range policy, but it pushed "too far, too fast," threatening to upset a delicate political and administrative coalition that Lloyd and her staff had helped to build and that had resulted already in more modest auto restrictions along Washington Street.

Downtown Traffic Restraints: Genesis of an Idea

The idea of restricting traffic on Washington Street went back to the early 1960s when Mayor John F. Collins and his aggressive redevelopment administrator, Edward Logue, were developing ambitious plans for downtown urban renewal. At the mayor's urging, a group of prominent businessmen formed the Committee for the Central Business District (CCBD) to help the city decide how to rebuild the retail shopping area. The CCBD, in turn, commissioned a study by Victor Gruen Associates, architectural and planning consultants. Gruen returned with a bold proposal that, in part, called for total pedestrianization of several blocks on Washington Street and two adjacent side streets, Summer and Winter streets. Gruen also proposed construction of underground truck delivery tunnels and a huge second-story walkway between the retail area and South Station, a nearby railroad terminal.

Reaction to the auto restrictions in the Gruen plan was largely negative. Although some small retailers were excited at the potential of pedestrianization for creating new business, the major department stores and others were skeptical. They particularly were concerned about impediments to delivery service—and were not reassured that tunnels were a feasible answer. They also were worried that pedestrianization would drive business away rather than attract it; people who could not drive their cars in the downtown area might not come at all. In the meantime the U.S. Department of Housing and Urban Development (HUD) let Boston redevelopment officials know that they would not receive the $77 million allotment necessary to proceed with the Gruen plan. HUD's decision killed plans for the pedestrian mall as well as other parts of the project, and the CCBD eventually disbanded.

However, the Boston Redevelopment Authority (BRA) never entirely lost interest in the project. By the early 1970s, under Director Robert Kenney, the BRA again turned attention to development of Washington Street. Several major projects were under consideration, including the privately financed construction of a new Jordan Marsh store and the publicly assisted development of a massive retail complex, Lafayette Place. In this atmosphere in late 1973, interest in the pedestrian mall was rekindled. To manage BRA planning Kenney selected John Sloan, a young architect on his urban design staff who had acquired a reputation for "getting things done."

Testing the Waters—Sloan's Work Begins

Recognizing that the mall never would be built unless the local merchants wanted it, in 1974 Sloan began soliciting their ideas about how to make the Washington Street environment more attractive to pedestrians. Sloan concentrated on small merchants first, anticipating that the major department stores would resist the idea. Even though Sloan had some strong opinions about what might be appropriate, he took no architectural drawings with him. To make the merchants feel they truly were being consulted before plans were drafted, he sketched out his ideas "on the back of an envelope" during informal conversations. These discussions showed Sloan that the small merchants were interested in the mall concept but were cautious about its potential impact on retail sales. Because their business was being diverted to suburban shopping centers, they were willing to contemplate innovative action but felt uneasy about the risks of dramatic change.

To develop support for his ideas, Sloan conducted studies of the amount of pedestrian and automobile traffic on Washington Street. According to his calculations, eight times as many pedestrians as auto passengers used the area, but pedestrians used only one fourth of the street space. Devoting more space to pedestrians, Sloan argued, would attract more shoppers to the downtown; they would have the chance to window-shop instead of being hurried along by the crowd or forced into the street by the crush on the sidewalks. Auto restrictions would make the retail district's physical environment more like the suburban shopping centers that were draining customers away from downtown Boston.

Sloan also began to hold meetings with various city departments whose operations would be affected by the Washington Street Mall. The BRA, an organization of several hundred professionals, is Boston's planning and redevelopment agency. But the BRA has no operating responsibilities; when its plans are completed, they are turned over to private interests or public agencies. Among the city agencies concerned with the mall project were the Public Works Department, which handles street construction and resurfacing; the Traffic and Parking Department, which is responsible for traffic control, parking facilities, and the "meter maids," who enforce parking ordinances; the Police and Fire Departments, which are concerned with public safety considerations; and the Law Department, whose attorneys give advice on legal questions.

Legally, the decision ultimately rested with the city's Public Improvement Commission (PIC), which consisted of the commissioners of Public Works, Traffic and Parking, Real Property, and Buildings. Boston's government structure creates a strong executive branch, so the city council had no role to play. By city ordinance, all street changes must be approved by the PIC. In principle, the PIC members are free to rule independently on proposed street changes; the mayor has no direct authority. In practice, however, because all four members hold their jobs "at the pleasure of the Mayor," they generally are responsive to issues on which he takes a clear stand. But the mayor does not routinely take a stand on most such issues. He regards the commissioners as both his experts and political advisers; often, therefore, he allows their judgment to shape his reactions to issues. Usually only when there is substantial disagreement among the PIC members—or among other advisers or agencies—does the mayor become deeply involved in such matters.

At this stage Mayor White was neither deeply involved in the planning nor committed to the mall project. BRA Director Kenney knew that the concept was consistent with White's general views on downtown development, and it is likely that he briefed the mayor on the planning process. Although they expected opposition from some city departments, Kenney and Sloan made no effort to engage the mayor directly in the policy discussions. When more detailed plans were ready, when other city agencies had commented on them, and when the merchants' sentiments had been probed, the BRA would seek the mayor's backing for the project.

Although simultaneously working on other projects throughout 1974, Sloan proceeded with the Washington Street Mall planning. After several months a specific proposal began to take shape: The mall would stretch from School Street to Winter Street; all but one lane of traffic would be barred from Washington Street; sidewalks would be widened substantially; benches and other pedestrian amenities would be installed; and a clear plastic canopy would be erected to "weatherproof" the pedestrian area.

The opposition Kenney and Sloan had anticipated developed quickly from several directions. The principal opponent was William Noonan, commissioner of Traffic and Parking, a traffic engineer with years of experience in city government, who reputedly was influential with both the major downtown merchants and with the mayor. Noonan feared the mall's impact on traffic circulation in the "Mickey Mouse maze" of old, narrow, downtown streets. To him, the issue was how to remove lanes from existing streets without enhancing traffic volume elsewhere. He argued that no other northbound street existed to accommodate the displaced traffic and, as a result, there would be severe traffic jams in adjacent areas. Moreover, he believed it was foolish to expect a single lane of cars to move on Washington Street. His department's studies had shown that most motorists were headed for downtown destinations and therefore wanted to park nearby; in addition, delivery vehicles frequently stopped along the street to bring cartons into stores. If only one travel lane were open, one illegal parker could totally clog Washington Street; and no one could expect anything close to 100 percent enforcement of parking regulations.

Besides these misgivings, Noonan believed that merchants who supported the mall plan were being misled: "I can sell you the greatest disaster in the world by telling you only part of the story," he said. What Sloan saw as improvements in the downtown environment, Noonan regarded as degradations in the traffic circulation system.

The Police and Fire departments also criticized Sloan's plan. Along with Noonan, they were worried that emergency vehicles—police cars, fire equipment, and ambulances—would be unable to maneuver in the downtown area. The Fire Department also was concerned that the plastic canopy would be a fire hazard or that it would make getting fire ladders up to second story windows difficult.

Building Support for the Washington Street Mall

Sloan's planning efforts and discussions with city agencies occupied most of 1974. By early 1975, frustrated by the resistance he was encountering, Sloan began to line up allies who would help him move the project along.

One supporter was Emily Lloyd, chief of Mayor White's small transportation policy staff. The staff had several responsibilities. First, it expedited action by city government on projects that the mayor was particularly interested in. Second, it monitored the activities of city agencies to identify issues with which the mayor should be concerned. Finally, the staff was permitted to nurture its own policy ideas until they were developed sufficiently to present to the mayor for consideration. Lloyd and her staff maintained both professional and political perspectives on transportation issues; they saw themselves advancing sound policy while also being protective of the mayor's political interests.

Lloyd and her aides, Sue Clippinger and Alex Taft, felt that the Washington Street Mall was an excellent project from both perspectives. If successful it would contribute to the downtown environment they knew White believed in, and they thought that the problems raised by Noonan and other commissioners could be overcome. They believed that the mayor ultimately would back the project, but knew he would want to see a supportive constituency among the merchants as well as his commissioners. Therefore, they became increasingly involved in Sloan's efforts to mobilize support for the mall project.

Sloan soon found more support in the merchant community. Alvin Schmertzler, vice president of Miles Variety Shop on Winter Street, was particularly receptive to Sloan's proposal. For years he had watched city government provide new street lights or paving to other downtown areas and had been trying to obtain similar improvements for Winter Street. With some encouragement from the BRA, he had begun to meet with other retailers to discuss ways to upgrade the area. Schmertzler was intrigued with the mall proposal because he had been impressed by similar projects in several European cities. In early 1975 Schmertzler wrote to the BRA on behalf of other Winter Street merchants, requesting that the street become a pedestrian way. Sloan urged Schmertzler to organize a formal association of local merchants, arguing that they would command greater attention and wield greater influence if city government believed they were a permanent watchdog group for Winter Street interests. Sloan advised the fledgling association about organizational tactics and helped them get stationery printed.

When Sloan felt that the small retailers were convinced of the mall's desirability, he urged them to begin a letter writing campaign to demonstrate their support. Sloan even drafted some of the merchants' first letters to Mayor White. (The mayor sent these letters to the BRA, where they routinely were channeled to Sloan as project coordinator. Sloan thus found himself writing replies for the mayor's signature to letters he originally had written himself.) Sloan also encouraged the merchants to write letters to Commissioner Noonan, who remained adamantly opposed to the mall plan.

At the same time, to expand his base of support, Sloan began talking with the Retail Trade Board, the primary organization of downtown merchants. The board moved carefully on controversial matters and tended to wait until its members reached agreement before taking public stands. The board was particularly sensitive to the opinions of Washington Street's major retailers; and Jordan Marsh, Filene's, and Gilchrist's did not respond favorably to Sloan's ideas. Their opposition stemmed from two sources. First, these retailers, much more than the small shopkeepers, equated cars with customers. They believed persons dependent on public transportation were less likely to be good customers than persons traveling by automobile. They were skeptical about the project because they feared that reducing auto access would decrease their sales volume. Second, they were concerned that vehicles delivering goods to their stores would be inconvenienced by the restrictions. They worried that delivery trucks would not be able to get through if the number of traffic lanes were reduced.

Sloan began meeting individually with key executives of the major stores, trying to win their support. These stores were the key to the downtown's economic health because, as large employers and attractive shopping places, they drew many people into the downtown area. Their views also carried weight with the editorial writers of the city's major newspapers. Consequently, the department stores were both directly and indirectly influential with the mayor. Their importance to Boston's economy assured them a full hearing. Furthermore, Mayor White would hesitate to identify himself with a proposal that the newspapers might tell the city's voters was economically irresponsible.

Sloan found that the department stores were not yet ready to take a firm stand. On one hand, they were suspicious of the project—all the more because

Noonan, whom they respected, was so strongly opposed. On the other hand, they were sensitive to the support evident among the small merchants. Filene's and Gilchrist's eventually were willing to go along with the mall project. Jordan Marsh was less eager to be accommodating; but, because its new building was under construction, it was not willing to block a plan that the BRA strongly favored. The BRA was too important for Jordan Marsh to anger.

In a meeting with top BRA staff in July 1975 Mayor White was presented with the supportive letters of many merchants as well as the personal urging of his own transportation adviser and the BRA director. In this atmosphere he agreed to the idea of a Washington Street Mall. Although he still was concerned with the large retailers' response, the project appealed to him. He did not see the mall as causing other major political risks; while it would inconvenience some motorists, he believed that they primarily would be suburban commuters and not Boston voters; he would not have to pay politically for their disapproval. City residents presumably would benefit from the project because it would create a stronger local economy and a more attractive place for them to shop. Disregarding memos from Noonan urging him to stop the project, the mayor agreed to let it proceed with the understanding that the BRA would make an effort to meet the objections of other city departments.

With the mayor's intentions known, Sloan's job became easier. White's support simplified Sloan's task of developing a proposal with which the reluctant city departments would agree. Although the mayor's approval did not obviate Sloan's need to compromise, it decreased the number and extent of changes he was compelled to make by increasing the bureaucratic cost of opposition. A department was less likely to block the project's development when it knew that the mayor wanted it to go forward.

Two changes were made in subsequent policy discussions in 1975. First, to accommodate the objections of the Traffic and Parking, Police, and Fire Departments, the BRA agreed to permit two lanes of traffic on Washington Street. Second, to reassure merchants who feared an adverse impact on retail sales, the BRA promised to design all physical construction as temporary facilities; if a test proved disastrous, the experiment could easily be dismantled. The BRA, however, insisted that physical improvements be attractive and substantial; it knew that mall experiments elsewhere sometimes had failed because not enough amenities were provided to lure pedestrians to the area.

The Retail Trade Board endorsed the project with these changes, and the mayor agreed to spend approximately $500,000 on the new facilities. These funds came from a bond issue for general downtown capital improvements that the city council earlier had approved.

With these agreements in hand, the BRA commissioned detailed architectural designs, which were completed in spring 1976. When Noonan saw the finished designs, however, he was furious: the "temporary" facilities looked permanent to him. He began to think that the BRA was backing out of its agreement to construct a temporary facility. Sloan defended the architect's work, saying that everything was demountable and that the project could be removed after a year if the results were not satisfactory. Sloan stressed that if the project were to succeed, the amenities had to be substantial enough to attract additional pedestrians. The BRA did not want to jeopardize the entire project by constructing incomplete and ugly temporary facilities.

To Noonan, however, the situation appeared otherwise. He called Deputy Mayor Robert Vey, who had been assigned to oversee city development projects, to inform him of the problem and insist that there be a test of the mall concept before construction began. On April 22, 1976, Noonan instructed a traffic and parking crew to simulate Sloan's proposed circulation scheme for Washington Street by using forty traffic barrels and some blinking lights. Little advance warning was given to the public. Motorists knocked over barrels, delivery trucks did not know where to stop, and traffic began to get snarled.

Merchants called the BRA, assuming it was responsible, to demand that the barrels be removed. The incident took Sloan totally by surprise. He called Emily Lloyd to find out what was going on. Fearing that Noonan's actions would sabotage the mall project by antagonizing the merchants, Sloan quickly gathered a few co-workers, rented a Hertz van, and swooped down Washington Street stuffing the barrels and flashers into the truck, hiding them at the BRA's waterfront project site. Noonan called on the police to trace the van; when he discovered the identity of the "thief," he bitterly complained to Deputy Mayor Vey.

Sloan and BRA Director Kenney met with Vey to discuss the incident and decide whether to modify the architect's plans. Acting at the direction of the mayor, Vey decided to go ahead with the project, making some design concessions to the indignant Noonan. With the mayor's support for the project apparent, the Public Improvements Commission approved the street changes. Construction contracts were put out for bid, and the project was completed in mid-1977.

UMTA's ARZ Demonstration Program

Even before the Washington Street Mall issue was settled, city officials began considering further auto restrictions for Washington Street and its environs. In September 1975 the BRA was approached by the federal Urban Mass Transportation Administration (UMTA) to see if Boston might be interested in competing for a grant to plan an auto-restricted zone (ARZ) in the retail district.

This ARZ demonstration grant was part of a larger program created by

Congress to encourage innovation in urban transportation systems. The program was overseen by the Service and Methods Demonstrations section in UMTA, a group of 10 staff members in Washington, D.C., who managed an annual budget of $16 million. Aside from the ARZ project, the section sponsored a number of other demonstrations in cities around the country. Congress had given UMTA substantial discretion in selecting the types and sites of demonstration projects but expected that these would in some way support transit service.

UMTA regarded ARZs as an excellent way to promote improved transit service, reduce traffic congestion, and facilitate economic development in major cities. Its demonstration project was designed to induce a few cities to experiment with ARZs in hope that their success would persuade other cities to adopt the innovation.

The UMTA Service and Methods Demonstrations section saw its function as applied research. As one staffer asserted, "the main business here is to take an idea, put it on the road, implement it, evaluate and test it. If it is a good idea, then we promote it to the [transit] industry." Some tension existed, however, between the "research/evaluation" function and the "promotion" function:

> There is no such thing as the ideal demonstration site. The city must be somewhat representative so we can generalize to other cities. But, if we are working with a transit agency, we prefer an innovative one, especially one that has a good data base to document the results. We are also looking for a physical and social geography, supply and demand of transit services, the orientation of management, data, sensitivity to the features of the demonstration. These are ideals, but you may not get the ideal. In the end you have to take what sites are available. Within the constraints of representativeness, and the implementation requirements of specific demonstration concepts, we look for sites that maximize the chances of success of the experiment. This is to help us with promotion of the experiment after the demonstration is complete.

UMTA staff contracted with a consortium of private consulting firms to carry out detailed planning and site selection for the ARZ demonstration. A national transportation consulting firm, Alan M. Voorhees and Associates Inc., the prime contractor, was responsible for traffic planning; Cambridge Systematics Inc., based in Massachusetts, analyzed the impact of auto restrictions on travel patterns and did the transit planning; Moore-Heder, a Cambridge, Mass., urban design firm, handled physical planning; and A. T. Kearny Inc., a Chicago firm, studied the problems of goods movement and commercial deliveries.

The consultants began work in June 1975, and by September they had contacted about 75 cities to identify potential demonstration sites. These cities were selected either because the consultants felt they were appropriate or because their officials responded to preliminary notice of UMTA's demonstration program. Forty-four of these sent the consultants information about the layout and activity of their downtown business districts, the operation of their transportation networks, the planning and implementation of related projects, and the political and administrative structure of the cities.

Boston officials received early word of the demonstration project through contacts in the State Executive Office of Transportation and Construction. (In January 1975 Mayor White's former transportation policy adviser, Fred Salvucci, had become secretary of transportation in the new administration of Gov. Michael Dukakis.) The BRA transportation planning staff made the first contacts with UMTA, and the mayor's transportation policy staff soon took an active role.

The ARZ program was attractive to key people in the BRA and to Emily Lloyd in the mayor's office. Such an experiment was consistent with their long-term agenda for transportation policy and downtown development. With the Washington Street Mall at so delicate a stage, however, they otherwise would not have considered additional auto restrictions so soon; but the UMTA program was too good an opportunity to pass up. Keeping very quiet about UMTA's invitation, to avoid stirring up more trouble with the Washington Street Mall planning process, city officials responded favorably to UMTA's initiative.

Using information provided by each city and the results of their own library research, the consultants narrowed down the list of potential demonstration sites to 12 candidates. Beginning around January 1976, representatives of the consulting team made visits to each city to speak with city officials, downtown businesses, and concerned citizens about the possible demonstration. They reported their findings to UMTA's Service and Methods Demonstrations staff, which decided how to narrow down the list of possible demonstration sites.

Early in the screening process, the consultants identified Boston as a prime site for an ARZ. The old, narrow streets of the downtown retail area suffered from severe traffic congestion and high pollution levels; an ARZ seemed to be an appropriate remedy for these problems. The area already was accessible by mass transit so the consultants had a strong base from which to design transit improvements. The city's character did not seem so unusual as to eliminate its use as a model for other cities interested in the program. The consultants noted that Boston had a long-standing interest in auto restrictions, as evidenced by the Victor Gruen proposal in the 1960s, and in pedestrian-oriented downtown development projects such as the Washington Street Mall project. With the BRA and city traffic agency, moreover, Boston had the institutional capacity to plan and implement an ARZ.

In April 1976, just before the final decision was made to go ahead with construction of the Washington Street Mall, UMTA announced that Boston was one of five cities selected for full-scale ARZ planning studies. The other cities were Providence, Rhode Island; Burlington, Vermont; Tucson, Arizona; and Memphis, Tennessee. Selection for the detailed study phase did not assure Boston that demonstration funds would be forthcoming; it merely meant that the four consulting firms would conduct in-depth analyses of each city's suitability. UMTA already had budget appropriations sufficient to pay for two demonstrations—about $1 million for each—and hoped for funds for another two demonstrations in the next fiscal year. In effect the five cities were competing for as few as two demonstration grants.

As intended by UMTA, the consultants carried out the planning studies, collaborating with local officials but not allowing them to control the work. In part this stemmed from UMTA's belief that some cities lacked the analytic resources and planning capability to do the job themselves. But it also resulted from the agency's desire to keep the project oriented toward UMTA's purposes. "Our objective is to work with the local area," noted one UMTA staffer, but "if you just let the urban area come and go at it, you might wind up with something different." While UMTA was prepared to adapt its ideas to accommodate local conditions, it was not ready to see its demonstration concept drastically distorted; if a city wanted federal funds, it would have to permit a meaningful ARZ experiment.

UMTA's Consultants Come to Boston

The consultants approached their work the same way in each of the five cities. As one key member of the consulting team recalled:

> Before we visited each city, we developed rough schemes of what might be done. The first step was to spend two days on site visits, meeting with a range of people, including transportation policy makers, people from the planning department, the mayor, merchants, perhaps the police and fire departments, local officials from the Federal Highway Administration [another unit of the U.S. Department of Transportation], state transportation officials, and any other people we could put together who might have an interest. We had a string of meetings, seeing them individually and in groups, trying to get as much information as we possibly could. We also spent time on the streets in between to get a feeling of what the cities were like. In later visits we were concerned with collecting the data and doing specific kinds of mapping so that we could do certain analyses about the use of streets, such as entrances to the downtown and volumes of use.

> We approached our analyses from two perspectives. First, traffic circulation systems. Second, physical and activity patterns. We were concerned with what patterns made sense for fitting an ARZ into the existing network of transportation and pedestrian activities. We wanted to fit them together. There were many rounds of negotiation on issues involved in such planning, both within the consultant team and with the folks in the city.

In Boston the consultants worked with Emily Lloyd and her staff—the principal local contacts—as well as with John Sloan at the BRA, the BRA transportation planning staff, and planners at the Massachusetts Bay Transportation Authority (MBTA), the independent metropolitan transit agency. The Traffic and Parking Department, hostile to the idea, was only peripherally involved. The process in Boston differed from that in other cities in one significant respect. In the other cities consultants made numerous public presentations and received a great deal of criticism that might otherwise have been directed at local officials. In Boston, however, officials were extremely sensitive about the delicate discussions surrounding the Washington Street Mall project. As a result, they did not permit the consultants to speak with anyone outside of local or state government. No publicity was given to their work, to minimize the chances of hostile reactions from the general public or the downtown merchants.

The consultants' work proceeded rapidly. Although city officials remained enthusiastic about the ARZ concept, by the summer of 1976 they had doubts about the scale of the project the consultants were designing. Their fears were confirmed when the draft proposal was finished in October. The consultants included a large section of Boston's retail area in the ARZ plans. The zone stretched from Government Center, past the department stores and smaller shops, to Essex Street on the edge of Chinatown; it extended from Tremont Street, on the edge of the Boston Common, to Devonshire Street on the edge of the financial district. (See Exhibit 1, p. 202.)

This proposal contained a complex circulation system for the ARZ, specifying patterns for autos, pedestrians, delivery trucks, and transit vehicles. The area of Washington Street from Court Street to Winter Street, a five-block area containing Jordan Marsh, Filene's, and other shops, would be for pedestrian use only. This added a few blocks to the original Washington Street Mall. In addition the narrow side streets of Winter (toward the Common) and Summer (toward South Station) also would be reserved for pedestrian use. Franklin Street (between Filene's and the edge of the financial district) would be primarily a pedestrian way, with auto access to a large parking garage. The plan envisioned construction of pedestrian amenities on streets where auto access would be eliminated.

Because of severe congestion in the retail district, MBTA bus routes ended at its periphery. The consultants' proposal would permit the transit agency to extend several routes so that passengers could debark in front of major department stores.

To assist pedestrians in getting from one point to another within the zone, the consultants proposed a shuttle bus system. It would run up Chauncy Street behind Lafayette Place, Jordan's, and Filene's, across two blocks on Franklin Street to Washington Street, and then up to Washington at the top of the zone. Additional routes would loop around the north end of the zone and also along the Common. This would facilitate access to the zone for elderly or handicapped persons who might have difficulty walking from the parking spaces and drop-off points on the area's edges. In addition it would serve other downtown shoppers.

Because many stores did not have off-street loading docks, or underground tunnels, the consultants needed to consider delivery vehicles in their overall circulation scheme. They gave these vehicles access to Washington Street before 11:00 a.m., when they anticipated levels of pedestrian use would increase. They also designated areas on adjacent side streets and on Tremont Street along the Common as all-day loading and delivery sites.

Official Reaction

City officials were shocked by the extensive UMTA consultants' plan and dubious about its rationale. As one recalled, "the consultants were saying that you *couldn't* do smaller areas for the ARZ. They believed it wouldn't work. However, they had no numbers to back this up."

Boston officials had grave misgivings about the consultants' plan for several reasons. First, the auto circulation plans were so sweeping that there was no assurance that the downtown traffic network would function adequately. The Traffic and Parking Department predicted massive tie-ups and difficulty for emergency vehicles; BRA transportation planners agreed. (Commissioner Noonan was suspicious of grand, untested schemes to solve complex problems. Planners, he believed, were too quick to propose dramatic change, simply sketching the outlines of an innovation and leaving it to others—like himself—to worry about or to be criticized for operational difficulties.) Moreover, many city officials were worried that such dramatic restrictions on auto use might damage the financial and physical health of the retail district. "If you wiped out vehicular traffic where there wasn't enough other activity, you would kill that street. It would become unsafe, deserted."

The project's capital and operating expenses also were a worrisome matter. City officials were aghast at the projected cost of the ARZ and associated facilities:

> The area that they ultimately delineated would have cost us several million dollars to resurface the streets and a few million more to channelize and resignalize the area. Halfway through the planning process we told them we were having trouble with money, that funds were simply not available for a project of this scale. After all, this was going to be a one-year demonstration with about $1,000,000 in federal funds.... There were no city bond funds because of the city's financial trouble.

Although the MBTA supported the ARZ concept, it was deeply concerned about how to finance the bus route extensions and the expensive shuttle

199

system. Because all MBTA services operated at a deficit, transit planners saw these service increments as a potentially large burden, increasing the need for operating subsidies from some source. The Boston Police Department, in turn, was concerned about financing the project. It saw that the plan required strict enforcement of traffic and parking regulations if it were to be successful. Would the department be expected to absorb the cost of additional officers' time in its existing budget?

Political factors also figured in city officials' calculations. Lloyd and her staff were concerned that the business community would react unfavorably. The large department stores had accepted the Washington Street Mall reluctantly, yet the consultants' plan covered an area far broader. No businesses had ever been approached in this larger downtown section. Many interests were involved: retailers would feel threatened by loss of sales and worry about disruption of delivery schedules; parking lot operators would fear drastic declines in patronage; insurance companies, stock brokers, and others would worry about commuting problems for their executives and employees; and real estate owners would fear instability in the market for downtown property. Lloyd also worried how the general public would react to such sweeping change. Would motorists blame the mayor for downtown traffic jams or for other inconveniences encountered while trying to shop?

The reaction of the business community and general public was important in the short run as well as the long run. If the city were selected as an ARZ demonstration site, a public hearing would be held on the project, followed by a city council vote to accept or reject the grant money. If substantial controversy surrounded the project, the council might balk at approving the ARZ demonstration.

What Next?

As Emily Lloyd and her aides, Sue Clippinger and Alex Taft, discussed the situation, they tried to conceive of a way to salvage the demonstration project. It was clear that they could not recommend, nor would the mayor approve, the UMTA consultants' proposal. But they still hoped to develop a smaller-scale alternative that would be attractive enough to UMTA to win the competition for demonstration funds and at the same time be acceptable to city agencies, the business community, and the general public. Several considerations were relevant:

• Mayor White was attracted to the ARZ idea. He wanted to discourage downtown traffic and believed that the area should be made more attractive to pedestrians. He also was enthusiastic about the demonstration project because it would bring federal funds to the city and enhance his administration's reputation for innovativeness, which would be helpful if he ran for reelection in 1979. On the other hand, he was cautious about losing the confidence and good will of the business community. And because he did not want to undertake a project that was technically unsound, he would listen carefully to the views of his operating agencies.

• UMTA was an essential participant because the project would be wholly infeasible without its demonstration grant. It was apparent from Lloyd's discussions with UMTA staff that they regarded Boston—the largest, most congested city among the five competitors—as the best site for the demonstration. However, UMTA had to be satisfied that Boston was giving the ARZ concept an adequate test. If Boston's plan was not a significant departure from its current situation, UMTA would select another city. Moreover, the plan had to include a transit element because of UMTA's mandate from Congress. The MBTA, therefore, was also an essential participant.

• If UMTA selected Boston as one of the demonstration sites, the city would enjoy considerable discretion in deciding how to use the $1,000,000 grant. UMTA would allow the funds to be used for any reasonable purposes connected with the ARZ demonstration. It also was possible that some additional federal grant money might be available for the project.

If it were willing, the MBTA might be able to persuade UMTA to give it a grant of $1,000,000 for a "bus priority" experiment. Bus route extensions in the ARZ probably would qualify. (Federal regulations did not permit this money to be used for operating expenses, however, only capital costs.) It also might be possible to get another $1,000,000 from Federal Highway Administration (FHWA) "urban systems" funds; the state Department of Public Works (DPW) got an annual grant from FHWA earmarked for the Boston metropolitan region. Because several highway projects in the region had been canceled in the early 1970s, however, much of this money was not being spent. Preliminary contacts with the DPW commissioner indicated a willingness to discuss—but make no commitments to—the ARZ project. Thus, money from several federal programs might be put together to meet the costs of the ARZ project. But there were limitations on how each "pot" of money might be used and uncertainty about its availability.

• The Winter Street Association, the organization of small retailers led by Alvin Schmertzler, already had gone on record in support of further auto restrictions, hoping to make their street into a pedestrian zone. They firmly believed that an ARZ would be *good* for downtown business. Because continuing downtown economic decline threatened their very existence, they were not inclined to be so cautious as the large department stores with their suburban branches. Lloyd and her assistants also knew that in a few other cities that had experimented with traffic restraints in the retail district—most notably, Philadelphia—merchants became strong backers of the concept, despite initial resistance, once the restrictions were in operation.

Together these facts gave Lloyd and her staff some hope that a politically feasible ARZ proposal might be developed. But the mayor's aides would have to take the lead in developing and promoting a revised ARZ plan. Otherwise, it seemed clear, the ARZ was dead in Boston.

EXHIBITS

Exhibit One:
UMTA Consultants' ARZ Proposal,
Primary Travel Corridors

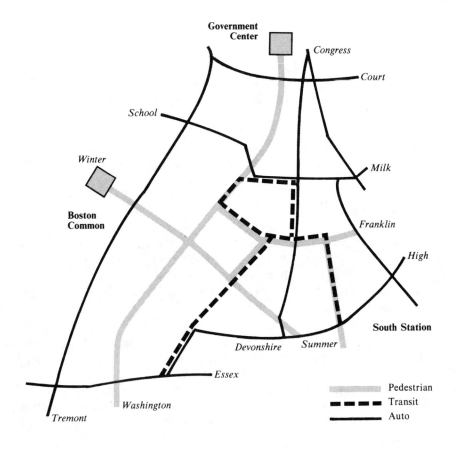

Discussion Questions

1. What is necessary to win city approval of a revised ARZ proposal?

2. From what source, and under what circumstances, are Lloyd and her staff likely to find allies?

3. What resources do Lloyd and her staff have to promote the ARZ project?

4. What is UMTA's likely reaction if the White administration proposes an ARZ covering less area in downtown Boston than UMTA's consultants had recommended?

5. Are the major department stores likely to be implacable foes of an ARZ project?

6. Do the actions of Lloyd and her staff go beyond the appropriate functions of mayoral aides?

Suggestions for Further Reading

Bardach, Eugene. *The Skill Factor in Politics.* Berkeley and Los Angeles: University of California Press, 1972. Assesses the roles and tactics of "policy entrepreneurs" in the development of mental health policy.

Howitt, Arnold M. "Downtown Auto Restraint Policies: Adopting and Implementing Urban Transport Innovations." *Journal of Transport Economics and Policy,* May 1980, 155-168. Analysis of the difficulties of planning and managing policies to restrict automobile use in central city business districts.

Meltsner, Arnold J. "Political Feasibility and Policy Analysis." *Public Administration Review,* November/December 1972, 859-867. Suggests a framework for taking political factors into account in designing public policies.

Yates, Douglas T. "The Mayor's Eight Ring Circus," in *Urban Policy Making,* Dale Rogers Marshall, ed. Beverly Hills, Calif: Sage Publications Inc., 1979, 41-69. Describes the features and dilemmas of the policymaking environment of big city mayors.

5. *Community Development in Gainesville*

INTRODUCTION

Securing federal funds is only one step in managing a successful intergovernmental program. The three parts of "Community Development in Gainesville" explore the different steps required to implement major federal programs in a small southern city during a period of 16 years. Through this case we can gain a better understanding of why program implementation is an extremely complex process and come to appreciate the dynamic relationship between federal legislation, funding patterns, and administrative oversight, on one hand, and local politics and program management, on the other. The case study's setting in a small community, moreover, permits us to observe some of the contrasts between big city politics and administration and the considerably smaller scale of government in Gainesville.

Case A describes the genesis and development of Gainesville's Urban Renewal and Model Cities programs from 1963 to 1973. As start-up problems unfold, we see again the importance of the policy entrepreneur's role (here played by several individuals) in turning a grant into a functioning program. In the process we see two dimensions of this role: a *political* side, aimed at winning acceptance of the program by key policy makers and active constituencies; and a *managerial* side, aimed at establishing and administering agencies to deliver services to the public.

Gainesville's experience in this regard is not unique. Because federal programs inevitably are entwined with the interests of local elected officials, public administrators, and interest groups, policy entrepreneurs must make coalition building a top priority. Here the problems encountered by Gainesville's mayor and the top staff of the Model Cities program are similar in many ways to the issues involved in "Restricting Traffic on Washington Street." Once the program has been accepted, though, there is another step: city government must establish the administrative capacity to handle the program effectively. Operational plans must be made; and working relationships must be established with other government agencies and programs, with nongovernmental organizations and firms, and with the general public.

As time passes, moreover, an effective policy entrepreneur must blend these political and managerial perspectives together to ensure the health of the program. A program must show results to maintain or expand its access to financial resources. It must adapt to changes in federal law and regulations, and it must adapt to changes in demands by the people affected by its operations.

Significant changes in a program's environment pose the greatest challenge to the policy entrepreneur. Case B deals with a crisis in the life of Gainesville's Model Cities program caused by the replacement in 1974 of several federal categorical grant programs, including Model Cities, by the Community Development Block Grant (CDBG). This case permits us to consider how changes in federal law are likely to affect the priorities, operating policies, and political relationships of the Gainesville program.

As was true of the block grants considered in the Washington State and Kentucky cases, transition from categorical programs like urban renewal and Model Cities to the CDBG freed local administrators from numerous federal regulations and program restraints. But it also introduced many new pressures at the local level. Politically, understandings of how federal funds would be used were subject to reexamination. Constituencies that were accustomed to having assured access to federal funds suddenly found that they had competitors; groups that previously had been excluded discovered that they could make claims for funds. The transition was unsettling for administrators as well as for interest groups. Agencies that had had guaranteed funding from the earlier programs learned that their resources were either drying up or were subject to claims by other agencies and programs; some employees found their jobs in jeopardy.

Case C tracks Gainesville's response to the new CDBG program from 1974 to 1979. For the policy entrepreneur, such a transition poses several challenges: to guide his projects through a period of change, protecting those that rank high in his priorities; to make shifts as painless as possible for those groups whose interests are damaged by the new program; and to establish a stable constituency for the revamped program to ensure its effective operation. This case thus focuses on the administrative and political changes that were required to consolidate the Gainesville Model Cities and urban renewal programs into a single administrative entity capable of running the larger program. It also chronicles a tale of "cutback management" in which the new Community Development Department staff attempts to promote effective programs under the threat of a drastic reduction in available funds.

Community Development in Gainesville (A)

THE CAST

Philip Landrum	Gainesville's U.S. representative to Congress
John Cromartie	Gainesville mayor and initiator of Model Cities
Robert Branning	first director of Gainesville Model Cities program
Carlyle Cox	senior planner, later director of the Gainesville Model Cities program
Charles Morrow	assistant director of Gainesville Model Cities program
Randolph Waters	Gainesville city commissioner
HUD	U.S. Department of Housing and Urban Development
OEO	U.S. Office of Economic Opportunity, created during the Johnson administration as part of the "war against poverty."
Southside	Gainesville's poorest, predominantly black residential area; selected as Model Neighborhood
Model Neighborhood	target area for Model Cities program
CDA	City Demonstration Agency, established to administer the Model Cities program in Gainesville
CDC	Citizens' Demonstration Committee, advisory committee formed to review plans for Model Cities program
CCDP	Comprehensive City Demonstration Plan, required as part of Model Cities application to HUD
TRC	Technical Review Committee, citizen advisory panel formed to review the economic and technical feasibilities of the Model Cities program
HRD	Housing and Relocation Department, established to manage several Gainesville Model Cities projects
NSC	Neighborhood Service Center Department, established to run several Model Cities projects

CHRONOLOGY

<u>1963</u>	Representative Landrum urges Gainesville officials to apply for federal urban renewal funds to rebuild the city's central business district. The city develops the required "workable program" and establishes the Urban Renewal Agency.
<u>1965</u>	Gainesville secures a federal grant from the Office of Economic Opportunity (OEO) to establish a Community Action Program to fight poverty.
<u>1965-1966</u>	Gainesville's urban renewal program becomes mired in controversy and is widely perceived as a failure.
<u>1967</u>	Mayor John Cromartie learns about the new federal Model Cities program and decides that Gainesville should apply. With Representative Landrum's aid, Gainesville is designated by the Johnson administration as a Model City and receives a planning grant.
<u>1968</u>	Planning for Gainesville's program begins. Cromartie recruits Bob Branning and Carlyle Cox from Atlanta to direct the program. Branning and Cox conduct a resident survey and establish citizen participation committees. Program staff, with citizen involvement, develop a detailed agenda of Model Cities projects and identify agencies that can carry them out. Cox begins to seek additional grants from federal and state sources to finance other projects and identifies agencies that can carry them out. HUD approves Gainesville's plan.
<u>1969</u>	Incoming Nixon administration delays start of Gainesville's program while desegregation dispute is settled and master contract is signed with HUD.
<u>1970</u>	Cox struggles to negotiate individual contracts with agencies to implement Model Cities projects and to get the contracts approved by the Gainesville city commission. As the year progresses, initial projects show good preliminary results. Detailed planning commences for second-year program.

<u>1971-1973</u>   Under Cox's leadership, Gainesville's Model Cities program secures many additional state and federal grants-in-aid.

THE CASE

Gazing out the window of his tiny office on a spring day in 1973, Carlyle Cox reflected on how both he and Gainesville, Georgia—a city of 18,000—had changed since he had moved from Atlanta in 1968. First as senior planner, then as director of Gainesville's Model Cities program, Cox had been instrumental in putting together one of the more innovative of the nation's 150 Model Cities programs. As he and his colleagues worked to bring millions of dollars to the city, Cox earned a national reputation as a skilled grantsman and administrator.

The outlook had not always been promising, however. Cox remembered the hostile reception residents of Gainesville's poorest neighborhood had given him at their first meeting; he also remembered the suspicion and skepticism of the city's political leaders and businessmen when the Model Cities planning process began. In those early days Cox had wondered whether a city as small as Gainesville could successfully implement a federal program as ambitious as Model Cities. He smiled at how wrong that first impression had proved to be.

'Queen City of the Mountains'

Gainesville, Georgia, is a small yet bustling community located in Hall County, 35 miles northeast of metropolitan Atlanta in the heart of the scenic Georgia mountains. Despite its modest size, Gainesville is the largest city and economic center of Georgia's Ninth Congressional District, an area encompassing 20 counties in the northeast corner of Georgia. As many as 50,000 people work, shop, and do business in Gainesville each day. The city also enjoys a brisk tourist trade from visitors and vacationers at nearby Lake Sidney Lanier, the most heavily visited man-made lake in the country.

This case was written by Kay Rubin under the supervision of Arnold M. Howitt. Its development was financed by a grant from the U.S. Department of Housing and Urban Development for use in the Program for Senior Executives in State and Local Government at the John F. Kennedy School of Government, Harvard University.

First chartered in 1832, Gainesville is an old city that has undergone many changes, particularly since the Depression. Prior to the 1930s Gainesville and surrounding Hall County had been a typical rural mountain area. Its economy depended on small-scale agriculture and forestry; its residents, mainly of Appalachian heritage, were proud, hard-working, and self-reliant. City dwellers were shopkeepers, teachers, professionals, or employees in one of the local businesses. County residents were primarily farmers, most of whom were small farmers or sharecroppers.

Area residents, like many southerners, believed in low-key, unobtrusive government. Gainesville was governed by a city commission (similar in function to a city council). The commission selected one of its members as mayor—mainly a ceremonial job—and appointed a city manager to serve as chief administrator of the city's service departments. Hall County elected a separate commission and provided basic services to the areas outside of Gainesville. In addition it performed some functions for the county as a whole. Both governments received their revenues from a low property tax.

The 1930s brought significant change to this economic and political situation. The Depression hit the rural South hard, and many families abandoned their farms in search of jobs in the city. Gainesville, inhabited by a new class of unskilled and unemployed workers, grew larger and poorer. Most of the newcomers were black. They built a new but poor neighborhood, the "Southside," on the southern edge of the city. Many of the town's smaller shops failed, and the local economy came almost to a standstill.

The problems caused by the Depression were compounded in 1936 by a tornado that ripped through Gainesville, destroying virtually the entire downtown business district. Prior to this disaster, the city commission had shown a conservative aversion to government "handouts" and refused to apply for federal relief funds being offered through President Franklin D. Roosevelt's New Deal programs. Following the tornado, however, the city was faced with a much greater emergency and had no choice but to seek federal help.

The WPA provided Gainesville with more than a million dollars over the following few years, putting many residents to work rebuilding downtown businesses and erecting a beautiful new county courthouse and city hall facing each other in the center of the downtown. Amid much fanfare, President Roosevelt himself came to Gainesville in 1940 for the dedication of the courthouse and city hall. The grateful city commission named the area Roosevelt Square. City leaders realized for the first time that the federal government could be a valuable source of funds.

1940-1960: From Farm to Industrial Center

The following decades brought another great change to Gainesville and Hall County. The Depression and tornado had made the city's business community painfully aware of just how fragile Gainesville's economy had been. The city needed more money and more jobs, and a group of businessmen set out to meet those needs by attracting industry to the area. Gainesville was an excellent location to sell—close to Atlanta, with a large land area and ready labor force, low taxes, inexpensive water and power, and cooperative city and county governments. Several textile and food-processing plants came to Gainesville, and Hall County became the home of Georgia's biggest new industry—poultry processing. The latter, in particular, was to become a dominant force in the local economy. Gainesville proudly proclaimed itself the "broiler capital of the world."

Industrial expansion in and around Gainesville brought a new prosperity to the people and a new urbanization to the city. Incomes rose, new shops, banks, hotels, and restaurants sprang up, and Gainesville, by the mid-1950s, began attracting workers, shoppers, and investors from all over northeast Georgia. This in turn enlarged the city's tax base, and the city became able to provide more and better services such as sewers, street lights, and parks. New schools were built in the city and county, and Gainesville's city schools ranked among the best in the state.

The county, benefiting from the increased tax rolls, also added a health department that served both the city and county. The city even added a small planning department so it could better manage the growth of new suburbs to the north, which had necessitated considerable annexation of land by the town. Yet despite the growth in services, the city was able to maintain its low tax rates and public debt (only one bond issue to build a new school), keeping a favorable atmosphere for business and property owners.

The Southside and Suburban Flight

While most of the city was experiencing an economic boom, life on the Southside remained much the same as it had been during the Depression. Throughout the 1940s and 1950s the Southside grew to encompass about one-fourth of the city's total area and population; most of the population was black. Gainesville's school system was segregated, and most of the area's larger industries refused to hire blacks. Thus most blacks were relegated to menial jobs in or near the Southside, and unemployment remained high even during the overall economic boom in the area. The conservative city government showed little concern for Southside residents. Because the Southside was divided among three electoral wards and commissioners were elected at large, Southside residents had little political power.

Because it was ignored by city leaders and most city residents, the Southside deteriorated steadily and by the early 1960s was a squalid slum of tumbledown wooden shacks, unpaved streets, open sewers and rat-infested garbage dumps. Crime and delinquency were much higher than in other parts of the city, yet police were a rare sight. The Southside schools received only minimal resources from the city. The only government assistance available for Southside residents was welfare and Social Security; moreover, welfare payments in Georgia were meager and Gainesville's state welfare office was small, inconveniently located, and lacked trained social workers or counselors.

The conservative city commission, though, refused to consider applying for any other federal assistance. Long after federal funds were made available to cities for education, urban renewal, and public housing, the city commission declined such aid. They feared federal control and opposed spending local taxes to provide the necessary matching funds or establish new departments to operate federal programs. As long as the city enjoyed a thriving economy, its leaders felt no compulsion to seek federal aid.

By the early 1960s, however, the city's overall economic boom had translated into suburban flight. More and more people were moving to the county, giving rise to dozens of new suburban shops and restaurants and damaging the economic health of the central business district. Worried downtown merchants and property owners began investigating possible government aid that could help revitalize Gainesville's inner city. They pressured the city commission to take steps to restore property values and business activity in downtown Gainesville and to improve the appearance of the adjacent Southside.

Gainesville Enters the Federal Grant System

As concern was growing over Gainesville's deteriorating downtown area, its congressman, Ninth District Representative Phil Landrum, had become an influential force in Congress. A ranking Democrat on the House Ways and Means Committee, Landrum also was a close friend of then Vice President Lyndon B. Johnson. A skillful politician, Landrum sought to use his influence to channel more federal funding into his district, particularly into its largest city, Gainesville. He urged Gainesville's leaders to consider urban renewal as a way to solve the problems of the central business district. In 1963 the commission instructed the city planning department to put together a "workable plan," the formal planning document required by federal urban renewal regulations as part of the city's grant application.

Inexperienced with the comprehensive planning methods prescribed by federal administrators and lacking knowledge of the Southside, the small city planning department staff relied heavily on the assistance of a federal urban renewal field representative to complete the plan. As a result the plan was very ambitious, calling for a $5 million, three-phase project to be completed over 10 years. More than 400 acres of deteriorated area on the Southside were to be cleared, with nearly one-fourth of the city's housing slated for demolition. Public housing apartments and new single-family houses would be built in its place, with some land reserved for private development and public buildings. A new Urban Renewal Agency (URA) would administer the project. The URA staff would serve at the discretion of the city commission; but once the workable plan was approved, the URA was bound to carry out the terms of the plan and adhere to federal requirements for its administration. This left the city commission with little practical control over urban renewal implementation. The commissioners, however, welcomed this administrative structure because it relieved the city of direct responsibility for the program. The commissioners also were pleased that the city's only financial contribution would be to provide the necessary streets, sewers, and utilities for the new development.*

While the urban renewal project was getting under way, another group of concerned citizens sought to take advantage of Gainesville's changing attitudes toward federal aid. A coalition of welfare caseworkers and local church leaders, encouraged by the city's acceptance and Representative Landrum's support of urban renewal, applied for and won a grant from the new Office of Economic Opportunity (OEO) to set up a Community Action Program. Chartered in August 1965, Gainesville's OEO program included a Head Start project for preschool children in the Southside, a nutrition information project, and a program to provide meals and basic health services to the elderly in the Southside. As the local match for the OEO grant, the city commission agreed to provide free space for the OEO center in a vacant, city-owned building. Other than this consideration, the commission largely was indifferent to the OEO program because it would require neither funds nor administrative involvement by the city.

By late 1966 Gainesville's federally funded programs were showing some results. The OEO program was slow in starting and suffered from a shortage of experienced staff. Gainesville, like many other small towns in the 1960s, simply did not have enough trained social workers to effectively manage a program of OEO's scope. The program's three full-time staffers and four VISTA volunteers were spread thin in trying to reach the entire Southside elderly and preschool population, and none of them had the experience or the time to adequately publicize the OEO program within the community. Thus most of OEO's intended beneficiaries simply were unaware that the programs existed, and many who knew about them were too proud to seek public assistance or were without the transportation necessary to take children or elderly people to the OEO center. The programs also suffered from a certain degree of insensitivity displayed by the VISTA volunteers who staffed them;

---

* Under urban renewal regulations cities were required to put up one dollar for every four dollars granted by the federal government; however, cities were allowed to count "in-kind" contributions such as streets and utilities as the necessary local match. Thus many cities were able to avoid any direct cash commitment to urban renewal.

apparently, many blacks sensed a patronizing attitude among the VISTAs.

Despite these difficulties, the intentions and goals of the OEO programs generally were seen as useful. OEO was intent on continuing them, blaming its difficulties on a lack of publicity and cooperation by the city. Local OEO staffers were certain that with additional funding and experience they could work out the program's problems and provide vital services to needy Southside residents.

OEO's problems, however, were minor compared with those the city encountered with its urban renewal program. In its rush to accept the $5 million in federal funds, the city's leaders had failed to notice that virtually no vacant housing existed in Gainesville in which to relocate families displaced by urban renewal demolition. Nor did they anticipate the climbing interest rates and land values of the mid-1960s, which made new houses unaffordable for most Southside families. The small URA staff (five program officials) had no previous housing experience and was unequipped to deal with the unexpected shortage of relocation housing. Fearing federal reprisals, the URA rigidly followed federal rules for relocation and demolition, even when this meant displacing families who had nowhere else to go. As a result, the urban renewal program's progress was slow and painful. Many families were forced to relocate to sections of Hall County outside of Gainesville (which meant sending children miles away to school) or charged rent to remain in their houses after they had been purchased by the URA. In most instances, displaced families moved to houses that were no better, and often worse, than those they had left.

The URA also acquired a reputation for favoring wealthy landlords. Prices offered to black homeowners usually were lower than those offered to these landlords. Some residents insisted that the whole program was designed to move blacks out, raise property values, and then give wealthy landlords a higher price for their property. More often than not, homeowners were forced to take legal action to obtain a better price from the URA; the many lawsuits further delayed progress of the program.

As a result of the delays, only 15 parcels of land were purchased in 1965 and 64 in 1966 (out of 250 planned purchases for Phase I), and the URA was unable to pursue a street-by-street clearance effort as planned. This led to haphazard street closings and snarled traffic around the central business district, which brought complaints from all over the city. Extensive newspaper coverage of urban renewal problems brought more complaints and embarrassment to the city commissioners, who were virtually powerless to take any remedial action.

By the end of 1966, the urban renewal program almost universally was considered a disaster for Gainesville. Displaced residents were bitter; those who had not yet been displaced were fearful of being ejected from their homes with no place to go. The city's leaders were embarrassed and disappointed, as were many of the businessmen who had pushed for acceptance of urban renewal funds. Virtually everyone was convinced that federal grant programs were "more trouble than they were worth."

Enter Model Cities

Despite the disappointments and frustrations of urban renewal, a few people in Gainesville still believed that only the federal government could provide the resources the city needed to bring relief to the distressed Southside. One of them was John Cromartie, president of the area's largest poultry-processing firm, and the new mayor of Gainesville. Cromartie took his position seriously even though the mayor had no official authority other than as a commission member and primarily was considered only the commission's ceremonial leader. Immediately after he was elected in 1966, he actively began seeking new programs that might help solve some of Gainesville's problems. By becoming actively involved in the Georgia Municipal Association and the U.S. Conference of Mayors, he learned of the many new federal programs that other cities were using to combat poverty and physical deterioration.

In January 1967 Cromartie and City Commissioner Randolph Waters attended the national mayors' conference in Washington, D.C., where they heard HUD Secretary Robert Weaver describe the newest Johnson administration program. The program was called Model Cities, and Cromartie immediately felt that it could help Gainesville.

The Model Cities Program

Model Cities was a response to growing criticism of the federal grant-in-aid system: too little federal money existed for aid to the nation's distressed cities; the available funding was allocated on the basis of skilled grantsmanship rather than on genuine need; most federal grant programs emphasized housing and physical improvements at the expense of employment training, counseling, education, and other needed social services; the existing programs were administered too rigidly; and the federal bureaucracy was unresponsive to varying local needs and capacities.

To answer these criticisms, President Lyndon B. Johnson in 1965 appointed a National Urban Task Force to design a new approach to federal aid for cities. The task force's work was given a high priority on Johnson's agenda. In less than a year the task force gave the president its recommendation: a pilot program to demonstrate the effectiveness of giving a large amount of federal funds, through both existing programs and additional appropriations, to individual neighborhoods in a few cities. Johnson embraced the idea, and, with an extraordinary legislative push, Congress enacted the program as Title I of the Demonstration Cities and Metropolitan Development Act of 1966.

Features of the Model Cities Program

The Model Cities program made available, through a new Model Cities Administration (MCA), nearly a half-billion dollars in federal aid to a maximum of 150 cities for a five-year demonstration program. In addition to providing funds, Model Cities established many procedures previously untried in federal grant-in-aid programs.

Participating cities would designate a "Model Neighborhood" (or, in the case of very large cities, two or more neighborhoods) within which all Model Cities projects would be concentrated. Rather than receiving funds on a project basis, cities would be granted Model Cities funds based on the overall "distress" of the Model Neighborhood. The cities would have discretion, within some program guidelines, to distribute their Model Cities allotment according to locally determined priorities.

Before any Model Cities projects were funded, cities would be given an initial planning grant and then be required to spend from six to eighteen months developing a five-year Comprehensive City Demonstration Plan (CCDP). The plan would outline a first-year action plan indicating specific projects to be undertaken in the initial year and establish overall goals for improvements of the Model Neighborhood. Both MCA and the locally elected governing body would have the right to approve, reject, or revise the plans.

Planning and coordination of the CCDP would be handled by a newly created City Demonstration Agency (CDA), which would become a regular department of city government directly responsible to locally elected officials. Local officials could choose to discontinue participation in the program at any time during its five-year life. The CDA would not be the implementing agency for Model Cities projects, but would only secure contracts for projects, coordinate their implementation, and supervise planning.

The CDA also would be required to establish a mechanism to ensure maximum involvement of Model Neighborhood residents in planning and implementation of the CCDP.

Cromartie Sets His Sights on Model Cities

As HUD Secretary Weaver announced at the mayors' conference in January 1967, Model Cities was an attempt to improve the planning and coordination of federal programs, increase local control and responsibility for those programs, and widen the scope of government assistance to depressed neighborhoods. John Cromartie instantly felt that this was exactly the kind of program his city needed. He returned to Gainesville and, unknown to the city commission, ordered the City Planning Department to draw up an application for a Model Cities program. The city's two planners were inexperienced with lengthy applications such as were required by Model Cities, and they had little idea of what HUD wanted other than a basic assessment of the extent of "distress" in the city's poverty area. The choice of the Model Neighborhood boundaries was fairly simple; the planners went back to the urban renewal plan and used basically the same site as the urban renewal area, which included nearly all of the Southside. However, the city had never before kept up-to-date statistics on housing, education, employment, and health. The planners had to go back to the 1960 census and try to extrapolate statistics for the Southside. The result was, in the judgment of a later Model Cities staffer, ".... the biggest piece of * * * you ever saw! They didn't know anything about filling out applications, they didn't have any real statistics.... HUD must have died laughing when they read it."

The application, however crude, was nonetheless good enough. As HUD began receiving and evaluating the dozens of Model Cities applications in the spring and summer of 1967, Congress was becoming more fearful of increased government spending and threatened to reduce appropriations for Model Cities. President Johnson, a skillful legislative strategist, ordered HUD to withhold announcement of the approved Model Cities applications until the appropriation bill passed. Although Gainesville was not on HUD's original list, it quickly was added as Johnson sought Representative Landrum's vote for the appropriation bill and his help in securing the support of wavering southern members of Congress. This process was repeated for other cities, and the appropriation bill narrowly passed. On November 15, 1967, a beaming Representative Landrum announced Gainesville's selection as one of the five Georgia Model Cities. (The others were Alma, Athens, Atlanta, and Savannah.)

Setting Up the Model Cities Program

Although Representative Landrum and Mayor Cromartie were ecstatic over Gainesville's Model Cities selection, the city commissioners hardly were overjoyed. They had not approved the application in the first place and had no desire to embark on another federal program, especially one that covered the same area as urban renewal. They were concerned that the small city staff would be unable to handle another large program, yet they feared hiring "strangers" from outside the city over whom they might have little control. However, the enthusiastic support of Landrum, and the outspoken public support of the local newspaper editor Sylvan Meyer, enabled Cromartie to convince the commissioners to accept the $98,000 Gainesville had been awarded for planning its Model Cities program. Finally, in January 1968 the commission agreed to begin planning, with a stern warning to Cromartie that this in no way meant that it automatically would approve the plans. But Cromartie had won the first battle and set out with renewed enthusiasm to develop a plan that the commissioners couldn't refuse.

Assembling a Staff

Cromartie knew that his first step, assembling a staff, could be the most crucial in determining the eventual success or failure of a Model Cities program. Knowing the commission's reservations about "outside help," but also realizing that no one within the city government had the experience or the capability to put together and manage a program the size of Model Cities, Cromartie looked to nearby Atlanta to find people who had the necessary experience and with whom the commissioners would feel comfortable.

While visiting city officials in Atlanta, Cromartie was told of two young men who were doing exceptionally good work in Atlanta's OEO program. He arranged to meet the two and was impressed with their enthusiasm and achievements. Bob Branning had served as director of Atlanta's largest public housing project, coordinator of several OEO service centers in rural Fulton County, and as a member of the Atlanta Community Planning Board. Cromartie was impressed with Branning's managerial ability and his experience in all phases of planning and implementing community service delivery. On the other hand, J. Carlyle Cox seemed to be especially talented at organizing and working with community groups. A Baptist minister, Cox had his first pulpit in Atlanta and was actively involved in the desegregation of the city's churches. He later joined Atlanta OEO as director of its VISTA volunteers—the largest VISTA group in the nation. He then became involved in planning and organizing several successful OEO neighborhood service centers in Atlanta's poorest neighborhoods.

Branning and Cox both were enthusiastic about the new Model Cities program, but it took a great deal of time and effort for Cromartie to convince the two to come to Gainesville. Impressed with Cromartie's commitment to the program and excited about the opportunity to see what they could do with a new program in a town where they would have to "start from scratch," they finally agreed.

Beginning the Planning Process

Branning and Cox had visited Gainesville twice; they knew something of the needs of the Southside, and Cromartie had warned them of the skepticism they would face from the city government and the Southside residents. However, it was still quite a shock when they were told that their jobs were "temporary." The commissioners gave them "unclassified" status, ranking Branning and Cox with the city's janitors and refuse collectors who were ineligible for city insurance and retirement plans. Their reception by the

218

Southside was not much better. At a preliminary public hearing on Model Cities, Branning and Cox were barraged with complaints and accusations about nearly everything from urban renewal to grocery stores. As Cox later recalled:

> Bob and I knew we were facing a challenge . . . but those first weeks made it feel almost like war. We both had our ideas about what kind of projects we should do, but it all went out the window. The main thing we had to do was "de-escalate"—to show the people we were there to answer their needs.

Before they could do this, however, Branning and Cox had to find out just what the people of the Southside needed. Because the city did not have an appropriate department to do this, they hired several students from the University of Georgia School of Social Work to design and conduct a survey of Southside residents. The students visited more than 100 Southside families; their responses gave Branning and Cox a clearer idea of the area's needs as well as the overall feelings of its residents. They were surprised to find— despite the prevailing opinions of federal Model Cities officials that depressed neighborhoods needed more social services—that Southside residents placed social services low on their list of priorities. Housing, education, physical improvements, and crime prevention were far more important.

Realizing the value of this input, Branning and Cox next began ensuring continued involvement of Southside residents in planning Model Cities projects. By law, they were required to form a committee of residents to review and approve all plans. However, they realized that this probably would not be sufficient to win real support for Model Cities; the neighborhood had to be involved from the very beginning in planning as well as review. In addition, Branning and Cox felt they could use the citizen-participation mechanism to involve, and gain support from, residents of all parts of the city as well as from city government officials. They knew that, because Gainesville was so small, the Model Cities program was bound to have a far-reaching effect, as did urban renewal, on the entire city. Thus Branning and Cox felt it necessary to devise a structure that would ensure planning input and review by all segments of the community. They devised an elaborate, three-tiered system:

- Seven planning subcommittees would work with CDA staff to devise actual project plans. Each subcommittee would develop plans for one specific component of the overall CCDP—housing, education, physical environment, social services, employment and economic development, health, and crime and delinquency. (These seven areas were chosen primarily at the suggestion of HUD in one of several technical assistance manuals provided to the City Demonstration Agency.) Subcommittees would be comprised of five Model Neighborhood residents and three non-Model Neighborhood residents (serving as volunteers appointed by the CDA).

• A Model Cities Technical Review Committee (TRC) would review all subcommittee reports and recommend adoption of each proposed project based on its economic and technical feasibility. The TRC would be comprised of three Model Neighborhood residents, a representative of each city department and several local professionals. Branning and Cox hoped that this committee could help "weed out" projects that might be very popular with residents, but infeasible given the city's limited resources.

• A Citizens' Demonstration Committee (CDC) would act on both the recommendations of the subcommittees and the TRC to give final approval to all project plans before submission to the city commission. The CDC was the centerpiece of the citizen participation structure, consisting of 15 Model Neighborhood residents elected to represent different sections of the neighborhood, and 10 residents from the remainder of the community, appointed by the city commission. In addition to reviewing plans, the CDC would meet on a regular basis to provide communication between the city's residents and the CDA and to review applications for additional federal grants for Model Cities projects.

Once they had decided on a structure, Branning and Cox began recruiting members for the subcommittees and holding elections for the CDC. This took about two weeks, during which time Southside residents began to show an active interest in Model Cities. The subcommittees were filled quickly, and all of them selected a Model Neighborhood resident as chairman. Spirited campaigns were waged for the CDC positions. Branning and Cox were elated, hoping that such great interest would lead to many new project proposals and to greater city responsiveness to the newly organized Southside residents.

These hopes were not completely realized, however. In March, when the subcommittees began weekly meetings, Carlyle Cox quickly found himself devoting nearly all of his time to refereeing the meetings. He was surprised to find that most of the subcommittee members saw their positions as opportunities to air bitter complaints about the entire city government. Only a few of them had real suggestions for Model Cities projects, and Cox found that most suggestions were "pet projects" that would affect only a small group of people within the Model Neighborhood. After a few weeks of these meetings, an exasperated Cox recommended to Branning that the subcommittees begin meeting every two weeks and that he and Branning start "brainstorming" to develop some ideas they could present to the subcommittees. Cox also quickly abandoned the practice of bringing one or two city officials to subcommittee meetings because this nearly always led to a barrage of complaints and invective against the officials.

Cox also learned that allowing subcommittees to elect their chairmen was working to their disadvantage; the elected chairmen had no experience in running meetings and often led the complaints. While he and Branning thought it would be unwise to change this structure immediately, they decided against allowing the CDC to elect its chairman. Instead, they allowed the city commission to appoint a CDC chairman and were dismayed when the commission chose a young, white businessman whose family owned a large poultry operation. He had lived in Gainesville only a few years after attending college and working in Atlanta and had little experience in community affairs. Newspaper accounts indicated widespread skepticism of the appointment, and many of the elected CDC members feared that he would make the CDC a rubber stamp for the city commission. Branning and Cox, in turn, feared that this could jeopardize the still fragile support for Model Cities.

Devising a Strategy

While Branning and Cox were ironing out the wrinkles in the citizen participation structure, they began intensive work to develop and propose some projects that would prod the subcommittees into action. In addition, Branning and Cox worked to develop an overall strategy for the Comprehensive City Demonstration Plan, which they hoped would ensure the plan's workability, its approval by HUD and the city commission, and its long-term success in combating the staggering problems of the Southside during and after the five-year life of the program. To accomplish these goals, Branning and Cox developed a fourfold strategy:

1. Devise projects that would provide broad and long-lasting benefits after Model Cities funds expired. This, Branning and Cox felt, implied emphasis on new facilities, job-creating projects, and comprehensive projects that would answer several needs simultaneously.

2. Devise projects that, if successful, would create constituencies within the Model Neighborhood or within city government, thus increasing the project's chances for city or state funding after Model Cities funds had expired.

3. Concentrate the first projects or problems that were most pressing and could be immediately and visibly affected to build early support and enthusiasm for Model Cities throughout the city.

4. Use as many Model Cities supplemental funds as possible for "seed money" to attract other federal and state grants. This would not only widen the scope of the Model Cities program but also would be attractive to the city commission and to HUD—since HUD guidelines stressed use of its own supplemental funds only for projects not fundable through other federal programs.

Cox felt such a strategy was a critical element in planning a successful program that would survive local political pressures and federal funding cutoffs:

> We tried early on to pick only the projects that would have a real impact and
> would continue after Model Cities; we took the five-year time limit seriously.
> We also felt we had to emphasize "hardware"—housing, buildings and
> equipment—rather than "software." We knew social services were important,
> but we knew a lot of the experimental programs being tossed around in the
> Sixties wouldn't last.... That was the thing that was so great about Model
> Cities—we could decide what most needed to be done and then do it.

Guided by this strategy, Branning and Cox developed preliminary
budgets for the seven subcommittees and began "brainstorming" some
projects for subcommittee consideration. Budgeting was a difficult task
because Branning and Cox had little budgeting experience or relevant data on
which to base cost estimates. They chose to simplify their task by allocating to
the committees straight percentages of the total $760,000 in supplemental
funds. Developing projects, on the other hand, was an area in which Branning
and Cox had considerable expertise. One obvious choice was a neighborhood
service center of the type both men had operated in Atlanta; another was a
whole range of housing assistance programs, such as loan guarantees, direct
assistance for down payments, and mortgage subsidies, to help families
displaced by urban renewal. Branning and Cox also felt that many OEO
projects that served Atlanta's low-income areas could be adapted to Gainesville, including special education, vocational training, elderly centers, and
youth recreation programs. Census data indicated a high birth rate among
Southside women, so Branning and Cox felt a family planning clinic would be
a valuable project. As indicated by the survey, rat control, cleanup, and street
paving projects seemed essential.

Cox found that approaching the subcommittees with these and other
suggestions was a delicate process: "I would listen to them talk about what
problems needed solving and then suggest, maybe we could do this to help
such a problem. I had to answer, not propose. We really tried as best we could
to make projects from their ideas."

The subcommittees were receptive to Cox's suggestions and, as Cox had
hoped, used many of them as a baseline to tailor projects to the specific needs
of the Southside. Still, some subcommittee members objected to Cox's
influence and complained that their suggestions usually were ignored. Cox's
response to this criticism was that many of the residents' suggestions would
cost too much, would not be workable, or would not provide lasting benefits after Model Cities was over. These opposing views surfaced many times
throughout the life of the Model Cities program.

Building Implementation Capacity

By late summer of 1968, Branning and Cox had a good idea of many of
the projects that would be included in the subcommittees' reports, and they

turned their attention to implementing those projects. This was the most difficult task of all, as Branning and Cox soon learned. Although both had brought considerable expertise in developing and overseeing public projects to Gainesville, there was little in their backgrounds to prepare them for the complicated work of finding appropriate organizations to implement projects and of negotiating the terms under which the projects were to be administered. Compounding their problem was the fact that the city had no experience with such a wide array of public projects as Model Cities, and few city departments had either the capacity or desire to undertake them. Yet Branning and Cox had little choice but to work with city departments; the only other organization that could be brought into Model Cities was OEO, whose expertise was limited to projects involving preschool children and the elderly. All other projects in the areas of health, housing, physical improvement, employment and crime, and most social service and elderly projects would have to be implemented by the city.

Fortunately, Branning and Cox had Mayor Cromartie and Commissioner Randolph Waters on their side. Both were highly respected by most of the city department directors. They were able to take advantage of this respect by using Cromartie and Waters as "go-betweens" to win arguments with the heads of the parks department, city school board, and police department for projects such as park construction, summer recreation, youth activities, learning disabilities treatment, and a police juvenile unit. Through his association with prominent local businessmen, Cromartie had no trouble locating a group to form a local Economic Development Agency to oversee construction of an industrial park. Cox recalled Cromartie's invaluable assistance in these efforts, "I don't know what we would have done without John. He was just absolutely determined to get Model Cities going. I doubt if a lot of the city people would have listened to us, but they sure listened to him."

Even Cromartie's support, however, was not enough to win over some of the more recalcitrant and conservative agency heads. For example, Branning and Cox met with early opposition from Dr. Donald Lancaster, the outspoken and highly respected director of the Hall County Health Department. Dr. Lancaster was convinced that Model Cities would undercut his department and weaken its authority, and he refused to cooperate in implementing any Model Cities health projects. (Among those proposed were a family planning clinic, home health aides for the elderly, and a mental health program). In July 1968, however, Dr. Lancaster accompanied Cox to a statewide meeting of health officials to review current plans for health projects in the five Georgia Model Cities programs. Cox described the meeting:

> Everybody presented their projects and showed how much they would cost, how many people would participate, etc. I was last and pulled out a CPM

chart [Critical Path Method, then a relatively new technique for mapping out the timing of various elements of a project] showing how all our projects would be implemented. The State Health Department had just started using CPM and they went crazy—we were further along than they were. Gainesville was the "star of the show." Dr. Lancaster immediately apologized for his opposition to Model Cities and offered to help us in any way possible.

This was a crucial event: word of Gainesville's sophisticated planning spread through the state bureaucracy, and Dr. Lancaster became one of the CDA's strongest allies, pushing other reluctant city department directors to agree to implement Model Cities projects. The dividends of this meeting would prove to be quite large for the CDA.

While most city and state departments began lining up behind Gainesville's Model Cities program, Branning and Cox found that some of the proposed projects did not lend themselves to implementation by either the existing city departments, state agencies, or Gainesville OEO. They especially were worried about housing-related projects; they expected housing to receive the bulk of first-year Model Cities appropriations, yet only the urban renewal agency had any experience in housing. The URA director privately had opposed Model Cities, but even if he had agreed to take on Model Cities projects, Southside residents would not have taken kindly to anything run by the URA. The only solution, they decided, was to create a new city Housing and Relocation Department to handle the proposed relocation and mortgage-assistance programs. The same solution was indicated for building a proposed Neighborhood Services Center (NSC). From their personal experience with NSCs, Branning and Cox felt that such a center, combining the offices of many state and local departments, had to be operated by a separate agency. In Atlanta the NSCs were operated by nonprofit community agencies, and Branning and Cox had always feared that those agencies would have to close the NSCs if OEO funds stopped. Thus they felt that it was important, especially in a small town such as Gainesville, that the city assume some sort of permanent responsibility for the NSC. Despite their confidence in these proposals, however, Branning and Cox knew they were taking some risks. The city commission easily could refuse to create the departments, and HUD could refuse to allow use of Model Cities funds for their operation (since they would technically be citywide departments and not confined to operation within the Model Neighborhood).

Hunting for More Grants

Throughout the months before the subcommittee proposals were submitted to the Technical Review Committee and Citizens' Demonstration Committee, Cox took on the responsibility of seeking out possible additional sources of funds for Model Cities projects. Having little previous experience in this area, he relied heavily on HUD technical assistance manuals to suggest possible federal programs and on Dr. Lancaster to suggest possible state programs that Gainesville could tie into through Model Cities. Dr. Lancaster helped Cox obtain his first grant agreement from the state Department of Human Resources (DHR) to fund Gainesville's family planning clinic through HEW's "Partnership in Health" program.

As he continued his search Cox found the CDAs were, as HUD had promised, receiving priority for grants from many federal programs. The availability of such grants influenced the several projects that the Gainesville CDA had suggested to the subcommittees, especially in the areas of crime and employment. The availability of federal Economic Development Administration (EDA) funds for industrial parks led Branning and Cox, in consultation with the City Planning Department and a HUD representative, to redraw the boundaries of the Model Neighborhood to include a large plot of land adjacent to the city's new airport, which the city had hoped to develop into an industrial park. The Employment and Economic Development Subcommittee subsequently incorporated plans for the industrial park into its long-range goals. Similarly, after contacting Law Enforcement Assistance Administration (LEAA) officials in Washington, Cox found that Model Cities were being given priority for that agency's grants. All of Gainesville's planned crime and juvenile delinquency projects would be eligible for LEAA funding.

However, Cox also found that many agencies would not give any guarantees of funding until he could tell them exactly how much money was needed and when the project would begin. Since Model Cities was still in its planning phase and no one really knew when its operation would formally be approved by HUD, this hurt Gainesville's ability to compete with other cities for many federal grants. As Cox recalled:

> We weren't working under any kind of deadline. Actually we thought the planning was really going slowly, and then HUD told us we were further along than almost any other "Model City." But, until the other cities caught up, a lot of people in the federal agencies were skeptical of promising us money. And we couldn't tell them when we actually needed the money. HUD sort of "forgot" about this.

As a result, Cox was able to secure only three grants for the first-year plan. But in the process he gained valuable experience and made contacts with state and federal officials that would be important in succeeding years.

An August Windfall

Just as the subcommittees finished their reports, Gainesville received an unexpected boost in August of 1968: Congress voted nearly to double the Model Cities authorization for FY 1970, increasing to one billion dollars the total supplementary funds available to the 150 CDAs. Gainesville's allotment was increased accordingly to $1.33 million dollars. Cox recalled the shock wave that went through the city: "A million dollars was just a tremendous amount of money," he said. "It wasn't hard to spend $700,000, but to spend nearly double that much . . . we had to scramble to figure out where to put it all. That was nearly half as much as the city's whole budget in 1968."

The windfall produced many fortunate consequences for the CDA. Cox went back to the subcommittees and told them that funds would be available for many of the projects that he previously had discouraged; more funds could be provided for housing development, and Gainesville could provide the minimum match for more federal grants. In two weeks of whirlwind meetings, the subcommittees expanded their proposals from a total of 46 to 66 projects, the housing budget doubled from $250,000 to $500,000, and the employment/economic development budget rose from $10,000 to $150,000 as funds became available to match the EDA industrial park grant in the first year.

Approving the CCDP

In September the seven subcommittees presented their final reports to the Technical Review Committee, proposing the 66 separate projects for the first-year action plan and extensive proposals of goals and objectives for the five-year Comprehensive City Demonstration Plan (CCDP). The reports were released to the press and the reaction was very favorable. Branning and Cox had "done their homework" in steering the subcommittees toward workable projects and in finding or creating the necessary capacity to implement the projects. As a result, the Technical Review Committee unanimously approved all of the subcommittee reports.

However, things did not go so smoothly when the reports reached the CDC. Despite the unanimous approval of the Technical Review Committee, many CDC members felt obligated to exercise their authority by voicing questions and objections to some projects. And despite Branning and Cox's efforts to avoid divisiveness, the CDC seemed to be split racially on many issues. Many Model Neighborhood members were inexperienced in dealing with meetings and negotiating, and the CDC meetings often ended in shouting matches. It took several meetings over a three-week period for the CDC finally to approve the plans, and the vote was not unanimous.

The fragile consensus of the CDC seemed to reflect the ambivalent attitude much of Gainesville had toward Model Cities even after the enormous amount of publicity given to Model Cities planning. Gainesville was basically conservative and still smarting from the urban renewal debacle. Public skepticism was typified in an article by a popular local columnist, E. P. "Hip" Palmour:

This OEO, Urban Renewal, VISTA-ridden town is now about to become a "Model City." This city ought to be renamed "Suckerville!" It is not governed by the people or their local officials. It is run by a bunch of imported experts who would make it a permanent experimental community of the federal government.

This sentiment was echoed in a public hearing in early October by two of the five city commissioners who now would have the final word on whether Gainesville would begin its Model Cities program. Cromartie and Waters, on the other hand, were outspoken supporters of Model Cities. The remaining commissioner, serving his first term, refused to take a position, fearing reprisals in the 1969 elections regardless of which side he joined. The Model Cities plan would have to pass by a majority, and Cromartie knew the wavering commissioner would vote "no" in a regular public meeting. So he, along with Branning and Cox, devised an ingenious scheme for getting Model Cities passed. Early in November they arranged an "information meeting" for the commissioners with all of the city department heads and members of the Technical Review Committee—more than 50 enthusiastic supporters of Model Cities. One by one they made detailed presentations of each of the seven CCDP components. After two hours of presentations, the commissioners were prepared to leave when, in a surprise move, Cromartie convened the commission and moved for adoption of the CCDP. As Cromartie recalled, "They knew they had been ambushed. They couldn't very well vote against the wishes of all those government and business people. So they voted unanimously for Model Cities." Branning and Cox were elated that Cromartie's strategy had worked so well. "We knew," said Cox, "that we wouldn't have stood a chance at an open commission meeting. If Cromartie hadn't done what he did, I doubt if we would have ever had a Model Cities program in Gainesville."

Waiting for Approval From Washington

After a year of arduous planning, Branning and Cox were anxious to begin implementing the Model Cities projects. They were encouraged by the quick processing of the CCDP and first-year plan by HUD's regional and national offices, culminating in an official announcement of approval in December 1968. However, national politics interfered with their plans, and it was nearly a year before any contracts could be drawn for the project to begin.

Gainesville had been one of a handful of cities whose Model Cities plans had been given "rush" processing in the closing days of the Johnson administration. At the same time, the lame-duck White House was seeking to commit as much of the Model Cities appropriation as possible and to ensure the continuation of the Model Cities program. The new Nixon administration responded to this tactic by ordering a second review of the plans that had received last-minute approval. HUD was ordered to investigate everything about the cities, and in Gainesville's case it discovered violations of federal school desegregation orders. Gainesville thus was informed in the spring of 1969 that its letter to proceed with Model Cities had been revoked indefinitely, pending compliance of its school system with federal desegregation laws. The city subsequently desegregated its schools, as many smaller cities did, by simply closing the high school and elementary school on the Southside. HUD then took Gainesville's Model Cities plan "off the shelf" and conducted a new review of all 66 proposed projects.

Gainesville finally received its "letter to proceed" in June 1969. Due to HUD's complicated funding procedures, however, this meant only a preliminary approval of funding; projects could begin, but Gainesville's CDA could not actually provide funds for the implementing agencies until it signed a "master contract" with HUD. The projects were to be funded on a reimbursable basis, with the agencies turning in vouchers for their services to the CDA; the CDA would then forward the vouchers to a local bank, which would reimburse the agencies and send the vouchers to HUD, which would repay the bank. The bank, unfamiliar with this process, refused to release any of its funds until the CDA could guarantee them reimbursement; in turn, the CDA was unable to complete any contracts with agencies to begin Model Cities projects. The entire program was delayed until HUD finally agreed to the "master contract" in December 1969—a full year after Gainesville originally had received its "green light" from that agency.

The only steps taken by the CDA during this time were to use some of the unspent planning funds—only $64,000 of the $98,000 grant had been spent—to hire additional CDA staff (including a physical planner, an information and evaluation officer, and a citizen participation director) and to determine the organizational structure of the CDA.

More than two years had passed since Representative Landrum had announced Gainesville's Model Cities planning grant, and not a single project had begun. Meanwhile, the CDA lost a valuable ally when Mayor Cromartie was defeated in his bid for reelection in November 1969.

Model Cities Slowly Begins to Move

The delay in finally beginning Model Cities produced uneasiness among city officials about the whole program. In the recent campaign some city commissioners had grumbled loudly about Model Cities, and newspaper articles were sounding increasingly impatient and skeptical that Model Cities actually was going to get off the ground. The CDA staff knew they had to get the projects started as quickly as possible in order to overcome this attitude. Unfortunately, the city and the CDA staff still largely were unprepared to handle the many intricate details of beginning new projects and of complying with federal regulations. As a result, the Model Cities program suffered even more delay.

Negotiating Contracts

Although Model Cities was supported by all of the agencies that had been asked to implement projects, Cox still found himself facing many difficulties in negotiating contract terms with the agencies. The CDA had to hire a lawyer to help work out the many legal details; it took several weeks to successfully explain complicated reimbursement procedures, overcome objections to limiting services to Model Neighborhood residents, counter the overall apprehension about government red tape, and work out the details of meshing the Model Cities projects with the agencies' current operations. Adding to Cox's troubles was the city commission's insistence on approving every contract. However, once he confronted the commissioners with the prospect of reviewing 66 contracts, they agreed to only an overall review after all contracts were negotiated. Then Cox moved to consolidate as many projects as possible, winnowing the 66 contracts down to a more manageable 20. Nonetheless, for HUD accounting purposes each project had to have a separate account, and the CDA hired a fiscal coordinator to handle the bookkeeping details.

Cox also had difficulty, as he had feared, in securing approval for the Housing and Relocation Department (HRD) and the Neighborhood Service Center Department (NSC). The commissioners were concerned about future city obligations to fund the departments; they were skeptical of HRD possibly duplicating the Urban Renewal agency's duties as well as suspicious of providing direct cash assistance to residents. They insisted on establishing a review board of private citizens to approve all grants for individuals' down payments or interest subsidies; they also insisted on directly hiring the staff of the two departments. The commission finally approved the departments in March 1970 and began hiring staff. The HRD was assigned four staff members, mostly by transferring personnel from Urban Renewal and the City Housing Authority (which operated the city's new public housing projects). The seven NSC staffers included, to no one's surprise, two commissioners' daughters. Unfortunately, both departments encountered even further delays before they could begin their long-awaited operation.

Regulations

By April 1970 only 13 of Gainesville's Model Cities contracts had been signed, and some of the most important projects were further delayed while the CDA worked out disputes with HUD over compliance with Model Cities regulations and for approval of additional federal grants. The Housing and Relocation Department suffered most from these delays. Cox went to

Washington to convince HUD officials that the HRD was not duplicating Urban Renewal duties and that its operations would be within the Model Neighborhood.

This proved to be the first of many Cox run-ins with HUD, which he felt was damaging the Model Cities program with unnecessary regulation and a lack of sensitivity to local needs:

> From the very beginning HUD was strangling us with regulation. For a program that was supposed to cut red tape, Model Cities had more regulations than I've ever seen. It was especially tough for small cities like us that were just getting started. HUD never took into account the different needs of big cities and small cities—which was pretty ridiculous when the program was supposedly founded on the principle of more local control.

Cox also cited the enormous paperwork and data collection requirements as a major burden on Gainesville's small Model Cities staff and recalled that nearly half of every year was spent preparing the next year's application. In addition to these delays, the HRD had to wait for approval from the federal Farmers Home Administration (FmHA) for use of its various loan and mortgage-subsidy programs and for the city commission to award a contract for the loan program to a local bank. Even after the FmHA-backed program was begun, its progress in securing mortgages for Southside families was exceedingly slow due to the many application and review procedures required by FmHA and the city and to a continued shortage of low-cost housing. Another HRD project, providing direct assistance through HUD for down payments, had awarded grants to only two families when HUD completely discontinued the program. By August 1970 fewer than a dozen families had actually moved into different homes with HRD assistance.

Frustrations continued to mount when HUD informed the CDA that its citizen participation program was not in compliance with Model Cities regulations and threatened to hold up all Model Cities funds. HUD tried to insist that the CDC should be made up only of Model Neighborhood residents or that another committee of neighborhood residents be formed with veto power over the CDC. Cox felt this was simply another case of HUD's insensitivity to the needs of small cities:

> HUD couldn't understand that we had to do things differently than cities like Los Angeles. L.A. had four or five model neighborhoods, each with five or six thousand people—they were like little cities, but they represented only a small fraction of the total population of L.A. We had just the opposite—a small model neighborhood that's a big portion of the city. Model Cities here had to involve everyone if it was going to work, because it would affect everyone.

Cox didn't have to go to Washington to work out this dispute, but he spent many hours on the telephone and collected several affidavits from CDC members attesting to its effectiveness before HUD finally approved the CDC structure. One of the most irritating delays of all was in staffing the implementing agencies. Although nearly all of the agencies had sufficient staff to operate the projects, HUD recently had instituted strict requirements for employment of Model Neighborhood residents in any Model Cities-created job. This requirement caused additional delays in the start up of the neighborhood service center and the JOY (Just Older Youth) center for the elderly. Cox recalled that the employment requirements were among the most unrealistic of all HUD regulations:

> Here was another case where HUD just wasn't being realistic with respect to small cities. We wanted to provide jobs for the neighborhood people, but it was almost impossible in such a small community to find enough people that were qualified to do the jobs and yet lived in the "right place." We ended up, in several cases, having to hire someone to train one or two people for jobs; and if one of them quit we'd have to do it all over again. How many people are out there waiting for jobs like counselors at the service center or the JOY center...? It was crazy.

HUD regulations also affected the staff of the City Demonstration Agency itself, much to Cox's chagrin:

> They told us we have to have so many clerks, so many "project evaluators," so many "community specialists," and the like. We had six people working just on citizen participation. One of them could have talked to every person in the whole neighborhood in two or three weeks! We had more than twenty people working for Model Cities and we could have done just fine with five or six ... all because of HUD regulations.

Progress at Last

These myriad delays were a blow to the confidence of the CDA, which became the target of much adverse publicity. Cox found himself frequently giving interviews to the press, usually apologizing and explaining the "external" causes of the delays. However, by the fall of 1970 he also was able to point to several encouraging developments in the Model Cities program.

Additional Grants. After the Model Cities funds began flowing to Gainesville, Cox continued to search for additional funding for the first-year projects. His efforts paid off as he secured four more sizable grants:

- $350,000 from HEW to construct a vocational wing at Gainesville High School. This grant required a match of $150,000, which CDA provided by delaying some education and physical improvement projects.
- $10,000 from HUD for a "Model Design Study" to update the city's statistical data and provide more pertinent information for future Model Cities planning.
- $10,000 from EDA for technical assistance to help Southside residents start new businesses.

- $40,000 from the Georgia Jaycees to sponsor a vocational rehabilitation center.

In addition Cox obtained HUD's approval to reprogram $400,000 of urban renewal funds to the HRD for land repurchases. These funds, combined with previous federal grants from the Economic Development Administration, Law Enforcement Assistance Administration, and Health, Education, and Welfare Department, brought the total outside funding of Gainesville's Model Cities program to more than $1 million in the first year alone.

First-Year Projects. Despite the disappointing delays, those projects begun early in 1970 had achieved some visible and well-publicized results. The rat-control and cleanup projects had markedly improved the appearance and safety of the Model Neighborhood. The two JOY centers were heavily attended, and the Health Department had conducted extensive outreach efforts to bring women into the family planning clinic. In addition, the CDA was fortunate to have the vacated Southside high school building available for its use; by late summer 1970, the building was almost fully utilized, housing the CDA offices, the NSC, indoor recreation for neighborhood youth, and a learning service center for University of Georgia social work students. The presence of these services in the heart of the Model Neighborhood was the CDA's largest source of pride and generated the most enthusiasm from neighborhood residents.

Reviews Show Gainesville's Success. When the city undertook an extensive review and evaluation of Model Cities in July, the impacts of the first-year projects and the additional funding secured by the CDA made quite an impression with the city commission. As a result, the CDA won a much needed vote of confidence from the commission and a "green light" to undertake more of the long-range projects that had figured so prominently in the original strategy of Branning and Cox. The CDA received an even greater boost in early August when HUD regional officials visited Gainesville for an on-site Model Cities review. Newspaper accounts indicated that regional Model Cities director Earl Metzger was impressed with Gainesville's program:

> We are very pleased with the progress indicated here in the first two quarters. We think Gainesville's program is one of the best in the region; we are encouraged by the many things we've learned here which might be very useful to other small cities like Gainesville. . . . My impressions indicate good racial and community relationships here in Gainesville; there certainly is no display of the kind of overt hostility you get in other areas.

Metzger also said he was "particularly impressed with the adeptness of the administrative staff regarding the number and quality of state and federal programs it has been able to bring into the city," especially the EDA technical assistance, the NSC, and the LEAA programs. The CDA was elated with these favorable reviews, which would bring considerable attention to Gainesville throughout the coming months.

Housing—A Continuing Problem

Despite the overall favorable impression of both HUD and the city commission with Model Cities, both indicated concern for the slow progress of the HRD in alleviating the critical shortage of standard housing in the Southside. To tackle the housing problem, Branning and Cox set up a task force consisting of themselves, the city commissioners, HRD director M. E. Cantrell, EDA director Jack Margolin, and several local housing developers and bank officers. The task force was charged with devising a method to speed up the development and sale of new housing at prices that Model Neighborhood residents could afford. Unfortunately, a legal opinion issued by Georgia's attorney general prohibited either CDA or HRD, as constituent parts of city government, from developing land and selling the houses. The only alternative was the establishment of a private, nonprofit corporation to purchase land, build houses, and sell them at cost. The developers indicated that they would be willing to form a corporation, but Branning and Cox questioned the validity of spending Model Cities funds to purchase land. However, with no other feasible alternative, Branning and Cox agreed to try to work out the details.

Cox was encouraged when the CDC voted unanimously to reprogram $310,000 from the largely ineffective loan programs to fund a nonprofit corporation and when a group of five local developers agreed to form Gainesville Non-Profit Development Inc. (GNPD). However, it took several weeks of negotiation with HUD to allow the actual reprogramming of funds and to work out the legal details of purchasing land outside of the Model Neighborhood boundaries with Model Cities funds. GNPD was approved in October 1970 and began purchasing land adjacent to the Model Neighborhood in November. Gainesville's plan for housing development was subsequently incorporated into a HUD planning manual as an example for other Model Cities—a great source of pride to the city.

Planning for the Second Year

While Branning and Cox were working out the details of GNPD the rest of the CDA staff was working with the Model Cities subcommittees, the Technical Review Committee, and the CDC to complete the second-year action plan. The CDA planners were given a great deal of responsibility for coordinating the planning process and for continuing the CDA's aggressive search for additional funding for Model Cities projects. Cox recalled the benefits of this delegation of responsibility:

> We kept the staff enthusiastic. They knew that their work was really important when each of them was given full responsibility for their area.

They developed expertise in their areas and learned a lot about running Model Cities in a short time. Also, the subcommittees and the CDC were probably tired of me and welcomed some new faces. . . . The same was true for the state program offices. I didn't have the time to properly follow up on all the grant applications, but the staff did. They developed good relationships with the state officials, which paid off.

Another change was the installation of CDA staffers from the citizen participation division as subcommittee chairmen. Although some of the CDC members objected to this policy, Cox stated in an interview that "the subcommittees themselves had requested this, since they had found the meetings and the planning process to be too unwieldy." As a result, the second-year meetings went much more smoothly and the entire planning process was completed between August and October. Only two projects were added to the twenty begun in the first year—paving Southside streets and construction of a new building to house the NSC. However, both were expensive, long-range projects and required new agreements with the city.

The construction of a new NSC building was suggested after social services planner Frances McBrayer found that it would be eligible for funding through HEW and HUD's Neighborhood Facilities Program. The city would have to provide only a third of the estimated $400,000 cost and could use Model Cities funds for the local match. However, such a multi-grant agreement would, by federal law, require a 20-year commitment by the city to continue the center's operation. The commissioners were hostile at first to this suggestion, fearing a huge expenditure after Model Cities funds expired. However, McBrayer and Cox met with the commissioners and convinced them that nearly all of the center's operating costs could be paid by the agencies that had offices in the center—including welfare, unemployment, and social security—and by federal grants from HEW. Their argument was reinforced when McBrayer secured over $100,000 in additional HEW funds for 1971, including $70,000 for the center.

The CDA found it more difficult to win the commission's approval for the street paving project. Several commissioners objected to paying the full cost of paving Southside streets because the city had historically paid for street paving through city bonds financed by the owners of property on the streets. At several commission meetings, the CDA presented evidence of the enormous cost of maintaining unpaved versus paved streets and argued that an owner-financed plan was infeasible for the Southside—resident homeowners couldn't afford to pay, and absentee landlords would raise rents as a result. The commissioners finally agreed to a compromise plan, suggested by the city manager, using general obligation bonds to pay a third of the paving cost, with property owners and Model Cities also paying a third each.

Following the compromise, the commission approved the second-year action plan, which called for expenditures totaling $2.8 million ($1.33 million in Model Cities supplemental funds). Gainesville had come a long way since 1968—and still had a long way to go.

The Second Year and Beyond

With most of its initial start-up problems worked out, Gainesville's Model Cities program swung into high gear, expanding services, adding projects, and securing still more outside funding. In the process Gainesville's city leaders and citizens developed a new appreciation of federal programs and an awareness of the continuing needs of the Southside. The CDA became a sophisticated planning and coordinating agency, handling not just Model Cities but all other grants obtained by the city. Carlyle Cox succeeded Bob Branning as CDA director in March 1970 and came to be widely regarded as a top grantsman and authority on small city redevelopment. And Gainesville itself, though not without its problems and failures, became an example used by many federal agencies to demonstrate the effective use of their programs in small cities.

Grantsmanship and Program Expansion

From 1971 to 1973 Gainesville's CDA continued to add to the city's "bankroll" of federal and state grants. To win these grants Carlyle Cox and his staff developed several different strategies and were assisted along the way by a fortunate turn of events.

One of the most effective strategies the CDA used to win both state and state-administered federal funds was devised by Cox in cooperation with the four other Georgia Model Cities. The five CDA directors held several meetings in late 1971 and early 1972 with state officials from the Department of Human Resources (DHR) and convinced them to use Georgia's Model Cities as test sites for all future DHR programs. The CDA directors agreed to fund several projects partially through Model Cities for two years, and DHR agreed to take over total funding if the projects were successful. Through this agreement Gainesville obtained DHR funds for a home health aides project, the family planning clinic, and a training program for mentally retarded persons. Gainesville also received favorable treatment from state grant administrators because the CDA staffers had developed a strong personal motivation to obtain grants; they were very persistent, became well-known in state offices, and had sophisticated data to present when requesting grants. Cox credited his staff's persistence as the reason they received several HEW grants through DHR. With these additional grants the Model Cities program was expanded to include an alcohol and drug-abuse education program, a preschool education program and an employment counseling program, which was operated through the Neighborhood Service Center.

Federal Grant Strategies. The Gainesville CDA's major strategy in obtaining federal grants was to "spin off" as many existing Model Cities programs as possible to other federal sources and thus to free more Model Cities supplemental funds for additional projects. The CDA was aided in pursuing this strategy by the many favorable reports on Gainesville's programs that HUD's regional offices began circulating through federal agencies in 1970 and 1971. Federal grant officials were more than willing to provide funds for a successful program. As one former Model Cities staff member recalled:

> It was certainly a case of "the rich getting richer." They [federal agency officials] were practically throwing us the money—they knew our programs were successful and we would make them look good. Why should they fund a new project when they can fund one with a proven track record?

Thus Gainesville had very little difficulty in obtaining additional grants from EDA, LEAA, and HUD. The HUD grants were especially "easy" to obtain because HUD was receiving mounting pressure from the Nixon administration to prove the effectiveness of Model Cities. In 1971 Gainesville received a $450,000 grant from HUD for a Neighborhood Development Project (NDP)—enabling the city to undertake an urban renewal clearance and redevelopment project in a small area of the Model Neighborhood. (The NDP was a success, answering many of the mounting criticisms of urban renewal.) The same year the CDA, on behalf of the city, also won a HUD Public Facilities grant to build a new Public Safety Building. (The previous city jail was located in the basement of city hall.) Following this award, Gainesville's city commission gave the CDA full responsibility for securing and administering all federal grants for the city. Subsequently, Cox was able to secure a $200,000 Water and Sewer grant to extend the city's sewer lines to both the Southside and to newly annexed suburban neighborhoods. In 1972 HUD awarded Gainesville a $50,000 Open Space/Historic Preservation grant for restoration of several landmark buildings near the downtown.

Gainesville had by 1972 become such a "prime target" for federal and state grants that the CDA actually was receiving offers of grants and turning some of them down. Cox realized that his staff was becoming overworked administering so many different grant programs. (By 1973 the count stood at more than 25 separate state and federal grants.) He recalled the difficult situation this created:

> Sure, we didn't want to turn down the money. For one thing, we could almost always find a use for it. And the other thing was that if we started turning down grants we were afraid it would look like we didn't need any grants. But the grants we turned down were for very specific projects, and we either already had the projects or we just didn't have the staff to put one together Remember, we had to find somebody else besides the CDA to run any project which was funded. It was very tricky. We had to tell the State, "Yes, we

really need the money, but we just don't have the capacity to administer it right now." We had to make sure nobody thought we had too much money or we might lose the grants we had. At the same time, we didn't want to sound ungrateful. It's always tough to say "no" when someone's trying to hand you a half-million dollars.

The Results

By the end of its third year, Gainesville's Model Cities program was attracting nearly $4 million a year to the city—a huge sum for a city its size. An elaborate brochure produced in 1973 cited several indications of the impact of Model Cities:

- average per-pupil education expenditures up by 50 percent

- 88 percent reduction in number of residents living in substandard housing

- development of 200 housing units through GNDP and HUD Section 8 rental program

- 400 families relocated into standard housing

- birth rate in Southside reduced by 54 percent

- 73 percent of unpaved streets paved

- all outdoor plumbing eliminated

- 95 percent reduction in major crimes reported

- 21 minority businesses assisted

- 2,700 individuals served at Neighborhood Service Center.

These and several other statistics spoke glowingly of Gainesville's Model Cities program, and many HUD officials concurred. However, the program was not without its critics nor without some admitted problems and failures. A common complaint was that the CDA and the city became absorbed in obtaining more and more grants and constructed its program with the primary objective of generating more funds. One CDC member recalled that, as the program went on, the CDC seemed to have less and less input into project selection and planning and became more of a "yes-man for the staff." The staff influence on the CDC became even stronger after the second year when the CDC chairman resigned and Carlyle Cox assumed responsibility for conducting the meetings. Cox and several city officials insisted that only one project recommended by the CDC was ever turned down; however, a longtime Southside resident and CDC member recalled that this was because "the staff had it all planned out before we could even ask for anything, and everything we did ask for seemed to be either 'ineligible,' or there 'wasn't enough money.' There was always enough money to tear down houses, but never enough for day care or a community center."

Cox admitted the problems with housing:

> It was amazing we did anything at all, especially in the first couple of years. There were many more unknowns than knowns; it was an enormous program for a town with no experience. The housing problem was terrible because of urban renewal. The Uniform Relocation Act of 1970 made it even harder to deal with, since we had to spend much more for relocation and then explain it to the people who had already moved and gotten less. It was hard to find developers who would build Section 8 housing [a federally financed rent subsidy program] and it was hard to get mortgages for the new houses built by GNDP. We were constrained by the housing shortage and by the restrictions on the federal money. Plus, no one in HUD really knew how to help us deal with housing. They were just as inexperienced as we were at that time.

Model Cities also came under fire in its later years from local businessmen and developers who were disappointed with the city's continued lack of attention to the deteriorating downtown business district. In 1972 the Gainesville Chamber of Commerce commissioned a study of its business activity and a plan for revitalizing the central business district, with the hope that Model Cities funds could be used as "seed money" for rebuilding downtown. Although the southern edge of the downtown was in the Model Neighborhood, HUD had informed the city that Model Cities funds could not be used for downtown redevelopment or for rerouting streets where traffic patterns had been greatly altered by urban renewal. City leaders began to echo the businessmen's sentiments; although they basically approved of Model Cities and were pleased with the funds attracted by the CDA, they still felt that many of the city's overall needs were not addressed by Model Cities.

Despite the criticism and dissatisfaction of some observers of Model Cities, the CDA defended its overall record and blamed problems on federal administrators and local conditions. Model Cities Assistant Director Charles Morrow, a lifelong Southside resident and the highest-ranking black in Gainesville's city government, recalled the Model Cities program this way:

> Model Cities was designed to fail. It was put together in a hurry and we knew from the beginning that it would be changed soon. That's why we tried to do things that would last, like the service center, the vocational wing, and the industrial park ... so when the funds stopped, we would still have something. The social programs that Model Cities was supposed to implement—we just felt a lot of them would eventually fail. . . . We also did the best we could to involve the people on the Southside. But they had really been "ripped off" by urban renewal and some people wanted Model Cities to do things it just couldn't do. I think Model Cities did a lot that would never have been done otherwise.

Discussion Questions

1. What were the main reasons that most of Gainesville's officials resisted the idea of federal programs for the city?

2. How and why were these attitudes overcome in launching the Model Cities program?

3. What were the key political and administrative tasks facing Branning and Cox in developing and implementing the program?

4. What accounts for Branning and Cox's success in "grantsmanship"?

5. What role did the federal government play in influencing the Gainesville Model Cities program—and what other effects did federal involvement have on the city?

6. How do small city politics and management differ from those in big cities?

Suggestions for Further Reading

Frieden, Bernard, and Kaplan, Marshall. *The Politics of Neglect.* Cambridge: MIT Press, 1975. A thorough account of the establishment of the Model Cities program and its early history, told from the perspective of federal program managers.

Pressman, Jeffrey L., and Wildavsky, Aaron. *Implementation,* rev. edit. Berkeley and Los Angeles: University of California Press, 1979. A now-classic case study and analysis of the difficulties of implementing major development projects; focus on Oakland, California.

Wolfinger, Raymond. *The Politics of Progress.* Englewood Cliffs, N.J.: Prentice-Hall, 1974. History and analysis of the urban redevelopment programs in New Haven, Connecticut, under one of the nation's most effective urban leaders—Mayor Richard C. Lee.

Community Development in Gainesville (B)

CHRONOLOGY

<u>1971</u>	President Nixon proposes Special Revenue Sharing programs to consolidate federal categorical grants-in-aid. Proposal seen as threatening to Model Cities, but it does not pass in Congress.
<u>1972</u>	Cox elected vice-chairperson of Model Cities Directors Association. He works to influence congressional action in revising Model Cities program. Cox begins to alert officials in Gainesville that legislation changing the program is likely to be enacted. He begins to feel that change will benefit Gainesville's program.
<u>1974</u>	Passage of Community Development Block Grant (CDBG) legislation fails to make small cities with predecessor programs automatically eligible for grants. Cox assesses potential impacts of new law on Gainesville's program.

THE CASE

By 1973 Gainesville's Model Cities program was in its third full year of operation, far ahead of most of the 149 other cities that had been designated Model Cities grant recipients. Gainesville's program was considered a success by both federal officials and most local observers. The local Model Cities staff knew, though, that in Washington the federal government was contemplating

This case was written by Kay Rubin under the supervision of Arnold M. Howitt. Its development was financed by a grant from the U.S. Department of Housing and Urban Development for use in the Program for Senior Executives in State and Local Government at the John F. Kennedy School of Government, Harvard University.

far-reaching changes in the nation's grant-in-aid system that might have a significant impact on Gainesville's future.

From Model Cities to Community Development

From almost the day Richard Nixon took office as president, his administration had sought to mold Model Cities and other HUD programs into a program that reflected Republican philosophy: fewer federal regulations and more local control over allocation of funds. In March 1971 President Nixon formally announced his "New Federalism" program calling for consolidation of hundreds of categorical grant programs into six "special revenue sharing" programs. For the next three years the president, the Congress, and state and local governments battled over the fate of the categorical grant programs, including Model Cities. The uncertainties created during this period were of particular concern to Gainesville because its Model Cities program was much farther along than most, and because it was participating in many programs whose future was in doubt.

Nixon's proposals, as well as other new policies, were seen nationwide as possible threats to the Model Cities program. Through correspondence and meetings at HUD seminars, the Model Cities Directors Association (MCDA) was formed to counteract those perceived threats and to influence HUD policy toward Model Cities. Gainesville Model Cities director Carlyle Cox was an early and active participant in the MCDA and became well-known through his frequent appearances at Model Cities seminars. In 1972 he was elected vice-chairman of the MCDA. That same year President Nixon introduced the first of several bills seeking to consolidate HUD grant programs and increase local control in the allocation of grants. Cox was called to testify before Congress on behalf of the MCDA. The MCDA favored consolidation of the categorical grant programs but preferred the congressional plan to the administration's; the administration's bill was blocked. Later in 1972 Cox returned to Washington to testify against an administration proposal diverting Model Cities funds to school desegregation. This measure failed also, and the MCDA gained recognition as an effective lobbying organization.

Some MCDA members also gained recognition. Carlyle Cox was among this group, which consisted of about a dozen directors who were young (Cox, at 35, was the oldest), outspoken, and whose Model Cities programs generally were viewed as innovative and successful. This group became the instruction team at many HUD seminars and was among those most active in the MCDA and National League of Cities lobbying efforts. According to Cox, the group soon was considered as "knowing more about HUD programs than HUD did" and was called upon several times during 1972 and early 1973 to assist in drafting new legislation for consolidation of HUD grant programs. Three different bills were introduced in 1972, with the House, Senate, and administration bitterly disagreeing on many key points.

Although the legislation was stalled throughout 1972, Congress seemed to be progressing toward a compromise; it appeared likely that some form of consolidated program would be approved in the next year. Late in 1972 Cox began informing his staff, Gainesville's city leaders, and the local citizen-review committee of the upcoming changes to be made in the seven HUD programs in which Gainesville participated. From his involvement in drafting the administration bill, Cox knew what the basic features of the new program would most likely be:

- Community Development Block Grants (CDBGs) would replace the seven categoricals;

- Cities currently participating in HUD programs would be "held harmless," or guaranteed their current level of funding;

- the CDBGs would be used for a wider range of projects than Model Cities funds, with emphasis on physical improvements;

- discretion of local officials would be increased in the allocation of the funds, and citizen participation would be required;

- the CDBGs would be distributed to cities by formula, rather than competition, with a certain amount set aside for small cities.

The major disagreements still to be resolved were the choice of the allocation formula, the method of distribution among large and small cities, and whether urban counties would be included among eligible CDBG recipients.

When Congress adjourned in 1972 Cox was confident that the new program would be good for Gainesville—"a sort of super-Model Cities" as he saw it. He looked forward to continued funding for the Model Cities projects that had become popular, both among the residents of the Southside (Gainesville's "Model Neighborhood") now receiving unprecedented attention from the city, and the city departments that received increased funding and expanded duties. With a wider range of uses for the funds, Cox also hoped to do more in the area of housing and to respond to the growing demands for downtown revitalization. He anticipated expanding his department's realm of operation to the entire city, making his and the department's positions more important within the city government and ensuring the city commissions' cooperation with the department's plans. Cox was unabashedly enthusiastic about the new program. Following several encouraging newspaper articles based on Cox interviews, the city anxiously awaited congressional approval and the start of a CDBG program in Gainesville.

Despite Gainesville's enthusiasm, however, the new Congress heard objections raised to the program that had taken shape in 1972. In 1973 Congress encountered an intense lobbying effort on behalf of urban counties. But inclusion of urban counties in the program would necessitate a change in the distribution method for the CDBGs because not enough funds were available to fully fund all large cities "entitled" to the CDBGs by the formula in addition to urban counties and small "hold-harmless" cities. Other complex issues kept Congress tangled in details of the new Community Development program throughout 1973 and well into 1974. Congress finally enacted the program in August 1974, after a five-week House-Senate conference committee had settled the remaining differences. It became the first piece of legislation signed by newly inaugurated President Gerald R. Ford.

The final legislation included a compromise on "hold-harmless" funding that was not reached until the last day of the House-Senate Conference. Cox, who had been watching developments in the debate warily, traveled to Washington shortly after the bill passed to learn in detail what the new legislation contained. He expected some changes in the revised bill that he and MCDA would not like, but he was unprepared for what he found. Only cities over 50,000 in population would be "entitled" to CDBGs. Small cities like Gainesville currently receiving HUD grants would be completely "held harmless" for only two years, after which their grants would be phased down to zero. Under the complicated formula, Gainesville's funding over the five-year program period would be:

- 1st year—$1,979,000 (100% of Model Cities and 100% of the average of all other HUD grants)
- 2d year—$1,730,000 (80% of Model Cities and 100% other)
- 3d year—$1,300,000 (60% of Model Cities and 80% other)
- 4th year—$780,000 (40% of Model Cities and 60% other)
- 5th year—$260,000 (0% of Model Cities and 30% other)
- After the fifth year Gainesville would receive no funds at all.

What Now for Gainesville?

As Cox returned to Gainesville with this unhappy news, he knew that he and his staff faced some formidable tasks and tough decisions. Nearly all of the points that had made the CDBG program so attractive to him earlier now would present major obstacles to its implementation in Gainesville.

First, Cox anticipated intense competition for the available funds. The established constituencies of the Model Cities program would make it nearly impossible to reduce funding for Model Cities projects at least until 1976 when Model Cities would officially expire. Meanwhile, Cox knew he virtually had promised his critics additional funds for new housing and downtown revitalization. The city commission wouldn't ignore the business community's demands for downtown improvements and highway reconstruction.

Cox also feared that the political difficulty caused by increased demand for reduced funds would be exacerbated by a loss of priority for other federal grants. Gainesville no longer would be one of only 150 Model Cities, but just "one of the crowd" again—and it would be a bigger crowd because many cities that would receive CDBG "entitlement" grants had never before competed for other federal funds. Cox also knew that consolidation of other categorical grant programs, advocated by President Nixon, could eliminate even the outside funding that Gainesville currently was receiving. Yet, as difficult as it would be to obtain additional federal funds, it would be nearly impossible for Cox to obtain any city funding because he had promised the city commissioners that such a request never would be made.

As he contemplated these problems, Cox also realized there would have to be some substantial changes in the current Model Cities administrative structure and that these changes would be made more difficult by the funding cutback. For example, urban renewal was merged with other grant programs under CDBG, yet the first of Gainesville's three urban renewal projects was barely half completed. Funds would have to be allocated to finish the project, and somehow the URA would have to be abolished. The Citizens' Demonstration Committee also would have to be altered to include more citizens from outside the Model Neighborhood; yet this would make it easier for the committee and the city commission to reduce funding of Southside projects and might destroy the hard-won confidence of the Southside residents. Even Cox's own position and department might now be in jeopardy; CDBG funds would go directly to the commission, which could choose to eliminate or drastically reduce Cox's staff in the interest of economy.

Although the potential problems were staggering, Cox knew that he and his staff would have to begin thinking about some immediate solutions. Within the next two weeks, meetings of both the CDC and the city commission would be held at which Cox would be expected to report on the development of the CDBG program.

Discussion Questions

---

1. What effects—both political and administrative—would the consolidation of HUD's categorical grant programs into the Community Development Block Grant have on Gainesville's programs?

2. In what ways must Cox change his perspective as program director?

Suggestions for Further Reading

Advisory Commission on Intergovernmental Relations. "Community Development: The Workings of a Federal-Local Block Grant Program." Washington, D.C.: Government Printing Office, 1979. Provides a legislative history of the enactment of CDBG and information about its operations during its early years.

Pressman, Jeffrey L. "Political Implications of the New Federalism," in *Financing the New Federalism,* Wallace E. Oates, ed. Baltimore: Johns Hopkins University Press, 1975, 13-39. A contemporary analysis of the likely effects of the Nixon administration's block grant programs on local governments.

Community Development in Gainesville (C)

THE CAST

Carlyle Cox	director of the Gainesville CDD
Charles Morrow	assistant director of the Gainesville CDD
Ernest Moore	Gainesville city commissioner
Virginia Canupp	CDD housing planner
Frances McBrayer	CDD social services planner
Bob Smith	CDD housing planner
CDBG	Community Development Block Grant, program that replaced several HUD categorical grants
CDD	Community Development Department, Gainesville's agency to administer CDBG

CHRONOLOGY

1974	Gainesville learns that under the new CDBG program its annual allocation will decline from $2 million to $0 over five years. Cox tells his staff to work immediately on the first-year application, while making plans for the transition. The city commission transforms Model Cities program into a new Community Development Department (CDD) to manage the CDBG program.
1975	Gainesville's preparation pays off; it is the third city in the nation to receive its CDBG allocation. CDD develops housing rehabilitation program, plans downtown redevelopment, and works on its second-year CDBG plan.
1976	Cox actively seeks new sources of financial support for the CDD; he secures grants from HUD and other federal and state agencies.
1977-1979	Cox prepares for the new Small Cities CDBG program. Grant helps stabilize funding for the future.

THE CASE

"I don't see why there should be any problem. After all, we're going to end up with just about the same money we had before, aren't we? I'm sure you'll be able to work it out." W. Ernest Moore didn't seem very worried. As one of five city commissioners in Gainesville, he was reacting to news he had just received concerning Gainesville's scheduled allocation of federal funds under the Community Development Block Grant (CDBG) program. It was September 1974 and Moore was in his first term as commissioner. But he was well aware of Gainesville's recent experience with federal programs. He had been impressed with the results of the Model Cities program since 1971 and had every reason to believe that the new CDBG program would be as successful. Even as he listened to news that Gainesville's CDBG allotment would be cut from almost $2 million to zero over the next five years, he felt confident that the able Model Cities staff would find a way to handle the situation as it had carried out the Model Cities program—with little supervision from the commission.

Carlyle Cox, director of the Model Cities program, had been afraid of Moore's reaction. After working for six years in the Model Cities program— the last four as its director—he had seen the city commission shift from a position of suspicion and close scrutiny of federally funded programs to one of benign cooperation. Although he credited his and his staff's efforts with encouraging this change, he now wanted to reverse it to involve the commission more in the CDBG program. Cox had just returned from Washington with news about the upcoming funding cutback, and he had hoped that the commissioners would be at least a little alarmed. Cox himself was worried; he knew that the CDBG program would be different from Model Cities and that managing the program would involve much more than simply dealing with the loss of funds. He did not want to be left "holding the bag" if some politically difficult decisions had to be made—and such decisions seemed certain. As he returned to his office, he gathered his thoughts and tried to decide what his staff should do next to prepare for the transition to the new program.

This case was written by Kay Rubin under the supervision of Arnold M. Howitt. Its development was financed by a grant from the U.S. Department of Housing and Urban Development for use in the Program for Senior Executives in State and Local Government at the John F. Kennedy School of Government, Harvard University.

Managing the Transition

Although Cox had discussed the probable implications of the CDBG program with his staff through 1973, he could not make any substantial moves until he knew the details of the new program. After coming back from Washington, he knew he would have to work fast to ensure a smooth transition and to set an "operational strategy" to manage the many program changes required by the CDBG phaseout. His first priority was to file the formal application for CDBG, including plans for using the funds, so Gainesville could receive its allotment as soon as possible. The more quickly the funds became available, he reasoned, the sooner the unfinished Model Cities projects could be completed, and the sooner Gainesville would have the matching funds necessary to attract other federal grants crucial to Gainesville's CDBG program. Cox knew that, because many more cities would be receiving grants under CDBG than under previous programs, Gainesville would need its CDBG funds early to "get the jump" on other cities competing for matching grants. Although he could not predict the actual date at which the CDBG would be phased in, he wanted to make sure that Gainesville's application would be "in the mail the next day."

Cox also knew it would be difficult to come up with an application quickly. For one thing, the first-year CDBG of $1.979 million was far more than his staff or the city had ever dealt with before. As he recalled:

> Two million dollars was just ... well, we'd never seen that much money before. It made our eyes pop out! What in the world were we going to do with that much money? We couldn't carry it over to the next year,* and if all the Model Cities projects were funded we still had over a half million left. Gainesville's a small town and that's just a lot of money—it was almost as much as the whole city budget.

He also worried that it might take a long time to get an application through the citizen review committee and the city commission. Cox especially needed close contact with city officials to explain the complex details of the program, many of which governed the choice of projects to be funded under CDBG. If the commissioners did not provide enough input into the planning of the application, he feared that his staff might make recommendations that the commissioners would later oppose, delaying the submission of the application to the federal government and hurting his and his staff's reputations. For this reason, Cox had tried to impress on the commissioners that they would have to

---

*Unlike the categorical grants, CDBG required cities to allocate their entire annual grant to specific projects and did not permit them to "carry over" unallocated funds to the next year. Cities that failed to allocate their CDBG in full could face a reduction or revocation of their grants. However, once allocated, funds for a particular project did not have to be spent in the year in which the funds were allocated.

be more involved in the planning of the CDBG program. But the commissioners seemed content to leave the planning to Cox and his staff.

Fortunately, Cox had a distinct advantage in dealing with the situation. Because he had been so deeply involved in the development of the CDBG program, he knew how the program would be administered, what the main program objectives and policies of HUD would be, and what parts of the program were likely to be amended in the future. Armed with this knowledge, Cox was able to gear up his staff quickly for the transition from Model Cities to CDBG and to help the city devise an effective strategy for dealing with problems posed by the CDBG phasedown.

Initial Steps

Cox first had to deal with the many administrative details of setting up the Gainesville program. His initial step was to get the city commission to designate his office as the operating agency for the CDBG program. Here he had another advantage: the Model Cities office had no serious challenges from other local agencies. In many larger cities, the Model Cities program remained a separate entity under CDBG, and a separate department was designated to run the overall CDBG program. In these cities the Model Cities program was relegated to the same status as any other nonprofit agency that sought CDBG funding. In Gainesville, however, the commissioners quickly renamed Cox's office the Community Development Department (CDD) and granted it status as a regular city department. However, they refused to grant Cox and his assistant director, Charles Morrow, classified employee status; they remained unclassified without city benefits or pensions.

Because no one knew when CDBG officially would begin, the "new" department was responsible not only for planning and organizing the CDBG program but also for continuing to coordinate Model Cities. Although this meant that preliminary CDBG planning would take some staff away from Model Cities, Cox was not concerned. He always had felt that Model Cities was overstaffed in accordance with HUD regulations. (Model Cities employed more than 20 people, in comparison with the five employed by urban renewal.) Cox realized that the transition would give him a perfect opportunity to trim his staff—thereby reducing administrative costs, which would be less and less "affordable" as CDBG funding declined. But laying off staff was an unpleasant task. As Cox later recalled:

> I knew we wouldn't need as much staff under CDBG, and I knew we couldn't justify the cost. But a lot of the staff had worked for three to four years, and many of them were black and from the Southside. We did two things to handle it. First, we took part of the staff and put them on planning for CDBG and let the others "run" Model Cities for the last year until March 1975. We also laid off an equal number of blacks and whites, including the mayor's

daughter, who was one of the first employees at the Neighborhood Service Center opened under Model Cities. We didn't want to look like we were discriminating—like once Model Cities was over we didn't care about blacks. But it was still hard to let go of some people when there were so few blacks working for the city.

Cox's strategy worked, and no controversy arose over the layoffs. Once the staff requirements had been worked out, Cox and his senior staff turned their attention to organizing the citizen participation component of the CDBG program. Citizen participation had been a somewhat disappointing exercise under Model Cities. Although at the program's inception many Southside residents showed great interest in its planning and implementation, attendance at the Citizens' Demonstration Committee (CDC) meetings had declined steadily, and fewer and fewer people were voting in CDC elections. At the urging of Assistant Community Development Director Morrow, a lifelong Southside resident who previously had served as citizen participation director, Cox agreed to retain the existing racial and residential composition of the CDC (60 percent black and from the Southside, and 40 percent from all other areas of the city). The city no longer was required to provide majority representation to Southside residents as it had during Model Cities. However, Morrow felt strongly that they "couldn't turn their backs on the Southside; people there were still suspicious of us and we had no reason to fan the fires." To encourage participation, Cox and Morrow decided to have the committee members appointed rather than elected, and Morrow met with members of the former CDC to "invite" them to remain on the new committee. Although most of them accepted, Cox still had six positions to fill to reach a membership of 29. He appointed people who were young and had been active in civic groups— some of them former Model Cities workers—with the hope that they would be more likely to attend committee meetings.

Cox and Morrow also decided to dispense with the seven subcommittees and the Technical Review Committee. These had been useful in ironing out many of the early problems of Model Cities and in suggesting new ideas for projects, but they had found that these two levels of review became overly cumbersome and had made the application process too long. They knew that the timely submission of applications would be important under CDBG. They planned, however, to wait until after CDBG had begun—and they could get a better idea of what the major components would be—before forming committees.

The First-Year Application

Cox was worried about what Gainesville's first-year CDBG application would look like and how quickly it could be put together. He and his staff had worked since late 1973 to develop ideas for feasible projects in light of the expected increase in CDBG money. But by the spring of 1974 Cox knew that many of those projects would be impossible to complete without eliminating Gainesville's existing Model Cities projects. He had to allocate nearly $2 million without creating costly programs or raising expectations within the community that could not be fulfilled later. As Cox recalled:

> It was a devil of a problem. We had so much money, and everybody knew it, and everybody wanted some. We knew there wouldn't be much money down the road, but it's hard to tell people that when all they see is two million dollars this year. It was also hard to explain the fundamental differences between CDBG and Model Cities. CDBG was a new concept—we thought it would be a great new program for Gainesville. But the problems which Model Cities dealt with were still there, and we had to keep a lot of those programs going too.

To resolve these conflicts, Cox assigned staff groups to work out different aspects of the first-year application. One group developed budget estimates for continuing the existing Model Cities projects; another group worked with regional and state authorities to determine where additional funds would be available for Model Cities projects. A third group "brainstormed" to develop new projects, especially in the area of housing—a critical problem area that Model Cities had failed to address adequately. The groups were small—three or four people—and Cox had given them only from mid-May until the end of June to make their recommendations. Cox believed, however, that the size of his staff was an advantage rather than a liability:

> Our staff was small, but it had a lot of experience and really knew the programs. Because we only had a few people, everyone had a lot to do and knew they were important to the success of the program. I know that in some bigger cities they had entirely new staffs working on CD that had worked on Model Cities and had real problems getting their act together. We were lucky. We had the experience, but also we were small enough so that everyone had a stake in doing this well.

During the latter part of June the entire staff met for several long sessions to draw up a preliminary list of projects and cost estimates for the first-year CDBG. They found that after full funding of all continuing Model Cities projects, about $700,000 was still left for new projects.* They then decided on several one-year expenditures that had been ineligible under Model Cities, including new firefighting equipment, three new parks in the Southside

---

* Model Cities projects included a multi-use Neighborhood Service Center, construction of an adjacent health center, educational programs for preschool children and adults, centers and nutrition programs for the elderly, and crime prevention and juvenile delinquency programs. Gainesville also used Model Cities funds to match grants for several projects in health care, education, recreation, housing, and physical improvements—all on the Southside of the city, which was the "Model Neighborhood."

neighborhood, and the removal of architectural barriers to the handicapped in the central business district. Another $300,000 was earmarked for land acquisition in and around the downtown area for a long-planned rerouting of Gainesville's highways. The "new projects" group, headed by housing planner Bob Smith, also proposed a comprehensive program of grants and loans for rehabilitation of deteriorating houses. Cox recalled the object of many of these additional proposals:

> We knew we had to do something big about housing. We hadn't gotten anywhere trying to relocate people out of the Southside, or into better houses, or in building new houses—interest rates were going up and nobody could afford new houses. So we thought a rehabilitation program would help people to stay in their neighborhood but have decent places to live. As for the other expenditures, some of them were for things we really needed—the street improvements and storm drainage especially. Others we chose because they could be done in a year or two, and they also helped to "parcel out" the money to some of the newly competing interests—the business community, some of the city departments, and people outside the Southside, who were wondering when their neighborhoods were going to get some of these federal dollars. These might have been political judgments, but they were no less necessary than the others in terms of the overall success of the program.

The suggested budget met with few comments or complaints when it was presented to the CDC. Some Southside residents were surprised that CDBG allotments would go to projects and expenditures outside the former Model Neighborhood, but they generally were satisfied that the Model Cities projects would be left intact. Cox and Smith were grilled about the proposed housing rehabilitation, however. Some committee members, remembering that many Southside residents had been forced to relocate during Gainesville's ill-fated urban renewal program, feared they would be compelled to leave while their houses were rehabilitated. Although they did their best to allay these fears, Cox and Smith realized that the rehabilitation program would be the real "acid test" of the CDBG program in the Southside; they knew they would have a difficult time securing the city commission's approval for the rehabilitation program and administering it successfully.

An important problem was that the city government had little influence with the local banking community, which was reluctant to cooperate in any public or private program to provide loans to low-income home buyers. The bankers also were not favorably disposed toward grants for housing purchases, as was apparent when a grant program begun under Model Cities was quickly terminated before any money was disbursed. However, the Community Development staff was convinced that the only way a rehabilitation program would work was through grants; most Southside homes needed such extensive repairs that even a subsidized loan would be unaffordable for residents. This program's design and implementation would be one of the most interesting and controversial aspects of Gainesville's Community Development program.

Cox and the Community Development Department staff were greatly relieved when the city commission approved the CDBG application in August 1974, shortly after President Ford had signed the Housing and Community Development Act that created CDBG. In January 1975 Gainesville was the third city in the nation to receive approval for its CDBG allotment. This speed often was repeated later in the program and became a key factor in Gainesville's successful management of its CDBG phasedown.

The First Year: Planning a Community Development Strategy

Although relieved to have successfully completed and submitted the first CDBG application, the CDD staff knew that they had more work ahead. From August to December, the CDD was occupied primarily with concluding the Model Cities contracts, arranging contracts for new CDBG projects, and completing the remainder of the paperwork required by HUD prior to the release of the CDBG funds. Because all but one of the eight CDD staff members had been part of the Model Cities staff since its inception, these procedures were routine—a marked contrast with the beginning of Model Cities when contracting and paperwork requirements proved to be major stumbling blocks to Model Cities' implementation.

However, Model Cities had been meticulously monitored and, in the end, heavily regulated by HUD. As the Gainesville staff learned, CDBG had far fewer regulations, and HUD seemed almost aloof to the cities (many of which were struggling to start their first community development program). Thus, as the staff turned its attention to implementation and funding problems Gainesville faced in its CDBG program, it got very little help from HUD and could find little direction in the broad guidelines Congress had set for the program.

The lack of guidance was acutely felt as the CDD set up its housing rehabilitation program. Many staffers recalled that no one in HUD seemed to know much about rehabilitation programs, and HUD had no "model" program to offer cities as it had in many program areas during Model Cities. Their concern was not so much that they could not devise a workable program, but that once they did, HUD would find some reason to disallow it,* or later

---

* Although Gainesville received its funds as an "entitlement," which meant it was entitled to a predetermined amount of CDBG funding over five years, HUD was empowered to conduct post-audits of local programs; and cities were required to submit performance reports. HUD also was empowered to withhold further funding from cities that did not comply with the intent of the program, demonstrate the capacity to operate the program, or unnecessarily delayed expenditure of funds.

would make regulations prohibiting it. They were worried especially that HUD would disapprove of a grant program (rather than loans), which they believed to be the best way to gain maximum participation of residents while protecting themselves from the local banking community's whims.

A bigger problem than HUD, though, was the city commission, which was known to be strongly averse to any kind of grant program. To win the commissioners' approval, Cox thought it necessary to make a tough political decision, and his staff agreed: they would propose a loan program first, knowing it would not work well and "allow" the comissioners to conclude later that the grant program was the better alternative. Cox explained this move as simply maximizing the net results given the political constraints; others on the staff later surmised it was designed largely to delay the start of the program so that funds budgeted for rehabilitation in the first year could be "carried over" to soften the blow of the CDBG phasedown.

Cox was taking a big gamble to suggest even a loan program; he knew he would need the cooperation of all six of Gainesville's lending institutions to make it acceptable to the city commissioners. This was no small task. Cox and housing planner Smith spent many long days tossing around plans before they finally decided on a strategy to approach the financial community. Cox described their risky and tension-filled approach:

> We knew that we could never get all of them [the lending institutions] together by being completely open about what we were doing. They never got together for anything—the animosity among some of these families that ran the banks went back years. So we asked the mayor to set up a meeting with us and the president of each of the lending institutions, telling each that we wanted his opinion on some financial matters of the CD Department. Of course, when they arrived at the meeting, they couldn't believe the other five were there, too. Knowing we had a captive audience, Bob and I then explained to them that we wanted to set up a low-interest loan program for housing rehabilitation, but we didn't know quite how to go about it. Of course we knew exactly what we wanted, but pleading ignorance made them all think we really needed their help. We told them that without their help we would have no choice but to give money directly to the homeowners, which of course made them blanch. I asked them to send me their best loan officers to work out a suitable program through which the city would guarantee their loans with the CDBG funds. Of course, none of them were especially thrilled with the idea—but nobody was going to say no in front of all the others and lose the potential loan business. So they all agreed. We were really sweating bullets for awhile, but afterward it seemed like it had been so easy; we had to laugh about it.

The bank presidents held to their agreement, and the Community Development staff learned a great deal from working with the experienced loan officers. Together they worked out a program, with the CDD agreeing to hold 30 percent of each loan as collateral; loans were not to exceed $5,000. This was favorable to the local lenders, because it put them at almost no risk in making loans to even the city's poorest residents, but it fell far short of the real needs of most Southside homeowners. "We knew it wouldn't work," Cox said. "Very few of these people could afford loans even at 5 percent and most needed far more than $5,000 to put their houses in decent condition."

The CDD made a valiant public relations effort to induce applications for the loans but by the summer of 1975, six months after the program was approved, not a single application had been made. However, because the CDD had "broken the ice" with the financial community and gone out of its way to accommodate the bankers' concerns, it was much easier to go back and convince them to drop the collateral provision, raise the loan limit and the income ceiling, and allow the CDD to make "supplemental" grants. Cox adamantly maintained that "We would never have done anything for housing 'rehab' any other way." However, it took almost another year for the revised program to produce significant results.

The delay in beginning the housing rehabilitation program indeed allowed the CDD to carry forward nearly $500,000 to subsequent program years. Whether or not this was intentional, it allowed the CDD much greater flexibility in its second- and third-year projects. This flexibility proved to be invaluable as the CDD came under increasing pressure during 1974 to use the CDBG program to respond to a previously unaddressed problem for Gainesville—the deterioration and abandonment of its downtown area.

Downtown Development

The merchants and land and property owners in downtown Gainesville were a powerful and influential group. Primarily due to their pressure, Gainesville had embarked on its ill-fated urban renewal program. Dissatisfied with the results of urban renewal, a group of these businessmen in 1973 privately had commissioned a major study of Gainesville's central business district and a plan for revitalization of the downtown. The study, completed by a prominent consulting firm in Atlanta, concluded that downtown Gainesville had lost much of its attraction for shoppers and visitors who preferred the many suburban shopping centers and the cultural attractions of nearby Atlanta. The consultants recommended that Gainesville redevelop a large section of its downtown area, highlighted by a civic center for meetings, exhibits, and concerts, and complemented by the rerouting of several main streets and highways that currently led into Gainesville in a haphazard fashion.

As the results of this study were circulated through Gainesville, the city came under increasing pressure to implement the plan using some of its large federal grants, including its CDBG. After refusing Model Cities support for the downtown plan (such projects were ineligible for Model

Cities funding) in 1973, the city commissioners spoke privately with Carlyle Cox early in 1974 about using CDBG funds to rebuild downtown Gainesville. Cox had been able to convince them that it would be to everyone's political advantage to wait at least a year, until the CDD could get a grasp of what other funds might be available and ways could be found to provide the CDBG funds without eliminating existing projects. Cox knew throughout 1974 that the CDD no longer would be able to resist the pressure for downtown development.

However, Cox also knew it would be dangerous to commit CDBG funds for downtown projects that would require long-term financing. First, he had the CDBG phasedown to consider. He also felt certain that HUD eventually would tighten regulations on CDBG allocations. Through conversations with HUD officials and community development leaders from other cities, Cox realized that many cities had taken the fullest advantage of the "local control" allocation of CDBG funds, and HUD was becoming alarmed at the number of cities that were using CDBG funds to finance hotels, office complexes, and civic centers—the latter exactly what Gainesville was planning.

Cox was right about HUD's revising the program guidelines but not about their effect on Gainesville. In 1975 Congress urged HUD to emphasize "economic development" as a major component of the CDBG program. Cox found that the proposed downtown development fell within HUD's new rules for eligible economic development projects, but CDBG funds could be used only for land acquisition, demolition of buildings, and rerouting of streets. The funds for the actual construction of a civic center and renewal of existing storefronts would have to be found elsewhere.

As the CDD staff examined the downtown plan, it realized that it would cost well over $1.5 million just to develop the site for the center and another $2 million to $3 million to construct it. Looking at their first-year CDBG budget, staff members noted that about $600,000 could be "reprogrammed" from other uncompleted projects (such as the unsuccessful housing rehabilitation program) and from several completed projects that needed no additional funds. In addition, Cox was able to convince the city commissioners to use city funds, primarily from its $700,000 in general revenue-sharing money, to take over some of the smaller Model Cities projects that had received CDBG funding the first year. Thus, since Gainesville's CDBG entitlement was reduced by only $250,000 in the second year, it was possible to begin downtown development without reducing funding for other projects.

The downtown project was controversial when the Community Development Committee began reviewing the second-year budget. Southside residents questioned allotting such a large sum for a project that would not directly benefit Gainesville's low- and middle-income families. One CDC member recalled that he was "surprised that we were going to spend so much to build this center when there were so many people laid off all over the city." The 1974-1975 recession indeed had hit Gainesville hard; unemployment in the city rose from 5 percent to more than 18 percent. While the CDD staff claimed both to the committee and in its CDBG application that the downtown project would create both temporary and permanent jobs and improve the overall city economy, many committee members were skeptical; even the local newspaper's editorials questioned the wisdom of embarking on such a major construction project during a recession.

The committee reluctantly endorsed the second-year CDBG budget, and the city commission enthusiastically approved it as well. However, the CDD still had to find the funds necessary to build the downtown center and to deal with a more drastic third-year CDBG cutback to $1.3 million.

The Third Year: Generating Additional Funds

Gainesville's first and second years under the CDBG program were significantly different from its experience in the Model Cities program. Not only were there more and different types of projects, but the city had relied almost exclusively on its CDBG entitlement to fund the projects. Two major reasons for this change from Gainesville's aggressive grant-seeking during Model Cities existed. First, the CDD staff felt that the first- and second-year CDBG entitlement was enough to implement the necessary projects, and additional grants might create expectations of future funding that would be difficult to fulfill later as the CDBG entitlement shrank. Second, as Gainesville went from one of only 150 Model Cities to one of nearly 1,000 CDBG recipients, the city lost some of its competitive edge in applying for additional grants. With these two factors in mind, the CDD held off on seeking other grants until it began contemplating its third year CDBG program.

In 1976 Cox directed his staff to renew efforts to obtain HEW funds for several of the social service projects that had begun during Model Cities. That year HUD had notified CDBG recipients that they should close out any remaining Model Cities, urban renewal, and other formerly categorical programs, and increase the emphasis on economic development and physical improvements in their CDBG program. Cities were encouraged to seek social service funding through HEW's Title IV and Title XX programs, which were block grant programs administered by the states.

Fortunately, Gainesville had maintained good contact with the state Department of Human Resources (DHR), primarily through CDD staff member Frances McBrayer, an expert on social service programs who had obtained and coordinated most of the outside grants during Model Cities. McBrayer worked throughout 1976 to obtain a DHR commitment of funds for several education and elderly programs on the Southside. She succeeded in obtaining a total of $350,000 from DHR for the 1977 program year.

Another important task the CDD faced was in finding funds for the downtown center. Cox had begun negotiations early in 1976 with the federal Economic Development Administration (EDA) to secure a three-year, $5 million grant to build the downtown center; however, EDA was demanding a local match from Gainesville that the city could provide only by increasing the allotment from its third-year CDBG. This meant that the CDD staff would have to come up with an additional $300,000 or else face reductions of other projects. Locating these funds would be especially crucial because Gainesville's fourth-year CDBG would be almost 50 percent less than its third-year allocation.

Anticipating the need for such additional funds in early 1976, Carlyle Cox had begun looking into the CDBG regulations to see if there might be an opportunity for Gainesville to obtain some of the CDBG funds that were reserved for "discretionary" allocation by the secretary of HUD. He was advised by some of his counterparts in other cities, and HUD officials as well, that these funds usually were reserved for cities and counties with no prior experience in Model Cities or community development; yet the application was required to demonstrate that it had the capacity to implement a CD program. This indicated to Cox that the county in which Gainesville was located, Hall County, might be able to apply for funds jointly with the city of Gainesville, with his department acting as the implementing agency.

Cox knew that Hall County, with a large population outside of Gainesville, needed many improvements in streets, roads, and utilities. The county government had long envied the city's ability to obtain and use so much federal money but lacked the type of planning and administrative staff necessary to win federal grants for the county. Both the city and county had come under fire during the past two years because the city's CDBG projects had to stop at the city limits; thus, there were many instances where homes on one side of a street were repaired while those on the other side were not, or where storm drainage stopped in the middle of a street. The city government routinely refused to annex such areas of the county. (Annexation could proceed only at the request of property owners on the street.) One CDD staff member noted that the city limits on the Southside had remained virtually unchanged for two decades, while urban renewal had forced many Southside families to relocate into adjacent county areas—making them ineligible for benefits of Model Cities and later of CDBG projects.

Cox arranged an information meeting with the Hall County commissioners, proposing an application for a $1 million joint city-county CDBG grant. In return for starting and managing the county projects, Cox requested that the city of Gainesville receive one-fourth of the funds awarded by HUD. Although the county commissioners were suspicious of the city government, Cox tried to assure them that the city intended to coordinate more of its community development efforts with the county and to work more closely with the county on other government matters; the joint CDBG would be a good way to begin. After winning Cox's agreement to allow the county full discretion on how its portion of the grant would be spent, the county commissioners approved the proposal, and the CDD drew up an application. The application was approved by both the city and county commissions and submitted to HUD in the late spring of 1976. HUD quickly approved the application and released the funds in August 1976. Gainesville received $250,000—just as the city was preparing the third-year CDBG budget. Gainesville was the only city in Georgia to receive both "entitlement" and "discretionary" CDBG funds in 1976.

The final sources of additional funds secured by the CDD demonstrated the increasing expertise and resourcefulness of the Gainesville planners. After obtaining the HEW and EDA grants, the staff looked into the regulations of both and found that "administrative and management" costs were legitimate expenditures for the grants. Thus the CDD designated two staff members as "project managers" for the social services program, transferring their salaries from the CDBG account to the HEW grant account; similarly, one other staff member was made project manager for the downtown project, and her salary also was paid through the EDA grant. Through such measures the CDD was able to minimize its administrative expenditures while budgeting the maximum amount (10 percent of the total grant) for administration, leaving additional funds that could be used for any CDBG project.

Income generated by the program itself was another source of such "contingency" funds. Gainesville owned a large amount of property that had been acquired through urban renewal and Model Cities, but the sale of this property would be a slow and cumbersome process. However, once the property was sold, the income reverted to the CDD account and could be spent on an eligible CDBG project. One CDD staff member commented that

> ... the "property income" made the difference. We sold a lot of land to keep the program afloat, and we still have some that we're waiting to sell. It's a "loophole" in the CDBG regulations because even after the project eligibility rules were tightened in 1977, income from land sales could be used for any project which was eligible at the time the property was acquired.

This "loophole" later became crucial in enabling the city to complete the downtown project, as well as in building a large city park on the northside of Gainesville—effectively a suburban area.

Through all of these inventive measures, the CDD was able to present a third-year CDBG budget that included an increased allotment for downtown development. A half million dollars for "close-out" of the urban renewal program continued funding for the Southside Neighborhood Service Center and education and elderly programs and for the acceleration of the housing rehabilitation program. Despite the reduction in the CDBG entitlement,

Gainesville actually spent more in total on its CDBG program in the third year than it had in the first.

The third-year budget was approved by the Community Development Committee, but committee attendance had declined steadily since 1974 and the approximately dozen members who regularly attended the meetings rarely disputed the recommendations of the CDD staff. In 1976 some Southside residents asked the committee members to request CDBG funding for a community center in the Southside because the area lacked any sizable meeting hall or function rooms. However, according to one committee member, the CDD staff put the project "on hold" for nearly six months. Only after repeated inquiries was the member told that it would be impossible to fund the community center because such a facility, as a social service project, ranked very low on HUD's priority scale. As CDD Assistant Director Morrow explained:

> One of the reasons we were so successful in managing the cutback was that we stuck to the rules as much as possible. Because we did this in Model Cities, for example, we didn't have as many projects that carried over into the CDBG program, so we didn't have the problems other cities had in trying to continue large social service programs. It was tough to keep telling people "their" projects were ineligible or low priority. But with the cutback, we were afraid that whatever program came after CDBG, the "feds" would favor the cities that stuck to the rules and might deny the funds to cities that didn't.

1977—Anticipating Changes in CDBG

The year 1977 was important for Gainesville's CDBG program. The Carter administration took office in Washington, and CDBG was due for review and reauthorization by Congress. The Democratic leadership had been critical of the program, particularly of the way in which CDBG funds were allocated. For Gainesville, the most important change proposed was one that would greatly increase the amount of CDBG funds available to small cities.

The original CDBG program guaranteed "entitlement" grants, distributed by a formula, only to cities of more than 50,000 people. The only small cities receiving entitlements were those like Gainesville that were "held harmless" for the funds they had received from the previous HUD programs; the hold-harmless grants were being phased down. Other small cities—and eventually Gainesville—would be forced to compete for the small amount of discretionary funds remaining after the entitlements were allocated. Many small-city officials, including Carlyle Cox, as early as 1975 had advocated setting aside a certain amount of CDBG funds for small cities.

The CDBG program was up for congressional reauthorization in 1977, and the Carter administration was anxious to put its stamp on CDBG. In response to pressure from small-city officials and their representatives in Congress, HUD organized a novel commission of local elected officials; local, state, and federal CDBG administrators; and outside consultants to consider the small-city problem and recommend ways to restructure federal assistance programs including CDBG. Gainesville's Carlyle Cox was a natural choice for this panel due to his long experience in community development, his activities as an instructor at various HUD workshops and a leading member of nationwide Model Cities and CDBG directors' groups, and in Gainesville's well-managed federal programs. Cox spent over half of 1977 working on the commission, helping to draft the administration's CDBG bill. Cox's participation provided Gainesville with invaluable "advance information" on what the new program would look like and how Gainesville could best qualify for funding. The Community Development Department staff knew it would have to work hard to make sure that Gainesville would be included in the new program—just as it had worked on the transition from Model Cities to CDBG a few years earlier.

In preparing the fourth-year CDBG budget, Cox told his staff that HUD intended to place much more emphasis on housing and infrastructure improvements in the revised CDBG program. Responding well to these new priorities, he thought, would help Gainesville to obtain whatever type of grant would be available to small cities. Accordingly, the staff devised a budget that slashed funding for all social service programs as well as for the downtown development project, while increasing allocations for housing rehabilitation, relocation assistance, street repair, and storm drainage.

The social service programs' cuts were lessened somewhat by the continuation of the HEW grants Gainesville had obtained in 1976. However, the programs were reduced in total, drawing scattered complaints—especially from the program managers who were forced to lay off some employees and scale down the programs' services. Nonetheless, few objections to the budget were voiced by the Community Development Committee, which generally felt that housing and street problems were far more important than social services.

In 1976 and 1977 the CDD had received many complaints about the housing rehabilitation program, although well over 200 homes had been repaired since the program was changed from loans to grants. Most complaints were due to shoddy workmanship or to insufficient funds to complete repairs once work had begun. (A housing boom in 1977 caused most larger and more established contractors to shy away from less profitable "rehab" work.) To bolster this program, which the CDD felt was the key to winning future CDBG funds, Gainesville obtained an additional $160,000 in federal loan funds through HUD's Section 312 program. These loans greatly increased the funds available per house and enabled the city to stretch the grant money further. Gainesville was one of the first small cities to make extensive use of this program, which began in 1964 but had relatively low visibility until high interest rates and housing shortages began to plague cities in the mid-1970s.

In addition to the HEW grants and the Section 312 loans, Gainesville and Hall County had obtained a one-year renewal of the joint city-county discretionary CDBG, giving the city a much-needed additional $200,000. However, Gainesville was unsuccessful in its attempt to obtain another joint grant with the town of Lula, a tiny community of fewer than 3,000 located in eastern Hall County. HUD turned down the application, which would have given Gainesville another $100,000 out of a total $500,000 in proposed grant funding. According to Morrow, HUD claimed Gainesville did not need the funds but was only trying to "use the town of Lula to feather our own nest."

While Gainesville's fourth-year CDBG budget was being approved by the Community Development Committee, Congress was putting the finishing touches on the Housing and Community Development Act of 1977. As Carlyle Cox had predicted, the allocation formula for CDBG was changed, with 20 percent of all funds to be set aside for cities under 50,000. A provision Cox had fought for especially hard was included, which gave priority funding under the small-cities program to cities whose "hold-harmless" grants were being phased out. Cities with prior CD experience were eligible for three-year comprehensive grants, while others were limited to one-year grants.

These provisions, combined with Gainesville's good "track record" under CDBG (the city never had received an unfavorable report from area or regional HUD annual reviews, nor had any application or performance report been questioned) made a small-city CDBG grant a virtual certainty for Gainesville. However, the timing of the grant, as well as that of all the other grants the CDD had obtained, was important in ensuring the overall continuity of the CDBG program. The timeliness with which Gainesville had submitted its first CDBG application enabled it to receive its annual allocation in March rather than in August when most other cities received their funds. The first joint city-county CDBG also was received in March 1977; however, the city was able to carry over this grant until the following year when Gainesville's CDBG entitlement fell from $1.3 million to $700,000.

When the small-cities program was activated, Gainesville was typically prompt in submitting its application, receiving the very first of the three-year grants, totaling $3 million. This was in November 1978, five months before the beginning of the fifth-year CDBG entitlement grant, which would drop to $264,000. HUD had reduced the first-year small-city grant by this amount but, because the grant arrived so early, it provided an additional cushion against the large fourth-year grant reduction. The following year HUD sought to reconcile all of its program accounts, putting them all on the same "program year" beginning in August. Thus Gainesville received its second-year small-city CDBG of $1 million in August 1979—only nine months after the first-year grant. This gave Gainesville well over $1 million in CDBG funding during the fourth entitlement year (1978), rather than $700,000.

Although this seemed extremely complicated, it was simple to the experienced planners in Gainesville. "You have to hand it to Carlyle," said housing planner Virginia Canupp. "He followed these programs so closely we always knew what was coming and responded very quickly. Many people fail to realize how important timing can be; but when you're in a small town like Gainesville and everything hangs on one or two grants, you learn to get that money as soon as possible."

Cox concurred. "Timing is everything," he said. "Why bust your tail chasing down other grants when you can get the job done by timing everything right? Even HUD still doesn't understand these kinds of things that the cities have been working out all along."

By 1979 Gainesville had weathered the storm of the CDBG cutbacks, celebrating its success as it dedicated the $6 million Georgia Mountains Center in the heart of a revamped downtown and an adjacent park in what was formerly Roosevelt Square. The guest of honor at these dedications was, appropriately, former Rep. Phil Landrum (who had retired in 1976), whose determination and political skill once had provided Gainesville with the federal funds it needed to begin its second downtown renewal.

Carlyle Cox and the Community Development staff were rewarded for their efforts when the city and county joined forces in 1979 to build a new administration building opposite the Georgia Mountains Center, funded by an Economic Development Administration grant.

From his window overlooking the center and Roosevelt Square Park, Cox reflected on the city's success:

> We tried to go by the rules, all the way back to Model Cities—even when we didn't like them. That's why we got the small-cities grant and the discretionary grant. Another Model Cities town in Georgia used its whole entitlement on social services, and they got nothing from small cities. Now they're scrounging for money. We knew what we had to do and did it. . . .
>
> We're a small town, but that meant we had a small staff, and it was easy to do things well. Only one of the seven of us [in the CDD] was not involved all the way back to Model Cities. The experience and dedication of the staff is remarkable; we all love Gainesville and wouldn't go anywhere else. That makes a world of difference.

Both citizens and program staff agreed, however, that there still was much to be done. Some residents were openly critical of the Community Development Department, claiming a lack of sensitivity to the changing needs of the Southside and an exaggerated emphasis on impressive statistics to keep the many federal grants. For example, in a heated argument over a proposal to use some of the final entitlement grant for "beautification" of the city's older public housing along a main highway, angry residents claimed that "camouflage is not an appropriate community development activity." CDC member

Jerry Castleberry, who headed an umbrella group of Southside neighborhood organizations, was bitter about the massive expenditures for the Georgia Mountains Center and other projects that

> ... will have no effect on the low- and moderate-income citizens of the community. That's what we all thought community development was about. Now they're going to have to spend even more money to keep it [the center] afloat. Meanwhile our people in the Southside still don't have adequate housing.

Many of the CDD staffers were candid as well in their assessment of the CDBG program. Assistant CD Director Charles Morrow expressed regret that the housing situation in the Southside had not greatly improved:

> We're really not much better off now than we were during Model Cities; we can fix up some of the worst housing, but then other parts of the neighborhood start deteriorating and make up for it. It's very frustrating. HUD says we have to have a "neighborhood strategy area" for projects like housing rehab, and it's hard to have to exclude areas which are outside the NSA [Neighborhood Strategy Area]. The program isn't designed to prevent deterioration. But I'd hate to see where we'd have been without it.

Discussion Questions

1. What strategy did Cox adopt to smooth the transition from Model Cities to CDBG?

2. What steps did Cox take to cope with the phase out of Gainesville's CDBG funds? Why did these prove successful?

Suggestions for Further Reading

Dommel, Paul R. *Decentralizing Urban Policy: Case Studies in Community Development.* Washington, D.C.: Brookings, 1982. Descriptions and analyses of CDBG programs in a number of U.S. cities.

Kettl, Donald F. *Managing Community Development in the New Federalism.* New York: Praeger, 1980. A comparative assessment of CDBG impacts in four Connecticut cities.

III. Citizen Involvement in Federal Programs

6. EXTENDING THE RED LINE TO ARLINGTON

7. CITIZEN PARTICIPATION IN OXFORD

6. *Extending the Red Line to Arlington*

Federal financing of state and local public works and development projects has made possible a wide array of improvements—such as housing, highways, transit facilities, sewage treatment plants, and public buildings—that otherwise might not have been made in America's metropolitan areas. Such projects provide benefits to millions of residents, delivering public services that greatly improve the quality of their lives.

Yet these projects have left a mixed legacy in some metropolitan areas. Particularly in the urban neighborhoods in or adjacent to construction sites, federally supported public works projects sometimes have generated suspicion, hostility, and bitter protest. The benefits enjoyed by many contrast with the costs borne by at least some residents of these communities.

Throughout the 1950s and 1960s two federal programs in particular—urban renewal and interstate highways—sensitized many urban dwellers to the potential costs of federally sponsored capital construction projects. In a number of metropolitan areas these early programs resulted in radical changes in the physical, economic, and social environments of the surrounding neighborhoods. Families, businesses, and social and religious institutions were "displaced"—forced to move away. The lengthy development process, moreover, often left land vacant for years and for additional years subjected remaining residents to dust, noise, and congestion from construction. Because of improvements to the area, rents and other living costs frequently rose beyond the capacity of longtime residents to afford, and newcomers swarmed into the area to live and work. Predictably, such results evoked intense public scrutiny of, and vigorous resistance to, subsequent development proposals.

Cries of protest were heard first by local public officials, but before long they had an effect at the national level as well. In the participatory climate of the 1960s, Congress enacted laws—as part of new programs or amendments to existing ones—requiring that citizens likely to be affected by such projects should be consulted and involved in the planning process. These statutes did not give veto power to the affected citizens, but they created procedural

267

protections to ensure that local residents' opinions were heard, and that citizens would have at least some access to decision making before project plans were etched in stone. In principle, these procedures were intended to help government officials weigh the benefits that a project would produce (often for many people who were spread out over a wide geographic area) against the harm it did to those who lived at or near the construction site.

As practice developed, local elected officials began to regard citizen participation in project planning with ambivalence. To the extent that participation is reasonably widespread and representative, citizen involvement affords an opportunity to find out how the community feels about a proposed project. By consulting with affected citizens, officials can better gauge community perceptions of need for a particular project, secure reactions to preliminary designs, and build public support for the idea. However, officials also view public involvement with hesitation or annoyance. From their perspective, the critical problem is to get representative participation at a stage of planning early enough for significant changes to be made in preliminary designs. It can be a very difficult task to make citizens aware that planning is in progress and that the project has potentially important impacts. In the absence of widespread involvement, many officials believe that citizen participation procedures may be manipulated by relatively narrow groups to thwart projects that would serve a wider public interest. They worry that the process may plant misconceptions in the public mind or simply delay planning long enough for rising costs to make the project economically infeasible.

From the standpoint of the average citizen, participation procedures also are problematic. Staying informed about government's planned projects, let alone becoming actively involved in shaping them, is a time-consuming and difficult task. Few people are willing to make the sacrifices needed to keep informed, think through the issues carefully enough to frame a position, and make public officials aware of their opinions and feelings—there are too many competing demands from family, work, friends, and recreation. For those few who do choose to become involved, making one's efforts effective can be frustrating. Will public officials listen if one articulates his or her ideas? If one feels that planning is going awry, how can he or she spread the alarm to the rest of the community? How can one inform like-minded individuals of the potential threat and persuade others of the danger? If making officials notice one's position requires having others visibly supporting it, how can one mobilize his or her neighbors and friends to get them actively involved? At the most general level, these questions point to a larger issue: what gets people involved in public affairs and what determines the nature of their participation?

The following case study, "Extending the Red Line to Arlington," explores the role of citizens in planning major construction projects. It permits the reader to consider the perspectives of both public officials and citizens.

First, raising the issue of how to solicit citizen views, the case describes a variety of methods by which public officials can get a sense of public opinion. These range from relatively informal methods, such as speaking to influential community members ("opinion leaders") or inviting residents to serve on ad hoc advisory panels, to more formal techniques. Among the latter are public hearings, mail or telephone surveys, and referenda. For the official trying to weigh public opinion, each method has certain advantages in depicting the *nature* and *intensity* of public sentiment, but each has noteworthy shortcomings, too.

This case also demonstrates that the *level* of public participation cannot be taken for granted. It lets us ask why there were so few residents of Arlington who wished to be involved during the early stages of the Red Line planning and why and how the townspeople's involvement could later escalate so precipitously.

Finally, the case raises questions about the *quality* of participation. How much information will actually be available to those who want to get involved? How representative of the community as a whole are the people who participate? Will citizens be consulted while project plans are still fluid enough to be changed in response to the public's views?

THE CAST

Margaret Spengler	chairperson, Arlington Board of Selectmen
Allen McClennan	director of Planning and Community Development for the Town of Arlington
Lawrence Susskind	professor in MIT Department of Urban Studies and Planning
John Cusack	state representative from Arlington
John Bullock	state senator from Arlington
Msgr. John J. Linnehan	pastor of St. Agnes Catholic Church, Arlington
Vincent Fulmer	resident of Arlington and member of St. Agnes parish
Robert Kiley	chairman of the board of directors and general manager of the MBTA
Donald Graham	MBTA master planner

Thomas P. O'Neill III	lieutenant governor of Massachusetts
William Cleary	president of the Boston Building Trade Unions and spokesman for the AFL-CIO State Council
Massachusetts Bay Transportation Authority (MBTA)	operates mass transit system in Boston metropolitan area
DeLeuw, Cather & Company	transportation consulting firm contracted by the MBTA
Citizen Involvement Committee (CIC)	citizen participation group organized by the Arlington Board of Selectmen
Summer Study Task Force	group of citizens who spent the summer of 1976 reviewing the MBTA's Red Line proposal
Cambridge Survey Research Corporation	performed telephone survey on the Red Line proposal for the Arlington Board of Selectmen

CHRONOLOGY

1972	Gov. Francis Sargent cancels implementation of major highway projects in the Boston metropolitan area.
May 1973	The Arlington Board of Selectmen requests that the MBTA extend the Red Line to Route 128 with stations at Arlington Center and Arlington Heights.
September 1974	The selectmen and Professor Lawrence Susskind organize the Citizen Involvement Committee (CIC).
April 1975	MBTA officials and consultants brief a small public meeting on Red Line extension plans.
1976 February	DeLeuw, Cather, & Company, MBTA consultants, propose a first-stage Red Line extension to Arlington Heights.

March	MBTA officials explain the proposal at a public meeting in Arlington.
April	1,200 Arlington residents attend meeting at St. Agnes Church to question MBTA officials about Red Line plan.
June	The selectmen appoint a Summer Study Task Force to investigate the Red Line plan.
September	The Summer Study Task Force publishes its study. State Rep. John Cusack files a bill to bar construction of the Arlington Center parking garage.
October	The legislature passes Cusack's bill.
December	A telephone survey of Arlington residents is conducted.
March 1977	The selectmen sponsor a nonbinding referendum on Red Line options.

THE CASE

"Who among you is ready to stand idly by and let Arlington become the end of the line?" demanded Msgr. John J. Linnehan of St. Agnes Church. Challenging the selectmen of the town of Arlington, Massachusetts, Linnehan spoke for hundreds of his parishioners and fellow Arlington residents who packed the town hall in the spring of 1976. They had come to express their views on the proposed Red Line subway extension, which would run out of Harvard Square to North Cambridge and Somerville and through Arlington before eventually continuing on to Route 128 in Lexington. (See Exhibit 1, p. 296.)

Earlier, when the Massachusetts Bay Transportation Authority (MBTA) first had made public its plan for extending the subway, Arlington townspeople were little concerned; such proposals had been made many times in the past. But as the MBTA's plans for Arlington became more definite, contro-

This case was written by Hester Barlow McCarthy and Arnold M. Howitt, with research assistance from Ben Dansker.

271

versy began to swirl around the rapid transit extension, and lines were drawn between supporters and opponents of the Red Line.

Proponents of the extension favored the jobs and commercial revitalization the project was likely to bring and believed it would improve living conditions in Arlington. As the town redevelopment board noted:

> The Red Line will clearly make Arlington a more desirable residential community. Arlington will be 15 minutes from Boston, yet removed from many of the problems and congestion of the Boston urban core. Residential as well as retail properties will increase in value. . . . The new zoning by-law will place physical limits on new housing and retail space. . . . Arlington will not become "citified."

Some opponents of the plan, however, saw their town becoming "the end of the line," where crime, traffic congestion, and neighborhood decline would occur. Others opposed the project as potentially interfering with the educational, religious, and community activities of Arlington. Linnehan expressed this view. "We are not opposed to the concept of sound mass transportation planning on a regional basis," he said, " but we cannot allow the MBTA to compromise the quality of life in Arlington at an unbearable cost to taxpayers and destruction of community values."

The Town of Arlington

Located nine miles northwest of Boston, Arlington is an inner suburb between urban Cambridge, with its educational and research centers, and suburban Lexington and Concord, with their historic and more rural airs.

The town of Arlington was first settled in 1630, originally as a precinct of Cambridge. In 1807 the community was incorporated as a separate town named West Cambridge. Finally in 1867 the town took its present name. As an industrial village, Arlington was the home of the first grist mill in New England as well as the center for the manufacture of saws and the shipping of freshwater ice. Arlington's growth closely followed the development of transportation facilities reaching out from Boston:

> During the nineteenth century, the town's development was enhanced by the development of a horse-drawn trolley line to Cambridge and the railroad from Boston. During the late nineteenth century and the first quarter of the twentieth, the town became increasingly urban, as electric trolley lines provided rapid transit service to Cambridge, Somerville, and Boston. Perhaps as much as sixty percent of the development of the town took place between 1905 and 1930 in the first great wave of western suburbanization of Greater Boston.*

In 1975 the town population had stabilized at 51,815; yet even without the rapid transit project subway planners expected it to start growing at a rate

---

* Town of Arlington, Massachusetts, Bond Rating Presentation, 1973.

of 5.7 percent over the following two decades. In contrast they estimated that Cambridge and Somerville would lose population at least until 1980.

In many ways Arlington still resembled traditional New England villages—but with the blemishes of encroaching urbanization. The town covered 5.5 square miles and was primarily residential in character. The Arlington Chamber of Commerce estimated that 59 percent of the tax base came from single-family houses, 25 percent from two-, three-, and four-family units, and 11 percent from larger apartment buildings. The remainder of the tax base, 5 percent, was occupied by commercial and industrial activities. Often characterized as a town of mostly blue- and white-collar workers, Arlington in 1970 counted only 4 percent of its families as having incomes below the poverty line.

The town's major retail area was Arlington Center, containing a line of shops and a municipal parking lot. While Arlington remained a pleasant residential community in the early 1970s, its shopping market was drying up as parking became a problem near the stores in Arlington Center. The physical condition of the shops was deteriorating because declining local commerce had left little money for upkeep and modernization. Shoppers and commuters easily passed the center by driving through it on the town's central artery, four-lane Massachusetts Avenue. Brighter shops and ample parking were found at Fresh Pond Shopping Center in nearby Cambridge or farther out in the suburbs.

As in other New England towns, much of community life in Arlington revolved around the churches, the main row of stores, and the parks in the town center. Built in 1856, the Victorian-designed First Parish Unitarian Church was an integral part of the community until it burned down in 1975. Plans soon were made to replace the church on the same spot. St. Agnes Church, also in Arlington Center, played a major role in community life. The St. Agnes complex, which included the church, rectory, grammar school, high school, and youth center, served approximately 12,000 parishioners.

Other major features of the town center were the town hall and historic public library, two public housing complexes with 236 units for the elderly, and two small historic parks. Approximately 28 structures and sites in the area had ratings ranging from "of primary historical importance" to "historically mentionable."

The land between Arlington Center and Arlington Heights was surrounded by industry, open space, and residential development; residential areas alternated with construction contracting companies, a water-supply pumping station, Arlington Coal and Lumber Company, and other businesses including a large A&P grocery store. Some sections were dominated by single-family houses, and numerous recreation sites dotted the area. Recreation areas included an ice skating rink, the Summer Street playground and tot lot, the

Arlington High School athletic field, a Little League baseball field, and Hill's Hill where go-carts and mini-bikes raced. Near the town's baseball field at the far end of Arlington Heights was Drake Village, a public housing complex for the elderly.

Many of the numerous parks and playgrounds in Arlington were moderately difficult or unpleasant to reach. Most children followed the Boston & Maine railroad tracks to the playing fields, a route that town planners hoped to reconstruct as a proposed landscaped linear park if the subway extension was built.

Arlington's town government consisted of two legislative bodies and an appointed executive. The representative town meeting, whose 259 representatives were elected from the town's 21 precincts, had the primary function of appropriating revenues. The Board of Selectmen was composed of five members elected at large on a nonpartisan basis for overlapping terms. The board set town policies and granted final approval to the town budget submitted by the manager and recommended by the representative town meeting. Appointed by the selectmen, the town manager headed the administrative arm of Arlington town government. He appointed the assistant town manager, formulated the town budget, and chose the heads of the operating departments.

The Massachusetts Bay Transportation Authority

The Massachusetts Bay Transportation Authority (MBTA) planned and promoted the Red Line project. Established by the state legislature in 1964, the MBTA managed nearly all public mass transportation facilities serving the Boston metropolitan area.

Four subway and streetcar lines extended out from Boston's central business district: the Blue, Orange, Green, and Red lines. The Blue and Orange lines served northern and southwestern parts of Boston and its inner suburbs. The Green Line primarily reached westward, branching out to serve Brookline and Newton. The Red Line extended both southeast of Boston to Mattapan and Quincy and northwest to Harvard Station.

The MBTA also operated buses, trackless trolleys, and commuter rail lines. About 950 buses ran over 711 route miles throughout the MBTA district. Another 50 trackless trolleys provided service on four other routes covering about 16 miles. Commuter railroads under MBTA management carried passengers into North and South stations in Boston, coming from as far north as Rockport (35 miles), as far south as Providence (44 miles), and as far west as Framingham (21 miles). Together these railroads covered 259 route miles.

In addition to operating this transportation network, the MBTA carried out numerous construction projects, including the extension of the Red Line subway. Funding for these capital projects came largely from the Urban Mass Transportation Administration (UMTA), a unit of the U.S. Department of Transportation, which paid up to 80 percent of a transit project's capital costs. Financing for the 20 percent state and local contribution came from bonds rather than from passenger revenues.

Initiation of the Red Line Extension

When Francis Sargent became governor of Massachusetts in January 1969 one of his first priorities was to evaluate current state transportation planning. He initiated the Boston Transportation Planning Review (BTPR) to help formulate new policies. The BTPR spent two years and $4 million assessing improvements needed in various travel corridors in the Boston region. The review was conducted by transportation consultants under the supervision of the governor's secretary of transportation.

In considering ways to encourage greater use of mass transit in the metropolitan area, the BTPR evaluated alternatives for extending the Red Line subway through the northwest corridor to North Cambridge, Somerville, Arlington and Lexington. (See Exhibit 1, p. 296.) Even the most enthusiastic proponents recognized that such a massive capital project would have to be constructed in phases because of the great cost and disruption during the construction period. Debate focused on whether the Red Line extension was needed at all and, if so, which parts should be built.

Some discussions concerned the route between Harvard Square and Alewife Brook Parkway in Cambridge. Several options were considered for covering this route, with stations planned at Porter Square (Cambridge) and/or Davis Square (Somerville) before reaching Alewife Brook Parkway (Cambridge). Other discussions concerned whether the rest of the corridor, stretching from Alewife Brook Parkway through Arlington and Lexington to Route 128, should be included in the subway extension. Options for serving this part of the corridor included:

1. A Red Line extension from Alewife Brook Parkway through Arlington, with stations at Arlington Center and/or Arlington Heights;

2. A Red Line extension including the two Arlington stations plus a final stop in Lexington at Route 128;

3. Express and local bus service from Arlington and Lexington to Alewife Brook Parkway.

The Boston Transportation Planning Review argued for a first phase extending the Red Line from Harvard Square to Alewife Brook Parkway. But when the MBTA seriously began considering the Red Line extension in 1973, it discussed the possibility of extending the line farther to the west through Arlington.

The Arlington Board of Selectmen encouraged the MBTA's interest.

Long concerned about a slumping local economy, board members were searching for ways to encourage commercial revitalization. They viewed the construction of Red Line stations in their town as a long-range solution for bringing shoppers to Arlington's faltering commercial center. Because of constant complaints from local residents about the dearth of parking spots near Arlington Center, they also wanted transit officials to include parking facilities in their project plans. A more definite proposal for the Red Line extension emerged as MBTA planning progressed from 1973 to 1975. Phase I was expanded to include the two Arlington stations. Although the MBTA foresaw a second phase that would extend the line from Arlington Heights to Route 128, no guarantees were made that Phase II ever would be built. According to MBTA planners, the proposed Red Line extension from Harvard Square to Arlington Heights would cover 6.5 miles at a total capital cost of $625,304,000. Construction would take nearly five years. The project plan included three parking garages: one at Alewife Brook Parkway, one at Arlington Center, and one at Arlington Heights. The final plan would require 10,850 person-years of employment and would represent 2,700 on-site jobs with a payroll of approximately $180 million. Related employment would increase the total project-generated payroll to $262,480,000.

Ridership forecasts for the new segment of the Red Line projected 42,700 daily boardings and 244 peak-hour bus arrivals at the new Red Line stations. These new stations would divert riders from direct boarding at Harvard Square and greatly reduce the congestion and circulation problems there; the number of peak hour bus arrivals at Harvard Station would decrease from 136 to 79. Inbound auto trips to Cambridge and Boston also would decline by 7,675 (or 9,210 person-trips) daily as a result of drivers being diverted to subway ridership. Shifting these transportation modes was thought to be an important energy conservation measure in light of the 70 passenger miles per gallon (PMPG) of fuel achieved on the Red Line compared with the 10 PMPG averaged by automobiles.

Two Red Line stations were planned in Arlington. A 750-car garage was proposed for Arlington Center with space for a "kiss and ride" passenger drop-off and transit parking. The existing Russell Common Municipal Parking Lot, accommodating 186 vehicles, was proposed as the site for the new structure. Adjacent to this site were some shops, St. Agnes Church, and its associated schools. (See Exhibit 2, p. 297.)

The subway between Arlington Center and Arlington Heights would use the Boston & Maine railroad right-of-way, eliminating that line's further service as a freight train route. Among the construction methods considered for this route were: deep-bore (where construction would be entirely below ground), cut-and-cover (where construction would be above the surface but the subway shaft later would be covered), and open-cut design (where the subway would be built and run in an open trench). The MBTA rejected the deep-bore tunnel construction option because of its high cost, suggesting instead an above-ground or open-cut design.

At Arlington Heights, the temporary stopping point of construction under Phase I, another garage and station would be built with parking space for 350 vehicles, a "kiss and ride" passenger drop-off area, and a bus terminal.

The Citizen Involvement Committee

Professional planners and engineers at the MBTA and various consulting firms did the bulk of the work in developing the Red Line extension proposal. But the MBTA made an effort to include local citizens in the planning process by meeting with local task forces in Cambridge, Somerville, and Arlington. In this regard, the MBTA's efforts meshed with a broader attempt in Arlington to consult residents about local issues.

In 1974 the Board of Selectmen invited Lawrence Susskind, a professor in the Massachusetts Institute of Technology (MIT) Department of Urban Studies and Planning, to organize a regular forum for citizen participation called the Citizen Involvement Committee (CIC). The CIC was intended both to educate the public on local issues and to give the selectmen information about citizen opinion on town policies. In the fall, at an open Arlington town meeting, Professor Susskind asked for volunteers interested in contributing directly to the selectmen's decision-making process. This group of about a dozen formed the CIC Steering Committee, which sought to recruit a cross-section of the town, including representatives of different income and age groups and people who had some familiarity with a range of economic, social, and environmental issues.

Few people responded to the initial call for CIC members, although churches and established community organizations were contacted about sending representatives. Because only a couple of residents came forward, the selectmen solicited additional people through the town newspaper and local contacts. People whom the selectmen knew in the business community were approached and convinced to join the group. Consequently, a number of early members of the CIC were businessmen, a fact that later brought accusations that the CIC largely represented the town's commercial interests. Participants in the CIC mainly had mid-level incomes and were fairly well-educated. A few blue-collar workers also were chosen.

The CIC Steering Committee created several task forces to study and report on various aspects of town affairs. One of these subgroups was the Land Use Task Force. Among its responsibilities was an examination of the Red Line subway extension.

The selectmen and Professor Susskind also organized small neighborhood task forces in East Arlington, Arlington Center, and Arlington Heights to evaluate the impact of the MBTA's Red Line proposal in each area. In contrast to the open membership of the CIC, participants in the three area task forces were chosen by the selectmen and group size was limited. These groups met privately in the afternoons. MBTA officials came to their meetings to present Red Line plans and proposals. The MBTA's proposals were scrutinized by the task force, whose feedback went directly to the transit authority without local dissemination.

In one major respect the MBTA altered its original plans. Arguments against a surface line running through the town between Arlington Center and Arlington Heights resulted in a compromise. The compromise plans called for a cut-and-cover design that was shallower than a deep-bore subway. Under this plan, the rapid transit line would run underground with a decking over it covered by soil and grass. Landscaping would create a linear park with pedestrian and bike paths over the subway, a popular plan with local residents. This linear park and pathway would replace the railroad tracks that were frequently used by children as a shortcut to nearby parks. The danger of pedestrians walking on the tracks had worried many residents, who also felt the tracks divided the town into two "wrong" sides of the tracks.

The First Town Meeting

What would an extension of the Red Line rapid transit system mean to the town of Arlington—its people, schools, shops, churches, playgrounds, and community environment? News of the planned project had filtered into the community for some time, but few residents had paid much attention to the idea. Over the years planners had suggested a Green Line subway extension to Arlington, a Red Line extension to Alewife Brook Parkway, or a continuation of the Red Line beyond Arlington to the northwest. Residents were skeptical about whether the latest plans were more likely to be acted upon than the earlier ones.

After months of planning, MBTA officials came to Arlington on April 20, 1975, to explain the Red Line proposal. The resulting public meeting was more than an effort to keep townspeople informed about the project; it was also part of procedures required to secure federal funding for the Red Line project. The Urban Mass Transportation Act, the federal law authorizing federal grants for transit construction, mandated public hearings to consider the economic, social, and environmental impacts of planned capital projects. The agency applying for federal funds—in this case the MBTA—had to submit a transcript of these hearings and a detailed statement about the issues raised. In subsequently granting funds under the act, the U.S. secretary of transportation had to certify that adequate opportunity was given for citizens to express their views and that "fair consideration has been given to the preservation and enhancement of the environment and to the interest of the community in which the project is located." (See Exhibit 3, p. 298.) The MBTA's consultations with the Arlington townspeople were an essential step in its efforts to proceed with the Red Line extension.

Only 70 Arlington residents appeared for the public meeting in April 1975. For two and a half hours they listened to Sylvia Donough and J. S. Mullaney, Jr., planners from the consulting firm of DeLeuw, Cather & Company, explain the proposed route of the Red Line extension from Harvard Square to Arlington Heights and describe the future Arlington transit facilities.

Following the planners' presentation, the residents asked a few questions about alternate routes for the subway. While the general sentiment of the meeting's town residents favored Red Line service to Arlington, some feared the possibility of a temporary terminus in their town. They knew that a terminus, as the end of a transportation line, becomes a storage place for transit vehicles as well as the site of commuter parking areas serving drivers from outlying suburbs. It is also the final stop for buses feeding into the subway system from the outer suburbs. As a focal point for transportation services, a terminus attracts increased traffic and congestion and often develops commercial establishments to serve the large number of commuters who pass through. Residents were concerned about what this would mean for the town's character. Several citizens sought reassurance from the transportation experts that the extension would not stop in Arlington Heights but eventually continue on to Route 128 in Lexington.

In reply, the speakers explained that none of their plans were definite. Design studies were continuing, and citizens' comments would be sought again as more definite plans emerged. In addition, the transit planners said that after completing the Red Line blueprints they would have to draw up an Environmental Impact Statement (EIS) on the project. The EIS and an application for a capital grant would be sent to the Urban Mass Transportation Administration (UMTA) in Washington, D.C., for approval. If UMTA approved the project plans, federal funds would be released for the initial construction stage.

The MBTA spokesmen told the audience that copies of the documents would be available for public inspection at the Robbins Public Library in Arlington Center where a special transportation area was being set up for information about the Red Line. Townspeople could read over the MBTA plan, express their approval, or make alternate recommendations before the papers were sent to federal officials.

Outcome of the Meeting

Despite this public meeting, Arlington residents knew little about the Red Line extension proposal. The MBTA had contracted with the Boston consulting firm of DeLeuw, Cather & Company to determine the feasibility of extending the subway line beyond Harvard Square. Until the consultants' study was complete, the MBTA would not make a firm decision about how far to extend the line during the first phase of construction. Thus their expansion plans remained vague, and they were insistent that all decisions were subject to change and final approval by UMTA.

Virtually no reaction arose to the MBTA's plans after the town meeting. Low attendance by Arlington residents and the transportation agency's failure to disperse information contributed to the attitude that the Red Line was not a pressing issue. "For a hundred years they've been hearing, 'It's coming! It's coming!' " declared John Cusack, a state representative from Arlington who remembered the early discussions of a Red Line extension. "Since Harvard Station was built as a temporary terminus in 1912, they've been planning a Red Line extension. Nothing ever happened, so no one paid much attention."

In Cambridge, in contrast, residents were urgently talking about the Red Line. In 1972 the Boston Transportation Planning Review had submitted its evaluation of various options for extending the subway past Harvard Square. The review's strongest argument supported construction of the Red Line to Alewife Brook Parkway in northwest Cambridge. Residents there knew that plans were quickly advancing for the rapid transit extension. They already were holding frequent neighborhood meetings on the MBTA proposals.

Planning in Arlington proceeded with much less public visibility. The small Red Line Task Forces at Arlington Center, Arlington Heights, and East Arlington spent 1975 in closed sessions with MBTA planners discussing local priorities and thinking about possible impacts on the Arlington community if and when the MBTA decided to extend the Red Line. The Arlington Center Task Force bargained with the MBTA about the center's proposed multi-level parking facility. Originally planned with a 750-vehicle capacity, the garage was reduced to 350 spaces. Additional compromises were reached between the two groups on details of siting and design.

Another Town Meeting

In February 1976, the Red Line issue assumed greater importance to Arlington residents. That month the consultants at DeLeuw, Cather & Company completed their study of transit needs in Boston's northwest travel corridor. They recommended that the Red Line extend from Harvard Square to Arlington Heights in the first phase, making actual construction a far stronger possibility.

In response the Arlington Board of Selectmen two weeks later announced an official town policy on the Red Line extension. While firmly supporting a plan for the extension through Arlington to reach ultimately to Route 128 in Lexington, the board recognized the need for phasing the construction project.

The selectmen would support this method as long as the construction phases overlapped. Also, they said they would prohibit any storage of rail vehicles or buses in Arlington Center, emphasizing the limited parking facilities in their town. While supporting the Red Line extension *through* Arlington to Route 128, the selectmen made no definite statement about the open-ended MBTA plan for Phase I in which Arlington Heights would become a "temporary" terminus as Harvard Square had in 1912. At the next stop, Lexington, town officials had commissioned a study called the Lexington Area Transportation Improvement Study to examine the feasibility of completing the Red Line to Route 128. The Arlington selectmen decided to wait for these results before taking a stand on where the line should end.

A month after the consultants' report was released, at the end of March 1976, MBTA officials returned to Arlington for another public meeting to explain the results. This time 300 residents attended the hearing.

Following the planners' presentation of the updated subway system plans, statewide leaders and heads of local organizations took the floor to express their opinions about the proposal. The speakers were almost unanimously enthusiastic about the improved transportation access to be provided by the Red Line in Arlington and optimistic about the town revitalization that was likely to occur.

Lt. Gov. Thomas P. O'Neill III exclaimed that the "Red Line extension into Arlington is one of the best, one of the most important things that has happened to the northwest corridor of Greater Boston for many, many years." He was followed by John Carroll, the Massachusetts commissioner of public works, who also favored the extension because of the relief it would provide to present traffic congestion problems. Speaking for the Boston Building Trade Unions and the AFL-CIO State Council, William Cleary enthusiastically supported the Red Line extension to Route 128 as "a great impetus for the construction industry."

State officials' stand in support of the Red Line was echoed by Arlington community leaders and town officials. State Sen. John Bullock, whose district included part of Arlington, joined in favoring the project, especially because of the commercial development it would attract to Arlington. He emphasized that the extension should go all the way to Route 128 and was eager for the construction to get under way after so many years of planning.

Allen McClennan, Arlington director of planning and community development, endorsed the project as "the single most important factor in Arlington for the rest of the century." The project also received unanimous approval from the Arlington Redevelopment Board, which cited the likely expansion of the retail district and redevelopment of existing stores and businesses in Arlington.

Margaret Spengler, chairperson of the Arlington Board of Selectmen, reiterated the board's unanimous approval of the MBTA extension to Route 128. However, she asserted the board's requirement that the line would have to go underground to protect the safety, economic interests, and aesthetic concerns of the town. The Citizens Involvement Committee also supported the plan, as did the local president of the League of Women Voters.

Finally, State Rep. John Cusack began to speak. The eighteenth speaker of the evening, he was the Red Line's first opponent. After patiently waiting and listening to repeated praise of the Red Line proposal, the state representative from Arlington was ready to blow his top. He found it unbearable to see the people of his district being cajoled into accepting the project. Not only were transportation officials planning the destruction of his community, he believed, but respected civic leaders were joining them in encouraging Arlington residents to support the subway extension.

To Cusack, the Red Line extension spelled trouble. Noise and traffic congestion would occur during construction of the Arlington Center station and parking garage. Digging and drilling activities would create air pollution, and the heavy construction equipment would cause severe wear and tear on the town's streets. Additional costs would be incurred after the subway system began operation. The influx of rapid transit commuters would be accompanied by a need for more police protection, traffic control, and enforcement of parking restrictions to keep overflow commuters from clogging nearby residential streets. With increased traffic would come more auto accidents and a subsequent increase in motor vehicle insurance rates, which were set according to the number of area accidents. Overall, Cusack foresaw deterioration of the "town atmosphere" of Arlington Center. The MBTA was describing only the regional benefits of the subway extension, not the costs to be borne alone by local residents.

The Arlington Center parking garage was of immediate concern to Cusack. He abhorred the idea of putting a five-level parking structure in the middle of the town's commercial and educational center near churches, parks, and residences. Cusack felt that it was up to him to inform residents of the damaging effects of constructing this parking garage. Recalling that night, Cusack explained, "Here they [MBTA officials] were looking for final approval for the plan and 99 and nine-tenths of the community didn't know what was going on! It was a total snow job by the MBTA." Speaking against the extension, "I felt like a voice in the wilderness."

Aftermath of the March Meeting

MBTA officials closed the session by announcing that they would review any problem areas in the plan. Cusack's remarks had struck a responsive chord among some Arlington residents who had attended the meeting. People began to wonder about the consequences of building a high-rise parking garage in Arlington Center. The next morning Representative Cusack received a phone call from Msgr. John J. Linnehan of St. Agnes Church. A parishioner had come early in the morning to see the monsignor, showing him the plans for the Red Line extension. Linnehan was shocked at the idea of an MBTA station and parking structure so near his church and adjacent parochial schools. He was hurt and outraged that he had not been informed of, or invited to, the previous night's public meeting, which he claimed had not been well advertised by MBTA or town officials.

Linnehan feared that increased traffic congestion around the garage would be a nuisance and hazard for the approximately 650 students enrolled at Arlington Catholic High School, 850 grammar school children at St. Agnes School, 2,500 participants in the interfaith youth center, and residents of the two neighboring public housing projects for the elderly. Because of the parking facility, he believed, traffic congestion and delays would occur on the one-way street next to St. Agnes, further interfering with people from weddings and funeral processions who used the street after services at the church.

Linnehan was a well-liked and vocal leader of the St. Agnes parish community. In opposing the MBTA plan he did not have to look far to find a way of organizing supporters for his cause; three groups already existed within the church. The grammar and high schools each had its own school committee, and the Parish Committee oversaw other church affairs. The congregation of St. Agnes Church provided a ready-made group of listeners, and the church a convenient place for meetings.

The monsignor contacted representatives of these committees. He wanted first to organize the parish and later draw the attention of the whole community to the MBTA's plan for their town. Under Linnehan's direction, church committee leaders prepared a petition to prohibit the MBTA from building a garage and bus terminal in Arlington. They also began organizing another town meeting. The monsignor called the Arlington town planner, Allen McClennan, to ask his help in bringing together officials for the public session. He in turn called the MBTA and its transportation consultants and arranged for them to speak to the people of Arlington again.

April 5th Public Meeting

Only six days after the previous public meeting, transit officials returned to Arlington to discuss the Red Line extension. Sponsored by Linnehan and St. Agnes Church, rather than by the town or the MBTA, this meeting was held at Arlington Catholic High School. The monsignor and his committee representatives hurriedly advertised the session, urging church members, parents of St. Agnes schoolchildren, and residents of the community to attend.

A standing-room-only crowd of 1,200 people jammed the hall that night, and 200 others were turned away. The review session on the Red Line extension plan also attracted Robert Kiley, chairman of the MBTA, and Fred Salvucci, Massachusetts' secretary of transportation, who were concerned that community opposition might threaten the rapid transit project. St. Agnes parishioners circulated a petition to send to the Environmental Protection Division of the attorney general's office, requesting reconsideration of the plan for a parking garage at Arlington Center.

While his church members gathered signatures, Linnehan addressed the crowd on the effects of an Arlington Center MBTA garage on St. Agnes Church and its educational facilities. According to the monsignor, parishioners and their children who attended the church-affiliated schools would suffer from the safety hazards imposed by construction and operation of the garage. Noise and congestion also would adversely affect the educational process, religious services, and the environmental quality of the area, as well as impose economic hardships.

Following the monsignor at the podium was an MBTA master planner, Donald Graham. Reviewing the Red Line plans, he asserted that considerable citizen participation already had been involved in the planning. Local officials and community study groups had provided input, he noted, and their suggestions had received careful consideration. The MBTA had made several alterations in the proposal as a result of citizen demands. For example, the above ground rapid transit line had been changed to a cut-and-cover design in response to public preference for underground construction.

Graham and other MBTA officials offered to answer questions from the floor. Citizens questioned the safety of placing a garage next to a school, the probable hazards and noise during construction, and the noise from the subway and outside traffic when the line was in operation. Concern for senior citizens also was expressed because the two Arlington Red Line stations would be very near the three elderly housing complexes. Several residents asked MBTA officials if the garage would be inconsistent with Arlington zoning requirements. The officials replied that although the area was currently zoned as residential, the MBTA, as a state agency, could override the local zoning law.

Arlington Planner Allen McClennan then spoke, adding some comments on the history of public involvement in planning the Red Line. At Porter Square and Alewife Brook in Cambridge, local residents had gotten together to review and discuss the Red Line stations to be located at those points. Likewise, the Arlington Center and Arlington Heights Task Forces had contributed ideas to the transit planners. On the matter of the Arlington Center garage site, McClennan noted that the MBTA had considered alternate sites but had abandoned them because of their adverse impacts on traffic congestion.

Several Arlington residents then spoke up strongly and emotionally against the Red Line proposal. Charles Bowser, a member of St. Agnes Church for 45 years, stated that the church was more important to him than anything other than his family. "If killing this garage means killing the Red Line, then I'm all for it." Another parishioner, Vincent Fulmer, pointed out that there were people at the meeting who were not planners, professionals, or town employees:

> These are Arlington parents, these are Arlington residents and taxpayers. They live here, they work here, they're bringing up their children here. And they care about their town. . . . How could you, or anybody, dare to blemish the center of our town with such a garage? How could you people of supposed intellect want to gloss over the economic and educational questions here in the name of progress?

Planner Allen McClennan replied that "no one was trying to blemish Arlington Center." He pointed out that several official and unofficial groups in Arlington had come out in support of the Red Line extension. As he listed those who had endorsed the project, the audience booed each one.

Emotions were running high as Linnehan brought the meeting to a close. He described the role of the 100-year-old parish and the school that was founded in 1888. He said the property was worth millions as a focal point of Arlington Center and would be isolated if the garage were built. When families and young couples were seeking a place to live, he argued, they looked at the general ambience of the community, including its schools, churches, and social life. The monsignor thought that Arlington should not be concerned about the benefits that neighboring towns would receive from the Red Line siting. Residents should think of their own town's future:

> There are ways to destroy a town by cutting its very lifeline. . . . To isolate the church in this manner by surrounding it with cars, buses, pollution and noise would allow it to die a slow death as an unpicked fruit ripening on the vine. . . . Let no one, no one, take our school and church so that it dies on the vine.

The Board of Selectmen Reacts

After the April 5 meeting Msgr. Linnehan tried to increase pressure on the Board of Selectmen. At that meeting, he had announced his intention to meet with the selectmen on April 20 at the Arlington town hall. Representatives of the St. Agnes Parish Council and other church committees were invited to attend. Because it was not a hearing, public participation was prohibited.

The monsignor's purposes in calling this session were threefold. First, he wanted to find out just where the selectmen stood on the issue of the Red Line extension to Arlington. Second, he hoped to discern what the board could (and would) do to help the St. Agnes groups fight the plan for an MBTA parking garage at Arlington Center. Finally, Linnehan wanted to continue to spread his ideas about the Red Line and to fuel opposition to the proposal.

At the April 20 session, members of the Board of Selectmen discussed the Red Line project, claiming that they had never agreed to either a temporary or permanent Red Line terminus in Arlington Heights. They appeared sensitive to public concern about the project's indirect costs, especially higher rates for police, fire, and insurance protection. The St. Agnes Parish groups left the meeting without a guarantee of support from the Board of Selectmen, but the board was beginning to take a more equivocal stand rather than directly supporting the Red Line extension. Discussion of these problems, moreover, drew greater public attention to the Red Line question, thereby generating the interest and involvement of other churches and organizations in the community.

It was a difficult time for the Board of Selectmen. MBTA officials were looking for support of the Red Line, which the board originally had welcomed and endorsed. Members also were sensitive to the commercial interests of the town. Improved transportation access and an increased volume of commuters could infuse sorely needed resources into the area's businesses. On one hand, the board had town planners working to incorporate a compromise on the MBTA line into Arlington's master plan; on the other hand, citizen groups under Linnehan's leadership wanted the elected board to oppose the project. The selectmen felt torn between a responsibility to guide the town's long-range development and the need to respond to residents' expressed interests.

The selectmen also had difficulty determining just who the subway opponents were and how many others they represented. Clearly, controversy over the plan had boiled up suddenly under the direction of Linnehan and a handful of avid supporters of St. Agnes Church. Yet the selectmen wondered whether one spokesman's view could be attributed to all church members. Just a few months earlier the extension had received nearly unanimous support except for Representative Cusack and some environmentalists who gave the proposal only a qualified recommendation. Had a complete turnabout in public opinion come about since then?

Mixed Signals for the MBTA

These reactions in Arlington raised serious questions for the MBTA. Transit officials were unsure just what to make of the local opposition, which had materialized and mushroomed in only a few weeks.

One problem was the Arlington Board of Selectmen, to which the MBTA had looked as spokesman for the community. In 1973 the selectmen had wholeheartedly supported the Red Line extension and specifically requested the MBTA to bring the line to Arlington. In the winter of 1976 they had expressed preference for a termination of the line at Route 128 in Lexington but recognized that phased construction would be necessary. Recently, a stipulation for underground construction throughout Arlington had been added to the selectmen's project acceptance requirements. Now, as public sentiment against the project became evident, the board was edging farther away from its early position of supporting the subway.

In the wake of the St. Agnes meeting the selectmen insisted that the Red Line continue to Route 128 without a terminus—temporary or permanent—at Arlington Heights. But the proposal for parking facilities in Arlington Center was causing the most heat. Ironically, that project had originally been added to the MBTA's plan at the urging of the selectmen, who felt that increased parking would encourage shopping and commercial revitalization in the town center.

As the selectmen hedged, the MBTA began to feel bewildered and betrayed by the town. The MBTA had followed the Board of Selectmen's original request for the Red Line and had encouraged citizen participation during the design stages. MBTA planners had met frequently with members of the selectmen's East Arlington, Arlington Center, and Arlington Heights Task Forces and had amended their proposals to meet public demands. Throughout the neighborhood task forces' meetings, the MBTA planners had sought the public's reaction to the problems and impacts associated with the Red Line. Focusing on residents' concerns, they hoped, would enable transit planners to anticipate which designs could be implemented and what modifications were necessary. Privately, the Arlington Center Task Force had bargained with MBTA planners until a satisfactory parking garage/station proposal had been arranged.

MBTA officials viewed opposition to the parking garage as a way for antitransit people to stop the Red Line project altogether. To MBTA officials, opposition to the temporary terminus status largely was based on false premises. In another town similar to Arlington, they believed, a temporary MBTA terminus had left the area "a sleepy neighborhood." The planners believed that people would be less opposed to "phased projects" if they had more confidence in the continuity of federal programs aiding mass transit.

Nevertheless, public reaction against the Red Line was escalating. This surge of community feeling threatened the entire subway extension. Final funding for construction had not yet been approved, and transit planners believed that the federal Urban Mass Transportation Administration would be reluctant to approve a project that faced significant community opposition.

The Summer Study Task Force

In June 1976, with pressure mounting from the MBTA on one side and local residents on the other, the Arlington selectmen turned to their citizen participation organization, the Citizen Involvement Committee. Although a number of scattered community groups were investigating the MBTA plan, little objective analysis of the Red Line proposal was available to Arlington's residents.

The CIC organized a Summer Study Task Force to carry out a thorough review of the Red Line extension proposal. The group was to examine the economic, social, and physical consequences of the subway extension as well as its impact on energy use. This information, it was hoped, would help Arlington residents make informed judgments about the Red Line project.

Just as it had done when seeking general membership in early 1975, the CIC Steering Committee contacted a wide spectrum of Arlington community groups and churches to gather volunteers for the Summer Study Task Force. This time the response was considerably greater. The issue now was far more visible. By the summer of 1976, moreover, organized citizen participation had become more common in Arlington and MIT's Larry Susskind was involving the CIC in a number of issue surveys. Furthermore, in contrast to the CIC's nebulous task of providing general citizen input into local policy making, the purpose of the summer study was concrete.

One of the first jobs the Summer Study Task Force undertook was an investigation of the Red Line feasibility study being carried out in Lexington. Task force members were worried about the eventual continuation of the rapid transit line beyond Arlington. Lexington's study was far from finished, and its results were important. The Lexington study could conclude that the extension between Arlington Heights and Route 128 would be unjustified. If the MBTA's plans for Arlington were completed prior to such a recommendation, Arlington might be the terminus forever. Consequently, task force members asked the Board of Selectmen to request that the MBTA delay sending its funding proposal for the Red Line extension to UMTA until the results came in from Lexington's feasibility study. The selectmen, however, rejected this recommendation. While they were increasingly cautious about supporting the Red Line extension, they were not prepared to turn their backs on the benefits the subway could bring to Arlington. So long as they remained unsure of community sentiment, they felt that the best tactic was to continue to study the issue and not to interrupt the MBTA's application for Phase I funds.

Throughout the summer the task force continued its evaluation of the subway plan. Unlike the St. Agnes committees that were working simply to block the Red Line, the Summer Study Task Force did not take a political stand on the subway issue, although many members were in fact opposed to the extension. They worked in earnest to produce an objective report investigating MBTA proposals, citizen reactions, and the costs and benefits of bringing the Red Line to Arlington.

By September 1976 the selectmen's Summer Study Task Force was ready to publish its conclusions. A detailed description of the Red Line proposal was written up in a special edition of *Feedback,* the Citizen Involvement Committee newsletter. The 11-page report described the MBTA plan, its history, and the procedures involved in its development. It provided a careful balance between the positive and negative arguments about the Red Line extension.

Red Line opponents interpreted the task force report and the selectmen's failure to oppose the MBTA plan as veiled approval of the subway. Others who read the task force findings thought its members neither accepted nor rejected the MBTA plan but provided information on both sides. But fears of adverse consequences from the subway were rising as the MBTA finished its draft Environmental Impact Statement that September. Those fears were accompanied by a feeling of powerlessness on the part of many Arlington residents.

Legislative Action Kills the Parking Garage

Representative Cusack had not moderated his feelings about the transit extension. At the same time the Summer Study Task Force published its Red Line review, Cusack submitted a bill to the Massachusetts House that prohibited any construction by the MBTA within 150 yards of Arlington Catholic High School.

When the joint legislative Committee on Transportation received Cusack's bill for discussion, the MBTA intervened, explaining that the 150-yard limit would prevent not only construction of a parking garage, as intended, but also construction of the subway extension itself. Although Representative Cusack's opposition had been aimed primarily at the siting of the parking facility, the railroad right-of-way that the Red Line would follow also was within the proposed 150-yard limitation. Because this limit had been chosen quite arbitrarily, and because its results were unintended, Cusack agreed with MBTA officials to reset the limit at 75 yards. The Transportation Committee decided to hold its hearing on the revised bill at Arlington Catholic High School. They were enthusiastically received by St. Agnes Church representatives who urged speedy action on the bill.

Soon after the hearings, in late September, the bill passed in both the House and Senate. Governor Michael Dukakis went to Arlington to ceremoniously sign the bill into law before a crowd in the Arlington High School gymnasium. Msgr. Linnehan called the passage and signing of the bill "democracy in action" and "the Legislature comes to the people."

"Terminitis"

Although opposition had existed all along to both the parking garage and the MBTA terminus, until this point community protest had focused on the garage at Arlington Center. When Representative Cusack's bill settled that issue, opposition turned to the proposed temporary terminus of the Red Line at Arlington Heights. The idea of becoming "the end of the line"—even temporarily—was anathema to many. In a letter to the editor of the *Arlington Advocate,* one town resident expressed these views unmistakably:

> ... [I]t is a fact that Arlington has historically accepted more of the "share the blight" programs than have its more affluent neighbors.
>
> In public transportation the present MBTA map shows rush-hour bus traffic in Arlington Center to be over one third that of hopeless Harvard Square.... As for housing, our low-income and elderly projects have long been fixtures here while Lexington, Newton, et al., detest and decline such developments with their snob zoning laws....
>
> Lexington, should you not realize, still supports (for Arlington) a "temporary" rail terminal, parking complex, and busing terminal. They will also suffer the inconvenience of Arlington traffic jams for a "temporary" duration. Once the die is cast, however, "temporary" is "forever"....
>
> For examples of "terminal towns" (double meaning intended) we look at Mattapan, Forest Hills, Harvard Square, and the relatively new mess at Quincy Center.... Why should the Harvard Square terminal be transplanted to congested Arlington when their B & M [Boston and Maine] tracks go all the way to 128?...
>
> There is much to be learned from observing the techniques of some of our more politically astute neighbors. From Lexington, we note how they paved over half of Mass. Ave. with sidewalk and made most of the streets one-way to severely discourage through traffic while encouraging local shoppers.... And from Cambridge, we learned ... that if you strongly object to something (like the now-defunct Inner Belt), you can stop it....
>
> If you wish to protect the quality of your home and investment in Arlington, you have but a few days left to act before your opinions will be ignored. Write to: UMTA, Dept. of Transportation, Washington, D.C....
>
> If the Red Line is ended in Arlington, Arlington is ended.

Horror stories of neighborhood deterioration dominated local discussions. Residents who rode buses daily through Harvard Square saw the congestion and pedestrian dangers there. They observed huge influxes of people crowded into a small area around the subway terminal, and they worried about extra cars, buses, and commuters in their own town. The temporary terminus at Arlington Heights, and the Red Line extension itself, became emotional issues throughout the autumn months.

In the meantime, the MBTA had been preparing the first draft of the Environmental Impact Statement on the Red Line extension project. The MBTA was assisted by Arlington's town planners who did not officially advocate or oppose the Red Line. The draft EIS was sent to UMTA in Washington in September 1976 but was not available to Arlington residents for another month. Claiming that the MBTA had promised a local preliminary review of the report, opposition leaders in St. Agnes Church resented being sidestepped by transit officials. Furthermore, although the plans for the Arlington Center parking facility already had been abandoned, the garage designs were inadvertently left in the EIS when it was sent to Washington. The mistake raised the ire and suspicion of many Arlington residents.

Citizen Outrage Boils Over

Although Arlington clearly was divided over the proposed Red Line extension, it was less obvious what proportions of the population favored and opposed the subway. Because town officials wondered not only which way the public leaned on the issue but also how strong were its convictions, the Board of Selectmen contracted for a telephone opinion survey in December 1976. An additional purpose of the survey was to help formulate issues for a later referendum vote.

Cambridge Survey Research Corporation (CSRC) conducted the telephone survey, contacting about 100 Arlington adults between December 8 and 11, 1976. The selectmen had assigned several tasks to the survey team. First, they were to measure the attitudes of Arlington residents toward the proposed Red Line extension. Second, the survey was to investigate what impacts the Red Line might have on community life. Third, CSRC was asked to make recommendations for a referendum advertising campaign based on what was found in the telephone survey data.

The following basic question was asked of survey respondents:

> The MBTA is proposing an extension of the Red Line rapid transit from Harvard Square to Arlington Heights, with likely stops at Porter Square, Davis Square, Alewife, Arlington Center, and Arlington Heights. It would run underground from Harvard Square through Arlington Center and then in an open cut to Arlington Heights. Do you think this is a good idea or a bad idea?

Of the adults surveyed, 49 percent said this was a "good idea," 40 percent said it was a "bad idea," and 11 percent replied that they did not know. Among the 17 short-term residents (less than five years in Arlington) 68 percent felt it was a "good idea," and only 29 percent thought it was a "bad bad idea." The 66 long-term residents ("over 10 years/all my life") were almost evenly matched, with 43 percent saying it was a "good idea" and 44 percent saying it was a "bad" one. Homeowners (70 respondents) also were evenly divided on the question, with 46 percent "good," and 44 percent "bad." Renters (28 respondents) favored the proposal 55 percent to 32 percent. Classified according to profession, the respondents replied as follows:

	Number of Respondents	Good Idea	Bad Idea	Don't Know
Professional	12	46%	42%	13%
White Collar	16	45	48	8
Blue Collar	9	51	41	9
Housewife	21	47	44	9
Teacher	6	62	26	12
Retired	20	48	35	7

When the question was restated to include underground construction throughout the extension and a continuation of the line all the way to Route 128 in Lexington, 61 percent came out in favor of the Red Line, and only 26 percent opposed it.

Those who favored the subway extension cited as advantages an easing of traffic congestion on Massachusetts Avenue, greater mobility, convenience, and especially increased business and redevelopment in Arlington. Opponents thought that the Red Line would cause neighborhood deterioration, an increased crime rate, more traffic congestion, and intensification of the parking problem.

Interestingly, those who had read the Summer Study Task Force's report on the Red Line, which had appeared in the September issue of *Feedback,* were more likely to oppose the Red Line than others. However, 60 percent of those surveyed claimed never to have received the *Feedback* issue, although it was sent to all town residents. As revealed by the survey, the "hardcore" Red Line opponent was a white-collar worker with a high school education, earning $10,000 to $15,000 and between 46 to 55 years of age. He or she also was well informed about the issue and owned two automobiles.

Cambridge Survey Research's analysis of the telephone survey was not widely distributed beyond Arlington town hall, but the survey results were discussed at two open meetings of the Arlington Board of Selectmen. The only widespread public information on the survey results came from an article in the *Arlington Advocate,* written after the selectmen's meetings.

Opponents of the Red Line were incensed by the results. Leaders of the fight against the subway denounced the poll as inaccurate and said the findings were based on faulty analysis. MBTA transportation planners were encouraged by the survey's display of support. Overall, the questionnaire further spotlighted the issue and attracted greater participation from both sides.

Despite increasing citizen opposition to the Red Line project, important sources of support still existed, especially within Arlington town government. Town planners were positive in their view of the Red Line and what it would offer for the future of their town. Never officially advocating a policy on the issue, they tended nonetheless to favor a careful implementation of the Red Line extension. The construction of a linear park over the B & M railroad tracks was an especially attractive sidelight of the proposal—one that planners had been dreaming about for a long time. Despite these benefits the planners knew that some people opposed the Red Line altogether. They believed this resulted from misinformation and a baseless fear that Arlington might change from a desirable community to a place more closely resembling the inner city.

The Arlington Redevelopment Board looked at the long-term growth and revitalization benefits of the Red Line. This group was anxious to regenerate the sagging commercial district and to attract new investors. The transit plan's provisions for serving elderly and handicapped citizens also were heralded by redevelopment officials.

With so many differing opinions on the proposal to consider, the Arlington Board of Selectmen was once again in a quandary; but pressure was building for a definite show of hands on the Red Line issue. Therefore, a few weeks before the March town election, the selectmen announced that four nonbinding referendum questions about the Red Line would be put on the ballot. They insisted that votes on the referendum would assist—but not obligate—them in determining the town's transit line extension policy. Linnehan believed the selectmen were using the referendum to get themselves "off the hook" about appearing to favor the extension. Others thought the citizens' votes would back the board into a corner and prohibit it from freely deciding on the issue. Still others thought the selectmen sponsored the referendum because of concern that the MBTA might think the majority of Arlington's residents approved of the Red Line extension. The telephone survey of a few months earlier had, after all, shown that many townspeople backed the MBTA plan.

The selectmen, the MBTA, and the St. Agnes committees were frantically busy prior to the election on Saturday, March 5, 1977. The Board of Selectmen sent mailings to every house in Arlington, explaining the proposed extension. The MBTA handed out flyers on all Arlington-bound buses leaving Harvard Square and was reported to have put pressure on employees who lived in Arlington to encourage their friends and neighbors to vote in favor of the extension. Simultaneously, Robert Kiley, the MBTA's board chairman, made conciliatory overtures to Arlington's voters:

> Those days when a state agency determined by itself, without sensitivity to the needs and wishes of a town, what was "right" or "good" for that town, are gone forever. I am committed to the residents of Arlington to ensure that their desires and concerns are heeded in the construction and operation of a safe, efficient public transportation system. We look forward to a positive and constructive planning process with the residents and officials of Arlington.

Meanwhile, church activists were out in full force counseling residents to vote "no" on all four questions. Claiming that the Red Line would never be extended past Arlington to Route 128, they discouraged voting for the Route 128 terminus option.

Meanwhile, another group formed around the referendum. Representing a small number of avid opponents of the Red Line extension, the Arlington Red Line Action Movement (ALARM) worked to counter the selectmen's and MBTA's efforts. They held a march down the B & M railroad right-of-way, carrying signs and protesting the Red Line extension. Just before election day they were busy passing out bumper stickers and leaflets opposing the rapid transit proposal. (See Exhibit 4, p. 299.)

On the top of the ballot for the March 5 annual town election were candidates running for town moderator, selectman, assessor, and school board. The nonbinding referendum presented by the Arlington Board of Selectmen offered four choices:

1. Do you support the extension of the Red Line/rapid transit through the Town of Arlington completely underground and ultimately to Route 128 with stations at Alewife Brook Parkway, Arlington Center, and Arlington Heights/East Lexington?
YES _____   NO _____

If the above extension (question number one) had to be in phases, which of the following would you support:

2. The Red Line/rapid transit extension into Arlington completely underground to a station at Arlington Center and continuing underground to a station at Arlington Heights/East Lexington with a temporary terminus at that point.
YES _____   NO _____

3. The Red Line/rapid transit extension into Arlington as far as Arlington Center completely underground with a terminus at that point.
YES _____   NO _____

4. Do you support ending the Red Line/rapid transit at Alewife Brook Parkway with a permanent terminus at that point?
YES _____   NO _____

At the time of the election, 31,821 voters were registered in Arlington out of a population of 41,178 eligible adults. The total number of ballots cast, 13,795, represented 43.3 percent of the town's enrolled voters. The referendum questions on the Red Line brought these responses:

	Yes	**No**	**Blank**
Option 1:	37%	60%	3%
Option 2:	35	56	9
Option 3:	8	69	23
Option 4:	16	71	13

Red Line opponents were overjoyed by the election. They called the vote an overwhelming victory for their side. To them the referendum results were unambiguous: under no circumstances did Arlington residents want a Red Line terminus in their town.

Others found reasons to question this viewpoint. A representative of the Arlington Planning and Community Development Department expressed doubt over the relevance of the results, citing the known tendency of those who felt most strongly about an issue being most likely to get out and vote. In addition, because only registered voters may participate in an election, nearly one-fourth of the adult population of the town was ineligible. Recalling the December telephone survey, the representative said it had been more indicative than the referendum vote because the strong Red Line opposition was not quite so well organized when the poll was taken.

The nonbinding referendum settled nothing officially. However, although neither the MBTA nor UMTA was bound to accept its results, the referendum had changed the political climate. Clearly, the project's future was uncertain.

EXHIBITS

Exhibit One:
Proposed Red Line Extension

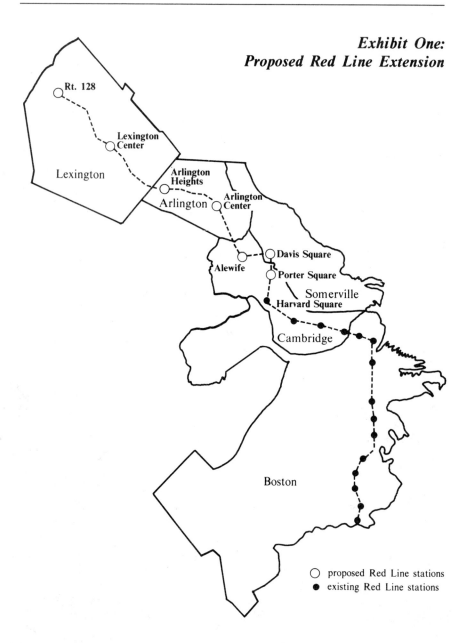

○ proposed Red Line stations
● existing Red Line stations

Exhibit Two:
Arlington Center Station Project Alignment

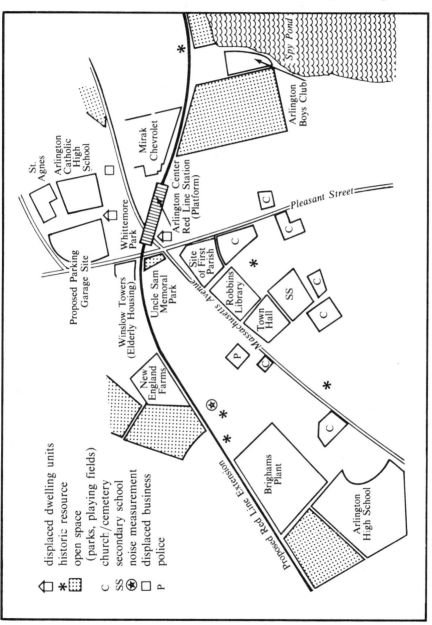

displaced dwelling units
historic resource
open space
(parks, playing fields)
church/cemetery
secondary school
noise measurement
displaced business
police

297

Section 1602 (d) Notice and public hearings

Any application for a grant or loan under this chapter to finance the acquisition, construction, reconstruction, or improvement of facilities or equipment which will substantially affect a community or its mass transportation service shall include a certification that the applicant:

(1) has afforded an adequate opportunity for public hearings pursuant to adequate prior notice, and has held such hearings unless no one with a significant economic, social, or environmental interest in the matter requests a hearing;

(2) has considered the economic and social effects of the project and its impact on the environment; and

(3) has found that the project is consistent with official plans for the comprehensive development of the urban area.

Notice of any hearings under this subsection shall include a concise statement of the proposed project, and shall be published in a newspaper of general circulation in the geographic area to be served. If hearings have been held, a copy of the transcript of the hearings shall be submitted with the application.

Section 1610 (b) Review of hearing transcripts

The Secretary shall review each transcript of hearings submitted pursuant to section 1602 (d) of this title to assure that an adequate opportunity was afforded for the presentation of views by all parties with a significant economic, social, or environmental interest, and that the project application includes a detailed statement on:

(1) the environmental impact of the proposed project.

(2) any adverse environmental effects which cannot be avoided should the proposal be implemented.

(3) alternatives to the proposed project, and

(4) any irreversible and irretrievable impact on the environment which may be involved in the proposed project should it be implemented.

Section 1610 (c) Findings; inadequate record; notice and hearing

The Secretary shall not approve any application for assistance under section 1602 of this title unless he finds in writing, after a full and complete review of the application and of any hearings held before the State or local public agency pursuant to section 1602 (d) of this title, that (1) adequate opportunity was afforded for the presentation of views by all parties with a significant economic, social, or environmental interest, and fair consideration has been given to the preservation and enhancement of the environment and to the interest of the community in which the project is located, and (2) either no adverse environmental effect is likely to result from such project, or there exists no feasible and prudent alternative to such effect and all reasonable steps have been taken to minimize such effect. In any case in which a hearing has not been held before the State or local agency pursuant to section 1602 (d) of this title, or in which the Secretary determines that the record of hearings before the State or local agency is inadequate to permit him to make the findings required under the preceding sentence, he shall conduct hearings, after giving adequate notice to interested persons, on any environmental issues raised by such application. Findings of the Secretary under this subsection shall be made a matter of public record.

March 5

Exhibit Four:
Arlington Voter's Guide to MBTA Referendum
Questions to Protect the Quality of Life

1. Do you support the extension of the Red Line/Rapid Transit through the Town of Arlington completely underground and ultimately to Route 128 with stations at Alewife Brook Parkway, Arlington Center, and Arlington Heights/East Lexington?

> **NO** Arlington Heights/East Lexington is *entirely* imaginary. Lexington will reject East Lexington and force Arlington Heights to become the "temporary" (10-20 years) terminus. We are *unanimously opposed* to any Red Line terminus in Arlington — temporary or permanent.

2. If the above cannot be funded as one project would you support the following?

    (a) The Red Line/Rapid Transit extension to Alewife Brook Parkway not to enter Arlington and with a permanent terminus at that point?

> **NO** Residents of East Arlington have made clear their strong opposition to Alewife as a temporary or permanent terminus — for environmental reasons. Until and unless more becomes known about the environmental effects of a terminus at Alewife, we strongly support East Arlington residents in opposing the Alewife terminus.

    (b) The Red Line/Rapid Transit extension into Arlington as far as Arlington Center completely underground with a temporary terminus at that point.

299

> **NO** We are *unanimously opposed* to any Red Line terminus in Arlington —
> temporary or permanent. Stations designed for local access are accept-
> able. A terminus is *not*. We are determined to use every proper means to
> prevent the MBTA from terminating the Red Line in Arlington Center.
> We believe a shortfall in federal or state funding of the MBTA proposal
> *or* cost escalation will result in a terminus at Arlington Center.

    (c) The Red Line/Rapid Transit extension into Arlington completely
        underground to a station at Arlington Center and continuing
        underground to a station at Arlington Heights/East Lexington
        which would be a temporary terminus.

> **NO** Arlington Heights/ East Lexington is entirely imaginary. Lexington will
> reject East Lexington and force Arlington Heights to become the
> "temporary" (10-20 years) terminus. We are *unanimously opposed* to
> any Red Line terminus in Arlington — temporary or permanent. The
> Arlington Heights/East Lexington terminus idea is an optical illusion.

THE ARLINGTON RED LINE ACTION MOVEMENT (ALARM)

Discussion Questions

1. Why were the citizens of Arlington relatively uninterested in the early planning for the Red Line extension? Why did so few members of the community initially learn about and become involved in the project's planning?

2. What accounted for—and made possible—the rapid mobilization of community members in opposition to the Red Line plans?

3. Could the Arlington Selectmen have anticipated the sudden emergence of bitter opposition to the project?

4. How representative of the community-at-large were the Red Line opponents?

5. Compare and contrast the following methods of soliciting citizen opinions about public policy:

        informal contacts by officials
        appointed advisory committees
        open membership advisory committees
        public hearings
        sample surveys
        referenda

Suggestions for Further Reading

Alinsky, Saul. *Reveille for Radicals.* New York: Vintage, 1969. The philoso-phy and tactics of the United States' leading theoretician and practitioner of community organizing.

Davidoff, Paul. "The Planner as Advocate," and Peattie, Lisa R. "Reflections of an Advocate Planner," in *Urban Government,* Edward C. Banfield, ed., rev. edit. New York: The Free Press, 1969. Two views of how planners can help unorganized citizens express their views in developing project plans.

Lipsky, Michael. "Protest as a Political Resource." *American Political Science Review,* December 1968. A theory of political protest that helps explain why a handful of protestors at City Hall can motivate policy makers and administrators to undertake changes in government policy.

Lupo, Alan et al. *Rites of Way: The Politics of Transportation in Boston and the U.S. City.* Boston: Little, Brown & Co., 1971. A history and analysis of how intense citizen resistance to highway building plans led to major changes in metropolitan transportation policy.

7. Citizen Participation in Oxford

INTRODUCTION

In the previous case study, "Extending the Red Line to Arlington," we took a broad look at citizen involvement in planning federally supported programs, emphasizing both the variety of ways that public officials can identify citizen sentiments and the factors determining whether individual community members will become politically active. In the case that follows, "Citizen Participation in Oxford," we closely examine formal, government-sponsored methods of soliciting citizen involvement in on-going program management.

This question became a matter of national attention with the enactment of the Economic Opportunity Act of 1964 and the consequent launching of an antipoverty program by the Office of Economic Opportunity (OEO), a new federal agency. Although citizen participation requirements did not begin with OEO programs, the controversy spawned by interpretation of the act's "maximum feasible participation" clause gave the issue enormous public visibility. Because the issue struck a responsive public chord, despite the controversy, Congress henceforth routinely inserted "citizen" or "public" participation requirements in the new federal grant programs that proliferated during and after President Johnson's Great Society. Neither these laws nor the regulations drafted by various federal agencies had standard language, but the general intent of the requirements was that ordinary citizens—who were neither elected officials nor full-time employees of government—should have significant "say" (either authoritative or advisory) in decision making and management of grant programs.

At the local level, citizen participation requirements created unusual pressures for municipal officials. These problems were all the harder to cope with when the substantive program decisions that had to be made were fraught with political conflict—as they were in the events described in "Citizen Participation in Oxford." In this case, the debate over how to structure participation revolves around a bitter argument over the division of a shrinking pool of Community Development Block Grant funds.

As in many other situations when the stakes are high, it is difficult to separate the procedural aspects of participation from the substance of the policies at issue. Yet there are fundamental—and highly practical—questions of democratic governance involved in designing citizen participation procedures. Exactly who ought to be represented? How should these individuals be selected? What is the proper basis of representation: territory, community organizations, or socioeconomic characteristics? How much authority should citizen participants actually have over program policy and operations? Should citizens be given "help"—in the form of technical assistance or strategic advice from municipal officials—in participating? The answers to these questions are not self-evident, but local officials have to find arrangements that conform to federal requirements and satisfy various constituencies both inside and outside of municipal government.

The question of which citizen groups should be represented is a particularly complex matter. Some observers argue that only those directly affected by a specific program should be entitled to participate in its management. In many instances, those individuals have been ignored in the past, even though their lives have been irrevocably changed by program operations. The poor, minority group members, and residents of inner city areas have seen their homes razed or their neighborhoods otherwise radically altered by urban renewal and other federally subsidized construction programs. Welfare recipients have lived with rules established by others for programs, such as Aid to Families with Dependent Children, even when those regulations have had harmful effects.

Other observers, however, argue for a contrasting viewpoint concerning representation. Government programs have impacts that go far beyond those people immediately affected, and the programs are paid for by the general public's tax dollars. The governance of federal programs, therefore, should be the responsibility of a broader segment of the community than just the people directly affected; otherwise, they argue, important interests and values of the public-at-large may well be ignored.

An equally difficult issue is the method of selecting citizen participants. Each different method has implications for the extent, style, and representativeness of participation. An election process is the obvious choice, as it was for OEO's antipoverty program, and this method has been adopted by many jurisdictions. Another possibility is appointment by public officials. Still other jurisdictions rely on open access by volunteers, thus allowing citizen participants to select themselves.

To establish a participatory system, public officials also have to decide on the appropriate basis of representation. Given their own experience, the most natural choice is territory: each participant represents a geographic area. Even with this specified, however, it still is necessary to decide how large a territorial unit is to be represented and how many people should represent each unit. Thus a city could be split up into small or large neighborhoods represented by one or more official participants; or those involved might be selected at-large from the city as a whole.

But geography is not the only conceivable basis of representation. Participants also might be chosen to represent organizations that play a major role in a community. Thus there might be representatives of churches, fraternal associations, community service groups, neighborhood civic associations, local business organizations, and the like. Yet this option requires assembling a list of all groups that ought to be included—and perhaps another list of those that do not "deserve" to be on the first list. This option also requires deciding whether each group should count equally or whether their voices should be weighted by some specifiable criteria.

Alternatively, participants might be chosen because they represent a particular socioeconomic category. Race, ethnicity, and economic status are the most common characteristics thought appropriate for representation; but other categories—including gender, religion, age, occupation, handicapped status, and even "sexual preference"—have their advocates.

An issue that causes tension in many jurisdictions is how much authority citizen participants should have over the programs in which they are involved. Federal regulations vary from program to program; and, within these regulations, each city has a good deal of latitude to decide just what role is appropriate. Public officials often face demands that citizens be given actual power rather than an advisory role. There also is frequent conflict over whether citizen involvement should be limited to policy making or should extend to oversight of day-to-day administration.

Controversy over authority often merges into controversy over procedures. Establishing a citizen participation system means deciding exactly how public representatives should be involved in adopting basic policy statements, recommending or approving the budget, hiring staff, hearing reports from program administrators, or dealing with public officials outside of the program. Disagreements about such basic but significant program processes can make relationships between citizens and officials quite difficult.

Finally, there also is disagreement about what aid citizen participants needed to perform their functions independently and effectively. Some program areas are relatively nontechnical, requiring little background or skill to conduct. But other programs involve substantial technical components or require esoteric knowledge about the regulations governing the use of federal money. Because most citizens are inexperienced in the mechanics of planning and managing government programs, they often lack skills and basic information necessary to make considered judgments about the issues. In many cases, they are left to flounder—often frustrated and ineffective or ready to challenge officials who are leaving them to struggle. In some cases, elected officials or program administrators provide technical advice, delegate city employees to work with citizen participants, or give money to citizens to hire staff who will be responsive and loyal to their perspective.

Taken as a whole, therefore, the problem of designing a citizen participation mechanism is quite thorny. Significant value questions are inevitably involved, as well as some compelling practical issues regarding program management. The task of sorting out these issues frequently is made more complicated, moreover, by an atmosphere of political suspicion—and sometimes rancor—between activist citizens and public officials.

THE CAST

Frank Whalen	Oxford city manager
HUD	U.S. Department of Housing and Urban Development
CDBG	Community Development Block Grant program
CDBG Citizens Advisory Committee	Citizen participation group for CDBG
CAP	Community Action Program, Oxford's antipoverty program
EOC	Economic Opportunity Committee, citizen participation group for Oxford's antipoverty program
CDA	City Demonstration Agency; administers Oxford's Model Cities program
CDA Advisory Board	Citizen participation group for Model Cities program
OHA	Oxford Housing Authority
ORA	Oxford Redevelopment Authority
Revenue Sharing Council	Unofficial group organized by EOC to give citizens views on CDBG allocation

CHRONOLOGY

<u>August 1974</u>	Congress enacts the Housing and Community Development Act.
<u>1975</u>	
January	City Manager Whalen announces a plan for citizen participation in the CDBG program; the EOC organizes the Revenue Sharing Council to denounce these arrangements and to propose an alternative CDBG budget.
January-April	Various claimants for CDBG funds compete intensely for a share of the budget.
April	CDBG Citizen Advisory Committee makes recommendations for the CDBG allocation; the Revenue Sharing Council proposes an "Alternative CDBG Budget." Facing strong citizen protests at a stormy meeting, the Oxford City Council adopts the CDBG budget. The next day the council majority expresses its displeasure to Whalen.
October	Whalen contemplates new citizen participation procedures for coming budget allocation process.

THE CASE

"We demand meaningful citizen involvement." "Decision making by the people, not bureaucrats," read the placards carried by 20 demonstrators marching back and forth in front of city hall. By closing his eyes, Oxford City Manager Frank Whalen could still visualize how these picketers had appeared

This case was written by Arnold M. Howitt and Kay Rubin. Although partially factual, this is a fictional case and is based, in part, on materials originally developed by Professor Lawrence Susskind of the Department of Urban Studies and Planning, Massachusetts Institute of Technology.

in early 1975 when they protested his handling of the new federal Community Development Block Grant (CDBG) program.

The protest followed the passage of the Housing and Community Development Act of 1974, in which Congress replaced several existing categorical grants with the CDBG. Local governments thereby gained discretion in using federal money for community development purposes.

The CDBG program, however, required that recipient communities provide substantial opportunity for citizens to advise decision makers about program expenditures. Oxford had a tradition of vigorous citizen participation in earlier federal programs. But during CDBG's first year (1975), the city's procedures for participation were bitterly criticized, especially by an active, articulate community coalition that previously had been deeply involved in Oxford's antipoverty program.

City Manager Whalen had been severely embarrassed by that uproar, and he had been rebuked—privately but firmly—by several influential members of the "independent" faction of the Oxford City Council for letting the situation "get out of hand." Now in the fall of 1975, as he prepared for the next round of CDBG allocations, Whalen knew that the council would be unhappy if a repetition of the controversy and conflict over CDBG occurred.

The City of Oxford

Oxford is an old, densely populated city of about 100,000 people located just outside the larger city of Metropolis in an eastern state. Rich in a history that dates to colonial days, Oxford is a heterogeneous city both in its economic base and in its racial and ethnic composition.

The city's dominant institution is Oxford State University, which enrolls 20,000 students in a variety of undergraduate and graduate programs. Surrounding the university campus are numerous small retail shops, two department stores, restaurants, and service establishments such as barbershops and laundromats. These businesses cater mainly to the Oxford student body and to middle-class suburbanites who shop and seek entertainment in the university area.

A growing number of businesses employing highly skilled professionals are spread widely throughout the university area: engineering firms, computer companies, management consultants, architects, educational and social science consultants, economic forecasters, and the like. These firms depend to a large extent on university graduates and part-time faculty consultants for their labor supply. Another large part of the city's economy is industrial, specializing in light manufacturing of products ranging from candy to coffins. In the past 20 years this industrial base has been shrinking as firms relocate to suburban sites or move to other regions of the country. Finally, Oxford supports many commercial establishments that cater to the rest of its citizens.

The city's population is quite diverse. Approximately 10,000 students live in dormitories on campus, while another 4,500 live in private rental units nearby. About 14 percent of the city's population is black and another 6 percent is Hispanic. Less than 1 percent belongs to the city's elite families whose roots go back for generations in Oxford. Many of the heads of these families are lawyers, physicians, investment bankers, or businessmen who work in nearby Metropolis. Another 15 percent of the community consists of young professional families who work for the growing "high-tech" sector of the city's economy. Oxford's largest group of citizens, however, is whites who work in the city's industrial or commercial firms. Many of these people are second or third generation "ethnics" of west or east European origin.

Oxford's City Government

Oxford adopted the council-manager form of government early in the twentieth century. Its principal policy-making body is a seven-member city council elected at-large (not by district) for a two-year term. The council appoints the city manager who is Oxford's top public administrator.

Oxford elections are formally nonpartisan, and city politics are quite separate from the state or national political scene. However, two loosely organized local political factions in Oxford—the "civic association" group and the "independents"—have competed closely for control of the city council over the past dozen years. The "independents" are traditional politicians, with deeply rooted ties to Oxford's working- and lower middle-class citizens. The "civic association" group, in contrast, is more closely identified with the city's elite and its growing population of young professionals. It rejects the "old politics" of "favors and deals" and supports "good government," meaning professional management and efficient, cost-effective service delivery.

In the 1960s the "civic association" group elected several stalwarts to the council but never won a majority. In the 1970 election, however, it achieved a breakthrough by winning five seats. The majority proved short-lived, however, because in 1974 the "independents" won four seats to recapture political control in Oxford. In 1976 both factions vigorously were preparing to contest the upcoming elections.

The city manager, serving "at the pleasure" of the council, can be dismissed by the council if his actions displease a majority of its members. Nonetheless, the city manager is the central figure in municipal government. Council members serve part time and therefore rely on guidance from the full-time manager, who can draw upon his five-person staff and the city bureaucracy for advice. The manager, moreover, has authority to appoint—and remove—most city department heads.

Frank Whalen, the incumbent city manager in 1976, was a seasoned professional. He had begun his career 15 years earlier in the public works department in Metropolis, then worked as assistant city manager in a small suburb until he ultimately became manager. When Oxford was recruiting a new city manager in 1971, Whalen was the first choice of the "civic association" majority on the council. He proved to be an effective public administrator: competent in running the city's service delivery departments and its finances, respected for his professional judgment and probity, yet sensitive to the political environment in which he operated. These qualities helped him survive as manager when the "civic association" lost its council majority in the 1974 election, although his hold on the job was weaker with the "independents" in power.

Citizen Participation in the Antipoverty Program

Before the Community Development Block Grant program, the city of Oxford already had experienced several different citizen participation methods in federal programs. The most visible and controversial participation occurred in the Community Action Program (CAP) funded by antipoverty money administered by the federal Office of Economic Opportunity. CAP began in Oxford in 1965 when four low-income neighborhoods (each containing about 5,000 residents) were designated as the primary CAP target areas.

In the spirit of the Economic Opportunity Act of 1964—the federal law that established the CAP program—Oxford's program provided for extensive powers for involved citizens. To oversee citywide planning and allocation of antipoverty funds, the city council created the Economic Opportunity Committee (EOC) composed of 35 citizens. Seven members were appointed by the council; the remaining 28 members were selected in special elections every two years by residents of the target areas. These elections did not coincide with national, state, or municipal elections. Seven representatives were chosen from each neighborhood. Any registered voter living in that area could participate and vote for as many as seven candidates on the ballot. In most elections there were long lists of candidates—often 30 names in each area.

Although the target areas were expected to show great interest in the EOC, the turnout in the special election was disappointing. In the first election in 1965, only 14 percent of the eligible voters cast their ballots; in subsequent elections, voter turnout averaged about 8 percent. Some of those elected were well-known community figures: ministers, lawyers, civic activists, and leaders of militant protest groups. Many others elected to the EOC were "unknowns"—people with no prior record of political activism who were able to persuade enough friends, relatives, and neighbors to back their candidacies. With a low turnout at elections and long slates of candidates, a person could be elected by as few as 25-35 votes. About two-thirds of the elected members of the EOC were black, another 20 percent were Hispanic, and the rest were white. The citizen participation procedures identified impoverished neighborhoods but permitted any area resident—whatever his or her income—to vote or run for the EOC. As a result, only about half of those elected were themselves "poor," as defined by the federal regulations establishing eligibility for CAP services.

Although the EOC did not operate any programs, it wielded a good deal of influence over the antipoverty program. Each year the EOC received proposals both from established social welfare agencies and from various community groups that wanted to get CAP funds to run specific antipoverty projects. The EOC decided which projects to fund, allocating money from the overall CAP budget of about $2 million a year. Although these choices, in principle, were made on a citywide basis, in practice the EOC tended to divide the funds among the neighborhoods and then defer to the judgment of the representatives from each area concerning which projects to approve. Federal regulations permitted EOC members to be employed by antipoverty projects—an option that about 15 members exercised at any one time. Other members used their influence to get jobs for friends or associates.

All available evidence suggested that residents of the four target areas generally were satisfied with the performance of the antipoverty program. In 1972 a public opinion survey (commissioned by the Oxford municipal government to probe citizen attitudes about local services) found that 65 percent of the residents of the four target neighborhoods felt that the EOC did a "good" or "very good" job of administering the CAP program. The result "rang true" to political observers familiar with politics in the target areas. Although periodic criticism was heard from a community group or leader, EOC had no organized opposition in the target neighborhoods.

By and large, the Oxford City Council ignored the EOC and the CAP program. Council members made no effort to influence EOC elections or policy, assuming there was no political payoff—and considerable risk—in becoming involved in neighborhood conflicts in the target areas.

The EOC, for its part, made few demands on the council. CAP funds came from the federal government, and, so long as the council made no attempt to interfere with the EOC, that group saw no reason to pressure the council. The only exceptions came in the late 1960s when the EOC lobbied vigorously against an urban renewal project in one target neighborhood and against a highway construction project that threatened housing in another target area. In both cases the EOC sought and won support from the council.

Citizen Participation in the Model Cities Program

The federal Model Cities program offered another—but quite different—opportunity for citizen participation by residents of Oxford's low-income areas. The Model Cities program was initiated in Oxford in 1967 when the city received a planning grant from the federal Department of Housing and Urban Development. The program—launched in 150 cities around the country—was designed to concentrate resources on specific distressed neighborhoods to facilitate a comprehensive attack on their physical, economic, and social problems. In Oxford the "model neighborhood" roughly encompassed two of the antipoverty target areas; its population was predominantly black and Hispanic. The program annually brought $2.1 million to Oxford.

By federal law, decision-making power in the Model Cities program was reserved to the city's municipal government; the program was run by a regular city department, the City Demonstration Agency (CDA), whose director was appointed by the city manager. But federal regulations also required an active advisory role for residents of the "model neighborhoods." The CDA Advisory Board consisted of 25 members—15 area residents appointed by the city council and 10 others named by leading community institutions or civic groups in the neighborhood.

The advisory board reviewed and made recommendations on annual program plans, budgets, and key personnel decisions. In addition the CDA staff actively sought volunteers, through advertising and community meetings, to work on advisory committees for specific Model Cities projects (for example, housing rehabilitation or a drug treatment center). These committees, which received technical assistance from CDA staff, were used extensively by CDA policy makers. Nonetheless, decision-making power in the Model Cities program rested with the CDA director and, ultimately, with the city manager and council.

Although several EOC members also served on the CDA Advisory Board, relations between the two programs were strained. EOC's key members felt that Model Cities staff overemphasized physical development activities at the expense of social services. They also were suspicious of the advisory relationship required for citizen participants in the Model Cities, believing that it was too easy for citizens to be manipulated, co-opted, or ignored if their ideas were inconvenient or incompatible with the staff's.

Citizen Participation in Other Federal Programs

Although the CAP and Model Cities programs were Oxford's low-income citizens' principal vehicles for involvement, there were two other federal programs that offered opportunities for citizen participation.

Since the 1950s Oxford had operated an urban renewal program and had built many units of public housing. The two operating entities—the Oxford Redevelopment Authority (ORA) and the Oxford Housing Authority (OHA)—were independent city agencies governed by separate, five-person boards of directors whose members were appointed for five-year terms, on a rotating basis, by the city council. Until the mid-1970s, both the ORA and OHA boards were composed entirely of white middle-class professionals and businessmen. Each also had an advisory council of citizens, but these bodies were largely inactive, meeting once or twice a year to hear reports from the agency staff. The ORA continued to function this way, but in 1972 and 1973 the "civic association" majority on the city council appointed an activist minister of a black church and a local Hispanic community group leader to the OHA board. These men, along with a liberal attorney already on the board, tried to shake up the housing authority. They appointed a "reform" executive director who began to treat the citizen advisory council more seriously.

The CBDG Program

Title I of the Housing and Community Development Act of 1974 consolidated several federal categorical grants-in-aid:

1. Open Space, Urban Beautification, Historic Preservation grants;
2. Public Facility loans;
3. Water, Sewer, and Neighborhood Facilities grants;
4. Urban Renewal and Neighborhood Development Program grants;
5. Model Cities grants;
6. Rehabilitation loans.

The intent of CBDG was to develop:

viable urban communities by providing decent housing and a suitable living environment and expanding economic opportunities, principally for persons of low- and moderate-income. This objective is to be achieved through elimination of slums and blight and detrimental living conditions, conservation and expansion of housing and housing opportunities, increased public services, improved use of land, increased neighborhood diversity, and preservation of property with special values.

Eligible activities included acquisition of real property that was blighted or deteriorating or that could be rehabilitated, conserved or preserved; code enforcement; removal of material and architectural barriers that hindered the mobility of elderly and handicapped persons; provision of public services not otherwise available to area residents; payment of nonfederal shares in other federal programs; housing rehabilitation; road, sewer, and water improvements; and relocation payments.

Congress enacted the block grant program to give local governments more discretion in disbursing federal funds for community development. The demise of the categorical grant programs—and the specific program regulations developed by the federal Housing and Urban Development Department (HUD)—meant that municipalities could determine their own spending priorities within the overall program objectives.

Unfortunately, from Oxford's point of view, the congressionally enacted formula for distributing the national CDBG appropriation resulted in a declining pool of funds for Oxford's own community development purposes compared with the levels of funding for the predecessor categorical programs. Oxford would receive $4 million in 1975, $3.75 million in 1976, and $3.5 million in 1977. Consequently, agencies and programs that had previously had a relatively assured source of federal money—provided by the programmatic limitations of each of the categorical grants—would now have to compete for a piece of the diminishing pie. The ORA, for example, was no longer guaranteed an annual urban renewal allotment from a federal categorical grant, but had to request a share of the overall Community Development Block Grant.

HUD regulations required that a local citizen participation plan be developed and made public. The plan, including a timetable, was to describe processes for disseminating information about available funds, opportunities for participation, available technical assistance, and participation opportunities for the future. No specific methods of organizing participation were required either by the federal statute or HUD regulations. (See Exhibit 1, p. 317.)

In Oxford's case, the broad range of eligible program activities, the phased reduction in spending, and the ambiguous citizen participation regulations all created a ticklish situation for City Manager Whalen in designing an appropriate citizen participation process. One possibility was to designate either the EOC or the CDA Advisory Board as the core of the CDBG Advisory Committee. Whalen knew that would be a disastrous policy because both groups had strong interests in getting a large share of the CDBG appropriation. The Model Cities appropriation was being folded into the CDBG program; and, while the antipoverty program had separate funding, the EOC was likely to see the new CDBG program as a means of boosting its own resources. Thus, if Whalen gave either the EOC or the CDA Advisory Board a leading role in citizen participation for CDBG, the "losing" organization no doubt would protest loud and long while the "winning" organization would have an unfair advantage over all of its competitors.

Whalen did not want to see the demise of any programs that had drawn funds from the categorical programs in CDBG. His solution was to create a citizen advisory committee composed of single representatives from the CAP and Model Cities agencies, from the ORA and the OHA, and from other community groups throughout the city—a total of 25 organizations. (See Exhibit 2, pp. 317-320.)

Almost immediately after Whalen's plans were announced, vehement protest arose. The EOC, along with some other groups, developed a competitive approach and created a Revenue Sharing Council elected from the four poor neighborhoods. At the first meeting of the CDBG citizen participation committee, members of the Revenue Sharing Council angrily denounced the process, claiming that the citizen participants would be co-opted by the city manager's "elitist" plans. They demanded that the process be changed. The Revenue Sharing Council called for a CDBG Citizens Advisory Committee elected from the city's neighborhoods—not composed of appointed, organizational representatives.

Although the city manager's staff had anticipated some form of demonstration, the vehement tone and extensive media coverage were surprising and embarrassing. The assistant city manager was intransigent (on telephone orders from the city manager), refusing to make changes in a publicly advertised and orderly process. The Revenue Sharing Council walked out of the meeting, casting a cloud on the legitimacy of the city-designed process. It continued its opposition for the next four months through press releases and other public statements, finally developing an "Alternative CDBG Budget" that emphasized expenditures in OEO neighborhoods, including large allocations for social services—especially day care. The council also claimed that the city manager's CDBG process was composed of groups with a vested interest in getting funds; it argued that the process was tainted with conflict of interest.

Despite the uproar over the CDBG allocations, the city's official participation process reasonably could not be called exclusionary: it involved weekly public meetings over a four-month period with a number of city staffers assigned solely to the CDBG program, including a significant time commitment on the part of the assistant city manager. The 25 community and civic groups invited to attend the weekly meetings gave their views on community development and housing needs and helped develop implementation priorities. The general public, too, had many opportunities to express opinions about program priorities. (See Exhibit 2, pp. 317-320.)

Nonetheless, bitter fighting occurred over the final CDBG allocation. Formerly the recipient of direct categorical aid, the Model Cities program was slated to receive only $527,000 in CDBG funds in 1975—$175,000 for a housing rehabilitation program and $352,000 for program continuation. This sum amounted to merely one-quarter of the amount model cities had received several years earlier. As this became apparent, the CDA Advisory Board grew more antagonistic toward the city administration (notably the city manager), striking a strident stance with regard to the advisory board's position as the representative of citizen interests.

The advisory board asserted that it understood best how to deliver services to its "unique" constituency. Observers agreed that the CDA Advisory Board was trying to build its neighborhood base by taking over key social service programs such as child care, recreation, and the overall administration of citywide citizen participation efforts. The Board ran head-on into competition with the Economic Opportunity Committee (EOC) to be the "best" representative of the same constituency. Each group made efforts to rally a grass-roots constituency through neighborhood organization—and the EOC, more experienced at this activity, seemed to be winning the "battle."

With the categorical programs' demise, the Housing Authority and Redevelopment Authority also found themselves in unusual positions. In the 1975 allocation, OHA received $52,000 for social services in public housing projects and $198,000 for modernization of public housing units. The CDBG decision makers believed that other agencies existed with less funding and more urgent needs. OHA competed with the Redevelopment Authority for funds for development activities, while the Model Cities group grappled with the OHA for service delivery dollars.

Meanwhile, the Oxford Redevelopment Authority, for the first time, had to justify its programs to the entire city. In 1975 it received only $550,000 for major infrastructure improvements in an area of East Oxford that contained several office and light industrial buildings and for traffic improvements in University Square, Oxford's major shopping district. In the advisory committee meetings, the ORA representatives generally were allied with the Chamber of Commerce and pushed for more funding for physical improvement projects that would help business and, they claimed, expand Oxford's tax base.

Whalen's Problem

The 1975 EOC walkout and the ORA, OHA, and CDA Advisory Board's animosity subjected City Manager Whalen to embarrassing publicity and a continuous barrage of complaints from organizations represented on the CDBG Citizens Advisory Committee. Following the final vote of the committee, the city council met in open session to approve the CDBG budget; the meeting turned into a four-hour shouting match that nearly resulted in fist fights among aggrieved community-group members. The next day several key members of the council majority called Whalen in for a private meeting at which they informed him that they would not tolerate a repetition of the 1975 squabble. They implied that Whalen might be dismissed as city manager if he could not resolve the situation before the meetings began on the 1976 CDBG allocation.

Thus Whalen faced the task of developing a system of citizen participation and CDBG decision making that would be regarded as legitimate by the various actors involved and also minimize conflict over the CDBG budget.

EXHIBITS

Exhibit One:
Excerpt from the Housing and
Community Development Act of 1974

"No grant may be made pursuant to ... this title unless an application shall have been submitted to the Secretary [of HUD] in which the applicant [i.e., the city]. . . :

(6) provides satisfactory assurances that, prior to submission of its application, it has (A) provided citizens with adequate information concerning the amount of funds available for proposed community development and housing activities, the range of activities that may be undertaken, and other important program requirements, (B) held public hearings to obtain the views of citizens on community development and housing needs, and (C) provided citizens an adequate opportunity to participate in the development of the application; but no part of this paragraph shall be construed to restrict the responsibility and authority of the applicant for the development of the application and the execution of its Community Development Program.

Exhibit Two:
City of Oxford 1975 Citizen
Participation Plan—Announcement to Citizens

The Citizen Participation Plan for the Community Development Block Grant Program in the City of Oxford will permit citizens likely to be affected by community development and housing activities, including low- and moderate-income persons, to articulate needs, express preferences, assist in the selecting of priorities and otherwise participate and be informed by combining the traditional committee or task force method of participation with a new unlimited input approach to citizen involvement.

The City Manager, Frank Whalen, has appointed a cross-section of agencies and organizations from throughout the city to send a representative to function as part of a citizen advisory committee. The committee will work

317

with the Community Development Department staff in the preparation of recommendations to the City Manager. The committee reflects primarily low- and moderate-income interests as well as those areas most likely to be affected by the block grant, including minority, housing, social service, business, industry and elderly interests. The committee will provide a broadbased advisory view towards the preparation of a three-year plan, a one-year action program, and a Housing Assistance Plan to be included in a Community Development Block Grant application.

The City Manager has also appointed Jim Meadows to the position of Citizen Participation Coordinator for the Community Development Block Grant Program. In this position Mr. Meadows will serve as the focal point for all citizen participation relating to the Program. All information, inquiries, notices and releases shall flow through the C.P. Coordinator who will be responsible for insuring maximum feasible citizen involvement.

Between November 12, 1974 and February 5, 1975 the Citizen Participation Committee will meet regularly to identify items for inclusion in the application. The purpose of the meetings is to identify problems, strategies, objectives and programs which can be dealt with by the Block Grant program. Those items identified by the Citizen Participation Committee will be presented to the City Manager, who will finalize all proposals in the application. The meetings are to be held in the City Council Chamber at Oxford City Hall and will be open to the general public. Notices of the meetings will be made available to all committee members and to the general public upon request.

In an effort to insure city-wide citizen input from persons who may not be committee members, or persons who may not contact representatives, or persons who do not attend the public meetings, the Community Development Department staff will be available to receive information and inquiries from other groups or individuals. The staff through the Citizen Participation Coordinator, Jim Meadows, will respond to telephone inquiries and office visits either scheduled or spontaneous. Spanish-speaking persons are available to assist in this effort whenever necessary. Such contacts are to exchange information, present facts, accept proposals, and generally increase involvement in and understanding of the program. It is anticipated that the interview approach will provide the vehicle for greater citizen participation in the planning process.

Additionally the staff will be reaching out into various neighborhoods to solicit input. Attending neighborhood meetings, promoting random exchange sessions, contacting established community sources and seeking new contacts will provide much information which would otherwise be unavailable. The committee, interview and out-reach approaches are the process by which affected citizens, primarily low- and moderate-income persons, may participate in the development of the application.

Citizens will also be provided assistance in understanding federal regulations, including Davis-Bacon, environmental policies, equal opportunity requirements, relocation provisions and like requirements and any other program requirements upon request, in ways that guarantee full understanding. Federal registers, program information and any and all printed material relating to the above items will be made available to citizens interested in those items.

A schedule of all public meetings and hearings is listed below. Once again, citizens will be invited to participate in the development of the application at these meetings and hearings prior to submission of the application for regional, state and federal approvals.

Copies of the application will be made available to all interested parties at the time of submission for HUD approval.

In the event that the City intends to make major revisions in the community development program, the citizens' participation structure will be involved in those revisions.

Additionally, it is necessary for the City to submit a Housing Assistance Plan which will establish future direction and policy for housing activity in Oxford. A Housing Assistance Task Force consisting of housing users and potential users of low- and moderate-income housing, plus providers and administrators will prepare the plan to submit to the citizen participation structure for inclusion in the application.

There will be cross-representation and regular communication between the Citizen Participation Committee and the Housing Assistance Task Force to ensure continuity and full citizen involvement. The Housing Assistance Plan must also receive the City Manager's approval prior to submission in the application.

Contact with line department heads and other city officials provides the staff with technical data to complement citizen input. That combination will make the Committee recommendations more realistic and practical. The City Manager will make the final selection of activities and funding levels to be included.

Finally, the purpose of all hearings will be to afford the citizenry the opportunity to present their views on community development and housing needs. Two formal, legal hearings will be a part of the eleven public meetings scheduled and will be advertised in the local newspaper for two weeks prior to the respective dates in order to satisfy local hearing requirements.

Subsequent to approval of the application, citizen participation will continue in a more localized manner intended to secure citizen input into the completion of funded projects. Each neighborhood will be involved in the design, construction and implementation of projects and programs, whenever appropriate. Neighborhood meetings will be held in order to reach a local consensus as to the particulars within each undertaking. Obviously there are established regulations and procedures which must be adhered to for safety, budgetary, continuity and other city-wide factors; but generally speaking plans will emanate from neighborhood sessions. These meetings will begin as soon as approval of the application is received. Again, any amendment to the program which will bring about changes to the budget of more than ten percent must be reviewed by the citizen participation structure previously defined.

Since the Community Development Block Grant Program is three years in duration, Citizen Participation will continue for the length of the Program. In both the second and third year it is necessary to submit applications to the Department of Housing and Urban Development to review, modify and complete the goals and objectives included in the three year plan. Citizen involvement will be included in the preparation of those applications and the completion of activities approved in those applications.

Listed below are the agencies and organizations invited by City Manager Whalen to serve on the CDBG Citizen Advisory Committee and a schedule of meeting times and places for the application preparation process:

Fenwick Neighborhood Planning Group
Oxford Chamber of Commerce
Oxford Committee of Elders
Oxford Community Center
Oxford Community Services, Inc.
Oxford Democratic Committee
Oxford Northside Neighborhood Assn.
Oxford Alliance of Churches
Oxford Hispanic Council
City Demonstration Agency (CDA)
Civic Unity Committee
Youth in Action
Community Education Committee
Concerned Black Parents, Inc.
Council on Aging
Department of Veterans' Services
Broadway House
Home Rejuvenation, Inc.
League of Women Voters
Mid-Oxford Neighborhood Assn.
Oxford State University
EOC Revenue Sharing Council
Jackson/Newton Community Corp.
Jackson Towers Tenant Senate
Riverton/Oxford Home Care Corp.

Discussion Questions

1. Evaluate the 1975 citizen participation process. Were the criticisms of these arrangements fair, or were they merely "sour grapes" from individuals and groups who did not get their way?

2. What are the comparative advantages and disadvantages of choosing citizen participants by a) elections b) appointment by public officials c) nomination by organizations d) self-selection/volunteering?

3. How and to what extent should the city manager "protect" existing programs that do not have widespread citizen constituencies—for example, the redevelopment program?

4. What changes should the city manager make in the citizen participation procedures for 1976 in light of the city council's message to him?

Suggestions for Further Reading

Advisory Commission on Intergovernmental Relations. *Citizen Participation in the American Federal System.* Washington, D.C.: U.S. Government Printing Office, 1979.

Gittell, Marilyn. *Limits to Citizen Participation.* Beverly Hills, Calif.: Sage Publications, 1980.

Jacobs, Bruce. *The Political Economy of Organizational Change.* New York: Academic Press, 1981.

Peterson, Paul E. and Greenstone, J. David. "Racial Change and Citizen Participation: The Mobilization of Low Income Communities Through Community Action," in *A Decade of Federal Anti-poverty Programs,* Robert H. Haveman, ed. New York: Academic Press Inc., 1977, 241-278.

Pressman, Jeffrey L. *Federal Programs and City Politics.* Berkeley, Calif.: University of California Press, 1975, Chap. 3.

Yates, Douglas T. *Neighborhood Democracy.* Lexington, Mass.: Lexington Books, 1973.